JOURNEY THROUGH
THE MINEFIELDS

Other books by Mendy Ganchrow, M.D.

Sason VeSimcha
An anthology
of Torah thoughts for Sheva Brachos

Entering the Covenant
An anthology of Divrei Torah
for Bris Milah and Pidyon Haben

JOURNEY THROUGH THE MINEFIELDS

FROM VIETNAM TO WASHINGTON
AN ORTHODOX SURGEON'S ODYSSEY

Mendy Ganchrow, M.D.

Eshel Books

Silver Spring
Maryland

Printed in the United States of America

Eshel Books
AN IMPRINT OF BARTLEBY PRESS
11141 Georgia Avenue
Silver Spring, MD 20902
800-953-9929

Library of Congress Cataloging-in-Publication Data

Ganchrow, Mandell I.
  Journey through the minefields : from Vietnam to Washington, an orthodox surgeon's odyssey / Mendy Ganchrow.
  p. cm.
  ISBN 0-910155-56-9
  1. Ganchrow, Mandell I. 2. Jews—United States—Biography. 3. Political activists—United States—Biography. 4. Religious Zionists—United States—Biography. 5. Physicians—United States—Biography. I. Title.
  E184.37.G36A3 2004
  296.8'32'092—dc22

                                    2003019807

JOURNEY THROUGH THE MINEFIELDS

FROM VIETNAM TO WASHINGTON
AN ORTHODOX SURGEON'S ODYSSEY

Mendy Ganchrow, M.D.

Eshel Books

Silver Spring
Maryland

Printed in the United States of America

Eshel Books
AN IMPRINT OF BARTLEBY PRESS
11141 Georgia Avenue
Silver Spring, MD 20902
800-953-9929

Library of Congress Cataloging-in-Publication Data

Ganchrow, Mandell I.
 Journey through the minefields : from Vietnam to Washington, an orthodox surgeon's odyssey / Mendy Ganchrow.
 p. cm.
 ISBN 0-910155-56-9
 1. Ganchrow, Mandell I. 2. Jews—United States—Biography. 3. Political activists—United States—Biography. 4. Religious Zionists—United States—Biography. 5. Physicians—United States—Biography. I. Title.
 E184.37.G36A3 2004
 296.8'32'092—dc22

                              2003019807

Dedicated to Sheila,
Whose companionship, love, and friendship have made
this odyssey a truly exhilarating partnership and experience

In memory of our parents
Rabbi Morris S. Ganchrow, OBM,
and Anna and Jack Weinreb, OBM,
and in honor of
my mother Kate
Their way of life has inspired me

Contents

Foreword by Rabbi Dr. Moshe Dovid Tendler / ix

Introduction / xi

Prologue: Vietnam Passover / 1

Early Life / 8

Medical Training and Marriage / 37

Vietnam / 63

From Grand Rapids to Monsey / 95

HUVPAC / 108

Presidency at the Orthodox Union / 154

The Bully Pulpit of the OU / 178

The OU and Other Orthodox Organizations / 193

From Oslo to the Rabin Assassination / 215

The Decline and Fall of Oslo /238

If I Forget Thee, O Jerusalem / 261

Relations with Bill Clinton / 266

My Minuet with Hillary Clinton / 274

A Jewish Candidate for Vice-President / 284

Meetings with Presidents and Kings / 291

Scoring Big in the World Zionist Elections / 307

The Pluralism Wars / 313

The Lanner Affair / 334

Summing Up / 371

APPENDIX: Selected Writings / 379

Index / 407

Foreword

Mendy Ganchrow's *Journey Through the Minefields* is a
mixed literary genre. It's an engrossing historical record
of major events in the life of the Jewish community,
as well as an autobiography of one who exemplifies the best of
halachic Jewry.

As a loyal citizen, and skilled surgeon, Ganchrow devoted
his skills to our soldiers in Vietnam. As a communal leader
on the local and national stage, he dedicates his life to the
service of Jewry in the United States, Israel, and to the rem-
nant of the once majestic Jewish communities of the Soviet
Empire.

The autobiographical vignettes depicting his tour of duty in
Vietnam and his meetings with presidents and kings these last
decades are an ode to the integrity, loyalty, and devotion to
Torah values of this orthodox physician turned statesman and
communal leader. His tireless efforts to foster "achdus," a recognition of the "peoplehood" of all Jews who accept the authority of Torah Law, as recorded in the minutes of his meetings with the leadership of the major orthodox organizations,
are his love song to Hashem who crowned us with the title
"Holy Nation."

When Moses was instructed to construct the Tabernacle in
the desert, he exclaimed in wonderment, can a nation of just
freed slaves accomplish this task? The G-d of Israel responded,
"one Jew can do it by himself if he is so committed" (Medrash
Rabbah Shmos 33:8).

Dr. Mendy Ganchrow, *shlita*, in this history provides the empiric evidence that indeed one Jew can do it all, if he is fully committed to G-d, his Torah, and his nation Israel.

Moshe Dovid Tendler
Yeshiva University
New York, N.Y.
6 March 2003

Introduction

I initially decided to pen an autobiography in order to leave a written account for my grandchildren and their progeny of the extraordinary people I have been privileged to meet during my lifetime and the world-transforming events in which I have had the opportunity to participate. Yet I was moved to actually sit down and begin composing this account by a somewhat discomforting vision I had several years ago while visiting a senior citizen center to which I had been invited by Linda Rothschild, the director of social activities there and a personal friend of mine.

There was an elderly gentleman sitting at a table in the corner gesticulating dramatically and speaking loudly as he tried to convince another resident of some point or another. I winced and said to Linda, "You know, that could be me a few years up the road trying to convince another senior citizen that, when I was younger, I had the opportunity to visit the White House on a number of occasions and to speak my mind directly to the President of the United States: I can visualize the other guy responding sarcastically, "Yeah, yeah, and I was once the King of England."

Shtarker is the Yiddish expression for a strong person. Yet, the word denotes far more than physical strength. When used colloquially, *shtarker* signifies someone with fortitude and strength of character—a person with the capacity to lead and to stand firm in the face of great odds.

In May 1986, a small group of grass roots Jewish communal activists that included myself, teamed up with Senator Alan

Cranston (D-California) to defeat a proposal by the Reagan Administration to sell 354 million dollars of portable Stinger missiles and other advanced offensive weapons to Saudi Arabia. The package included 1066 Sidewinders and 100 Harpoon air to surface missiles. Stung by this setback, President Reagan immediately vetoed the bill as passed by Sen. Cranston and then summoned several Republican senators who had voted against his position to the White House. Turning on all of his considerable powers of persuasion, the "Great Communicator" appealed to the errant senators for their support in the upcoming vote in which Cranston and his allies in both parties would attempt to override the President's veto.

The senators responded to the President that while they hated to oppose a foreign policy initiative that he saw as a high priority, they had given ironclad commitments to oppose the arms sale to certain pro-Israel activists around the country who happened to be providing backing for their re-election campaigns that year. Therefore, the senators said, they could only consider changing their votes if the Administration could convince the individuals in question to release the senators from their commitments. Among the names of pro-Israel activists that came up in those meetings was Dr. Mandell Ganchrow, a little known colorectal surgeon from Monsey, New York, who was said to have personally secured commitments to oppose the Saudi arms package from three Republican senators: Jesse Helms of North Carolina, Paul Trible of Virginia and Steve Symms of Idaho.

Shortly thereafter, I received a call from the White House. The President of the United States, I was told, wanted to see me at a meeting in the Roosevelt Room of the White House several days hence. Under almost any other circumstances, I would have been thrilled by such an honor and opportunity, but on that occasion I was, frankly, deeply apprehensive of the prospect of going one on one with the President. I understood what he would ask of me, and the last thing I wanted to do was to tell President Reagan, a man I had voted for and admired deeply, that I opposed his wishes on an issue he considered critical. Rather than do that, my first instinct was to try to get out of the meeting even if it meant making up an excuse that was less than truthful.

I therefore called the White House scheduling office and told them in a regretful tone that while I would try my best to attend the meeting with the President, I might have to decline in order to stay in my hospital in Rockland County that day to perform a previously scheduled surgical procedure. I was off the hook, but instead of feeling relief, I was beset by conflicting emotions. Suddenly, the phone rang, and the voice on the other end of the line was that of Doug Bloomfield, an official of the American Israel Public Affairs Committee, the leading pro-Israel lobby. There are no secrets in Washington and he was well aware of my White House invitation. Never one to mince words, Bloomfield asked me bluntly, "Are you a shtarker?" "What do you mean?" I said, to which Doug replied, "I mean, can you say no to the President of the United States?"

"Yes," I responded with a conviction I hadn't felt until that moment. "I can say 'no' to the President if I believe truth is on my side."

"Then you must go to the meeting with the President to present the pro-Israel point of view," Bloomfield said emphatically.

I have always considered myself a disciplined soldier for the pro-Israel cause so I immediately picked up the phone and informed the White House that I had managed to clear my schedule and would be coming to the meeting after all. I entered the Roosevelt Room with my heart in my mouth, but when the moment of truth came, I looked President Reagan in the eye and said that while I was normally a staunch supporter of his Administration and believed in his priorities for America, I was convinced that his arms sale to Saudi Arabia was not in America's own best interests. My statement served to stiffen the backbones of several other pro-Israel activists at the meeting, who subsequently made statements confirming that they too would not drop their opposition to the Saudi arms sale.

A few minutes later, the President pleaded a scheduling conflict and left the room. Shortly thereafter, while we were still in the meeting with other Administration officials, we were informed that the Administration had decided to drop its plans for the Stinger missiles to the Saudis and leaving the arms package with a far more modest sale of defensive weapons. There was jubilation among the pro-Israel advocates in the room. In the face of intense pressure from an Administration headed by the most popular president in decades, we had stood our ground and we had won.

I had been involved in pro-Israel activism since 1981. But

until that triumphant moment at the White House five years later, I sometimes wondered whether the enormous amounts of time and energy I was devoting to lobbying and networking with senators and congressmen in Washington and in building HUVPAC (Hudson Valley Political Action Committee), a formidable pro-Israel political action committee, was really having a discernable impact in terms of strengthening the U.S.-Israel relationship. Were the considerable financial and professional sacrifices I was making to devote myself to pro-Israel activity—not to mention all the time I was spending away from my wonderful wife Sheila, and children Malkie, Ari and Elli—really worth it?

Those were questions I never asked myself again after my trial by fire that day in the White House, because I never again had the slightest doubts about my course. I realized that I had taken on a mission in life that was larger than myself and that I had been privileged to find myself in a position in which I could make a difference in helping to ensure the safety and well being of the people of Israel. I knew from that moment on that I was prepared to make whatever sacrifices were necessary to go on fulfilling that mission to the absolute best of my ability.

This book details how I went from a religiously vibrant but economically straightened childhood in Brooklyn to becoming a highly successful surgeon with a booming practice that allowed me to provide my growing family with a comfortable lifestyle in bucolic Monsey, New York. Then, well into middle age, I found a new purpose in life and transformed myself into a fiercely committed and politically astute pro-Israel activist in the halls of the United States Congress. I became widely known as the person who reached out to Sen. Jesse Helms and made him kosher to a pro-Israel community that deeply distrusted him; and as the man who created the Hudson Valley Political Action Committee in the early 1980's and quickly built it into the largest local pro-Israel PAC in the United States. Then in the 1990's, I became president of the Union of Orthodox Jewish Congregations (OU), the premier modern Orthodox communal organization in the country, and dedicated six years to streamlining, energizing and opening up a body that many had considered stodgy and insular.

If in 1962, when I completed medical college, someone had told me that 35 or 40 years later—at the top of my surgical career—I would retire early and devote myself full time to community service, I would have considered that person crazy. I would have felt the same way if someone had said that in 1999 the *Forward* newspaper would choose me Number two of its Top 50 Most Influential American Jews list or that the centennial edition of the *Rockland Journal News*, a Gannett paper, would label me as one of the 10 most prominent Rockland residents in the last 100 years. Yet the events of our life often overtake our best-laid plans and lead us in unexpected directions. During my college and med-school years, I never would have imagined in my worst nightmares that I would shortly thereafter find myself in the jungles of Vietnam, hunkering down for life and limb during all-out fire fights with the Viet Cong and working feverishly around the clock as a surgeon to save the lives of as many badly wounded G.I.'s as I possibly could. Nor would I have guessed that as hellish as those experiences were, I would come to see my service in Vietnam as a highly positive experience that gave me on-the-job surgical training while teaching me crucial life lessons that have stood me in good stead ever since.

It is impossible for any of us to predict the unexpected twists and turns our lives will take. It is possible, however, to build one's life work around certain values and beliefs. I pray that throughout my own life journey, I have succeeded in being a *shtarker* in defense of the causes my conscience told me were just; ensuring the freedom and security of Israel and the United States, and building a better future for the Jewish people by upholding a Torah-true way of life.

I want to emphasize that throughout this book, and especially in the chapter concerning my response to the Baruch Lanner affair while president of the Orthodox Union, I have not violated anyone's trust by revealing things that were said to me in confidence. Nor have I revealed any information from the confidential report on the Lanner affair by the Richard Joel Commission. Everything I have written here about the Lanner affair is either already public knowledge, or represents an airing of events related to the case as I experienced them in my last months as president of the OU. The opinions in this book are purely my own and do not represent the thinking of any organization.

I would like to thank the following people for their help and support to me in the preparation of this book. Walter Ruby played a major role in writing and editing the document. He came to the project with a leg up, having covered my political activities for many years on behalf of the *Long Island Jewish World* and *Jerusalem Post*. His rich knowledge of Jewish politics sometimes allowed him to recall events from 15 years ago or more in which I had been involved that I myself had forgotten. His good humor and understanding made him a pleasure to work with.

My secretary at the OU, Fran Breiner, was an enormous help. This volume was more than four years in the making and she patiently tracked my progress and pushed me forward during all of that period that I was at the Union. I am very grateful to Rabbi Dr. Moses Tendler, my Rabbi, teacher and friend for over 40 years, for not only making suggestions but also reviewing a number of chapters and making sure that my description of events and individuals throughout this volume were within the spirit and letter of *halacha* (Jewish law). Marcel Weber, my friend and partner at the Orthodox Union, reviewed both the OU and Lanner chapters for accuracy and fairness. Early on, when I started to write this book, Charlotte Friedland, the editor of the OU magazine *Jewish Action* and Mike Cohen, who was in charge of the internet at the Union, were quite encouraging to my efforts. Beverly Kirshblum, my secretary at HUVPAC helped with the final corrections in the manuscript.

Phil Friedman who in the past has reviewed legal questions for HUVPAC and Howard Kohr, Executive Director of AIPAC, kindly reviewed the chapter on political activism, and Charles Stillman, a "lawyer's lawyer" and his partner John Harris checked the Lanner chapter. I am deeply appreciative of their efforts.

My daughter-in-law, Banji, spent a great deal of time helping me prepare the Vietnam chapter. She did an excellent job and only her obligations to her family prevented her from editing the entire book.

Linda Rothschild, a close friend, was kind enough to carefully read and critique my ongoing efforts. I am deeply grateful to her. There were many who volunteered for the task and I am appreciative of all of them. However, living in a tight-knit community, I felt extremely comfortable having Linda and my wife Sheila undertake this project. I wish to express my appreciation to Tuvia Rotberg, the well-known owner of a Judaica bookstore in Monsey, and Manny Polak of M.P. Press, who sits near me in synagogue, for their technical advice. Morry Schreiber and Jeremy Kay, my publishers, were a delight in co-ordinating all of the various facets that go into publishing such a volume.

Speaking of Sheila, this volume would not have been possible without the encouragement and support of my wonderful wife and partner of over 40 years. Her advice and her mere presence were of critical importance at those difficult moments when I felt that my ability to author an autobiography was a pipe dream. As she has been throughout our marriage, Sheila was always there for me during the writing of this book as a critic and a friend.

PROLOGUE
Vietnam Passover: Next Year in Jerusalem

I t was almost Passover, 1969, and I was happily looking forward to one of the duties for which I had regularly volunteered since arriving in Vietnam the previous summer—assisting the Jewish chaplain in officiating at services marking Jewish holidays and the Sabbath. This time, I would be working with my friend, Rabbi Harold "Chico" Wasserman, the chaplain at the sprawling U.S. base at Long Binh, where I myself was stationed at the 24th Evacuation Hospital. We were to officiate at a Seder for nearly 400 Jewish soldiers from bases and field posts around the surrounding area. I believe our seder was the only one of the four or five scheduled by the U.S. Army that year in Vietnam to be Orthodox-officiated. Only a handful of the soldiers who would be attending the two Seders and staying with us at Long Binh for the first two days of the holiday, were halachically observant. Wasserman and I were excited about the opportunity the holiday offered us to reach out to a large number of non-observant Jews and to share with them the spiritual beauty of a traditional Seder performed according to the tenets of Torah-true Judaism.

We had been given permission from the chief of the 24th Evac hospital, Col. Hammond, to use two contiguous wards that were normally kept empty in readiness for emergency mass casualties as a venue for our Passover Seder and for sleeping accommodations for some of the visiting G.I.s. The Jewish Welfare Board had sent us several thousand kosher TV dinners and a huge supply of matzos. We had such an overabundance of kosher wine that the Catholic chaplain would ask me several days later if he could use some for the sacrament, which I was happy to agree to.

So, as we approached the big event, everything seemed to be in order.

Yet things rarely went according to plan in Vietnam and sure enough, hours before the onset of the holiday, Wasserman informed me that he had developed a bad case of laryngitis. He asked if I could take the leading role in conducting the service and guiding the singing during the Seder while he played the back up role that normally fell to me. In fact, I had run seders many times before, so I didn't miss a beat in telling Wasserman I would be happy to pinch-hit for him. As I made last minute preparations and watched hundreds of Jewish soldiers arriving at the base, I resolved to make the Seder as traditional as possible without cutting any corners or adding the sort of new-fangled additions common in Reform Passovers. To say I was charged up and ready to roll would be an understatement.

The first part of the Seder service went wonderfully. Even though the vast majority of the soldiers were non-observant and some had never even been to a seder before, they responded with evident enthusiasm to the warmth and sense of acceptance that Wasserman and I conveyed together with the few soldiers who had experienced traditional seders before. As far as I could tell, no one in the room seemed impatient about sitting through the full Orthodox Seder. I certainly didn't discern any rustling or groans of "Lets eat, already." Naturally, the enthusiasm peaked during the singing, especially of *Dayenu*, which was familiar to nearly everyone. As we sang, I felt myself being overwhelmed by a sharp pang of loneliness for my family; especially for my sweet wife Sheila and little daughter Malkie. I had never been apart from my loved ones at Passover before and even as I sought to inspire enthusiasm in the 400 men sitting in front of me, I couldn't help but ask myself; "What am I doing in this G-d forsaken place with hundreds of complete strangers on this most special of holidays?"

Yet as fast as that feeling arose in me, I pushed it determinedly away and redoubled the fervor of my singing. After all, I reminded myself, I was not only responsible for leading the service, but as a major, I was the senior officer at the Seder. The men in that hall were looking to me for leadership and inspiration and it was up to me to project an aura of confidence, zest and joy, even at moments when I was not feeling so upbeat. In a life and death situation like Vietnam, leadership was a sacred responsibility, and I resolved anew to do everything I could to rise to the occasion.

Finally, we finished the first half of the seder and the meals were served. While not freshly made, those TV dinners were delicious, at least by Vietnam standards. An aura of contentment suffused the room. After finishing eating, many of the men drifted out of the ward and went outside the building into the central quadrangle to watch a movie on a large outdoor screen where every night they showed films for patients and staff. I realized that many of the non-observant G.I.'s who had gone outside would likely not be returning for the second part of the seder, but I figured that was understandable. Some of them had probably absorbed more *yiddishkeit* (Jewish spirituality) in the preceding two hours than they had gotten in years, if ever. Let them go and watch the movie.

Suddenly, out of nowhere, came a loud whoosh, the unmistakable sound of incoming enemy rocket fire. We knew instantly what it was because one of the first things a soldier learned upon entering the war zone in Vietnam was to distinguish between the powerful thud produced by outgoing mortars and the sinister whistle of an incoming missile. Seconds later, we heard several medium-sized explosions; evidence that Viet Cong missiles—probably mortar-or rocket-propelled grenades—had impacted somewhere inside the huge base, perhaps 500-1000 yards from where we were sitting. Instinctively, those of us inside the ward tensed up, preparing to hit the deck if the missiles hit any closer. Within seconds, the men who had gone out into the courtyard came pouring back into the ward. There was confusion and a sense of disorientation among many of the men, but no discernable sign of panic. Many of them appeared to be looking expectantly at me, waiting for orders as to what to do next.

As I pondered the situation, I was acutely aware that, unlike myself, most of the men who had come to the seder did not live at the base and were unfamiliar with the surroundings. Nearly all had left their flack jackets and helmets in the rooms they had been assigned for the night and at that moment, many seemed confused as to where those rooms were. As I struggled to maintain order, the sound of the incoming rockets ceased, but who knew whether they might not start up again in a minute or two? Suddenly, the sirens went off, sending a series of loud wails across the sprawling base. Standing orders at Long Binh were that at the first sound of a siren, everyone was supposed to crawl to an underground bunker and stay there until the all-clear was sounded.

Having been through many similar situations, I realized instantly that if we followed those orders and went directly to the shelters, we might be there for hours while U.S. helicopters searched for the source of the incoming fire. As the senior officer in the ward at that moment, I knew it was my responsibility to direct the evacuation. Yet I simply could not bear to contemplate a premature end to the wonderful seder I had shared with 400 fellow Jewish soldiers.

I seethed with a variety of strong emotions at that moment. I bristled with a feeling of defiance of the enemy and was damned if I was going to allow "Charlie" to shut down our beautiful seder with a little rocket fire. I could feel the evident spiritual uplift that the holiday was providing to those men; and my *neshama*, my Jewish soul, rebelled at the prospect of ending it. I also felt a deep conviction that this was a case of *shluchai mitzvah* (the performers of a mitzvah) and recalled that the Talmud says that he who is performing a mitzvah cannot be injured.

All of this raced through my mind within a matter of seconds and then, amidst the bedlam happening around me, I jumped up on the table and shouted.

"Men, I am the ranking officer in this room. I give you my solemn word that G-d will allow no harm to befall you if you now perform the mitzvah of sitting back down and finishing the seder."

My confidence and conviction must have been infectious, because the room became almost instantly quiet as all of the soldiers in the ward sat down in their seats at the dinner tables in perfect discipline. No one walked out of the room, and not even one of the men shouted back to me, "Are you out of your mind?" or "Hey, Doc, finish the seder if you want, but where do I go to hide?" For the next 45 minutes to an hour, we completed the seder in almost surreal tranquility. As though in confirmation of my promise, the Viet Cong shelling did not start again.

Then something amazing happened; something I would not

believe credible if I saw it in a movie. As we finished the formal seder, Wasserman and I rose from our seats and spontaneously began dancing around the huge table, singing the words from the Haggadah; "L' Shana Ha'baa Bi'Yerushalyim," (Next Year in Jerusalem). Within a few moments, virtually everyone in the room joined in. I could see tears running down scores of faces, including my own. Men were unashamedly hugging each other. For me, it was emotionally overwhelming to join with hundreds of American GIs in the distant jungles of Vietnam in professing our shared love for far-off Jerusalem. It felt too at that moment that we were affirming our faith in the God of Israel to protect us from the deadly unseen perils that threatened us every day in that ravaged land. I could see that many in that room—and not only the "religious" ones—felt that they were participating in a transcendent moment that felt truly miraculous.

Despite the beauty and emotional power of that moment, which always remained vivid, I would hardly claim that my decision not to order the troops to the shelters was either wise or morally correct. Looking back on that seder after more than thirty years, I simply cannot justify having done something that was not only in flagrant violation of U.S. Army regulations, but also of the Jewish moral imperative to preserve and protect life at all costs. Through my arrogance and stupidity I could have gotten us all killed, and if, God forbid, even one of those men had been hit by flying shrapnel and wounded as a result of my insistence that we finish the seder, I would have been deservedly court-martialled. Still, no one can change the past, and I did what I did. Perhaps the old saying that "God protects fools" is true, because none of our group was injured. Certainly, many of us felt that God was with us that night.

I have long reflected that my behavior at the moment we came under fire shows that I have some Lubavitch blood in me. My insistence on continuing the seder was reflective of a determination to accomplish something I have continued to do all of my life; to try to bring the joys of Torah and yiddishkeit to my Jewish brothers and sisters who, unlike me, did not have the privilege to grow up in the warmth and beauty of a Torah-true home. It is for this reason that I have continued to teach a weekly Talmud class to non-Orthodox doctors at Good Samaritan Hospital near my home even though I retired from my medical practice at the hospital eight years ago.

If the experiences of that unforgettable Passover buffeted me with an artillery barrage of strong feelings and impressions, it was hardly the first time in Vietnam I had felt beset by emotional overload. Many times during my seemingly endless twelve-month tour of duty, I had the feeling that more was happening to me than I could possibly absorb and remain sane. Many times I pondered the question, "How did I end up here?" Indeed, what was I, a nice Orthodox Jewish boy from Brooklyn who grew up to be a doctor, doing in the hellish jungles of a killing zone? It often seemed to me that someone in authority must have made a mistake somewhere along the line, because just as Vietnam had never been part of my game plan, I was hardly a prize catch for the army either. After all, I was a sedentary and overweight surgeon—not a gung ho physically toned Green Beret. When my moods of self-pity set in, as they often did during my down time away from the operating room where I struggled daily to save the lives of G.I.'s whose bodies had been blown apart in combat, I would frequently reflect bitterly that the whole thing just wasn't fair.

At those moments, I found myself beset by a host of fears beyond the primal one that I might be killed at any moment. Assuming that I managed to survive, would I be psychologically damaged by the violence I had witnessed or by the deaths of so many friends, including two of my fellow doctors? Would I be able to readjust successfully to civilian life? Could I ever again be a good husband to Sheila and a good father to my children or had the brutal experience of Vietnam forever shattered my ability to be kind and loving?

I knew men from my father's generation who had fought in World War II and had never succeeded in readjusting to civilian life and I knew others who had come home and built strong and wholesome lives. As a boy growing up in Brooklyn in the late 1940's, I had grown accustomed to Holocaust survivors with numbers etched on their arms. All of them had been through mind-bending horrors and yet while some seemed broken by the trauma of what they had endured in the death camps, many others managed to build happy and successful lives in their new country. Would I myself fall into the first category or the second?

As it would turn out, in many ways Vietnam was the best thing that ever happened to me. That searing trial by fire exponentially increased my overall self-confidence and my belief in my competence as a surgeon. Serving as an officer in Vietnam taught me leadership skills I have applied successfully both in my medical career and parallel life as a pro-Israel activist and Jewish organizational leader. The experience of having witnessed friends cut down by flying shrapnel only yards from where I was standing taught me to conquer my fears of the possibility of imminent death and to appreciate every day of my life as though it could be my last.

Serving in Vietnam also strengthened my abiding sense of American patriotism. I certainly hadn't chosen to go to Vietnam, but despite my bouts of self-pity and self-doubt, I hadn't run away either. I believed then, just as I believe today, that Communism was evil and I continue to consider that our own cause in Vietnam was just despite the eventual bitter outcome of the war. Loyalty to my country has remained a very basic tenor of my value system my entire life.

That understanding lay far in the future, however, as I lay in bed that night in 1969 after the end of our seder, with the fresh images of the extraordinary events in which I had participated cascading through my mind. Reflecting on my decision to go forward with the seder in the face of enemy fire, I wondered why it was that my commitment to Judaism had transcended everything else—including life and limb—at that moment, and from whence I had summoned the conviction that everything would come out all right if we went ahead with the seder. To understand all of that, I reflected, I would have to let my mind wander back to my very earliest days, back to the struggling but vibrant Orthodox Jewish world of Crown Heights, Brooklyn in the late 1930's.

CHAPTER ONE

Early Life

I was born February 6, 1937 in East Flatbush, New York. Yet to make vividly clear who I am, where I came from, and what I am all about, I need to take you back long before my birth to the world of my parents and even my parents' parents.

I never had the opportunity to meet my father's parents, both of whom died long before I was born. I experience an electric sense of personal connection whenever I look at one of the few remaining pictures of my paternal grandfather, Mendel, and see the unmistakable family resemblance between the two of us. He was a Lubavitcher Hasid who came to New York from Yanovitz in White Russia in the early years of the century and ended up as a Rebbe (teacher) in East Flatbush, where he died of cancer at the age of sixty four in 1933. His wife, my grandmother, Sara, also died prematurely of cancer four years earlier at the age of fifty four.

My father, Morris Ganchrow, was a strong man, even a tough man, but also a profoundly good and decent one. He was almost universally beloved by everyone who had dealings with him. I loved him deeply until the day he died at the much too young age of fifty seven in 1962.

My father was not a politically correct parent by modern-day standards. He was a sharp disciplinarian with a strong temper who believed in hitting his children with a strap when they did something wrong. Yet he was, above all else, a kind man, a devoted family man who loved his wife and children with all his heart and soul and was totally dedicated to providing for us. And when it came to corporal punishment, the threat was usually enough to make unnecessary the actual act.

Morris Ganchrow was born July 5, 1905, in Brooklyn, but he spoke Yiddish perfectly. He was one of four surviving children, himself and three sisters, but he was the only child who stayed truly Orthodox; that is, lived an Orthodox lifestyle throughout his adult life. Perhaps that is because my father received a rock-solid foundation whereas his sisters did not; he went through the yeshiva system from his early childhood until the end of high school; attending Yeshiva Chaim Berlin and then the new Yeshiva University High School (Talmudic Academy) before getting a private smicha (rabbinic ordination).

Economic survival necessitated that my father go to work right after graduating. I do not recall him ever making mention of being sorry or disappointed that he was unable to attend college, but he did give the impression he was distinctly aware that he never had higher education and was therefore sharply limited in what he might otherwise have accomplished.

If Morris Ganchrow maintained strong links to the faith and traditions of his parents, he was unmistakably a native-born American. My father's spiritual home was the Young Israel movement. Young Israel, which opened its first congregation in a storefront shtiebel (synagogue) on the Lower East Side and soon expanded to Williamsburg and Brownsville in Brooklyn, where Morris was a member, was composed of young American-born and English-speaking Orthodox Jews who were very different from their Yiddish-speaking fathers and grandfathers who had arrived a decade or two earlier from Eastern and Central Europe. The Young Israel movement encouraged the singing of songs during services, which explained why so many young men like my father became *chazanim* (cantors). The young people conducted their own services and had parties where young men and women could meet in an Orthodox context. I believe it is not too much to say that in the 1920's, 30's and 40's, it was Young Israel that saved Orthodoxy in America. The movement certainly created a network that has lasted a lifetime. Even today, I often meet old men at Orthodox events who will approach me and say, "I remember your father so well. He was such a wonderful guy."

Morris Ganchrow was a product of his own time and place, specifically of the America of the 1930's, the Depression era. My father had seen his own parents modest savings go up in smoke when the stock market crashed, so he never tried to save money after that. He never bought a stock or bond in his life and he didn't trust banks. Indeed, when he died he left my mother nothing more than eight hundred dollars in the vault and considerable debt.

For if my father did not save money, he did do what he had to in order to provide his family—my mother, myself, and my two younger brothers—with the nicer things in life. He bought a house with a considerable mortgage that he struggled to come up with every month, and always rented the family a summer bungalow in the Catskills (He never had the "courage" to put the money down to buy a summer house despite all the dollars he continued to pour into rentals). When I was growing up we had a car, unlike most of the struggling families around us. But clearly the experience of the Depression had caused my father to conclude that putting money aside was a bad idea; who knew if it would be there tomorrow?

My father scrambled to find a variety of ways to pull together a living. Possessed of a marvelous singing voice, even though he had no formal musical training and could barely read a note, he made a living as an itinerant or free-lance cantor, serving in a wide variety of congregations around Brooklyn and also traveled widely around the United States and Canada. Always a public personality in the Jewish community and beyond, he served as a host for a time of a Yiddish-language program on WEVD, a Jewish-oriented radio station with a large audience. He was also a highly talented public speaker. In his determination to provide for his family, my father considered no job, however humble, to be beneath himself. Even though he was a renowned cantor and radio personality, he also taught the *haftorah* (readings from the prophets) to bar mitzvah kids. From the time I was conscious, I used to sit in my playpen and listen and by the time I was three years old, I could sing the whole haftorah. Indeed, as a toddler I would sing the haftorah while my mother wheeled me in my carriage down Eastern Parkway. Sometimes, women would eye me disapprovingly and say to my mother, "This is an *ayin hara* (evil eye), a devil. Its unnatural for such a small child to be able to do that."

Although music was my father's first love, he had to do other jobs to make ends meet for his growing family. As a young man, he delivered kosher chickens to people's homes. Much later, during the last twenty years of his life he became a professional fund-raiser, primarily for Yeshiva University. He was also an honorary chaplain to the Shomrim Society and the Ner Tamid

Society (respectively the Jewish fraternal orders of the New York City Police and Fire Departments), as well as to the Sea Scouts and the Police Athletic League.

In all of the many professional and honorary roles that he played, my father was absolutely incorruptible. For him nothing could be worse than taking a bribe or even cutting corners in a quasi-legal way and his proximity to politics caused him to stress the evils of corruption and bribery by public officials. He was adamant that his own children should absorb that lesson. He explained to us sternly that not only are all forms of bribery against the Torah, but that when a person is in public service, he has an obligation to uphold the public trust by being scrupulously honest with public money. My father said that a person is honor bound to uphold an even higher ethical standard with public money than he would with his own finances.

That training made a lifelong impression on me. Although I have served in top leadership positions in several Jewish organizations, I have never wanted to touch money, to serve, for example, as an organizational treasurer. When I started HUVPAC in 1982, we didn't have a computer. In the beginning I would sit for hours in our kitchen with my wife Sheila and my kids making mailing labels by hand. Several times when I spoke in synagogues on behalf of HUVPAC in the early days someone would approach me and ask, "How do you keep your records? Are they computerized?" I would respond in the negative and the person would offer to help us computerize our records until I asked, "By the way, can you do it on a volunteer basis?" Invariably, those eager beavers would look at me like I was crazy and walk awkwardly away.

Finally, realizing that the labeling and record keeping was becoming an impossible job as HUVPAC grew rapidly, I broke down and spent $3000-$4000 of my own money on an IBM computer. For many years, my total computer expertise was generating labels. I no more thought of billing HUVPAC for that considerable expense than I did for the scores of telephone calls I made every month from my own home and business phones to senators and congressmen in Washington and around the country. That sense of personal rectitude came to me thanks to the training I received from my father.

Morris was first and foremost a people person. People loved him and he responded in kind. He loved politics and had friends in high places. He had close ties with the Brooklyn Democratic machine and many good friends in the labor unions. My father was very close also to Abe Stark, the Borough President of Brooklyn. I remember vividly that when my parents celebrated their twenty fifth wedding anniversary, Mayor Paul O'Dwyer presented them with a beautiful tea set as a gift.

My father had many non-Jewish friends, especially Italian-Americans. He had a particularly close friend named Johnny Votta, who was a World War II veteran and American Legion leader. Johnny and his large family and friends apparently didn't trust their priest very much, because they all used to come to my father for advice. When my father's sister desperately needed blood for an operation, ten members at the American Legion showed up at the hospital to donate blood. When Israel needed guns in 1948 to stop an invasion by Arab armies, the same group from the American Legion collected firearms to send to the new Jewish state. On one memorable night, we learned that one of my father's Italian-American friends had been stopped by the police on Ocean Parkway for a traffic violation and promptly been arrested when they found the car contained a cache of firearms. The man had been on the way to deliver the arms to a ship that was about to sail for Israel.

My father's friendships with people like Johnny Votta taught me an invaluable lesson about how to conduct my own life. My father never made a distinction between Jews and non-Jews. He taught me that all people—Jewish and non-Jewish—are equal human beings and that you should treat all people, as you would want them to treat you. Certainly, I never heard my father preach hatred against anyone. At the same time, he was emphatic to my brothers and I that it is important to live as a strictly observant Orthodox Jew. He taught us that people of all backgrounds will respect you if you uphold your own traditions honestly and proudly, but that they will despise you if you try to hide who you are.

The neighborhood where my father and mother raised my two younger brothers and I, East Flatbush and Crown Heights, was very different then than it is today. It was a friendly middle class neighborhood that was overwhelmingly white—primarily Jewish, but with a large Italian population. Not only was the Lubavitch community, that has come to loom so large in recent decades, very small at that time, there were relatively few Orthodox Jews in general in relation to the larger Jewish population, which was mainly non-affiliated with substantial Conservative and Reform communities. Later of course, as the American black and Caribbean population of the area grew apace, the non-Orthodox Jews and Italians mainly fled to the suburbs. Many mainstream Orthodox Jews also left for the Five Towns and other suburban areas or relocated to Boro Park and other heavily Jewish parts of Brooklyn. Only the Lubavitch community chose to stay, since they believed that the highest blessing was to live close to their Rebbe, who had let it be known that he would never leave Crown Heights.

When I was growing up, the neighborhood was warm, *heimisch* and safe. One rarely heard about people getting robbed and my childhood was unscarred by incidents of anti-Semitism. My family never had much money, but neither did most of the families growing up around us. Unlike so many other diaspora Jews who have grown up with a sense of marginality, I felt secure and at home, loved and provided for by my parents and truly at home, in a vibrant community that was overwhelmingly Jewish. Still, I attribute my sense of self-confidence; the belief that I could accomplish whatever I set my mind to, primarily to the inspiring example of my father. He combined a mixture of high expectations, encouragement, and love toward me and my brothers.

My father was best known in the community as a cantor. Synagogues advertised for the cantors in the Yiddish newspapers, and my father would grandly arrive with a double choir in tow. People literally mobbed the shuls to hear them, and my father and his company traveled to synagogues throughout the U.S. and Canada to perform.

My father taught us to appreciate cantorial music and sometimes we would walk two or three miles on a shabbos to hear a particular cantor perform. Often, we would take the guest cantor home with us for lunch, walking the same long shlep (trek) home in reverse. Song was always in our house. My brothers Saul and Jacob and I learned the repetoires of some of the great choirs of those days like the Oscar Julius Choir, the Henry Spector Choir or the Abe Nadell Choir. I loved to sing *chazunis* (the cantorial chant), but the only problem was that I had no voice. I had good *nusuch* (tune or melody), but no voice. When I was in the shower or driving alone in the car my voice was "terrific."

Perhaps because he felt he himself had not received sufficient education, my father was very strict with my own schooling.

Every few weeks, he would show up unannounced at my school to ask my teachers how I was doing. God forbid the consequences for me if I got a bad mark on my report card. On the few occasions it did happen, my father insisted that I bring a note home from my teacher every day explaining that I was making sufficient progress. Thank God, I mainly did quite well academically.

My father loved baseball and imbued me with an almost fanatical devotion to the Brooklyn Dodgers. He took me to Dodgers games all the time. Often, he would pick me up from school around 4PM and we would drive down to Ebbetts Field together to catch the last few innings of a day game. Since my father knew all the cops in the area, we were able to park right next to the ballpark and walk right in. I also got a fire line card through my father's *proteksia* (connections) that allowed the bearer to pass through police lines to get close to a fire. On a couple of occasions, I was driving around on a date with Sheila before we were married and hearing the wailing of a fire engine siren would shout impulsively, "C'mon we are going to a fire." No doubt she thought I was completely crazy.

Morris Ganchrow was a wonderful man, but when I did wrong, I knew I might be in line for punishment. When I was little, I used to try to call my grandfather on the phone to tell him to protect me from my father and occasionally my mother so I wouldn't get punished—except that I didn't know how to dial the phone and would keep getting the wrong number. Finally, the phone company called my mother and asked who was making all those wrong number calls. After that, my mother taught me how to dial correctly.

What I learned from my father was controlled anger. If you are angry all the time, people will avoid you, but if you never get angry, people will take advantage of you. Indeed, ninety nine percent of the time, my father was a soft and giving person, especially in his relationships with his children. I have sweet memories of many times when he came home from work with toys for me. Other times he would surprise and thrill me by saying out of the blue, "Hey, Mendy, lets go to a movie" or "I have two tickets for the Dodgers game. Do you want to come?" Of course, I did!

I myself feel today that spanking, or the threat of it, can be an effective disciplinary tool, provided it is not overdone. Often, it will suffice for a parent to show the errant child a scowl or point to his belt buckle. The truth is that kids need discipline, just as I did in my childhood, if they are to learn to function effectively in the world. I was a high-spirited kid and was frequently full of mischief. I respected and loved my father and knew if he struck me, it was because I did something wrong. I also knew that if I did something good, I would be rewarded. Believe me, I was rewarded many more times than I was disciplined.

My mother, like her late husband, is a person of great intellect and goodness. Blessedly, she is still with us and in 2001 celebrated her 90th birthday. She did not seek to make her mark in the world, but like other women of her generation did everything she could to give her children the foundation of love and understanding we needed to build successful lives. She remains totally aware of current events and seems to have forgotten no episode or personality from her rich life. She was always a voracious reader of books and newspapers; but, sadly, is no longer able to read due to partial blindness caused by macular degeneration. Nevertheless, she is still able to enjoy watching movies and shows, and listening to talking books.

My mother's father, Jacob Wallach, came to America from Poland in 1904 when he was already married with a small child, but waited six years until he had made enough money to bring over his wife and child to Brownsville, Brooklyn. One year later, July 16, 1911, my mother was born. My grandfather had been a yeshiva student in Poland, and during the years he lived alone in New York, despite the economic pressure, he never violated the laws of kashruth or shabbat. I knew him only slightly and remember him as a thin person who always rolled his own cigarettes. Of course I loved him very much and complained to him if I felt my parents were picking on me.

After his family joined him in Brownsville, Jacob Wallach tried a number of ways to make a living, but was never very successful. For a time, he worked as a presser in a factory, and then opened a business that was soon destroyed by a fire. Later, he opened a fruit stand in East New York that went bankrupt, and finally operated a series of fruit pushcarts—until he broke his leg and became disabled.

My maternal grandmother, Anna Wallach, was extremely religious. She covered her hair and was meticulous in keeping the Shabbat and the laws of *mikveh*. As I grew up, I often went to her house to pick her up to walk together to shul on the Shabbat. As an adolescent, my mother helped her father at the fruit stand, until she got a job as a secretary at a local bank shortly after graduating from high school. It was while working at the bank that she met my father. Since my own mother grew up with such an observant mother and had a number of other religious aunts and uncles, she readily acceded to my father's desire that his wife-to-be should keep a rigorously Orthodox home. They were married July 7, 1935.

She continued to work even after they were married, but quit when the children were born. Later on, she went back to work as a statistical typist. She worked for many years but never received health insurance or the benefit of a pension.

Like her husband, my mother was American-born, but absorbed much of the culture and flavor of Jewish Eastern Europe in her mother's milk. She was a very good cook in an old world sort of way, but her concept of vegetables were *kishke* and *kugel* (stuffed derma and potato or noodle pudding). Each Friday morning, we would awake to the sound of my mother chopping pike, white fish and carp in a wooden bowl to prepare gefilte fish. If we didn't finish all the food on our plate, she would remind us of all the children in Europe who were starving.

My mother was the peacemaker in the family. Whenever my father was fighting with one of his sisters, my mother would be the one to patch things up. To this day, even though she is in her 90's, if I don't call my brother, Jacob, for two or three days, she will call me and say none too subtly, "I spoke to Jacob today and he says he hasn't heard from you for a while."

I have two brothers, Saul who is three years younger than myself, and Jacob, who is six years younger. Saul and I shared a bedroom when we were little. We grew up being close, going to baseball games, and doing many other things together. Because of the substantial age difference between my younger brother Jacob and myself, I related to him more as a baby brother when growing up, but we began to feel like equals after his reaching adulthood. Both of my brothers went on to teaching careers in the New York City public school system, and both worked every summer as chefs in Zionist camps in the Catskills. Just as I have, they and their children and grandchildren have remained rooted in the traditions and lifestyles our parents implanted in us so many years ago.

As for my mother; while she may have deferred to my father

in many decisions, if she felt strongly about something, she was adamant about putting her foot down. For example, when it came time for me to go to elementary school, my father wanted me to follow in his footsteps and attend *Yeshiva Chaim Berlin*, which was located near our home. However, when he and my mother entered the building to register me for class, my sharp-nosed mother smelled urine in the hall. She immediately turned to my father and said emphatically, "That's it. Mendy is not going here. I will never send a child of mine to such a school." Nothing my father could say would change her mind, and he agreed that I would instead be enrolled at the Crown Heights Yeshiva, a more modern Zionistic-style school where Judaic studies were taught in Hebrew instead of Yiddish. Being transferred to the *Crown Heights Yeshiva* had fateful consequences for me. If I had gone to *Chaim Berlin*, I would surely never have become a physician, because higher secular education was not a prime goal of that devoutly religious, old world style institution.

Actually, the truth is that my father never wanted me to become a doctor. He badly wanted me to be a rabbi or failing that, a lawyer. But from a very early age, I knew I wanted to be a doctor, in particular a surgeon who saved peoples' lives. When I was a young boy, my father was often sick and I would always marvel at the ability of the doctors who would frequently come to our house to treat him. Then, when I was nine or ten, my father became desperately ill with pneumonia. We were unable to visit him in the hospital and I was fearful that he would die. I prayed hard and recited psalms. I can't recall whether or not I made a formal pledge, but I recall promising God that if he allowed my father to live, I would become a better Jew and a better person. Miraculously, he recovered, and I resolved to serve God to the best of my ability.

Ironically, as I grew older I came to understand that the best way for me to accomplish that was not to make my life's work as a rabbi. I saw too many Orthodox rabbis making compromises in upholding *halacha* (Jewish law), for the sake of securing and maintaining lucrative rabbinical positions. For example, I was appalled to observe Orthodox rabbis accepting positions in synagogues without separate sections for men and women or where the rabbi spoke with a microphone from the *bimah* (center podium).

Once when I was a college student at Yeshiva University, I was sent to an Orthodox shul in Rochester, N.Y. to serve as a guest rabbi during the High Holy Days of Rosh Hashanah and Yom Kippur. The shul had a balcony for women, but in the middle of the afternoon service, two women came downstairs to sit in the back. I asked someone to go over to them to ask them to sit in the women's section, but the reply came back to me that they did not want to leave where they were sitting. Their response was a flagrant violation of Orthodox law, which requires that the sexes should be separated by a divider, a facet of Jewish religious observance that originated in the Holy Temple in Jerusalem.

Feeling that I had no choice, I stopped the service. I announced that I did not want to embarrass anyone but that the service could not go on unless the two women in the back vacated their seats and went to the women's section. At that point, they got up and went upstairs, but later I was informed that I would not be rehired the following year because I was too "rigid."

This tendency by a growing number of rabbis to cut *halachic* corners so as not to offend powerful congregants was part of a wider phenomenon that began after World War II and has continued until this day known as "checkbook Judaism." If you had the money, you could make yourself into a "Jewish leader" and gain, in effect, the ability to set Jewish law. Throughout American Jewry, there was the same distasteful picture; the ascendancy of Jewishly illiterate so-called communal "leaders" who attained their exalted positions because of the fortunes they had made, or even because of what I have called "lucky sperm," being the son or daughter of one of those self-made tycoons.

This virus was even affecting the Orthodox community, which until now had been the most devoted to upholding Torah-true Judaism. Jewish institutions have had guests of honor at their dinners and events that are intermarried. Sadly, intermarriage has not proven an insurmountable barrier to becoming president of a "major" Jewish organization if the person in question has a large enough checkbook and is willing to contribute lavishly. I find this tendency to be completely unacceptable.

Actually, I am not so rigid by nature. I am a pragmatic person in many aspects of life, and have often, for example, been willing to make compromises on political issues. But I will not compromise on the basic tenets of my Orthodox Jewish religious faith. I therefore decided early on that I would be more valuable as a strong Jewish lay leader than as a rabbi.

In truth, I had another, perhaps less noble reason, for deciding against the rabbinate. I certainly had the intellect to be a rabbi, but I decided early on that I doubted I had the *zitzfleisch*, the perseverance, to sit and learn Judaism for so many years with the kind of intensity I would need to become a first-rate rabbinic leader. I have never wanted to do anything halfway, so unless I believed that I could become top of the line at anything I set my mind to do, I chose not to start.

There was another field that attracted me greatly—politics. Fascinated by my father's closeness to the world of politics in Brooklyn, I myself started mixing it up as an aspiring politician when I was still a school kid. My first campaign was for president of the General Organization (Student Council) of Crown Heights Yeshiva, a position for which I ran in seventh or eighth grade. My uncle, Dave Greenberg, who had a printing shop, printed up cards and posters for me with the legend "Vote for Mendy Ganchrow." I lost that race, but got hooked on the process. I went on to become president of the student body of the Brooklyn Talmudic Academy (Yeshiva University High School), not once but two times.

What was it about politics that so appealed to me? Since my childhood, I have loved the game—the art form—of politics. I love the "art of the deal." It is like watching Marlon Brando in "The Godfather"—that little whisper in the ear and the handshake—the expressions of loyalty. Politics is filled with fascinating ritual and is replete with the best and the worst of human relations. I was fascinated by the power of Carmine De Sapio, who was the undisputed leader of Tammany Hall during my youth and who ended up going to jail.

From an early age, I read the *New York Times* and followed national politics. During the summer of 1948, when I was eleven, I placed the radio under my pillow late at night so that I was able to listen to the Republican and Democratic Conventions. The latter event was especially exciting when the delegations from the southern states took part in a dramatic walkout over civil rights. I would also stay up way past my bedtime, listening to speeches by Henry Wallace, who ran a quixotic but memorable campaign on the Progressive ticket. It was an incredible political year; right down to President Harry Truman's stunning come-from-behind victory over the heavily favored Republican nominee, Thomas Dewey.

In 1951, I got to see Harry Truman in person, when he came

to speak at the Eastern Parkway Arena in Brooklyn. Needless to say, it was the first time I had ever seen a President of the United States and I was giddy with excitement. My father knew the Secret Service agents in charge of security, and I was allowed into the arena before it opened and got a seat in the second or third row. The President was in the middle of his speech when the mother of a Korean War soldier suddenly rushed toward the podium; screaming something like "You killed my son!" Six Secret Service agents instantly materialized, wrestled the woman to the ground and then carried her off as though she was a piece of flypaper. Amidst the pandemonium, someone in the audience shouted, 'Give 'em hell, Harry!" Gesticulating dramatically with his arms, the president responded in his distinctive Missouri accent; "I'm gonna, if you give me a chance." The crowd applauded wildly in appreciation.

So given my love of politics, one might have expected that, having decided against the rabbinate, I would have applied myself in getting into a good law school, in preparation for a political career. But by the time I was in high school, I had already decided that I didn't want to become a professional politician. I realized that, all too often, politics has a very high level of dishonesty and corruption. I decided that it would be better to dabble in politics in order to advance causes in which I believed, while making my living from a medical practice, rather than becoming a professional politician. In this too, I would be like my father, who knew the key players of the political world, but was not directly part of it.

I was an excellent student at Crown Heights Yeshiva—I had to be, what with my father checking up on me all the time. But I also knew how to have a good time. Like my father, my first love was the Brooklyn Dodgers. For most of my childhood, I went to about twenty five or thirty Dodger games a year, and the ones I was unable to attend I listened to on the radio. Whether sitting in a bleacher seat at Ebbetts Field or listening to the game on a radio at home, I would score every pitch, including foul balls. My knowledge of the minutia of the game was awe-inspiring. How many times did I correct Red Barber on the radio? He'd be calling the balls and strikes when the other team was up and he'd say something like, "This batter has a .242 record." I would immediately shout out, "You jerk, he is batting .239." A minute later Barber would say, "Sorry, folks, I was mistaken. His actual batting average is .239." I impressed a lot of people that way. In fact, I can still recite by heart the batting averages of all of the members of the 1950 Dodgers.

How many people today remember that there was also a Brooklyn Dodgers football team that played in the NFL for a few years? I even went to see one of their games at Ebbetts Field. Like I said, I was the truest of Brooklyn sports fans and literally bled Dodger blue.

I ended my sports mania at the age of twenty, when the Dodgers suddenly deserted Brooklyn for Los Angeles after the 1957 season. I had been such a rabidly loyal fan, living and dying with the team and I just couldn't take the betrayal by Dodgers owner Walter O'Malley. Like so many other Brooklynites, I realized in a flash that I had been snookered. O'Malley, had been doing it all along as a business—and it was definitely not my business! Then I thought, "Hey, this guy is making millions and I'm making nothing. Why should I give him love, affection and loyalty?'"

I did follow the Dodgers for a few years after they moved to Los Angeles. When I was in medical school in Chicago, I went to see them play the Cubs at Wrigley Field a couple of times. Once, I was watching the Dodgers in batting practice and shouting at my favorite player, Carl Furillo, like we did back in Brooklyn. "Hey Carl, how ya doing baby? Good eye, Carl, good eye" and the next thing I know this hillybilly from Wisconsin goes over to the ushers and asks them to have me evicted for making too much noise. Obviously, he had never been to Ebbets Field. So the ushers come over and tell me to tone it down and I say, "Whaddaya mean? That's what you do at a ballgame." Anyway, the ushers eventually left me alone and gave the guys who complained some other seats.

Later on, they built an apartment house on the site of Ebbetts Field, called the Ebbetts Field Apartments. When I was a resident rotating through pathology at Brookdale Hospital, I got a job making house calls at night. I got a call to the Ebbetts Field Apartments. I went there and saw the patient, but when I left I started to cry. I said to myself, "That's it. I will never take another call at Ebbetts Field. It just hurt too much."

Today, my children and grandchildren don't understand my seeming lack of interest in sports. They ask; "How can you live in this world and not be interested in sports? They follow various sports like hockey and basketball in which I have no interest whatsoever. What they don't understand is that I actually loved sports, was a more hard-core fan than any of them will ever be, but that when the Dodgers left Brooklyn, I felt that sports had abused me. I also find it obscene nowadays to see ball players making twenty million dollars a year while teachers and civil servants are struggling. For me, that is a sign that there is something seriously askew with the values of our society.

When I was in college I used to spend the summers working as a busboy or waiter at various hotels in the Catskills, and often played on the hotel softball teams. On one memorable game day morning during one of those lazy, long-ago Catskills summers, a player from the other team called me to confirm we would be playing them that afternoon and then said, "Oh, by the way, Johnny Podres will be pitching for us. Do you have any problem with that?" I laughed, assuming he was pulling my leg. The idea of Johnny Podres, the Dodgers pitching ace, showing up to pitch for a Borscht Belt team composed mainly of overweight Jewish kids seemed about as likely as if he were to say that President Eisenhower would be playing center field.

Anyway, when we arrived at the ball field, sure enough, there was Johnny Podres with a big convertible car and a beautiful girl on his arm, signing autographs. When I had recovered from my shock, I went up to him and said, "Johnny, we are honored to have you here, but I should warn you that we play seriously, sliding into bases and things. We don't want you to get hurt." Johnny gave me a none-too-friendly look and sort of growled, "OK, kid, just play the game."

He pitched—not like he pitched in the majors of course—but underhand, according to softball rules. He had a terrible team behind him so our team won the game and since I was the pitcher opposing him, I have been able to claim all of these years that I beat Johnny Podres. It was remarkable to watch Johnny run the bases with all the beauty and form of a top-notch professional athlete. When I picked up the New York Post the next day, there was a column on the sports page mentioning that Podres had been sent home for a few days in the middle of a Dodgers' road trip so that he could rest his ailing arm. And there he was making a few bucks pitching softball in the Catskills — which was definitely a "no no" for major league pitchers supposedly resting their arms. I doubt the Dodgers had any idea that Johnny was moonlighting during his "down time."

As much as I adored baseball as a kid, I actually offered to give up going to Dodger games in 1948, when I was eleven, so that my parents could save on all those sixty-cent bleacher tickets and buy a television for us. Television had suddenly become the craze of America, with Howdy Doody and Milton Berle. I pleaded with my parents for a TV set, but they kept insisting it was too expensive. One day my father came home from work and found me standing in front of our house with a picket sign shouting that my parents were not fair because they were denying me a television. When that didn't work, I swallowed my pride and offered to give up baseball games and trips to the movies as well.

One of my friends in those days and a classmate at Crown Heights Yeshiva was Erich Segal, later to go on to fame as the author of *Love Story*. On Sundays, the gang would go to his house, a big sprawling place that looked like a castle and hang out with our club, which we called "The Sages."

Nineteen-fifty was a big year for me. I was both bar mitzvah'd and graduated from Crown Heights Yeshiva. My father wrote my bar mitzvah speech for me in Yiddish which I did not understand, but which I memorized to recite in the synagogue. I recited it by heart and somehow managed to repeat a page without anyone noticing. It must have been a real spellbinder. Overall, though, it was a gala event at which my father served as cantor with a 24-piece-choir in the Park Place Synagogue in Brooklyn. Somehow over two thousand people packed into the shul for the event, which had been advertised in the Jewish newspapers.

After the services, my parents had a small reception for family and friends with herring, kugel and kichel, followed by a formal affair the following evening at a catering hall.

Under my picture in my yearbook from my graduating year at Crown Heights Yeshiva is the notation that I wanted to be a physician as well as a surgeon. Then it was on to the Brooklyn Talmudic Academy (BTA), which was another name for the boys' school at Yeshiva University High School. I vividly remember the school, which had two small buildings at the corner of Bedford and President Streets, just three blocks from Ebbets Field. We had no gym; but we played all kinds of sports outside in an adjoining used car lot and in the street.

I thrived at BTA both academically and socially. I was inspired by two rabbi-teachers, Rabbi Harold Kanotopsky and Rabbi
Peretz Yogel, of blessed memory. Rabbi Kanotopsky, whom I
considered to be my Rebbe, was an American-born mathematics
teacher who was also rabbi of the Young Israel of Eastern Parkway. He was a great Torah scholar, whose method of imparting
both the intricacies and the majestic sweep of Torah Judaism was
so lucid and eloquent that to this day when I am preparing a
major talk, I refer to his books for incisive lessons in the teachings of our tradition. He was also a very approachable all-Ameri-
can kind of guy who used to play baseball with us. Often when
I was pitching, he would be right behind me playing second
base and I would shout, "C'mon Rabbi, make that play." Here
was a man with immense moral authority but who never held
himself aloof. He was very informal and treated all his students
with respect and kindness.

Rabbi Kanotopsky used to say that it is proper to stand up
whenever the Torah is being read in the synagogue as a show of
respect to the Torah, which was given to us by God. Still, he
cautioned one should not stand if the local rabbi himself did not
stand up, as one should never do anything to embarrass the
rabbi. This is a lesson that I took very much to heart and passed
along to my own children.

Rabbi Yogel was a very different kind of rebbe; a refugee from
Europe who fled Hitler together with the rest of his yeshiva by
way of Japan and Shanghai, where he spent the war years. He
was a deeply devout Jew who dressed in a black frock, but was
extremely knowledgeable on a wide range of secular subjects, from
Shakespeare to medicine. One morning in class Rabbi Yogel noticed that I seemed distracted and said to me, "Nu, Mendy, you
don't seem like you are paying attention to the Talmud." I responded that I was nervous because my brother was in the hospital that morning having an operation to have his appendix removed. So he sat me down and drew me a detailed diagram of the
appendix and adjacent organs and explained the whole operation
to me in detail, emphasizing that having one's appendix out was
gornischt (nothing) and there was absolutely no reason for me to
worry. By the time he was finished, my mind was totally at ease.

Rabbi Yogel was a warm and compassionate person who cared
deeply for his students and had a wonderful philosophy that
emphasized that there is ample time for many aspects of life.

Unlike some teachers who used to bemoan summer vacation as wasted time when students ought to continue studying, Rabbi Yogel would urge us to use our summers in camp to relax and enjoy ourselves so that we would come back to school in September well rested and ready to study hard.

As I mentioned, I spent a lot of time and energy in high school perfecting my political skills in student government. I figured it wouldn't hurt my re-election bid if I used some of my father's political contacts to dazzle my fellow students, so at my behest, my father invited his friend, New York State Supreme Court Justice Hymie Barshay to come to speak to the student body on the subject of "Justice." Barshay was himself running for office at that moment, so the speech he delivered before our student body came across as an out and out campaign speech about why he should be re-elected. It was sort of embarrassing, so when Barshay paused in the middle of his speech, my father leaned forward and whispered in his ear; "Judge, you are supposed to be speaking about justice." Barshay smiled and addressed the student body, saying, " I have just been informed by Rabbi Ganchrow that I am supposed to speak about justice. Well, it would certainly be justice if I was re-elected."

Besides running for political office, my favorite extra-curricular activity was the school debating team. The manager of our team was an individual one class behind me named Avi Dershowitz, who later became Professor Alan Dershowitz, the famous Harvard Law School professor, author and television commentator. Another member of the team was Steve Riskin, who later became Rabbi Shlomo Riskin, the Chief Rabbi of Efrat and a famous figure in Israel and throughout the Orthodox world. I have had the honor of introducing Rabbi Riskin at various events over the years, and always point out on those occasions that among the three people pictured in the front row of the debating team of the 1954 school yearbook, the Elchanite of BTA, two of them, Riskin and Dershowitz had changed their first names. Only Mendy Ganchrow kept his original name, but, alas, did not attain the world renown of the other two.

Sometimes, when people meet me the first time, they assume that because I am an Orthodox Jewish leader, I must be prim and straight-laced. Actually, nothing could be further from the truth about me or about the world I grew up in. In fact, it was a milieu of fun and good-natured practical jokes in which I often took part. At BTA, we used to take advantage of some of our teachers, including a soft-spoken and chronically forgetful Spanish teacher everyone called "Senor." We would sometimes put bricks in his briefcase and then break out into laughter when he would pick it up and frown, not understanding what was weighing him down. He would walk down the halls of the school lugging his briefcase, leaning to the right at close to a ninety-degree angle.

The most memorable prank I can remember was played by a notorious *kibbitzer* (practical joker) in our class on our own dear Rebbe. At that time, the whole country was abuzz about news that the notorious bank robber, Willie Sutton, had been recaptured after an escape from prison due to information supplied by an FBI informer named Arnold Schuster. Shortly thereafter, Schuster was himself murdered and a substantial price was placed on the head of the murderer. One day, our kibbitzer brought a toy phone to class, which had a genuine sound ringing mechanism. When the phone rang, the kid stood up from his desk with the phone in hand and said, "Hello operator, get me the police. Hello, police, do you know who killed Schuster? It was—." At that point another participant in the joke, seated on the other side of the room, jumped dramatically to his feet, extended a cap pistol and shouted, in fake mobster style, "Take this you dirty rotten rat. Die you stoolie!" and fired several rounds. The *kibbitzer* clutched his chest with a hand he had smeared with ketchup and cried, "He got me. He got me." The Rebbe, who had been completely taken in, cried out, "Oh no! They shot him! They shot him!" and rushed over to the fallen student. The class was hysterical with laughter, but the Rebbe was so intent on trying to save the student's life that it took a few moments before he realized he had been taken in.

During my freshman year at BTA, I myself went too far with a practical joke and ended up in a brush with the law. At the time, my whole family was angry with our landlady, who would often fail to provide heat and hot water to the four-family-house in which we were living—even in the winter. I belonged to a youth club at Young Israel of Eastern Parkway, from which we used to send postcards to remind members of upcoming sports and social events. One night, in a giddy mood, I took one of those postcards, addressed it to our landlady, and then crossed out the world "Young Israel" and wrote "I will meet you in the graveyard." Urged on by a friend of mine, who is today a well-known rabbi, I went outside and put the postcard in a mailbox. Upon receiving the prank postcard, our landlady turned it over to the postal service, which informed the police who commenced an investigation. I was quickly discovered and, scared out of my wits, I had to go down to the Postal Service, which made me sign a pledge that I would never do anything like that again. The police promised to expunge the incident from my record if I did not get into further trouble by the age of eighteen. After that I was careful to avoid practical jokes that could remotely be construed as crossing the line between good fun and juvenile delinquency.

I don't want to convey the impression, however, that I was a smart aleck sort of kid who didn't take his studies seriously. Nothing could be further from the truth. I grew up imbued by my father and the environment around me with the ideals of *torah u madah* (bringing together Torah and modernity), and I upheld these values not only in primary and secondary school, but also when I headed off to Yeshiva University. From my childhood, I was committed to the idea of living a Torah-true lifestyle while also adopting the best of the modern world and I realized early on that those of us growing up in the world of the modern orthodox yeshiva would have to study twice as hard as non-yeshiva students, who studied only secular subjects. But neither I, nor any of my friends, complained about the heavy load we had to master. We loved the culture of *yiddishkeit* we were growing up in, and wouldn't have traded it for the world.

But to return to myself in my younger days, I must acknowledge that I remained given to occasional displays of high spirits, even after I had entered the hallowed halls of Yeshiva University. On Simchat Torah, when I was seventeen or eighteen and a freshman at YU, I literally got high on spirits. In those days, after the celebratory dancing was finished, we used to go around the neighborhood from house to house singing and happily carousing. In many of the homes, the woman of the house would invite the young men in; providing them with stuffed cabbage, gefilte fish, chopped liver or some other treat, together with plenty of liquor. The dining rooms were small, so those at the table passed the food to those standing and sitting beyond. On that occasion, my college roommate, who lived in our neighborhood, kept passing me shot glasses filled with schnapps and, pretty much a novice drinker, I kept belting them down. Unfortunately, he forgot to pass the food along with the liquor. Pretty soon, my head was spinning wildly and I was more light-headed than I had ever been before or have ever been since.

When we reached the last house of the afternoon, I threw up and passed out on the living room rug. When I woke up some hours later, I stumbled out and headed home, after apologizing profusely. The next day, I couldn't remember in whose house I had been when that mortifying incident had happened. Then one day in the fall of 2001, some 45 years later, I was paying a shiva call after the death of a friend, when his uncle, a man in his nineties, came up to me, shook his head gravely, and then said to me with a mischievous twinkle in his eye, "Hey Mendy, you still owe me for that rug you got dirty." I did a double take and asked, "You mean that was your house?" and he replied, "It sure was."

Although I'm considered a veritable pillar of the Orthodox community, I like to think that I retained a highly developed sense of humor, as anyone who has ever heard me tell jokes about my proctologic practice can testify. Still, I tend to share that side of myself mainly with family and friends. In general, I am not someone who lets it all hang out with people I am not close to. Over the years, I have shared my wild and crazy side mainly with my children and grandchildren, filling their heads with all sorts of tall tales. I've always been a Walter Mitty type, so it was very much in character that I used to tell my kids when they were small that I had once played for the Brooklyn Dodgers. I assumed they figured out along the way that I had been telling *bubbameisers* (fairy tales), but recently when I was babysitting for one of my grandchildren, one of his friends came up to me and asked suspiciously; "Is it really true you played for the Brooklyn Dodgers?" Trying to appear modest, I confirmed I had been on the Dodgers, but only for several years and hadn't hit many home runs. The kid eyed me suspiciously and then said, "Wait, then there must have been a baseball card of you. Do you have one?" "No," I responded straight-faced without missing a beat. "That was in the days before baseball cards."

When I was about seven or eight, we lived down the block from a muscle-bound vaudeville and circus performer who styled himself "Mighty Adam." I never actually met Mighty Adam, but we used to see him driving around the neighborhood in his truck, upon which he had painted the legend, "Mighty Adam— the Strongest Man in the World." His shtick was that he could bend iron and perform other feats of great strength. My father, from whom I inherited my penchant for wild yarns, used to make up stories about our colorful neighbor; telling me that Mighty Adam could pull trains with his hair or that he could stop small airplanes from taking off. My father also told me similar tall tales about a mythical strong man he called Muttaleh.

When I had my own children, I used to regale them with stories about Mighty Adam and Muttaleh; how the two had worked together performing heroic deeds. When I had grandchildren a generation later, I told them the same stories. Yet like my kids before them, when my grandchildren got to a certain age they would say, "Grandpa, stop telling those silly stories. There is no Mighty Adam or Muttaleh in real life." "No," I would reply, "There really was a Mighty Adam. He lived down the street from us." My son rolled his eyes and said, "C'mon Dad, stop feeding the kids all those *bubbameises*." Even my mother's assurances that Mighty Adam had really existed were to no avail.

Anyway, not long ago, I was at a wedding, sitting alongside my youngest son Elli, who is today a happily married lawyer. I was making conversation with a man my age whom I had never met before when we discovered that the two of us had lived on the same street in Brooklyn when we were small kids. Suddenly, he turned to me and said, "Wait a minute, if you grew up on that block, you must have known Mighty Adam." I could see my son's jaw drop in astonishment, and for a moment, the sophisticated Manhattan lawyer he has become disappeared and was replaced by the child he once was. "You're kidding," he said to our new acquaintance. "You mean there really was a Mighty Adam?" The man confirmed that Mighty Adam had lived on Park Place in Brooklyn, and explained to my fascinated son how his own father had told him that Mighty Adam had once rescued a Jewish woman from an attack by a bunch of anti-Semitic toughs. My son just stood there shaking his head in bemusement.

Looking back, I am struck by how little I myself was concerned about anti-Semitism when I was growing up. I do dimly remember one incident when I was a child of eight or nine of being taunted by a group of gentile boys about my yarmulke. There was an exchange of insults, a bit of pushing and shoving and then I ran into the house. But the incident had little impact on me and I don't want to blow it out of proportion. Certainly, it has never been my thing to go through life claiming to be an oppressed person. Not only have I very rarely encountered anti-

Semitism from gentiles, yet more frequently, I have experienced the opposite reaction to my Jewishness. For example, during my time in medical school in Chicago, I had a Catholic professor who would often say to me around noon on Friday afternoons, "Mendy, shouldn't you be heading home? The Jewish sabbath will begin soon." I would thank him for his concern, but explain that Shabbat would not begin for another four or five hours. The professor would respond, "OK, but shouldn't you get moving now, so as to avoid traffic?"

Over the course of my life, I have usually had very good personal relationships with gentiles. Actually, I have often had more trouble with Jews than with non-Jews. I believe this has been the case because of the training my father gave me of treating every person, Jewish or gentile, in the same way I would want to be treated. I treat gentiles as my equals, neither looking up or down at them. Over the years, I greeted every person I met in the hospital, from the top administrator to the men and women who swept the floors and washed the bedpans with a smile and a friendly "Hello, how are you?" I believe that because I came across as respectful of all the employees of the hospital, including African-Americans, Haitians, Puerto Ricans, that my medical practice got a lot of referrals from those communities. But I certainly didn't do it for that reason.

A lot of people in the Jewish community have asked me how I have managed to form warm and productive relationships with senators and congressmen from southern and western states with whom I seemed to have little in common culturally or religiously. I respond that I have not been successful in this respect because I am a great raconteur or a world-class storyteller. Rather, when meeting these legislators I try to put myself in their shoes and ask myself, "What is it that this guy wants from a doctor from Monsey, New York?" Usually, what they want is someone who is honest and fair; who will be upfront and explain clearly what he is looking for. Apparently many senators and congressmen relate to me in that way.

I believe that another reason I have interacted easily with non-Jews is that I have never felt a conflict between being American and being Jewish or between loyalty to America or Israel. I have always felt totally comfortable to be an American. I proudly served my country in Vietnam and am unselfconsciously patriotic. I get goose bumps every time I salute the flag and sing our

National Anthem. Yes, I also love Israel deeply and worked for many years to build support for the Jewish state in the White House and on Capitol Hill. Yet, I have undertaken that work with the conviction that what I am doing is as good for America as it is for Israel. I believe passionately it is good for America to support the only democratic state in the Middle East and bad for us to subsidize undemocratic nations like Saudi Arabia that also happen to oppress women.

In 1954, I graduated from BTA and moved on to Yeshiva College, the undergraduate portion of Yeshiva University. It was a natural progression. Half of my high school graduating class ended up on the Yeshiva College campus at Washington Heights. Sixty percent of the freshman class came from Manhattan Talmudical Academy and thirty percent from our school. As for myself, it never occurred to me to go anywhere but Yeshiva College and in fact, I applied to no other school. It was the only institution of higher learning where one could remain true to the values of *Torah u Madah*, science and modernity in a Torah atmosphere.

In fact, it is the precept of *"Torah u Madah"* that most fully describes my outlook on life. This weltanschauung, which is the trademark of Yeshiva University, has been my guiding principle throughout my life. It was my time at that noble institution that ensured that I would carry those principles forward into adulthood. I have always felt that it is unfortunate that Yeshiva University did not expand into a national institution and open branches in cities like Chicago or Los Angeles as well as New York. I believe if YU had done so, we would not have seen the sharp turn to the right of so many Orthodox Jews, which is in its essence a rejection of Torah u Madah, the principle that one can be a fully halachic Jew and yet live in the modern world. YU has proven that such a synthesis is possible; indeed, in my opinion, that it is the most Torah-true, internally consistent way for a Jew to live.

If I ended up going to college where most young men from the modern Orthodox community went, I was no more original in my choice of a major. In fact, it appeared that three fourths of the freshmen class at YU that year declared for pre-med. Yeshiva University's Albert Einstein Medical School had just opened, and it seemed that every Orthodox boy in those days wanted to be a doctor. But getting to med school was a very tough grind. Of the seventy to eighty young men who declared pre-med in the beginning, only twenty to twenty five were left at the end of the four years of undergraduate work and of that group only sixteen or seventeen got into American medical schools.

The daily regimen at Yeshiva was difficult and occasionally exhausting. At the time though, with all the energies of youth and a determination to do well, my classmates and I managed to surmount the challenges. Our days began at 7AM with the morning prayers. From 9AM-12PM, I would be in the Bet Midrash in a small study group preparing together to make a presentation to the rabbi in the afternoon on the section of Talmud we happened to be studying that day. We would meet with our rebbe from 1-3PM. Then we would begin our secular subjects; not only courses, but also lab sessions. We finished around 6 to 8 PM and then had to deal with homework. Friday was a half-day, but on Sundays we got up bright and early for full regular classes and labs.

Despite how difficult it all was, I remember Yeshiva College with enormous fondness and great loyalty; indeed I saw to it that all of my own children studied there as well (My daughter followed Sheila's footsteps and went to Stern College, which is the women's branch of Yeshiva University). For those of us in the modern Orthodox community, Yeshiva College represents a way of life that is extremely precious to preserve.

Looking back on those days, perhaps the most amazing thing was that despite the grind of the daily schedule, I found time for a wide range of extracurricular activities. I got involved in campus politics right away. I ran for class president in my freshman and sophomore years, but lost both times to my friend Lenny Shapiro, who had the advantage of having come from Manhattan T.A. (Today, he remains a good friend, is a resident of Monsey and happens to be my ophthalmologist). Finally in my junior year, I was elected school secretary. I also became chairman of *The Affiliated Young Democrats*. My dormitory room in college was known as the "Governor's Mansion." A wide circle of friends and acquaintances congregated there. Years later, friends would stop me on the street and say, 'Hey, Governor, how are you?"

I was also very active on the YU debating team. I vividly remember the excitement of traveling to other schools and taking part in pressure-cooker debates. One year we were at Howard University in Washington D.C. for a debating match that would help decide the national championship. Normally, the outcome of debates were decided by three professors serving as judges, but when we arrived at Howard, we were informed that they had decided to change the rules and allow students in the audience to vote on the outcome. Our side was furious because obviously the students at Howard would be biased in favor of their own squad. More importantly, because the rules had been changed, the debate could not be counted in the National Collegiate Debating League, in which we were in contention for the championship. I decided to make clear exactly what I thought of that tactic by clowning a bit. When it was my turn to speak, I came down off the speaker's platform and walked into the audience shouting and flailing my arms like a southern preacher in the middle of a fire and brimstone sermon. I must admit I was pretty good at it, and the funny part was that not everyone understood I was having some fun. One of the Howard professors came up to me afterwards and said, "Son, I can see you practicing before the Supreme Court of the United States in a few years."

In fact, I was probably too active in school politics and in extracurricular activities like the debating team for my own good. Those were years of turbulence between the students and administration at Yeshiva. As Secretary of the Student Council, I was in the middle of the fray. I was very fortunate that I had as a roommate Shimmy Kwestel. Both he and Seymour "Skippy" Jotkowitz often tutored me in preparation for my exams. Shimmy, of course, went on to become president of the OU a few years before I did, as well as becoming a professor of law. Skippy became a professor of neurology. They really saved my butt a few times during those long ago college years and I remain forever in their debt.

I was also sort of a jock, or actually a *nochshlepper*—someone who loved sports and hanging around the players even though I myself wasn't good enough to make the team. I was a bench jockey for the YU basketball team, helping transport equipment to the games and sitting on the bench with the players. I remember once YU played a game in Madison Square Garden before the New York Knicks came on to play an NBA game. After the YU game was complete, the Knicks came out and for some reason no one noticed me or asked me to leave, so I managed to sit with the Knicks on their bench for an entire game. The Knicks then had two brothers named McGuire on their team and that day one of them got hurt and they took him to the dressing room. After a while, another player named Sweetwater Clifton came out of the dressing room and I said, "So how's he doing, Sweets?" Clifton responded, "Well, go into the locker room and check for yourself." I stayed where I was, though, because I realized that if I got off the bench I'd probably never be allowed to return.

In those days, every student at Yeshiva College had to take one or two credits of physical education. Yet because Yeshiva had a paucity of athletic facilities, most of the Phys-Ed program was off campus in rented venues. Today, thank God, Yeshiva has a pool and a real gym. Like a lot of other students, I was loath to deal with the Phys-Ed requirement. Don't forget that we studied Talmud and religious studies from nine AM to three PM every day and from three to eight we took our secular studies. Who had time or energy to futz around a gym in short pants? So I came up with one of my patented Mendy brainstorms. I approached the head of the Phys-Ed department and suggested we have bowling as part of the program. He said, "Its OK with me if you organize it," and I agreed to do that. So I put up a notice on the bulletin board that anyone who wanted to do their Phys-Ed requirement as part of the bowling team should register with me.

The problem was that up until that moment, I had never bowled in my life, and had no idea whether it was better to have a high score or a low one. (The first time I ever bowled was at Fort Monmouth, N.J. in 1967, right before I shipped off to Vietnam). Yet that didn't stop me from organizing a fictitious bowling league, one that helped many of my fellow students get through their Phys-Ed requirement. Every week, I would post scores in the Phys-Ed office as though we had actually bowled and the head of the department bought the whole thing. We managed to continue the charade even after Falcaro's, our supposed "home bowling alley" burned to the ground. I simply told the head of the Phys-Ed department that we had relocated to another bowling establishment.

During the summers of my years at Yeshiva College, I would head for the Catskills, where I worked from June to September as a busboy or a waiter at Borscht Belt landmarks like the Hotel Fuirst and the Hotel Pineview. During the course of a summer I was able to make $1000 or more, which covered much of my tuition costs. The hours were long, and the food and living conditions were truly terrible, but I was young and strong, and had many great friends up there, so the summers went quickly and were a great deal of fun. I continued to work in the Catskills during the summer of my second year in medical school. The greatest benefit of that summer turned out to be that it was there that I met a wonderful young woman named Sheila Weinreb.

But I am jumping ahead in the story. During my senior year at Yeshiva, I applied to medical school and was accepted by two of them; the University of Alabama and Chicago Medical School. I chose Chicago because several of my friends were going there and it was obviously an easier place to live as an observant Jew than Alabama would have been.

As my last year of Yeshiva College was winding down and I was preparing to head for the Catskills for my final summer before leaving for Chicago, one of my father's "political" friends invited me to his office. I already knew that the gentleman was running for the position of Brooklyn Borough President, but I was stunned when he said he wanted to hire me for the summer as his campaign manager. He said he had heard about my work as head of the Young Democrats at YU and thought I could be especially helpful as a liaison to the Jewish community.

I replied that I was flattered by the offer, but needed to know how much he would pay me. My would-be employer replied that he would not be able to pay me right away, but promised solemnly that once he was elected he would appoint me as a "hole inspector." I must have looked totally confused, so he smiled and said, "You know that Con Edison digs up the streets and they are required by law to fix them afterwards. Therefore, the Borough president appoints 'hole inspectors' to make sure that Con Edison fills up the holes they make in the streets. In fact, it's a patronage position that pays very well."

Then I understood. The man was promising me that if I served as his campaign manager on a volunteer basis, he would assure me a good salary for a pretend job once I went off to medical school. Of course, it was brazenly illegal, but that was how things were done in New York City clubhouse politics in those days. I explained as nicely as I could that even though I thought he had a good chance of winning, I could not afford to take the risk of working all summer for nothing and seeing him lose the primary or election. I needed a guarantee of several thousand dollars for medical school tuition and would hardly be able to explain to the bursar's office in Chicago that I couldn't pay my tuition costs because my job as a hole inspector had not come through. He shrugged and said I was passing up a great opportunity, but I left his office and headed back to the Catskills. As it turned out, he lost the primary.

The night after Yom Kippur 1958, my parents helped me lug all of my belongings to Newark Airport for the flight to my new life in Chicago. I could tell something was on my father's mind and finally, just before they announced that the plane was boarding, he turned to me and said, "Mendy, if you change your mind and decide to continue your formal *smicha* (rabbinic) studies toward ordination, I can arrange a position for you as assistant rabbi at Prospect Park Jewish Center." I replied with both tenderness and firmness, "Thank you, Dad, but no thanks. I really want to be a doctor." He never questioned my career choice again.

My father would die four years later, just as I was completing medical school, so he never had the chance to see me become a doctor. Whenever I visit his grave, the thing that disturbs me the most is that he never had the opportunity to see me as a doctor, to come to my wedding, to meet my children, grandchildren and all the rest. I believe he would have been very proud of what I accomplished in life. I do know that at that moment, as I boarded the plane to Chicago, I had truly become a man, an independent human being in charge of my own destiny. But so much of who I was then, who I am today, my values, my beliefs, my inner being, my *neshama* (soul) had already been given to me by my wonderful father, Morris Ganchrow of blessed memory.

Chapter Two
Medical Training and Marriage

I had never lived outside the safe and comfortable confines of the Orthodox Jewish community until I flew off to Chicago to attend medical school in September 1958. I understood that I would face situations where my Jewish religious obligations and convictions might be put to the test of facing an apparent conflict with my requirements as a medical student and later as a physician. Still, I hadn't realized until the last minute that this test would arise so immediately and intensely upon my arrival in Chicago.

It turned out that the first several days of classes fell on Succot, which is an eight-day-long holiday. During the first and last two days of Succot, observant Jews are required to refrain from driving, writing or putting on electric lights. That meant that those days I would have to walk three miles back and forth between campus and the apartment I was sharing with two other Jewish students—one of whom was Orthodox and the other a young man who had decided that he wanted to live an Orthodox lifestyle. I was young and strong and didn't really mind the long walks, but once I arrived at class each day, I faced more difficult dilemmas. Because of the holiday, I was forbidden to write, which meant I could not take notes from the professors' lectures or even turn on my microscope, which made it nearly impossible to take part in lab work unless someone would turn it on for me.

Needless to say, those days were extremely stressful for my roommates and I. We were all extremely motivated to succeed as doctors, and deathly afraid that we would fall hopelessly far behind in our class work right from the get-go because of our religious obligations. We also did not relish appearing weird and difficult in front of our instructors and classmates. As it turned out the roommate who planned to live an Orthodox lifestyle decided after the first day that he could not tolerate the tension and began taking notes. On the second day he started to drive. I was determined not to compromise on my own Jewish observance and held strong even in the face of considerable difficulty. Fortunately, I was able to copy the class notes from my roommate after the holiday.

By the end of Succot, I felt reassured that I had the emotional strength and constancy to keep up my Jewish observance and succeed in medical school. My anatomy professor that year was the Catholic professor I mentioned in the first chapter; a very decent and caring person who was extremely solicitous about my Jewish observance. His warm understanding reaffirmed my confidence in the belief that if I were clear about who I was as an observant Jew and refused to compromise on it, the outside world would both accept that and respect me for it. Shabbat also presented problems because my classmates came in on Saturdays to review the anatomies of their cadavers. Yet with my professor's permission, I came in by myself or with the several other Sabbath observers after sundown on Saturday.

One evening, two weeks into medical school, I walked into an operating room at Cook County Hospital for the first time to view an operation in progress and was startled when the anesthesiologist called me over and asked, "Doctor, would you mind giving anesthesia for me during this operation?" I told him I was new in med school and barely knew anything, but he replied, "That's all right, I'll help you out and show you what to do if you have any questions." He turned away and I had the strange sensation of being there all alone practicing anesthesiology. All of a sudden, the patient seemed to stop breathing. My own heart must have nearly stopped for a second and I screamed, "Doctor, quick come over here. He's not breathing." Then I saw the surgeons at the table who were observing the full scope of the aorta pulsating with well-oxygenated blood flowing to the tissue burst into laughter at my inexperience. It turned out I had the patient's mask on wrong, which created the illusion he wasn't breathing. It was an embarrassing moment, but I was so giddy with relief that I hadn't killed my very first patient that I remember laughing along with the other doctors.

Overall, I did well and found myself gravitating toward surgery. I came home for the summer of 1960, expecting another relatively uneventful summer working in the Catskills, but things became considerably more exciting.

Shortly before the Democratic party was to hold its National Convention in Los Angeles that July, one of the busboys at the hotel I was working at informed me that he had seen notes in the archives of the Nazi German Foreign Ministry—some of which were at Columbia University in New York—which potentially might be detrimental to John F. Kennedy's candidacy. He explained that the archives portrayed Kennedy's father, Joseph Kennedy during his time as U.S. Ambassador to England, right before the outbreak of World War II as having asserted to the German Ambassador in London that the Jews controlled the American press. This was in addition to other charges regarding the elder Kennedy's feeling toward Jews.

I had already been supporting Lyndon Johnson, Kennedy's chief rival for the nomination. After hearing what the busboy had to say, I felt I had to do something. I arranged for him to get a day off and he went down to Columbia to make copies of the incriminating documents. We then mailed the documents by special delivery to Johnson's campaign manager, Oscar Ewing.

On the following day, I was excited beyond belief when LBJ held a press conference to release the documents. As it turned out, my action barely zinged JFK's rush to the nomination, which was unstoppable at this point. Johnson's going public with the documents we had sent also did not prevent Kennedy from choosing him as his vice presidential running mate in order to be able to capture Texas and other southern states in the election. Perhaps I had not changed the course of history, but I had still learned an important lesson for the future; namely that knowledge is a supremely important commodity in politics and, indeed, one of the defining aspects of "power."

As to the other event of that summer—well, let me preface it by noting that, I don't give up easily. If I believe in a principle or in a goal, I will pursue it with all my energy and will refuse to take 'no' for an answer. Of course, I sometimes run into a fair amount of rejection along the way, but I never take that rejection personally or let it get me down. I take a step back and make a clear-headed evaluation of whether with time and persistent charm I can achieve my goal. If there is even a small possibility of that happening, I will continue my campaign with all the force at my command, and hopefully not destroy my credibility in the process.

I have displayed this ability to persuade people to see things my way many times in my long career as a Jewish activist. It was certainly no easy feat to bring Senator Jesse Helms or Senator Steve Symms around to a pro-Israel position or to convince much of the organized Jewish community to cotton to those conservative Republicans who had long been mistakenly seen as anti-Israel. Yet never in my life have I proven how determined I can be even in the face of the most formidable opposition than I was in my dogged pursuit of Sheila Weinreb. Compared to winning over Sheila, charming Jesse Helms into becoming a supporter of Israel was a piece of cake.

I first met Sheila in the summer of 1960 after my second year in medical school. I had come home from Chicago and my brother Saul and I were on our way up to the Catskills for another summer. Each of us was driving his own car, which we had both filled with a group of guys and girls who were going to work with us at the Pineview Hotel in South Fallsburg. We had just pulled into the parking lot at the Psychiatric State Hospital in Middletown, New York, where we planned to visit an old family friend named Dr. Zlatlow, when I saw an attractive young woman emerging from my brother's car. What went through my head at that portentous moment was, "What an adorable girl!"

I had dated a fair amount before, both while at YU and out in Chicago where my friends were always setting me up with different girls. Yet none of those relationships had really clicked and never until I caught my first glimpse of Sheila had I experienced that electric sense of knowing instantly that this was the girl I wanted. Anyway, I "got it" right away. It took Sheila a whole lot longer to figure it out.

Sheila was from Far Rockaway, NY and had just finished her second year at Stern College. She was just nineteen, having been born on December 29, 1940, four years younger than I. It turned out that she was a counselor at the Pineview. So I had all summer to court her and figured, with my customary positive thinking, that if I was persistent in my pursuit, Sheila would come around to seeing I was the right guy for her in a couple of weeks. Was I ever wrong! Sheila made clear from the get-go that she had absolutely no interest in me. One night a group of us went to the nightclub at the Pineview and I must have been gazing at

Sheila with love in my eyes, because she suddenly turned to me and asked sharply; "Why are you staring at me?" I replied with total sincerity, "Because I am going to marry you." Sheila rolled her eyes and responded, "You're crazy. Leave me alone."

It wasn't like I was the only boy who had noticed Sheila. She had a few guys running after her, and one steady boyfriend for most of that summer. Overall, it appeared like a most discouraging situation, but I resolved to campaign for her hand as intensely as I had formerly campaigned for positions in student government. I did have a few cards up my sleeve. One was the fact that I was one of the few young people at the hotel who had a car so Sheila found it convenient to use me—for example to drive her on her day off to visit her parents who were staying for a few weeks at a hotel a few miles away. For my part, I used the opportunity to befriend her mother and father, Anna and Jack Weinreb, who, unlike Sheila, found me positively charming. Soon, they were telling Sheila what a wonderful young man I was—the last thing she felt like hearing at that moment!

Soon, the end of the summer was approaching and Sheila had given me no indication she would be willing to see me again once we left the mountains. I didn't panic, but kept up my campaign in the hope of turning her around. I finally caught a break in a very strange and unlikely fashion. The chef at the hotel, who was a rather churlish person, had suffered second and third degree burns on his legs early that summer. Because of my medical experience I was the lucky guy who got 'volunteered' to change the chef's bandages every morning. Not only was it difficult work, but the ungrateful guy never even thanked me for what I was doing for him. Finally, on Labor Day, the last day of the summer season, I asked the chef, whether in recompense for all I had done for him, he might send out a juicy steak for me to eat. The "hired help" at the hotel never got quality food. The chef understood that he really owed me one and agreed to serve me a steak in the children's dining room, where my brother was a waiter.

Concerned that the hotel owner would glimpse me eating such good food which was not supposed to go to the lowly likes of me, I hunkered down behind a pole, swallowing the steak as fast as I could. Sheila came into the dining room with her campers and, seeing me wolfing down my food in a less than elegant fashion, asked, with just a trace of sarcasm in her voice, "So, is the steak good?" I replied, "Of course it is." She responded, "Not as good as my mother makes." I shot back; "How would I know what kind of steak your mother makes?" Sheila said, "Well, the next time you are in Far Rockaway, come over for a steak, and you'll see how good it is."

Eureka! I had my opening. Before Sheila could think twice and retract her "invitation" I riposted, "Look, I can't just show up on your mother's door and ask for a steak. Lets make a definite date, like tomorrow night and I'll be there." She saw her mistake immediately, but apparently felt trapped. After all, she was the one who had offered the invitation. So the next evening I showed up at Sheila's place, where her mother, who was crazy about me and strongly in favor of my getting together with her daughter, had fixed me a terrific steak.

Sheila's version: I don't know why I mentioned to Mendy that he should come to Far Rockaway and try my mother's steak. Sometimes things just pop out of your mouth that you don't really mean to say. I certainly did not have the remotest romantic interest in Mendy. In fact I had a very serious boyfriend all that summer. But I knew Mendy was crazy about me, so honestly, I was stringing him along a little bit; using him when I needed a lift or some other favor. Honestly, I was still a little immature at that point.

On the other hand, my parents, who had come over from Europe and thought in kind of old-world terms, thought Mendy was terrific; a serious young man who was religiously observant and was studying to be a doctor. So when I told my mother he would be coming over for dinner the next night, I cautioned her, "Mom, its no big deal. He's just a friend." In my own mind, I meant that he was a friend I was going to get rid of—and quickly. I had made my mistake inviting him over, but it wasn't going to go further than that one night."

Still, my mother got all excited that Mendy was coming and made a terrific meal. So we had dinner at our family's table and, as usual, Mendy totally charmed my parents. At the end of the evening I took him aside and told him, "OK, that's it. You've had your steak. You've had your dinner, but that's it. Please do not call me any more. I don't like you, I don't want you, so go back to Chicago and have a good life."

My version: What was my reaction to what seemed to be the definitive rejection from Sheila? "It didn't bother me in the least. I wanted this girl and was determined to press ahead in my pursuit of her no matter what. I had two weeks left before I was supposed to go back to Chicago, and was determined to break down her resistance before I left.

Sheila's version: I couldn't imagine a guy continuing to pester a girl after the kind of firm "no" I had given to Mendy, but I knew him well enough by that time to understand that he was so determined that he might call back anyway. So I told my mother, 'If he calls, just tell him I'm not home.' But my mother said, 'Oh come on, Sheila. He's so nice. He's going back to Chicago in two weeks anyway. Why not see him in the meantime?'

But I insisted I would not see him, so the first time Mendy called, my mother told him I wasn't home, but with so much hemming and hawing that he probably figured out she was fibbing. My mother was from the old country and even the most innocent lie was something she was not capable of. So after that she said to me, "Look, I won't do that again. If he calls again, you'll have to speak with him yourself and tell him whatever you want." Sure enough, Mendy called the next day, and reminded me that he was leaving for Chicago soon and he only wanted to see me one more time. I guess I felt sorry for him and figured since he would be leaving soon anyway, I might as well go out with him one last time. But that date wasn't much fun either and afterwards, I told Mendy, "Look, you had your date, but that's enough. Lets not prolong this agony any more. Please don't call me any more."

Yet even that "clear as crystal" message didn't discourage him. Mendy kept calling and finally I said to myself, "Look, its now only a week till he leaves. Let me show him a little rachmones (mercy) and spend the time with him. He didn't have any money in those days so we kept going to the zoo—first the Brooklyn Zoo, then the Bronx Zoo. Zoos didn't charge admission in those days. I just remember us doing a lot of walking and talking.

In addition, as I never had tasted alcoholic beverages and didn't care for soda, I guess I must have qualified as a 'cheap date.'

Then Mendy went off to Chicago, but he kept calling me from there, and then gradually my feelings for him began to change. He was so sweet and devoted to me, and thought I was so beautiful. Mendy was just so persuasive—he is really the kind of guy who can sell you the Brooklyn Bridge. Anyway, before I knew it we were in love and two years later, after I finished Stern College and he finished medical school, we got married."

Back to Mendy: I returned to Chicago that year with a definite skip in my step. I had a wonderful girlfriend back home, and felt I could conquer the world. But medical school was tough and kept giving me all the challenges I could handle and then some. Late that year, I worked in the Home Maternity Program at the Chicago Maternity Center for two weeks. We would go to peoples' homes together with student nurses and deliver babies. The conditions were rather primitive; we were given one pair of rubber gloves per week and had to keep re-boiling them. We would roll up newspapers over coke bottles and put them at the end of the bed so that patients could bear down against them during the delivery. I had some rugged experiences as a maternity doc. Once I went to an apartment situated above a bar to assist a woman who had gone into labor and found out that she was the wife of the bartender, who happened to be an American Indian. He looked like a pretty rough guy, especially in that he had a fingernail that must have been eight inches long and very sharp, which he obviously used as a weapon. Every half hour, he would come upstairs to see if the baby had been born yet and each time I noticed that he had become a little bit more inebriated. By the time I had delivered the baby, he was drunk as all get out. He didn't like the way the baby looked, claimed it wasn't his own and started shouting threats at me. I had to call the police to get me out of there.

On another occasion, after I had delivered a baby, the new mother told me she didn't know what to name the infant and asked my advice. I facetiously suggested the name "Mandell I. Ganchrow Washington" and to my surprise, she said she thought it was a good one. The father of the baby, a strapping African-American guy, apparently didn't agree, because the next day he came storming into the maternity center demanding to get his hands on me. I hid in a back room, while my colleagues helped him to change the name on the birth certificate.

One of my classmates was a very bright guy, but extremely naïve and believed almost everything he was told. As a practical joke, several of the other students informed him that a new technique, known as the "Shickelberg test," had been found to easily diagnose sickle cell disease—a particularly severe form of anemia that primarily effects African-Americans. The only way to diagnose sickle-cell disease is by a blood test to determine if the red blood cells are "sickling" but this student was made to believe that it was also possible to diagnose the disease by holding a patient's finger up to a very bright light in order to see the cells sickling. Some months later, Dr. Zimmerman, the chairman of the Department of Medicine at Mt. Sinai Hospital gave a "Grand Round" attended by professors, hospital staff and medical students on the subject of Sickle Cell Anemia. At the end of the lecture, Dr. Zimmerman asked if anyone had any questions. Before we could stop him, our classmate raised his hand and asked, "Dr. Zimmerman, why didn't you mention the Shickelberg Test as one way to determine sickle-cell. "What in blazes is this Schikleberg Test?" asked the clearly perplexed chairman. As the confused student began to stutter out an explanation of how the test was conducted, the entire audience burst into laughter.

During my fourth year, I worked at a kosher nursing home where I was provided with room and board plus a few dollars in exchange for taking care of the patients at night. With so many elderly people, we had a lot of medical crises. I made a bit of extra money working the night shift in the hospital psychiatric ward; often playing pool with the patients. A nursing home can be a depressing place, but the warm and *hamische* atmosphere was a nice change after some of the other places I had worked.

During that year, we medical students performed a lot of surgery. On one occasion during that year, a man came in who had cut his lip badly and needed several stitches. Two of my friends, both Jewish doctors were working on him, when the guy began to make a series of bigoted comments about Jews. At that point, the two doctors began sewing his two lips together and one of them said, "You bastard, I'm a Jew." The guy got wild-eyed with fear, jumped off the emergency room table and high-tailed it out of there.

I loved doing surgery and became quite good at it, but there were some embarrassing moments as well. On one occasion, our professor of vascular surgery was demonstrating to a group of visiting surgeons in the amphitheatre of Cook County Hospital how to perform a certain procedure involving putting a vein in to replace an artery. I was standing on a stool behind the professor intently watching his demonstration, wearing a surgical gown that I had not tied well in the back. When I took my hands out of my pockets, the gown suddenly flipped up over my head, over him and onto the instrument tray, thereby contaminating all the surgical instruments, which had to be re-sterilized. I ran out of there as quickly as I could and disappeared for a few hours. Then I came back as though nothing had happened, and it turned out the professor hadn't seen which student klutz had bollixed up the operation. I didn't volunteer the information that it had been me.

Sheila and I had become engaged during my third year in medical school and had set our wedding for June 1962, right after I was to graduate. Throughout that pressure packed final year of med school, I was getting ominous reports from my mother in Brooklyn that my father's health was worsening. He had a heart condition as well as diabetes, which made it difficult for him to work. On Purim Eve of 1962, he was admitted to Beth-El Hospital in Brooklyn. I returned home to visit him for a few days and when he seemed to improve, I returned to Chicago to complete my last three months of medical school. A week later, however, he developed staphylococcal endocarditis, a potentially fatal bacteriological infection of the heart tissue and his kidneys began to fail. The attending physician informed my mother that my father's odds of survival were not good, and she called me to ask that I come home immediately.

I took a cab directly from La Guardia Airport to the hospital. When I walked in, he looked up at me quizzically from his bed inside an oxygen tent, and asked; "Mendy, what are you doing here? Aren't you supposed to be in school?" Trying to preserve the illusion that everything was OK, I replied, "I had a few days off, Dad, so I decided to come home and check on you." He seemed touched I had come, but assured me that he was doing well. I told him that I was going out of the room for a moment to find his doctor and come right back. I couldn't find the doctor in question, but when I returned to my father's room, I saw a group of other doctors and nurses scurrying around. My father was on the floor and they were frantically pumping his chest. But it was no use. He was gone. It was March 26, 1962. Amidst my overwhelming grief, I felt a sense of deep consolation that G-d had kept him alive until I had a chance to see him one last time. Clearly, my father had waited to see me before passing away. He was only fifty seven.

I recall very little of my father's funeral or the days of shiva (mourning). I only remember that I was plunged into enormous grief. I felt that the props had been knocked out from under my life. I had not only lost a father who I had loved very much, but a role model and the person most in life who I had sought to emulate and please. Amidst my deep sorrow, however, I resolved to be strong for the sake of my mother, who would somehow have to pick up the pieces of her life, and of my younger brothers. Saul had already married a few months before but Jacob was still in school. Sheila, who was then three months away from her graduation from Stern College, volunteered to move in with my mother in order to keep her company. I returned to Chicago to finish school.

Meanwhile, our wedding was fast approaching and I had a difficult decision to make.

Once I would graduate I would be liable for the military draft. I had two options; either to go take my chances of being drafted into the Army as a general medical officer or to defer military service through the Berry Plan, which allowed would-be doctors to finish their medical training before going into the military. The second option mandated a two-year tour of duty as a trained specialist, whereas the first option meant gambling that I might not be drafted, but if drafted, I would be a general medical officer. I decided to go with the Berry Plan. I wanted to complete my medical education before having to deal with the military.

When I made my choice, there was no war in Vietnam yet on the horizon. My experience there still lay five years ahead.

In June 1962, Sheila, my mother and my brothers had come out to Chicago right after her graduation from Stern College to celebrate with me my own graduation from medical school. Immediately after that event, which took place on June sixteen, we all headed back to New York in two cars. My mother's gift to me for my graduation was a set of Talmud (Shas)—one I have cherished ever since. Sheila and I decided that we would live at home with my mother for a time after our wedding in order to help her get back on her feet. It was a significant sacrifice for Sheila as a young bride to give up her privacy for the first year of her married life, but we both felt it was the right thing to do.

Our wedding took place on June 26, 1962 at the Park Manor in Brooklyn. It was characterized by great joy on our part and that of all the celebrants. Yet everyone's joy at the *simcha* was tempered by the awareness that it was exactly three months to the day that my father had passed away. We had gone ahead with the wedding after some soul-searching and much discussion because *halacha* specifies that if plans for a wedding have already been made, the death of a parent should not be the cause of a cancellation. Conversely, if the plans have not already been made and announced, Jewish law specified that we would have had to wait the full year of the mourning period before rescheduling the event. Given how much Sheila and I loved each other, we were thankful we didn't have to wait and, knowing my father, I am certain he would not have wanted us to.

Sheila and I rarely fought with each other, but we had two pretty good arguments in advance of the wedding. The first was over the choice of a band. I was determined to have an old-world klezmer band headed by a crusty, much-renowned musician named Dave Tarras; Sheila wanted a more modern-sounding, American-style Judaic band. Also, given that in my childhood I myself had often sang as a choir-boy at weddings, I insisted that there should be a small boy in a white robe at our wedding who would march down the aisle at the proper moment and sing the *vemale*; a prayer calling on G-d to fulfill the wishes of the couple during which said choir boy dramatically raises his arms in the style of a benediction. Again, Sheila objected to the concept as too old-fashioned and sarcastically dubbed the boy as "The Angel." I insisted on both points and, as has often been the case in our lives ever since, she allowed me to win.

We had a lovely three-day honeymoon weekend at the Pioneer Country Club in the Catskills. We had to return to Brooklyn Sunday morning June 30, as I had an orientation at Beth-El Hospital that afternoon for my internship, which was to start the following day. My mother had planned a big Sheva Bracha party for us that Sunday evening. *Sheva Brachos* is celebrated for seven days after a Jewish wedding in honor of the bride and groom.

Imagine my dismay when I was informed at orientation that because the outgoing intern class had left to start their residencies I was to be on call starting that very night. When I explained about the party, they decided that since I lived only about a five minute drive from the hospital, that I could call in periodically from home to find out if any medical emergencies had arisen that necessitated my presence. Thankfully, we got through the party without my getting called into service, but at 2AM that night the hospital called and informed me that a patient had an infiltrated intravenous. I asked whether it could wait until I got to work at 6:30AM. They said they would check and ended up calling back several more times until deciding that it could indeed wait until the morning.

I was thankful I had been able to spend that night at home, but Sheila was noticeably disgruntled about the frequent calls from the hospital and complained to me that she wasn't sure she would be able to tolerate an ongoing regimen of telephone calls during the wee hours. Indeed, it took her a few weeks, but she began adjusting to that unpleasant fact of life and soon didn't even wake up when the phone on my side of the bed rang loudly in the middle of the night. For my own part, once we started a family, I must admit that I rarely heard the babies crying in the middle of the night either. Sheila was the one who had to get up.

Beth-El Hospital in 1962 was a wonderful place to be an intern. The chief of medicine was a world-renowned academician named Dr. Isidore Snapper, a "Damon Runyon" character of pronounced old world civility. Incredibly, in his illustrious career, Snapper had been professor of medicine at the University of Amsterdam, had occupied an important medical position in Peiping, China as well as at Columbia University in New York. His knowledge of medicine was legendary and his textbook on "Bedside Medicine" did not require references or a bibliography. Everything he wrote or spoke about was in the context of "I saw, "I did" or "It is known."

Our chief of surgery was Dr. Charles "Charlie" Ripstein, the first director of surgery at Albert Einstein College of Medicine. "The Chief," as we referred to him, had pioneered many operations, including the "Ripstein procedure" for rectal prolapse.

Not only did Beth-El provide me with outstanding medical mentors, it also had kosher food, a rarity in hospitals in those days, and initially gave spouses of the house staff the privilege of eating dinner in the hospital cafeteria nightly. Still, even at Beth-El I did not have an easy time performing both my medical duties and religious obligations. Every day that year I managed to attend thrice-daily kaddish services as part of my one year obligation in memory of my father and still keep up my rotating internship duties. But Shabbat was a tougher problem. At Beth-El, as at most hospitals in those days, Saturday happened to be the biggest day of the week for elective admissions. Today we have no such obligation as most of the patient workup is done on an outpatient basis. Yet back then, as the medical intern on call every other Saturday, I might be expected to "admit" twelve to twenty patients; which typically involved writing down their information in long hand, doing a physical and ordering tests as well as medications in conjunction with the resident and attending physicians. Jewish law proscribes writing on the Sabbath except for saving a human life and, even then, it should be done in an unusual manner such as writing with the opposite hand. In any event, "saving a human life" hardly applied to the majority of elective admissions I was dealing with—patients who were typically there for workups involving x-rays, EKG's and blood work.

Especially in the summer, when Shabbat did not end until eight or nine at night, I could not postpone the examination of patients until after sundown. Nor could I remember the pertinent information on so many patients without writing it down. Deeply perplexed, I went to Rabbi Moshe Tendler, a renowned rabbinical authority who had been my professor at Yeshiva College. What distinguished Rabbi Tendler from other learned rabbis was his knowledge of medicine and his willingness to make critical decisions. After considering my request, he gave me a *heter*, (rabbinical dispensation) to use a portable tape recorder for this purpose, which allowed me to transcribe the material after sundown. Because of the nature of its transistor components, the tape recorder was not considered to constitute a violation of "Biblical law." Since all the patients were sick and hospitalized, an accurate recording of their status was vital to help them on the road to recovery. Thus the "rabbinic" prohibition involving the use of a transistor tape recorder could be permitted in the absence of a non-Jew to record data. This dispensation did not apply to the use of such a device under any other circumstance, nor for any other person.

Because I wanted desperately to avoid writing on Shabbat, I used to fill out a number of death certificates in advance, absent only the names of the deceased and the times of their deaths. I asked the nurses who worked on Saturdays to write in the actual names of the people who passed away during their shifts. I also filled out laboratory request forms in advance so as to meet whatever medical emergencies might arise for all of the patients for whom I knew I would be responsible on Shabbat. Thus someone admitted for chest pains would have all of his forms already filled out for EKG, chest x-ray and certain blood work. I did the same for other usual causes of Saturday admissions.

Once Dr. Snapper, who maintained, with considerable justice, that what I was doing amounted to "cookbook medicine," chewed me out. He was not mollified even when I explained to him the supreme spiritual significance of maintaining the Sabbath. Today, of course, computerization, phone dictation and oral orders have resolved most of these problems. In addition, a number of hospitals have *shomer shabbes* internships and residencies.

The conflict of medical ethics versus religious ones not only came up for me in my own performance of my medical duties. It also came up for patients as well; occasionally with life and death stakes riding on how it was resolved. One afternoon, a woman came to the hospital with a severe gynecological problem that was causing her to lose blood at a rapid rate. I told her she needed a blood transfusion, but she responded that she was a Jehovah's Witness and would rather die than accept a blood transfusion. Judaism commands that saving a life comes before even the strictest religious injunctions. However, this young woman was adamant about refusing a transfusion. Even if that meant risking her life, she surely had a right to follow her religious convictions even if I did not agree with them. That was her prerogative. She based her moral stand upon the Old Testament injunction of "not drinking blood." Jewish theologians interpret that to mean that the blood of an animal previously slaughtered should be salted and koshered, but not as an injunction against blood transfusions.

The woman was taken to the operating room and while she was waiting for anesthesia, I heard the attending surgeon and resident discussing among themselves giving her blood without her knowledge. I strongly objected to this, reminding them forcefully that such an act would be a criminal one, constituting assault under New York State law, and would not be covered by malpractice insurance. The two physicians became incensed and ordered me out of the operating room. I never wanted to find out whether or not they had ended up giving the patient a blood transfusion against her wishes, but I am aware she survived the operation.

As my internship year was coming to an end, I decided that despite the warm and accepting atmosphere at Beth-El and the presence of mentors like Drs. Snapper and Ripstein, I was ready to be exposed to a larger, more world-class type hospital center. I therefore sought and was accepted at Montefiore Hospital in the Bronx for a first year surgery residency. The atmosphere at Montefiore was more brisk and business-like than at Beth-El, and, although nominally a Jewish hospital, considerably less *hamische* and not kosher either. When I would be making rounds in the morning at breakfast time, I would become nauseated by the sight and smell of the sausage being served to the patients. This was something I had never been exposed to before.

There was a hierarchical atmosphere at Montefiore and much competition among the residents, with some more than ready to snitch to the chief, Dr. Elliot Hurwitt, if a fellow resident, such as myself, could be shown to have done something wrong. All of this made not only for a less congenial atmosphere than at Beth-El, but a less professional one as well. But it certainly taught me some survival skills that have come in handy along the way.

My first rotation at Montefiore was in orthopedics, and the first surgical procedure assigned to me was a spinal fusion. This was a challenging procedure that normally would be given to a more experienced orthopedic resident. However, in 1963 Montefiore had no orthopedic residency, and, therefore, each first year resident spent two months as the "orthopedic resident." In any case, I was the only resident available at that moment to perform the operation. I was given forty eight hours notice to prepare for the procedure. I ran to the library and took out every orthopedic textbook I could find and memorized every single page relating to spinal fusions. I went in to surgery two days later confident I had mastered all the material in the textbooks, but concerned about one thing; all of the books I had managed to get my hands on were thirty or forty years old.

Sure enough when I met the attending physician that morning and he asked me what my plans were for carrying out the operation, he looked dismayed when I informed him what I planned to do. "But that procedure went out 30 years ago," he exclaimed. I immediately confessed that I had never done a spinal fusion before and had gotten all the information from old textbooks. Fortunately, unlike some of the other medical personnel at Montefiore, that doctor was a real mensch, and said to me, "Don't worry. Watch me do one side and then you can do the other." His decency and reassuring manner helped me get through that operation with flying colors.

One of the more disturbing experiences I had at Montefiore took place in the urology service. In 1963, there was a paucity of indigent or walk-in patients upon whom to conduct urologic surgery. They overcame this deficiency by having the surgical residents go to flop houses on the Bowery once or twice a week, where they had an arrangement with those facilities. Some of the male alcoholics who frequented those shelters would be informed that they would not receive their customary free meal unless they agreed to submit to a rectal examination. Since it was not unusual for alcoholic males at advanced stages of their lives to have enlarged prostates, the resident would carefully tell the men, "Having examined you, I cannot tell you for certain that you do not have prostate cancer." That statement was, of course, technically correct. Indeed, 10 percent of all elderly men have microscopic cancer cells in their prostates; a fact of which the ultimate medical significance is not clear. In any case, that comment would usually do the trick in convincing the men that they ought to come in to Montefiore for further testing.

Once or twice a week, the department would arrange to transport a group of such men, filthy and smelly, from the Bowery up to Montefiore, where they would be defumigated and then put through a series of tests. Occasionally, the doctors would discover that a patient was carrying another disease they had been unaware of. A few days later, they would again be told that after all the examinations, they could still not be certified as being free of all evidence of prostatic cancer. They were advised that in order to be safe, they should agree to undergo a surgical procedure known as an open perineal prostatic biopsy (OPPB). Ten percent of these would come back with evidence of microscopic prostate cancer and undergo radical prostate surgery. Yet, at that time no hard facts were available to quantify the clinical significance of being among the unfortunate ten percent. This was in the days before the PSA blood test. What percentage of the "ten percent" subset would have lived a full and normal life without developing clinical carcinoma? No one knew.

As I noted, each of the residents found his own patients for these operations. I was indignant about the entire procedure, which I considered profoundly unethical and immoral. Therefore I was the only resident that year in the urology department who refused to go to the Bowery looking for patients, and consequently the only one who did not perform a single prostatic biopsy. My colleagues, of course, were aware of my feelings, but did not see it my way.

For forty years, memories of this period have continued to trouble me. What the Montefiore urology department was doing in this situation was, in my opinion, fundamentally inconsistent with good medical care. I probably should have blown the whistle on this practice. In retrospect, it is difficult to believe that higher ups at Montefiore were ignorant of these activities. I am sorry to acknowledge that at that stage of my life I simply did not have the strength of character to risk my medical career to take a stand I knew to be right.

Indeed, I had a lot to lose. On December 31, 1963, in the middle of my first year of residency, Sheila gave birth to our first child, Malkie, at Beth-El Hospital. Shortly thereafter, I decided to leave Montefiore for my second year of residency and go back to Beth-El, which on January 1, 1964, had changed its name to Brookdale. Doing that would give me the chance to return to the program of Dr. Ripstein, who was my surgical hero. I was already leaning in the direction of doing a residency in colon and rectal surgery after finishing my general surgery residency. Ripstein's expertise in colitis and his worldwide reputation for the Ripstein procedure for rectal prolapse made him the perfect "rebbe" in that speciality.

I was a bit worried that "the chief" might not accept me given that I had left a year earlier for Montefiore, but he welcomed me back. I couldn't have been happier, especially when he gave me permission to take a month off to make my first trip to Israel together with Sheila.

We left Malkie at home with Sheila's parents and headed off to do Israel on a shoestring budget, traveling the length of the country, from Metulla to Eilat by Egged bus. It was June 1966, and scaldingly hot, especially in the unforgettably awful non-air conditioned bus we took down to Eilat. After three weeks of such exhausting schlepping, we decided to relax in our final week in a seaside hotel in Netanya. We ended up at a kosher hotel that served two heavy meat meals every day. We asked if we could instead have a dairy meal for lunch served at a separate table from the other guests. The manager readily agreed, giving us separate dishes with butter and milk.

Everything seemed fine until Sheila noticed that the silverware at our table appeared to be the same silverware they were using at the tables with meat dishes. We called over the maitre de, but he assured us solemnly that our silverware came from a different place than the rest of the cutlery. We put aside our serious doubts until the next night when Sheila realized that some of the guests at a wedding celebration taking place in the hotel dining room were eating meat and milk together. I went to the desk and began to shout emotionally in English about how disgraceful it was that a hotel passed itself off as kosher, with a rabbinic certificate on the wall, and yet indulged in such practices. The manager shouted back at me "*daber Ivrit*" (speak Hebrew), and then tried to convince me that the man I had observed mixing meat and milk dishes was not Jewish, which of course, even if true, would not excuse the violation of kashruth. I kept sputtering away indignantly in English. While I could converse in a slow Hebrew, my anger mode was only in English.

Sheila and I checked out the next morning and moved to the Deborah Hotel in Tel Aviv, which was known for being rigorously kosher. There, I happened to meet the secretary of the Israeli Chief Rabbinate, and breathlessly informed him of the terrible violations of kashruth I had observed in Netanya. He looked at me like I had been born yesterday and said, "C'mon, you know you can't trust a kashruth certificate here in Israel." Although Israeli kashruth standards have improved significantly in the decades since 1966, even today in many areas they do not come anywhere near the rigorous standards of the Orthodox Union or other kashruth organizations in America.

While I was at Brookdale, Sheila and I moved into a two-bedroom apartment on the top floor of a Lefrak building within walking distance of the hospital. I felt truly blessed; I had a happy marriage and a beautiful baby and loved what I was doing in my surgical residency. Certainly, being in the operating room was my favorite time of the day. To have the opportunity to scrub with and operate alongside Dr. Ripstein was a great pleasure. His technique was nearly perfect and he was a consummate gentleman who almost never lost his temper. Most important, his knowledge of surgery and medicine in general was almost encyclopedic and he was extremely generous in his willingness to devote time and energy to nurturing myself and the other residents and in sharing his knowledge and insights with us.

During the last year that I was chief resident at Brookdale, I was working like a *meshuganah* (nut case). I was practically on call every single night and chronically exhausted. On one occasion, I had been on call more than thirty six hours without a break. I came home about 11PM and immediately fell asleep. Sometime shortly after midnight, however, Malkie began to cry in the next room, and strangely, considering how tired I was, it was I, and not

Sheila, who heard the baby. As I was stumbling out of bed to check on Malkie, I was startled to hear the unmistakable sound of footsteps on the roof, right above our top floor apartment. I had a sensation close to panic, thinking it could only be prowlers who could be expected at any moment to come down the fire escape and try to break into our apartment. I ran to the phone to call the police, only to find that the line was dead. With my throat in my mouth, I banged desperately on the phone several times, and felt a flood of relief when the line suddenly came back. I dialed 911 and breathlessly informed the police operator that there were prowlers on our roof. She took our address and told me to hang on; that the cops were on their way to rescue us. I then ran around our apartment putting on all the lights so that the prowlers would know we were awake and, hopefully, decide not to break in after all. When I got to the living room, I saw that the keyhole to the door in the entrance was open and the light from the hall was shining in. I peeked through and saw that the hallway was filled with all my neighbors, as well as policemen, ambulance corps personnel and dogs. Utterly mystified, I opened the door. Our next-door neighbor, Mrs. Feinbloom took one look at me and cried out, "Oy, Dr. Ganchrow. Thank G-d you are alive."

Amidst the general bedlam it took a few minutes to make sense of the situation. I finally realized that what had happened was that the emergency room had phoned me for a consultation shortly after I had gone to bed. Given how exhausted I was, I had apparently picked up the phone without fully waking up, had spoken a few incoherent words and then dropped the receiver to the floor. The person on the other end of the phone heard only snoring or a labored deep breathing and, fearing that there might be something wrong, had dispatched an ambulance to my building. Unfortunately, given that it was so late at night and the neighborhood was not as safe as it once had been, no one wanted to open the door.

After that, the hospital called the police who apparently banged on our door, but neither Sheila nor I heard anything. Fearing that we might have been victims of foul play, the cops then went to the apartment of one of our neighbors and climbed up onto the roof with the intention of coming down to our apartment through our fire escape. The police were chased away by barking dogs in our neighbor's apartment. So, it was the sound of the policemen on the roof that I heard and mistakenly assumed to be robbers.

When I finally pieced together what had happened, I felt very foolish but also quite touched that the hospital had immediately sent out an ambulance corps when they thought I might be sick. Given the escalating crime level in the area, I was also more than a little relieved that the cops had gotten there so quickly.

Indeed, the life of a surgical resident in a hospital in central Brooklyn that had seen better days was not an easy one. On New Year's Eve 1966, a night I spent in the emergency room, there were so many stabbings and shootings in Brownsville and East Flatbush that we ran out of chest tubes to insert into the chests of victims with lung injuries. I think I put in something like eighteen chest tubes that hellish night. We did what we had to do, but sometimes we felt we were like King Canute trying to hold back the tide of violence that was rapidly sweeping over the area.

Violence was building on the international scene as well. In May of 1967, Egypt blockaded the Straits of Tiran and Israel suddenly stood poised on the brink of war against all of the Arab nations surrounding her. Like many other American Jews, I felt that I should go to Israel and volunteer my services in that emergency. If war broke out, I wanted to be near the front line as a surgeon, fighting to save the lives of gravely wounded Israeli fighters. I went to Dr. Ripstein and requested a leave of absence to go to Israel, which seemed eminently reasonable, given that I only had two more months to go before finishing my training. Ripstein said he would be happy to allow me to leave, but reminded me that I would also need to get the approval of the American Board of Surgery, which is the governing body for the training of surgical residents. To my dismay, they informed me that if I were to leave, I would not be considered to have completed my surgical training and would have to repeat an entire year.

I was very upset and angry, but finally concluded that as much as I felt I ought to be in Israel at that moment, I could not go. I had a wife and a small child to consider, and simply could not afford to lose an entire year of training. In any case, I would get my chance to serve as a front-line surgeon soon enough.

At that point with the army staring me in the face, I had to make a decision about which area of surgery I would specialize in after leaving the army. Chest surgery would involve two years of training and other areas of specialization did not have their own Boards. The only area of surgery that was of interest to me that had its own Boards and only one year of training was colon and rectal surgery. The fact that Ripstein was an expert in the field and had taught me much about it also clearly played a role in my decision.

As for the more immediate prospect—the Army—I felt I had lucked out when I got an assignment in the summer of 1967 to Patterson Army Hospital at Fort Monmouth, New Jersey. After all, the base was located only one hour from Far Rockaway, Queens where we were often able to go on shabbos when I was not on call. We rented an apartment in a town house occupied primarily by army personnel about half a mile from the base, a relatively easy walk from the hospital.

To say I was ignorant of the basics of how the army worked would be a vast understatement. On my first day on duty, I was told I had to buy my own uniform and headed to a PX store that specialized in uniforms. As I passed by three individuals who were partly blocking an aisle, I accidentally brushed one of them lightly on the shoulder. To my surprise, I heard a series of shocked 'oohs and ahs' and realized that a couple of them were fixing me with some very angry stares. It turned out that the man I had brushed against was a general. He himself didn't seem to mind, but his entourage was quite upset. One of them said to me sharply, "Don't you realize you touched a general?" I responded, "Sorry, but how was I supposed to know the guy was a general?" "And who the hell are you?" he demanded. When I replied that I was a doctor, he rolled his eyes and said in a tone of near-disgust, "Oh, a doctor." As I was to learn, a lot of military people expected that kind of gauche behavior from physicians, who were known not to take the military too seriously.

I myself, improbable though it may seem, was given the rank of captain, together with the uniform and bars that came with it. The following day, I reported at the Fort Monmouth Motor Vehicle Bureau in order to get a driver's license. I had put on my uniform for the first time as best I could, and placed my captain's bars on my hat as well as on my shirt. As I waited on line to obtain my permit, an MP (military policeman) came over to me, saluted and whispered in my ear, "Captain, your bars are on upside down." I was totally embarrassed, but not sure how to fix them, because I did not have the slightest idea whether the bars should be placed vertically or horizontally.

I settled into the hospital, performing hernia operations and the like, but the specter of Vietnam hung over me, as it did nearly everyone else on base. Every day doctors were getting their orders to leave for Vietnam. The situation was even more nerve racking for Sheila than it was for myself. Both of us were already enduring culture shock in an environment where almost no one had seen an Orthodox Jew. A general's daughter, who lived in the next apartment to us, acknowledged to Sheila that she had believed Jews have horns. It was very difficult to get the people there to understand why we said 'No' to their kind invitations to come over for a barbeque.

Finally, three months into my training, my orders came, but they were to report to Fort Sam Houston in San Antonio rather than go directly to Vietnam. Sheila, Malkie and I made the long drive all the way to Texas, with a stop off for shabbos in Tulsa, Oklahoma. Throughout some of the trip, I had my left arm hanging out the window as I drove; somehow managing to tear the rotator cuff in that arm in the process. I didn't realize at that point how serious the injury was or how long it would take to heal.

The Army had gathered several hundred physicians and dentists at Sam Houston and seemed determined to prove to us we were no better than any other draftees—by treating us like dirt. As soon as we arrived and assembled as a unit, we were ordered to sing the theme song of The Mickey Mouse Club and march in formation to that tune. Many of the wives of members of our unit, who were standing off to the side, could not hold in their laughter as they watched their husbands following orders, marching left, right, left turn, right turn, company halt while belting out the words "Who's the leader of the club that's made for you and me? M-I-C-K-E-Y M-O-U-S-E!!!" For the next six weeks, we suffered through a regimen of marching, firing ranges and scrambling under barbed wire. It was not as rigorous, it was true, as the basic training course endured by the regular G.I.; just enough to give us some important basic knowledge while continually making the point to us that just because we were doctors, we were no better or more important than any other officer.

At the end of our basic training course, we had a graduation ceremony in which we were required to wear a set of dress blues. The uniform cost about $350, a considerable expense in 1967. Loath to spend so much money on a set of clothing I would wear only once in my life. I managed to avoid that expense by borrowing a set of dress blues from an individual shaped more or less like I was, except that he was substantially wider and plumper. I didn't realize how big a difference there was between us until I put on the uniform and felt my pants slipping precariously from my waist. As we walked to the ceremony, I desperately tugged at the pants with one hand to keep them from falling while I tried to pull the jacket on tighter with the other. Things got considerably dicier during the inspection ceremony when we had to stand at attention. As the commanding officer walked up and down our row, I desperately pinched my pants with my left hand when he was to the right of me and with my right hand when he was to my left. During this ordeal, I confess to offering a devout prayer that I would not be the first U.S. Army officer in history to have his pants fall down during an inspection ceremony.

I managed to take some time off in order to prepare for and pass part one of my surgical Board tests, which were given in Galveston, Texas. Then we were ordered to return to Fort Monmouth. Shortly thereafter I received my orders to go to Vietnam as a surgeon. I was to ship out in about a month. It was an enormously trying time psychologically for both Sheila and I. For my part, the issue was not that I was so frightened at the prospect of facing Vietnam, but rather felt agonized about leaving Sheila and four year old Malkie all alone. Sheila was extremely fearful for me and was also going through a stressful time trying to become pregnant with our second child.

Meanwhile, the torn rotator cuff in my left arm was causing me more and more pain. It got so bad that I had to excuse myself from doing surgery. Under normal circumstances, such an injury would have been enough to prevent me from going to Vietnam. However, under army regulations a physician cannot be excused from combat duty by a note or diagnosis from a physician in his own hospital. Therefore, I was sent to Walter Reed Army Hospital in Washington, where the chief of orthopedic surgery of the entire United States Army examined me. Obviously, the decision of such an august figure would be final. After a thorough examination, he confirmed to me that I indeed had a torn rotator cuff. Then he smiled and said, "Son, the best treatment for you will be the hot sun of Vietnam. I just got back from there, and you are going to love it." When I reminded him that because of my bad arm I would not be able to move patients on stretchers, he responded, "Don't worry, we have plenty of other people to do that." So there was nothing further to be done. Despite our fears and unhappiness I prepared myself psychologically for a one-year-hiatus away from my family in a war zone and tried to help Sheila do the same.

Sheila's version: I was extremely depressed by the whole situation. I desperately wanted a second child and had not managed to get pregnant before Mendy left. I was fortunate to have loving parents who insisted I move back home with Malkie during that year and gave me a great deal of psychological support. Throughout the whole time I was terrified that Mendy would be killed. I was teaching in a public school that year, and every afternoon, on my way home from school, I'd get a panic attack, fearing that when I turned the corner I'd see two soldiers standing at our door to tell me that my beloved husband had been killed. In fact, I did have a good friend whose husband was a doctor in Vietnam who was killed during the time Mendy was over there. So it was really terrifying.

Probably what pulled me through was that I had to be strong because I had to take care of my daughter. Also, of course, I was kept busy with my school teaching job. I had Mendy's two R&R (rest and recreation) breaks to look forward to. The first time, which came at Thanksgiving, 1968, we met in Tokyo. On the second R&R trip, which was to Hawaii, I took Malkie along so she could remember what her father looked like. Mendy used to call about once a week, though it was hard for him to predict in advance when he would be given the opportunity to call. I used to frequently baby sit in the evenings during that time so as to make a few extra dollars. One such evening, my mom called me and told me to come home immediately; that Mendy had called and would be allowed to call back again shortly. All in all, it was certainly one of the most difficult periods of my life.

Just prior to leaving for Vietnam, I spent a day at Fort Dix, New Jersey learning to take apart and shoot an M-16. Just after lunch, as I, together with several hundred other men, was preparing to head for the shooting range, an enlisted man came over to me, saluted, and said, "Sir, you are the ranking officer of these two hundred men. Please line up your men and march them to the firing range. For a moment I was totally speechless. I knew only one command and that was "Attention." So I yelled it and everyone formed into a line. Then I followed with "left face" and everyone turned left. Finally, I shouted out what seemed like the obvious command under the circumstances, "Forward, march." Immediately, everybody started marching. Hey, I kind of liked this role.

The problem was that about fifty feet ahead was a large truck blocking their route. I had no idea how to tell them in "army language" how to move around the truck so I began yelling, "Watch out for the truck! Watch out for the truck!" Many of the men broke up in laughter. If that wasn't hard enough on my dignity, there was the fact, that most of the recruits were thinner and stronger than I was. I was overweight and out of shape, carrying a 75- pound-sack on my back in the hot June sun. The next thing I knew I was falling far behind my troops. The young sergeant who had originally asked me to march the men, came back to me with a smirk on his face and said, "Sir, would you like me to take over?" All I could get out was "Please." The sergeant ran ahead and directed the entire group to the firing range, which was more than a mile away. When I finally arrived there, huffing and puffing from the exertion, the troops had already received their instructions. They informed me, "Sir, as you are the ranking officer of this group, you will be in firing pit number one. That sounded good, until I realized that there were 100 pits running in descending order, which meant that pit number one was the last pit, another three quarters of a mile away. After a hard slog, I arrived there and was greatly relieved to find that my partner, a young soldier, had already set everything up so as to make things easier for me. I took my shooting practice and did reasonably well. At the end, the original sergeant came up to me, saluted again, and said, "Sir, march your men back to where they came from." This time, however, I had learned my lesson and quickly replied, "Sergeant, you take over." After the men marched off, I walked over to the road, stood right in the middle of the asphalt and flagged down a truck driven by an enlisted man. I did not ask for a ride, but taking advantage of my rank, I ordered him, "You are taking me back." Dutifully, he drove me back to the place we had started from.

CHAPTER THREE
Vietnam

The moment that I had dreaded for years, but never really expected to arrive, had now come. I was going to Vietnam. All appeals had been exhausted. Sheila was tearful and distraught in the face of the magnitude of the moment. As for myself, I was calmer, but, in truth, felt sort of stunned. I could hardly believe this was happening.

In the first week of June, 1968 I travelled to Travis Air Force Base in California. There were hundreds of uniformed men, privates, corporals, and sergeants, who were awaiting transfer to Vietnam on commercial jets. They all looked very young. While surveying the crowd, I noticed a chaplain wearing the insignia of the Star of David and the Ten Commandments, indicating that he was Jewish. He, too, was on his way to Vietnam. I struck up a conversation with him and learned that he was a Reform Rabbi named Mark.

While we were talking, an individual in civilian clothing approached and introduced himself as a Conservative Rabbi representing the National Jewish Welfare Board. He had been informed that the two of us were going to Vietnam and had been instructed to greet us and send us off. We had about three or four hours before the plane took off, so the chaplain invited the two of us to be his guests for lunch at the Officers Club. Because the food was non-kosher, I, the Orthodox Jew, had only a bourbon; the Conservative Jew had fish; and the Reform Jew had steak. On the way back to the Air Force Base, we stopped off at the Jewish Welfare Board office. The Conservative rabbi gave me a huge bag containing cans of kosher chicken parts, chicken soup with matzo balls, and a variety of other foods for the plane trip and for my first few days in Vietnam. I had already shipped over some cases of canned kosher meat from a New York butcher— which turned out to be so horrid I ended up throwing it away. I would have rather died of starvation than eaten that stuff. It truly tasted like warm dog food.

The food I received from the Jewish Welfare Board helped a little, but until I was able to get some new shipments from Sheila, I lived mainly on Coca Cola. I was drinking so much of it, in fact, that I was gaining weight, despite my otherwise spartan diet. In fact, I wrote a letter to the Coca Cola Company apprising them of my situation, and they shipped me a few cases of Diet Coke, which was not available otherwise in the canteen.

Mark and I finally got on the plane. Given the gravity of the moment, it was a relief to have someone alongside me on that endless flight that I could talk and relate to. The overwhelming reality that when the plane touched down, I would be in Vietnam, in the middle of a war, felt utterly surreal to me. We spoke about various topics—trying to pass the time. Mark, though a Reform rabbi, told me he had gone to visit the Lubavitcher Rebbe after receiving his orders. He seemed to have done that both for the spiritual encounter with a great Torah scholar and also, perhaps, for some personal guidance. While we were talking, we were served dinner. It was ham. Mark got very upset. He started yelling, "I am a rabbi. This is an insult to me. How could you do this?" He created such a scene that I became embarrassed and tried to calm him down. The crew, who worked for a civilian airline that had leased its planes to the military, replied firmly that there was no choice of food—that it was ham or nothing. I invited Mark to share my canned food with me. He accepted my offer and we opened a few cans of Horowitz-Margareten matzo ball soup and chicken.

We arrived in Vietnam at about 5AM the following morning; landing at Bien Hoa Airport. After getting some things in order, I went to the corner of a hooch (shack) to pray. While I was putting on my tefillin (phylacteries) and talit (prayer shawl), Mark asked me if he could use my tefillin, and if I could show him how to do it as well. I was more than happy to accommodate his request. Normally, to my knowledge, Reform Jews do not don a prayer shawl or tefillin on a daily basis. I felt pleased he had made the request and naively thought that perhaps after the episode with the ham he was "seeing the light." When we finished, we went to our first Vietnam breakfast at the mess hall. I had a whole orange, corn flakes, milk, and a cup of coffee. To my surprise and considerable consternation, Mark had bacon and eggs. "Mark," I said to him. "It is really none of my business, but yesterday on the plane, you were screaming about ham, and now you are eating bacon. It's from the same animal." "Yes, you are right," he acknowledged, but then said, "Look, a Jew is not allowed to eat ham, but bacon, I love!" That priceless remark has lingered in my memory all of these years.

Mark left the following day, and I did not see or hear of him again after that until his name was attached to an announcement on the bulletin board about Rosh Hashanah services in Na Trang, which is located on the coast. The sign read that everyone should come to services and bring their bathing suits. If I had any doubts that Reform represented a totally alien Jewish worldview than everything I had grown up with and was about, my experience with Mark removed those doubts.

I had arrived in Vietnam. It was four months after the Tet Offensive, during which the Viet Cong and North Vietnamese Army had stormed into Hue, Da Nang and Saigon itself, and before being driven out with heavy losses. This badly embarrassed the United States Army and the Johnson Administration. The weather at that time of year in Vietnam is very hot and muggy. It became so muggy at times that although I put on a freshly starched uniform every morning, I became totally sweated up the moment I walked out of my hooch. We quickly learned that wearing underwear was an impediment. During monsoon season, it was impossible to find protection from the torrential rain and powerful winds.

After several days of orientation and a lot of just hanging around, I finally received my assignment. I was going to be at the 45th surgical hospital at Tay Ninh. This hospital was the successor of the MASH 45 unit of book, movie, and television series fame. It was a Friday morning when I was given the orders to take a helicopter to Cu Chi, which later became famous for the Vietcong tunnel system, and from there, to catch a second copter to Tay Ninh. The only problem was that the first leg of the trip had brought me to Cu Chi late Friday afternoon, and it was getting very close to the Sabbath. For religious reasons, I did not want to fly on the Sabbath. I knew I was in Vietnam and had military obligations, but I was determined not to compromise my religious convictions.

Fortunately, I managed to find some old friends from civilian hospitals who were happy to greet a familiar face. They basically hid me until Sunday morning when I proceeded on to Tay Ninh. In fact, doing so was not particularly risky for them, because I would not be considered part of the 45th Surgical Unit until I had actually shown up and reported for duty. Taking an extra day or two to arrive, as I did in that situation, was not all that rare in Vietnam.

In any case, my shabbat in Cu Chi proved to be anything but tranquil. I had been instructed to stay inside the hooch, which wasn't a problem for me, because I was exhausted and welcomed the uninterrupted rest. At around ten or eleven at night, I was awakened from a deep sleep to feel the earth literally shaking. I stood up for a second, but was knocked to the ground by the force of the vibrations. I had no idea what was happening. Then, everything was silent and I half wondered if maybe I had dreamed the whole thing. Yet, fifteen or twenty minutes later, the violent shaking began again. A series of twenty explosions or more—lasting for thirty to sixty seconds— shattered the quiet of the night.

Terrified, I remained on the floor in the hooch, with my helmet on my head. Yet no one else in the camp seemed particularly concerned about the "earthquakes, " and eventually I began to understand that the explosions presented no immediate threat to my survival. At that point, I fell back to sleep. In the morning, I inquired about the incident and was laughed at. Apparently, these were B-52 explosions miles and miles away. I was also to learn in time to welcome the sound of B-52 bombing rather than fearing it. Indeed, several months later a planned B-52 attack within a half mile of our camp saved my life and the lives of many other members of my unit by decimating and scattering the enemy forces that were surrounding us.

Later on in the year, I was on a two-day "in-country" R+R in Natrang and ended up in Cu Chi again on Friday afternoon. There I met an oral surgeon, Dr. Arnold Jutkowitz, who is today a fellow resident of Monsey. He was preparing *arbis* (chickpeas) for Friday night, and I joined him at a pre-Oneg Shabbat. It is hard to describe the wonderful feeling I had to be able to sit and talk about Torah so far away from home and with someone who was much like myself and experiencing similar emotions. All of that and I was able to get back to Tay Ninh before sundown.

Tay Ninh is a city close to the Vietnamese border with Cambodia. The army base where I was stationed was approximately two to three kilometres from the Ho Chi Minh Trail, the main supply line used by the North Vietnamese to funnel troops and supplies into South Vietnam. Directly opposite the base was the tallest and most-sacred mountain in Vietnam, called Nui Ba Din. The Americans controlled the bottom of the hill and had posted their communications center at the top of it. However, the middle of the hill was completely dug out and contained a Vietcong hospital, supply base, and enemy R+R center. Every night, we would fire on the center of the mountain. All the doctors not on call would gather outside in their casual attire, have barbecues, and watch the fireworks as the tracers lit up the night sky. It was really quite beautiful to watch, sipping our bourbon and smoking cigars.

Unfortunately, the helicopter pad of the base was right next to the hospital, and came under frequent rocket attacks. Two doctors were killed in Vietcong attacks shortly before I was stationed at the base. I recall that on one occasion I was standing outside the kitchen speaking with another doctor. After we said goodnight and walked away from each other, a rocket hit the exact spot where we had been thirty seconds before. Hundreds of fragments hit the back of the kitchen and the refrigerator. It was truly a miracle that no one had been injured.

The small base at Tay Ninh became extremely dangerous at times and, quite often, we were put on "red alert." There was an ever-present danger that we could be overrun by the Vietcong or North Vietnamese troops and, in the interest of safety, we always had to walk around in helmets and flak jackets and carry 45 automatic pistols. Considering the medical corps to be notoriously poor soldiers, the military brass gave us passwords to use when we needed to get to the operating room during the red alerts. An armed guard was usually sent to accompany us so we wouldn't be shot by accident.

On a number of occasions, the mamasans, the Vietnamese women who cleaned our rooms and washed our clothes did not show up for work as scheduled in the early morning. In each of those situations, red alerts were immediately sounded, because our intelligence people feared the women had been warned about an impending enemy attack. However, on one or two of these occasions, our supposedly crack intelligence corps was apparently not aware of a more innocent reason for the mamasans' absence that even many newcomers like myself had learned about; the women had not shown up for work because of an obscure Vietnamese national holiday.

I recall one particular red alert when we were in an underground shelter under extremely heavy bombardment. We could see that one of our colleagues was sleeping in his bed above ground across the way in a drunken stupor. He did not stir despite our attempts to wake him. He remained there throughout the entire attack, but miraculously, was not hurt. This doctor had a very interesting personal story. Apparently, he had been a medic in the field and on one occasion flew down to Saigon with a lot of money from his fellow officers to purchase electronics. The helicopter he was in was shot down, and everyone was killed except for him. Somehow, because he was short, wiry and fast, he managed to outrun the small firearms and mortar fire directed against him. As a reward for his survival, he was assigned to our hospital—even though he was neither a surgeon nor a specialist. Unfortunately, however, the trauma of what he had endured was too much for him to bear sober, and he usually drank himself to sleep. The memory of this physician has always stayed with me. I often wonder what became of him.

Once a week, the Jewish chaplain of our sector of Vietnam, Rabbi Harold "Chico" Wasserman, came by helicopter to Tay Ninh to visit me and bring me kosher food. He was a graduate of Yeshiva College and, under normal circumstances, would have had to undergo an additional three-to-four-year program in New York in order to receive ordination. However, he wanted to be in the U.S. Army as a chaplain so badly that he went to Israel to study so as to be able to receive his rabbinical ordination in a shorter period. He then returned to the States, joined the Army and went to Ranger training school. He also took parachute training, since his desire was to become RA (Regular Army). He was a short and thin individual, full of energy. He was never able to walk straight or slowly, so if you were walking in a normal fashion, he would be running in semicircles around you. Luckily for Wasserman and the observant Jewish military personnel he served, his father owned or managed a large supermarket in New Jersey, and was able to send his son shipments of canned vegetables. I was one of the fortunate people he shared the food with.

Each week Wasserman would ask me why I was stuck in this G-d-forsaken area, since to my knowledge I was apparently the only Jewish physician in the 45th surgical unit. I responded that I had absolutely no chance of being moved out of the hospital in Tay Ninh to a less exposed dangerous place. The protocol in Vietnam was that no transfers would be granted until a physician had been in the country for at least six months. When Wasserman first began asking, I had only been in the country for six to eight weeks. Still, Rabbi Wasserman constantly attempted to get me transferred.

During this time, the Vietcong and the North Vietnamese had surrounded our base. Intelligence warned they would likely attack us, in the hope of drawing troops away from the defense of Saigon, seventy miles away. However, the U.S. military brass back in Saigon decided that the enemy was engaged in a clever ruse and had no intention of actually attacking. Therefore they would not commit the troops to our defense. On the other hand, our intelligence officers informed us that we might be overrun and that we should therefore expect the worst. As it turned out, only helicopter gun-ships and frequent B-52 carpet bombings saved us.

While all of this was going on, I would write to Sheila who was living with her parents, that I was having a wonderful time playing volleyball and sitting in the sun. I would then write to Rabbi Louis Bernstein of Queens, N.Y., who was a good friend of mine, as well as to my brother Saul, to let them know what was really transpiring. I remember telling them I was not at all sure I was going to survive this siege. The fact that Sheila's sister Rona was at home helping with Malkie, and Sheila's other sister Judy lived only a few blocks away was a consolation to me.

The commander of the Tay Ninh base decided that the best way to counter the overpowering enemy imperilling our base was to allow them to crawl right up to our perimeter fence and then open up concentrated machine gun fire in order to kill them. Every morning after enemy troops would attack the base, our sentries would have to go out and remove the bodies from the fence. One major reason for the vulnerability of our base was that our unit was primarily composed of support personnel. I never knew the overall size of our force in Tay Ninh, but I believe it was around 1000 men, including troops from the helicopter unit and the hospital, along with cooks and other supply personnel. We had only a few troop carriers and a squadron of helicopters with which to defend ourselves.

Intercepted enemy documents made clear that they knew we had no real fighting personnel, and had therefore decided to make Tay Ninh a genuine target for attack. Even after reading those documents, however, headquarters again told us we could not expect reinforcements, because Saigon was the key defense point and the Americans could not commit any troops for the defense of Tay Ninh. It was not pleasant to discuss this information with my fellow officers, and to contemplate that there was no way out in case of attack. But that was the grim reality we faced, and all of us were aware of it.

Each unit at Tay Ninh sent one officer to the daily intelligence briefing, and on several occasions I was the one who attended. After hearing the grim assessments in those briefings, I definitely came to know the meaning of "foxhole religion." As I said, we owed our salvation to the B-52 bombers. As grateful as we were to those pilots, we were acutely aware of the frightening fact that B-52's released their 500-pound bombs from a level of some thirty to forty thousand feet. We knew that from that height it would not take much for the navigator to misjudge his mark by a couple of hundred feet and that such a mistake would have placed the bombs directly on top of our hospital unit. We prayed a great deal and thanked G-d for the expertise of the crews of the B-52's and the helicopter gun ships who saved our lives.

I remember vividly the panorama of the huge craters and enormous destruction inflicted by the bombs which I observed on a helicopter trip through the countryside. Years later, during the Gulf War or Afghanistan, when I heard that the B-52's were being sent to the Middle East for use in carpet bombings against the Iraqi army or the Taliban, I knew there was no way those armies could withstand the type of punishment the B-52's deliver.

We doctors sometimes performed operations on Vietcong and North Vietnamese prisoners who had been wounded. On one occasion we were under enemy attack, with B-52's bombs exploding right outside the base. As I was operating on a POW, one of our medics volunteered to leave the area to get a full length splint for the enemy soldier's broken bones, risking his own life in the process. The B-52 bomb explosions caused all of the instruments to fall on the floor. We quickly put the patient on the floor and finished the operation lying down. I often thought while in Tay Ninh of the irony that I might possibly get blown to pieces by errant American bombs while operating on a Vietcong prisoner.

When not on duty, I found our base to be a boring place. Some of our doctors used their off-duty time to volunteer at a French children's hospital in Tay Ninh City. They would then go out to eat in a French or Vietnamese restaurant. I regretfully decided not to join them. Not only could I not eat non-kosher food, but I also was aware that the roads were mined and I had solemnly promised Sheila not to take any unnecessary chances. I reflected grimly that there were certainly enough ways to get killed in Tay Ninh as it was.

Even though they were not actively involved in combat, many of my medical colleagues liked to get dressed up in flak jackets, rows of bullets, helmets and 45 caliber revolvers, as though doing that could render them into fighting men. It seemed sort of "dumb macho" to me, especially since such dress up games increased our chances of getting involved in combat situations we were not adequately trained for. I vividly remember driving through Saigon in a jeep with several of my doctor friends, with one of my legs hanging out in case a VC motorcyclist drove up alongside us and dropped a hand grenade into our jeep.

After I had been in Tay Ninh three months, Rabbi Wasserman went to see the chief of surgery of Vietnam, a Colonel Cohen. Wasserman explained to him that there was an Orthodox Jewish surgeon in Tay Ninh named Ganchrow who was depressed. He pointed out that I had no religious services to attend and no access to kosher food on a regular basis. Cohen replied that his hands were tied because of the six-month rule. Wasserman then went to see a Colonel Maldonado, a Puerto Rican physician who was Cohen's superior due to a few days difference in seniority, and who was in charge of medicine for the U.S. Army for all of Vietnam. Wasserman explained that he had just come from seeing Cohen and the latter had turned down his appeal on my behalf. Moldanado exclaimed, "I can't believe you went to see Cohen. Everyone knows that he is not sympathetic on these issues." He immediately signed the orders for my transfer to Long Binh's 24th evacuation hospital.

Cohen's face showed total shock a few days later when he ran into me at Long Binh and found out I had been transferred. But he never asked me directly how my transfer had gone through despite his opposition.

Naturally, I was relieved and gratified to receive these orders, but they arrived at an extremely precarious moment. It was about one in the morning, and we were under attack. The enemy was attacking right up to our gates, and we had just endured a B-52 raid from thirty-five thousand feet, a pinpoint bombing around the area. Suddenly, the enemy blew up our munitions dump. It was becoming a massive battle. Helicopters were evacuating some of our most seriously wounded men who needed neurosurgical care (we had no neurosurgeons at Tay Ninh) and transferring them to Long Binh, which was only fifteen miles from Saigon. Since I myself was supposed to go to Long Binh, I decided to seize the opportunity, despite my fear of flying at night. I quickly packed my bags, and ran to the helicopter. After the hellfire in Tay Ninh, we had an uneventful flight to Long Binh and landed there with the birds chirping and the night extremely quiet. However, that tranquillity proved to be fleeting. Long Binh, too, would soon become the target of enemy attacks.

The hospital in Long Binh, known as the 24th Evacuation Hospital, was much larger than that of the 45th in Tay Ninh and had all types of specialists on staff. There were neurosurgeons, urologists, plastic and dental surgeons, orthopedists, and an entire medical unit. Many of the surgeons had academic teaching positions and were far more experienced than I. Some of them encouraged me to write medical papers while I was there. One of my papers on "mini-laparotomy" was published in an army medical journal in Vietnam. In a second paper, I compiled a study of two hundred and forty colon injuries. The study was subsequently published in the Archives of Surgery, a prominent U.S. surgical journal, after being presented to the Western Surgical Society. Since I was still somewhat lacking in self–confidence, I invited two other doctors to co-author the paper—even though I had done the majority of the work.

The saddest department in the 24th was the neurosurgical ward. The patients here were young soldiers who had suffered spinal injuries and were paralyzed, as well as others who had incurred severe head injuries and had lost most of their ability to talk or even breathe. The ward was truly a horrific sight that burned itself permanently into my memory. As I went about my rounds, I tried to avoid walking through the ward, even though doing so meant going considerably out of my way. Even as a physician who had seen so many terrible things, I found that ward unbearably depressing.

The young soldiers out in the field often tried to feign illness so they could escape combat. One classic case I remember was that of a young boy who came in and told me he had appendicitis and needed an operation. I told him his case sounded highly irregular, since normally the patient comes in describing symptoms and the doctor diagnoses and prescribes the treatment and not vice versa. The soldier was adamant. "Doc," he said. "Don't you believe me? I have appendicitis. Please operate!" It was quite obvious upon examination that he did not have appendicitis—that he was simply afraid of going back out to the field. I could not blame him for doing what he was doing. I wished I could have helped him. But the matter was out of my hands, since his white blood cell count was normal, and his abdomen showed no signs of a surgical condition.

One of the lessons I learned and carried with me during my surgical career was the value of having nurse anaesthetists. Previously, I had only seen anaesthesia administered by anaesthesiologists, who were, of course, trained physicians. For some reason, the army had a shortage of these. I do not recall a single anaesthesiologist in the 45th surgical, and we might have had only one or two in the 24th evac. However, the competence level of the nurse anaesthetists we had there was incredible. This was the result of a number of factors. First, almost all of the patients were young and prior to being wounded had been in good health. Second, the nurses had developed a technique of rabid intubation, which meant the patients were put to sleep very quickly with a breathing tube in their tracheas. Third, although any individual surgery could be long, it was repetitive in that we were dealing with acute injuries to organs or systems, rather than more-complicated cancer operations. When I went into practice later on, I found that I often preferred, and was very comfortable with, nurse anaesthetists coming into the operating room and being in charge of the anesthesia for smaller and mid-sized cases.

Since I planned, after Vietnam, to do a colon and rectal residency, I became the resident expert on colon disease. During my time there, I diagnosed one case of amebiasis via a sigmoidoscopy and biopsy, a rare condition no one else had detected. Thereafter, I was considered something of a "hero."

Under normal circumstances, we performed our operations in teams. We would have twenty-four hours on call, twenty-four hours off call, and twenty-four hours on second call, though we rarely got called on second call. Every few weeks, we could expect to confront mass casualties, either because our side was on the offensive or the enemy was. Because of the expectation of casualties, we would change the schedule to a twelve-hour-on and twelve-hour-off shift. What I learned from the twenty-four hour on-call experience was that I had the ability to sleep on a stretcher for five to eight minutes and wake up feeling rejuvenated. That ability has stayed with me to this day, when I can pull my car over to the side of the road if I feel sleepy, close my eyes for five minutes, and then continue on my way.

The sounds of a helicopter or medi-vac approaching was almost always the first warning we would have that casualties were being brought to our hospital. The nurses, lab technicians and, of course, surgeons, became extremely proficient at triage. While in the classroom, we had been trained that in battle situations we should place mortally wounded patients who were expected not to survive on the side so as to concentrate on those who had a strong chance for survival. Yet now that we were actually being confronted with mass casualties, we often found that our training did not adequately prepare us for the excruciatingly difficult decisions we had to make.

On a number of occasions during my tour, our medical corps was simply overwhelmed by more casualties than we could effectively deal with at once. At such moments, we doctors had to make instantaneous life and death decisions; effectively drawing the curtain on young men who had been alive and healthy only an hour before. Because we had no choice but to focus our limited resources on those with a fighting chance to survive, we could not even go through the ritual of making a good faith effort to try to save many critically wounded men.

At least we were kept well supplied and had up-to-date facilities. Blood was plentiful and our x-ray machines worked at full capacity. We even had the capacity to measure arterial blood gas. The surgeon of the day assigned the cases to the surgical teams that were on call. We often had two or three teams specializing in different disciplines operating on a patient at the same time; such as abdominal surgery, neurosurgery and orthopedics. This team work was key to the successful approach to patients with multiple traumas.

Watching the members of the admitting team perform their varied tasks was akin to watching a choreographed ballet. Each member of the medical team knew the tasks to which he was assigned and there was little confusion or duplication of functions. Among the medical equipment we routinely deployed were IV's, blood work, x-rays, antibiotics, Foley catheters, central venous pressure monitors and naso-gastric tubes.

Every surgeon who served in Vietnam became a master of a complex "art form." It was medicine at a very high level, but it was also often excruciatingly difficult and emotionally exhausting. I confess that once I returned to practice medicine in the United States and had to rotate to emergency room calls for surgery, I often tried to avoid the trauma drill that is so familiar to viewers of emergency room programs on television. It brought back to me all too vividly many terrible memories of the days and nights I spent desperately trying to save so many young lives.

Today, I occasionally flip on a television program featuring emergency room triage in war-like situations. And though we have new modalities such as CAT scans, MRI and angiography, the basic elements of the job are still the same.

We did everything we humanly could to save lives, but we also had a sad motto: "Fatal wounds are always fatal." There was a line of massive trauma beyond which the patient was predetermined not to survive, no matter how hard we tried and how many blood transfusions and surgeries we administered. Still, the statistics showed that the percentage of GI's with life-threatening injuries saved by army surgeons in Vietnam was significantly higher than was the case in World War II and the Korean War. This upsurge in the survival rate was primarily due to the use of helicopters in Vietnam to bring patients quickly in from the field. We were also able to cut down on infections compared to earlier wars through the use of antibiotics, massive debridement of necrotic (dead) tissue, leaving extremity wounds temporarily open, and doing delayed primary closures within a few days. The system for evacuating wounded GI's to Japan and the U.S. allowed military hospitals in Vietnam to concentrate on acute injuries. In addition, vascular surgery saved thousands of limbs through the use of vein grafts.

The calibre of military surgeons in Vietnam was extremely high. Most of them had academic appointments and a few even were members of the faculties of major medical centers such as Stanford and the University of Pennsylvania. Almost all specialties were represented. As mentioned, we dispensed cutting edge medicine that was often significantly ahead of what was being done stateside. For example, long before hyperalimentation became standard in American hospitals as a means of saving patients by using a high-calorie, high protein solution given by a large bore venous catheter in the neck, we in Vietnam were already using it on sick and wounded GI's.

On one occasion, I recall opening the chest of a badly wounded soldier and finding a flap of heart muscle hanging out. Apparently, a bullet had bounced off the patient's rib and sliced off a piece of his heart with cardiac muscle flapping around like a page in a book. I asked one of the cardiac/chest surgeons to assist me as I reattached the muscle with sutures. Our joint efforts in this case were so successful that my patient's post-operative EKG showed only a small amount of permanent damage to his heart.

On another occasion, a Vietnamese civilian came to us with a fragment wound in the neck that was already several days old. The wound had a large and growing pulsating mass which, strangely, had an audible bruit, or sound of rushing blood that was indicative of an A.V. fistula (a connection between the artery and vein). It was a challenging case, and every surgeon at our hospital wanted to perform it. Since I was the duty officer that day, I got to do the operation with the help of a vascular surgeon. We actually filmed the whole operation, and I assume that film is today in the Walter Reed surgical film library.

One situation I will never forget involved a pregnant Vietnamese woman who had been hit by a heavy U.S. truck and seriously wounded. It was clear she was going to die, but we were determined to try to save the unborn baby. I had never done a Caesarean section on my own before, so I called a friend of mine from residency days, who was a trained obstetrician stationed at Cu Chi. He was terrific; explaining the procedure to me on the phone in minute detail. I then performed the operation flawlessly, but unfortunately neither the mother nor the baby survived.

There were plenty of such tragedies, but there were also many moments of medical triumph when we managed to save the lives of people who appeared to be goners. Overall the medical situations we surgeons confronted in Vietnam would probably have taken us decades to witness and experience in an American trauma center.

I quickly became accustomed to the almost daily loss of life in Vietnam. What I was witnessing did not overwhelm me emotionally until month ten of my twelve-month stay. Gradually, it came over me that our side was suffering a tremendous toll of human life for reasons not really clear to me, especially since there were no front lines near us. Every day lives would be sacrificed to take a certain paddy, and at the end of the day, we retreated. Then, the next day, the same rice paddy would be captured with a further loss of life. Two particular incidents seemed to me so senseless that they brought me to the brink of not being able to endure the situation in Vietnam.

The first was the massacre at Nui Ba Din in Tay Ninh province. An unofficial truce had been declared between the Vietcong in the center of the mountain and the American rangers who controlled communications from the top of the mountain. There had even been an article in the *New York Times* about the sharing of water between the two sides. One American commander decided it would be best to lock up the soldiers' guns on top of the mountain, since having them out in the open was "dangerous." He unaccountably forgot they were in a war zone. One morning, the Vietcong tunnelled up through the mountain and massacred all of the Americans, who did not have a chance to defend themselves. I recall the bodies being brought in bags in multiple helicopters to our hospital. The scene was absolutely horrific. The American general who came to investigate what happened noted that if the commanding officer had survived the attack, he would have been court-martialed. Very oddly, I do not recall reading about this incident in any newspaper.

The second event occurred very close to the end of my eleventh month in Vietnam. A veterinarian was driving in a jeep from another base to the base at Long Binh. Sandbags had been placed on the bottom of the jeep in order to protect the driver in case of an explosion, even though the roads were swept twice a day for mines. Approximately one hundred yards from the entrance to the base, the vet and his driver got a flat tire. In order to get the spare tire out of the trunk, they removed the sandbags and did not put them back because they were so close to the base. They hit a mine after driving only a few feet. Their legs had to be amputated, as did the vet's rectum and buttocks. It was a horrendous injury that later proved to be a fatal journey through the minefields. I went into a corner and started to cry because of the fate of these two young Americans. It seemed such a point-less loss of human life.

I did many more operations on POW's in Long Binh than I had in Tay Ninh, since our hospital was located right next to a prisoner-of-war hospital camp. The 24th Evac was also very close to the Long Binh jail, which we sardonically referred to as "LBJ." Most of the prisoners there were black Americans who had been convicted of smoking marijuana or similar illegal activities. One Sabbath, I awoke from a nap to the foul odor of gas. I thought we were under enemy attack, but it turned out that there was an out-of-control riot going on at LBJ. In an effort to get things back under control, helicopters had dumped tear gas into the prison, and the wind had wafted the gas over to our area.

Long Binh was quite a sprawling base, where recreational activities co-existed somewhat surreally with war-related ones. In addition to two major hospitals and the prisoner-of-war camp and jail I mentioned, Long Binh boasted a huge PX, tennis courts, and a swimming pool. When not on duty, we could usually walk around in shorts and polo shirts. Each night, the off-duty staff and patients in wheelchairs and on crutches and canes gathered in the hospital quadrangle to watch movies. For entertainment, there was one television channel and, of course, the *Stars and Stripes* newspaper, as well as pocketbooks to read. My closeness to southern colleagues introduced me to bourbon and coke, which quickly became my favorite drink.

Sometimes, I preferred more serious forms of recreation. My friend and college roommate, Shimmy Kwestel, had sent me a present of the *Chumash*, Five Books of Moses, with an English language version of Rashi. I often found perusing these sacred texts to be enormously comforting.

We had a large contingent of dedicated nurses at Long Binh. On one occasion I recall, members of the company in charge of experimental weapons such as the Gattling gun decided to invite the nurses' contingent for a demonstration of the weaponry so as to impress them and hopefully to convince some of them to go out on dates. Our commanding officer insisted, however, that either the entire hospital should be invited to the demonstration or no one would be allowed to go. This was such a large number of people, however, that they had to divide up the hospital staff into two sessions.

The entire event struck me as a terrible waste. The army had to provide security for those valuable doctors, nurses and technicians, and therefore armed vehicles; helicopters, tanks and roadblocks were set up as the demonstration took place far away from the hospital. Each nurse and doctor was given the opportunity to throw a hand grenade, fire various small arms and to watch a demonstration of massive firepower. The probable cost of this exercise in overkill was certainly tens of thousands and perhaps hundreds of thousands of dollars—all for the purpose of impressing those nurses.

Many movie stars and sports figures came to visit the troops. One of these visitors was Arthur Ashe, then one of the world's greatest tennis players. Obviously, he used our tennis courts. On another occasion, a famous movie star, who had previously been a nurse, came to entertain the troops. After visiting the officers club and having a few drinks there, she wanted to see the operating room. A general was happy to oblige and escort her. I happened to be operating on a seriously wounded GI at the time of her visit. He was losing a tremendous amount of blood. The movie star asked if she could be of any assistance. The nurse anaesthetist and I told her she could pump the needed blood. She actually did a wonderful job, and we caught up with the blood loss.

Yet when I asked her to stop, the movie star became indignant. "How can you tell me to stop?" she snapped "I know what I'm doing." Perhaps her irritability was the result of the considerable amount of alcohol in her system. In any case, the general signalled to us not to say anything else that might anger her. We ended up taking blood out of one arm of the patient, as the movie star was pumping blood into the other. Fortunately, this lasted only for a few minutes, and no harm was done.

I also had the opportunity to meet Jimmy Stewart. He looked old and gray, and when I later saw him in the movies with his hair dyed and makeup on, I could not believe it was the same person.

I took up jogging in Vietnam, which together with the dearth of kosher food helped me to lose about seventy pounds. Toward the end of my stay in Long Binh, they had built latrines with flushing toilets. This was a real luxury. One evening, I went out to wash up before going to bed. Since it was so hot out, I walked out undressed from the waist up. As I was returning from the latrine, rockets started coming in overhead. Our vast experience with both incoming and outgoing mortar and rockets made us able to discern between the two. The very distinctive whistle of these rockets made me realize immediately that they were in-coming. The rockets landed five hundred feet from me, and I immediately dove to the gravel and rock-covered ground. I started crawling to an underground shelter that was approximately three hundred feet away. All the doctors in the hootches came running out looking for shelter. One of them was carrying a bottle of scotch. When I finally got to the shelter, my heart was racing as fast as it possibly could. I was all cut up and bloodied from crawling on the rocks and gravel. Though I normally hate scotch, I gulped it down in order to calm my nerves.

As I glanced over the bleeding superficial wounds I had in-curred in that incident, I realized I had just legally qualified to receive a Purple Heart. However, in order to be certified, I would have needed to go to doctors in another hospital to be examined because, according to the rules, my own colleagues were not per-mitted to attest that I deserved a Purple Heart. Since such a trip was impractical, I decided to forget about it, but I always remem-bered that I should have qualified for one. That incident brought back memories to me of going to the orthopedic surgeon at Walter Reed Army Hospital for my torn rotator cuff because the doctors at Ft. Monmouth Hospital could not disqualify me from service to Vietnam. I blanch when I recall the nasty sense of humor he manifested when he told me that the heat in Vietnam would be the best thing for my shoulder and I would "love" the place. His sense of humor was wasted on me then, as it is now.

During the course of my nine long months in Long Binh, the war drew ever closer to the sprawling base and we came under attack many times. Toward the end of the year, I had the grati-fying experience of being promoted from captain to major. I was given an Army commendation medal. I have always assumed I received it because I didn't run away.

As terrible as Vietnam was in so many ways, it was a terrific clinical experience for me. During my residency, I had operated with a junior resident and an intern; in Vietnam, except for major vascular cases, I mainly operated alone with just a nurse. We became quite proficient at taking care of trauma cases—an expe-rience whose value would last me throughout my entire surgical career. Vietnam brought me not only volumes of experience, but self-confidence. Of the medical papers I wrote during my career, half a dozen came from my clinical experiences during the war.

While in Vietnam, I had the opportunity to visit Japan a number of times. Since I had arrived in Vietnam in June, I had taken only my summer uniform. On one trip to Japan, I wore this uniform—although it was wintertime. It was raining and snowing and quite cold. While I was walking through Tokyo, a Japanese individual came up to me with an umbrella. He asked me where I was going and volunteered to walk with me so I would not get completely drenched. I remember thinking at the time that something like that would never happen in New York.

On another occasion, we took a planeload of sick and injured individuals to Japan. I was the medical chaperone on board. This was a two-day experience, which was a reward, of sorts, for good behavior. While I was there, I visited Chaplain Victor Solomon. His wife had two remaining kosher steaks in the freezer, which she was kind enough to prepare for me. I was extremely grateful to them. I also had a chance to meet my old friend from elementary, high school, as well as college, Marvin Tokayer, who was the rabbi in Japan.

I was able to see Rabbi Tokayer again later while on my first R&R (rest and relaxation) with Sheila on Thanksgiving 1968. Sheila and I visited his home. Moshe, as I called him, had earlier discovered a Jewish cemetery in Kobe Japan and wrote the book called *The Fuji Plan*, about the desire of the Japanese to protect Jews during World War II. Years later, to celebrate our 25th wedding anniversary, Sheila and I joined Moshe as he led a tour group to Japan, Hong Kong, and China.

Sheila and I spent that week at the luxurious New Otani Hotel in Tokyo. After six terrible months of separation, it was wonderful to be together. The six days we spent together were like a second honeymoon, an opportunity to renew our love and to just cuddle together. We also managed to visit Mt. Fuji and as many other tourist sites in the Tokyo area as we possibly could.

Sheila was able to bring some kosher food with her from the States, which I very much appreciated. We had Friday night dinner in the synagogue with Rabbi Herschel Schacter, a visiting Jewish chaplain in the reserves who became a good friend of ours. Rabbi Schacter had served in the U.S. Army during World War II and had been with the liberators of the Nazi concentration camps. He later went on to become president of the Religious Zionists of America and chairman of the Conference of Presidents of Major American Jewish Organizations.

The synagogue in Tokyo was not an Orthodox one and did

not have a *mechitza* (a separation for men and women), so I said my actual prayers alone in a small room. Still, Sheila and I felt obligated to manifest our shared Jewish heritage with the tiny Jewish community of Tokyo by sitting in on their services. We have returned several times since. On one of my visits to Tokyo, the Jewish community had a memorial service for Jews who had been hung in Syria as supposed spies for Israel. On that occasion the Tokyo synagogue was completely full.

Leaving Sheila at the end of the week felt exceptionally cruel. I could not stand seeing her trying to hold back her tears as we said goodbye at the airport. She recalls that as she sat in the airport sobbing, a hundred pair of Japanese eyes looked upon her with obvious sympathy, but also with evident sadness that they could do nothing to help. Years later, when we were back in Tokyo on another visit, we were pleased to again be able to stay at the New Otani. Being there brought back memories of a bright moment in a long year that was often filled with feelings of despair.

My second R&R took place in Hawaii for a five-day period during March 1969. What made this trip so special was that Sheila brought along our daughter Malkie. Sheila had been nervous that Malkie, who was five years old at the time, would not remember her father. When I first caught a glimpse of Malkie getting off the plane, she was dressed up as such an adorable young lady that I almost did not recognize her. We stayed in an apartment near the beach that was provided by the government at a low cost to soldiers serving in Vietnam.

While in Honolulu, we did plenty of sightseeing, including the U.S.S. *Arizona* Memorial at Pearl Harbor. Since I was in the armed forces, we were able to go out on a Navy launch. Sheila and I were stunned to hear a sudden roar from the sky as dozens, perhaps a hundred, airplanes flew by. When we looked up, we saw what appeared to be Japanese Zeroes coming out of the sky releasing bombs—with subsequent explosions. For a moment, I felt totally disoriented and confused and felt like I was hallucinating. Then, through the din, I heard our guide on the Navy boat saying, "Please do not be frightened. They are filming a movie called Tora, Tora, Tora, about the attack on Pearl Harbor." Later, when we had the chance to see the film, I could pick out the scene we had witnessed.

The end of our R&R get-together in Hawaii, like the earlier one in Tokyo, was very difficult for us all. It broke my heart to leave Sheila and Malkie. Yet one thing about Vietnam that differed from World War II or the Korean War was that each soldier's assignment lasted only one year unless he re-enlisted. Even though it was hard saying good-bye, I knew exactly how many days I had left in Vietnam before I would be back home in New York. Each daily letter I sent to Sheila had the exact number of days I had remaining in the war zone clearly noted both on the envelope and in the letterhead. In my last letter home in June I thanked the postman on the envelope for a year of deliveries, noting I was coming home. Even today, I thank G-d every day that I made it through my 12 months in the middle of a terrible war and was able to make it home again.

As I noted, I had the opportunity to act as assistant chaplain at Long Binh; officiating at services marking Jewish holidays and the Sabbath. Soon after I arrived at Long Binh, one of the Orthodox Jewish chaplains was killed in a plane crash, and I volunteered to be his replacement. I then arranged a schedule with the Conservative rabbi at the base to conduct services every other Shabbat, so that he could serve elsewhere on those occasions.

What was deeply upsetting to me, however, was that the rabbi, who outranked me at the time, came in a jeep every Sabbath carrying the Torah scroll. I asked him to please leave the Torah in the shul (synagogue), or with me so as not to involve it in a desecration of Shabbat. Whether one is personally Reform, Conservative or Orthodox, I felt it was an insult to the Torah to be driven around in a jeep on the Sabbath. After several weeks of prodding, he finally agreed to my request, and the Torah was kept in the chapel. I believe he did so because I had embarrassed him into changing his mind.

On Rosh Hashanah and Yom Kippur, I volunteered to serve as the cantor of the Orthodox services, which I conducted together with Chaplain Wasserman at Di An. We drove a considerable distance to conduct the services. Five hundred men came in to attend the services from various parts of the region. There were also Conservative and Reform services being held in other parts of the country. The services were very meaningful to me, but some of the soldiers complained they were too Orthodox, even though we went out of our way to include much English language liturgy.

One highlight of the occasion for me was sharing with several of the men a smoked turkey that Sheila had sent me for the holidays. Conducting the services alongside me and Rabbi Wasserman, who graduated Yeshiva College in 1965, were William Levy, who was on leave from Yeshiva University, Dr. Shelly Feldman, a graduate of the class of 1962 at Yehiva College and Dr. Joel Eisner, a 1963 graduate of Albert Einstein College of Medicine.

I have already written about that unforgettable Passover seder of 1969. Certainly, the incident was not only overwhelmingly emotional for all of us who experienced it, but it also felt genuinely miraculous to many of us. I later wrote an account of that amazing Seder for the National Council of Young Israel's Viewpoint newspaper.

My religion affected many other events during my stay in Vietnam. Throughout my life, I have grappled with the challenge of being an Orthodox Jew in America, but found that it is many times more difficult during times of war. For example, the army has a rule that each soldier must go through a test to make sure his or her gas mask is working and that he or she knows how to use it. In combat situations, as existed in Vietnam, one is required to go through this procedure twice a year. The exercise involved getting into an enclosed truck when gas is present, calling out some mumbo jumbo, and then slipping one's gas mask on or vice versa. It seems like a lifetime ago today, and the exact details are not clear.

I had gone through one such test before arriving in Vietnam, but before I knew it, six months had passed and it was time for the entire hospital to take another one. The test was scheduled to take place on a Shabbos, and we would have to travel a few miles from the hospital by jeep to take part in it. I told the commanding officer I would be more than happy to take the test on any other day, since the "gas truck" was there at all times, but because I did not deem the situation worthy of violating Shabbos, I requested that I not be expected to take it that day. The officer in charge of this particular operation was my surgical partner, Colonel George Lavenson, who was regular army. Despite our friendship and partnership, Lavenson informed me sternly that if I did not take part in the test on that day, I would be court-martialed together with a young conscript who was a Seventh Day Adventist with similar objections to mine. Only the intervention of my chaplain, who went far up the chain of command, prevented my being court-martialed. This episode could have been really serious, since being court-martialed in a combat zone is not a frivolous matter.

Toward the end of my service in Vietnam, I received notice that Joel Kaplan, a classmate of mine from Yeshiva University, and today a psychiatrist in Nassau County, N.Y., would be arriving at Bien Hoa Air Base from America in order to begin his year of service in Vietnam. I made a special effort to be there to greet him when he arrived. Somehow, Chaplain Wasserman and I managed to obtain the manifest of planes landing in Saigon and Bien Hoa. We once even went out to Bien Hoa on one occasion thinking Joel was going to be there, but it turned out to be a false alarm. When he finally did arrive, he had no idea there were going to be any friendly faces there to greet him. We embraced him with open arms, knowing there was nothing more frightening then being far from friends and family in such a strange and threatening environment.

Many years later, Sheila and I received an invitation to Joel and Harriet Kaplan's eldest son's bar mitzvah. In the course of the affair, Joel stood up, greeted Sheila and me from the podium and reminisced how much my greeting him when he arrived in Vietnam had meant to him. In 2000, when I was honored by the Orthodox Union, Joel took out an ad in the journal that read, "Thank you very much for the hot pastrami sandwich in Vietnam." He had been very impressed with the kosher food we were able to acquire for him as he stepped off the plane. Indeed, ultimately, I never ate in the cafeteria. Between what the chaplain brought and what Sheila sent me in the mail, supplemented by the canteen, I was never lacking in that department. I was able to pick up cold vegetables on my own. Joel recently told me that he in turn welcomed another orthodox physician, Dr. Albie Hornblass, to Vietnam in a similar manner.

Sheila had the food deliveries down to a system. On a given date, every other week, she would go to the post office in Far Rockaway just prior to the plane taking off for San Francisco, which would carry the parcels to Vietnam. With this schedule, I was able to get four challahs, pickled herring, and other kosher goodies every two weeks. There was only one occasion where the challahs arrived green and moldy. The smell was so bad I ran to throw them out. Then I noticed that the mamasans would take them out of the garbage and eat the challahs themselves. I begged them not to, but to no avail.

Another "perk" of life in Vietnam was that automobile dealers advertised in the *Stars and Stripes* newspaper. At a hundred dollars over cost, I was able to buy a car via the mail for delivery in Grand Rapids, Michigan, where I knew I would be headed after my discharge. I have always had a weakness for new cars, and usually buy a new one every three years. Indeed, even in the immediate aftermath of our wedding, when Sheila and I had very little money, I managed to buy a new car with predated checks, which is not a typical Jewish approach.

I was able to communicate with Sheila by letter, tapes, and an occasional phone call. The phone calls consisted of a phone hooked up to a short- wave radio operator in the United States who would then place a collect call to whomever you were trying to reach. For example, if my call was picked up by a short-wave radio operator in Little Rock, Arkansas, my wife would have to pay the cost of a phone call from Little Rock to Far Rockaway, where she lived. During the summer, Sheila and Malkie had gone to Camp Eton in order to keep busy. Since the phone calls were collect, one of my calls came into the camp. The owner of the camp refused to accept the charges, since Sheila did not have the money in her pocket at that moment to pay him back. Angered by this treatment, Sheila left the camp immediately.

I wrote Sheila several poems when I was away. She saved them and it is quite a nostalgic experience for me to read them again after all these years. Here are a few of them:

5 July 1968
A Poem of Love to Sheila

How does one start a poem of love?
For a woman whose love he doth share,
Her eyes sparkle like 2 bright lights,
The thought of which are beyond compare.

Her beautiful form I dream of always,
It is enticing to say the least,
Her features are like a golden goddess,
She makes me feel like a beast.

To think that I cannot have her now

To hold my hand and give me support,
Is something that is quite unfair,
The reason for which there is no retort.

Her warm smile and gentle personality,
Are among the qualities that I adore,
There could never be another,
To take her place on this or any shore.

An Original Poem by A Loving Husband
Dedicated to my wife Sheila – 11 September 1968

Ode to a beautiful wife but alone,
Waiting for husband so far away,
Combating depression and boredom for which she could be prone,
Waiting for her lover to come home to stay.

A more faithful woman could not be found,
For this lily of the field is pure and true,
With love for her mate she does abound,
And with dedication and devotion she does imbue.

She counts the days for his return,
How cruel of man that they must war,
To take her husband away on more than a mere sojourn
To fight senselessly on another shore.

One sees the politicians bicker for the sake of votes,
They really couldn't care less for the lives of the boys over there
How could they understand what tensions and hardships the war
  provokes?
Between a husband and wife who only want to keep living like a
  pair.

Her fellow citizens at home go about life normally,
Regarding Vietnam they are without tension or commitment,
The war is ten thousand miles away,
Only statistics at night over TV makes them grimace for a minute.

But this loving wife of mine,
Thinks about me with great contemplation
And prays for that period of time,

When together we will be,
Free to live out lives as lovers without separation,
As normal human beings in society.

    From your darling dedicated husband
                  Mendy

    This next one was titled "Sheila."
    10 Oct 1968

I miss my Sheila more than ever
Our separation seems like a hundred years
Each day is an experience of torture
To fight back the hidden tears.

The fairness of this war has escaped me
I would not mind serving for just cause
But I'd much rather be frolicking with my daughter playfully
Than operate on young Americans who are simply listed as a "battle
  loss."

This war has no end in sight
Only my constant thoughts of my wife
Help me to ease the spectacle of the surrounding blight
And make my spirit come to life.

She is the essence of my whole existence
Without her I would be lost
Her daily letters and tapes are the only matters of significance
That keeps me going in this unreal world
That is only measured in "military cost."

Poem III – December 19, 1968
To Malkie and Sheila

Sitting alone and feeling blue
My spirits soar when I think of my spouse
A woman of valor who above all is true
In the love for her husband who at this moment
Feels like a louse.

To be so far away and for no real cause
To live like an animal for a year
And watch battle casualties, which the generals call
    "only minimal loss"
Of life and limb of eighteen year olds
Who are almost too young to taste beer.

But my wife and my daughter are my life
The thought of them gives me the strength
To observe the continuing toll of civil strife
In a war which seemingly is of endless length.

The diplomats talk about table shape
The Vietnamese politicos wives don their golden brooches
As American units are fighting in another scrape
And American fighting men sleep in their muddy hootches.

The hippies back home riot in every season
And the right-wingers would use the atomic bomb
What has happened to the American sense of justice and reason?
When is this war going to be properly managed by
    men of stability and calm?

These arguments are not new
So one should not get upset or depressed
Every survivor of this has something to look forward to
For me it is my wife and daughter-they are the best.

    My political thoughts on the situation in Vietnam are readily apparent in this next piece that I sent to my wife.

January 21, 1969
To Sheila

A new administration has taken office,
And a new set of politicos can steal from the coffers,
But the American soldier involved in the this mess,
Is used as a pawn as in a game of chess.

No one cares for the sweethearts and wives,
Suffering a forced separation that may ruin their lives,
But grateful I am that my wife is a like a saint,

To suffer as everyone but with minimal complaint.

I miss her more than words can describe,
If only I could simply imbibe,
To repress my insatiable love for my girl,
Which is ever present in me like a shell's pearl.

The time is slowly coming to a close,
Perhaps in the future I will not need to resort to long distance
  prose,
To articulate the feelings that I possess,
That distance and inexpertise do not allow me to express.

Only our wonderful past and prayfully a glorious future
Allow my sanity to remain at an even keel
The rest of the time I am working with a suture
To do my best as a physician to heal.

But even the most dedicated get tired
Of ceaseless grenade wounds, mortar fragments and such
In a war in which these boys here had not conspired
To be killed and maimed as easily as the politicians eat lunch.

That is why I am everlastingly grateful to my Sheila
She allows me to function in this atmosphere of war, death and
  frustration
There is none to me like my Sheila
Halfway around the world she is at my side
      to allow me to keep my life in proper equilibration.

During my second month at the 24th Evac, Robert Reinhold,
a reporter from the *New York Times*, came to Long Binh to do a
story about the military's medical-evacuation system by following an individual soldier going through the process of being
evacuated from the war zone. It turned out that I had operated
on the badly wounded soldier they chose to cover, Douglas
Schwinn; conducting a difficult operation involving multiple
injuries to his chest and abdomen, as well as repairing an injured
artery in his leg. I was interviewed for the story by Reinhold
before Shwinn was removed to Japan to recuperate from his
wounds and on October 28, 1968, Reinhold's article was a front-
page story in the *Times*. He was kind enough to send me a copy,
which I still keep on the wall in my basement.

The disgust, horror, and sadness I felt about what I had experienced there made it impossible for me to read or watch anything about the country or about the war I had been a part of. This went on for about ten years, until one day, while skimming the *Times*, I came across some pictures from Vietnam that were very familiar to me. It turned out Robert Reinhold, the reporter who had interviewed me in 1968, was doing a follow-up story on Douglas Schwinn, the badly injured soldier whose life I helped to save. Sadly, Reinhold's story showed that the soldier had been divorced and had suffered considerable misfortune in his personal life after returning from Vietnam.

This was the first time I had been exposed to an account of the harrowing long-term effects of Vietnam on one of the soldiers I had operated on. The impact of the war has stayed with me too. To this day, I keep on my desk at home, several large shrapnel pieces, rocket propelled grenade fragments, and a bullet I removed from the body of one of my patients. Those items are constant reminders to me of the horrors of war.

The final few weeks were extremely nerve-wracking, especially at night. I harboured a secret fear of being killed by a mortar as I lay in my bed. Despite the great heat we were enduring during those days, I slept each night in a flak jacket. I tried wearing my helmet as well, but it would not stay on in bed.

On my last day, I received a citation from the Jewish Welfare Board for my work as a chaplain. Then I flew to Saigon in preparation to be flown back to America. Getting on the plane in Saigon to fly out of Vietnam for the last time was an extremely happy moment, but more joyous still was the moment when that plane touched down on U.S. soil in Anchorage, Alaska. I immediately rushed to a telephone at the airport to tell Sheila I was back in the USA and on my way home to her. Tears come to my mind even now when I think of that moment.

From there, I flew on to Fort Dix, New Jersey, where I received my discharge from the army while in full-dress uniform with all my medals. I remember taking the bus from Fort Dix on a Friday to Port Authority in New York City. An MP came over and asked for identification. I proceeded to show him my discharge papers. When he was satisfied with my ID, I asked him why he had stopped me. He said he had never seen such a young major with so many battle ribbons. What he did not realize was that doctors start out as captains and usually get promoted to major within a year if they are serving in a battle zone.

I arrived at the station in midtown Manhattan and got off the bus at about four or five in the afternoon on a Friday in June, lugging two duffel bags with me. Unlike the MP at Fort Dix, none of the people streaming past me at the station anxious to catch their buses home at the end of the workday, seemed to notice me passing by in my uniform and medals. It occurred to me that they were completely indifferent to what I had endured during the preceding year; that they could no more care that I had just come back from Vietnam than if I had just returned from the moon. Indeed, I found the sensation created by the people pushing at me in order to get to their buses a little bit quicker to be quite unsettling, even nerve wracking. I had been away from crowds for quite a while and almost suffered a claustrophobic reaction from the hustle and bustle at the Port Authority.

Over the years, many people have asked about my reflections concerning my experience of witnessing the devastation of the war in Vietnam up close and personal. I always reply that, first of all, I am not a pacifist. I believe one must be prepared to fight for one's country, especially for the sake of democracy and freedom. Nevertheless, what left the greatest impression on me was seeing first hand the immense, horribly wasteful loss of lives and limb endured by our boys. The U.S. government quite evidently did not have any sort of plan to win the war. We did not know where the enemy was, and in many cases even who he was. So often, after capturing a hill or a town at enormous cost, we quickly withdrew. When the enemy came in, we attacked again. It all came to seem so senseless.

I also was left with the feeling that the indigenous population really had no interest in democracy or in supporting the South Vietnamese government. To the contrary, the determination of the Vietcong to fight and die for their cause appeared to me to be truly heroic. They could survive on very little food, stay in the ground in small holes, and live on almost no rations in order to lie quietly for hours or days to perpetrate a surprise attack on our forces. On one particular occasion, I operated on a prisoner-of-war who had lost his upper extremities at least two weeks before. Under normal circumstances, his arms should have been infected and full of gangrene. But because this POW had been lying quietly in a water barrel in order to avoid detection, the maggots cleaned up his wound—so it was beautifully debrided, and he was able to live. Some of the prisoners-of-war I treated were fifteen and sixteen years of age.

I believe that in Saigon, the people had some education as well as a certain level of appreciation for the concept of democracy. I did not discern any such feeling, however, in the small towns and villages. Moreover, there are many stories of Marines and other allied forces going into towns and Montagnard villages to teach the people hygiene—such as not to defecate into the drinking water, to wash soiled clothes, and use the latrines. This worked well enough until the Marines left—and the people went back to their old ways.

Despite my disillusion, my tour was a great experience for me from a medical point of view. I had the opportunity to practice medicine with surgeons and doctors from all over the United States. It was quite interesting to see that so many surgeons used different techniques for the same operation; yet the results were quite similar. For example, one of the most-common injuries was to the bowel, requiring a division and *anastamoses* (resuturing). There are many technical ways to do this, and surgeons have become accustomed to the way in which they are trained.

Once or twice a week we had grand rounds, going from bed to bed to discuss our problem cases. The chief of surgery in our hospital, the 24th evac, was Dr. Donald Brief, who was a major at the time, but came from a private practice in Maplewood, New Jersey. He was tall, handsome, quite intelligent, a natural leader, and an excellent surgeon. On one occasion, we came to the bedside of one of my patients who was in a coma. He was a Vietnamese civilian who had been hit by a huge army truck and had wounds to the abdomen. I operated on the wounds, but, sadly, the patient never woke up.

Trying to dispel the sorrow all of us felt, I introduced a little light humor, telling my colleagues in the ward room that the patient was lying there "like a lox," a common slang term used in New York hospitals. When I looked up and I saw approximately twenty blank or quizzical faces staring back at me, I remembered that "lox" is not a common food or commonly used colloquialism in the rest of America. I began to explain to them that on a Sunday morning in New York, many Jews go out and buy bagels—whereupon, again, I got another collective stare. This was before bagels became a nationwide craze. I explained to them that bagels were rolls with holes in them that you slice open, cover with cream cheese, and then take smoked salmon and smack it on the bagel—where it lays there without moving. As I gave this explanation, I animatedly stuck my tongue out and cocked my head to the side to give an approximation of lox lying on a bagel.

Looking back from thirty years remove, my stay in Vietnam appears to have been a trial by fire that, despite the horrors I witnessed, had some important positive consequences for me. Not only did I come home a far more mature and self-confident surgeon, but I also had the opportunity to save money, because most of what I was paid—including bonuses for battlefield and overseas pay—was non-taxable. Sheila was living with her parents and paid no rent.

When I returned from Vietnam, Sheila became pregnant almost immediately. Ari was born on Purim, March 22, 1970. We had a third child, Elli, born August 14, 1975, when we moved to Monsey. We were not able to have the fourth child we wanted, but were more than thankful for the three wonderful children we did have.

Though I could not have predicted it then, my year of service in Vietnam proved to be an immense benefit for me when I started my political work over a decade later. It turned out that I was one of the few pro-Israel activists in Washington who had actually served in Vietnam. As such, I was considered an American hero, especially by political conservatives, and had much greater credibility in making my case on behalf of a strong U.S.-Israel alliance than I otherwise would have had. John McCain (R-Ariz), Larry Pressler (R-South Dakota) and other U.S. Senators who had served in the war greeted me as their "Vietnam buddy." My Vietnam experience became a calling card that allowed me to say that I was, and still am, a conservative, a Jew, and a proud American. I see no contradiction among any of these.

CHAPTER FOUR
From Grand Rapids to Monsey

While I was still in Vietnam, I learned that I had been accepted as a resident in colorectal surgery in two hospitals—Baylor University in Texas and the Ferguson Clinic in Grand Rapids, Michigan. I chose the latter because that 120-bed facility was the only hospital in the country that devoted itself exclusively to treating colon and rectal diseases. It was modeled after St. Marks Hospital in London. In 1970, the Ferguson Clinic performed close to 2000 ano-rectal procedures and about 800 colon resections annually.

The Ferguson Clinic was also known for treating its medical residents very well; arranging, for example, for each resident and his family to live rent free in a private home. So shortly after I had returned stateside, Sheila and I packed five-year-old Malkie and all of our belongings into our Corvair, and headed for Michigan. Upon arrival we took ownership of a brand new Pontiac Bonneville, which I had ordered while still in Vietnam.

It was culture shock when the Ganchrows hit Grand Rapids. First of all, it turned out that the new pastel short sleeve shirts that had recently come into vogue in New York had not yet reached Grand Rapids. Had I not been known as a Vietnam vet, I would doubtless have been labeled a hippie or a communist for wearing those shirts. More significantly, while I may not have been the first Jewish surgeon ever to do a residency at the Ferguson Clinic, I was definitely the first Orthodox Jew. The clinic had a fancy private dining room for the residents and attending physicians where waitresses served steaks and lamb chops to the hungry surgeons. For me they had cottage cheese and ice cream. Most of the people who knew us in Grand Rapids never had the slightest previous exposure to an Orthodox Jew and must have found our ways bizarre, but they were always very nice to us.

Sheila's version: "One family who lived two doors down from us was of Nordic descent. A couple of days after we arrived they showed up on our doorstep with cookies and cakes to welcome us. I started to explain to them apologetically that we were Jewish and had our own dietary laws that would not allow us to eat the cookies, but how touched we were by their kindness. But as I was rambling on, I noticed that they had gone pale and seemed to be in a state of near shock. Was it something I had said? She stuttered a bit and finally said, 'Dear, please don't take this the wrong way, but we were really taken aback when you said you were Jewish. You see, we have never met Jewish people before, and always heard that Jews have horns.' So I put my hands on my head, ruffled my hair a little and said, "Well, I'm Jewish and see, no horns."

"I wasn't really angry because I could see our neighbor hadn't said that Jews had horns in order to be offensive. That was what they had been brought up to believe. Overall, they were as nice as they could be and I came to trust them so much that I left Malkie with them on a few occasions when Mendy and I had to go out. Still, they could never comprehend the whole kashruth thing. The lady of the house just kept bringing us over things she had baked no matter how many times I explained to her why we couldn't eat her cakes and cookies. Looking back, it seems unbelievable to me that in 1969 there were people in the United States of America who actually believed Jews had horns."

Being the only Orthodox Jews at the Ferguson Clinic really kept us on our toes. I have never been a handy person, especially when carpentry work has to be done. So when the high holidays came around, I went to Dr. James Ferguson, the head of the clinic and asked him if he could give me some pointers about how I might build a small free-standing structure. Dr. Ferguson asked me exactly what it was I wanted to construct, and I responded, "I need to build a succah." He looked at me blankly and I told him that a succah was more or less a hut, and explained briefly what it religiously signified, which he seemed to find fascinating. Anyway, he could tell from my questions that I would have a lot of trouble with the construction, so he kindly offered to send some people from the clinic's engineering department over to my house to build the succah according to my specifications. The covering for the succah was provided by several hospital workers who also grew Christmas trees for a living.

While the men from the clinic were building the succah in my yard, I could see most of our neighbors standing around watching; trying to figure out why the crazy Ganchrows were putting up a little shack next to their house. Yet a few days later, there was an article in the Grand Rapids newspaper about a succah at the local Conservative temple, and soon all of my neighbors were bursting with pride that our block had its very own succah. On the first night of the holiday, Dr. Ferguson and his wife came out to have a meal with us in our succah and had a wonderful time. So the succah turned out to be a grand success.

Our son Ari was born while we were living in Grand Rapids and Dr. Ferguson and his wife accepted our invitation to come to the *bris* (circumcision). My college classmate Moe Berlin, who lived in Detroit, helped arrange to bring a Detroit mohel and a few other Orthodox Jews to help us complete a ten-person minyan. This was a two-or-more-hour drive from Detroit to Ari's bris. Ferguson's son-in-law, who happened to be a big strapping guy, was fascinated by the mohel and wanted to watch him perform the circumcision, but ended up passing out dramatically at the sight of blood.

Our neighbors could not pronounce "Ari" until the film Exodus was shown on television and Paul Newman played Ari Ben-Canaan. Here again they were proud to have an "Ari" on their block.

Because there were no Jewish day schools available, we sent five-year-old Malkie to first grade in a public school in Grand Rapids and tutored her at home in Jewish subjects. Soon however, she began complaining that none of the other kids could pronounce her name; they were calling her 'Milky' and 'Mawlkey' and all kinds of other derivations of her name. Sheila and I began to get a little alarmed the day she came home from school and begged us to let her change her name to Mary Jane or Mary Beth. We knew we planned to live in the all-Jewish environment of Monsey, New York in a few months time, so we decided to humor her for the time being and told her she could call herself

Mary Jane if she wanted after we arrived in Monsey. Of course, she went back to being Malkie as soon as we left Grand Rapids and arrived in Monsey.

I wrote a number of top quality surgical papers while at the Ferguson Clinic, which certainly added to the prestige of the institution. When it was time for Sheila and I to leave, Dr. Ferguson extended his hand to me and said simply, "Mendy, send us another Jew." It was his way of saying that I had been a terrific resident at the Ferguson Clinic, and that there must be highly positive values in Judaism that had contributed to making me the person I was. For me, it was another one of those moments in my life when I realized that most non-Jews would accept and respect me if I openly observed my religious faith and tradition and did not try to hide or downplay it.

Dr. Ferguson also gave me an important piece of advice that day which I have never forgotten and have sought to apply ever since. He told me, "Always sell Ganchrow!" Indeed, if I was not to make the case for what Mendy Ganchrow had to offer as a colorectal surgeon and as a Jewish political activist and organizational leader, there was no one else around who was likely to do so.

While I was winding up my residency in Grand Rapids in colorectal surgery, I was offered a full-time teaching position at Wayne Medical School in Detroit. It was a position I would have been strongly inclined to take, except that Sheila and I had already made a down payment on a house in Monsey. Sheila badly wanted to return to the New York area. We had many friends in Monsey who had urged us to come, including old classmates such as Doctors Abe Becker, Dave Hammer, Barry Hochdorf, Bill Klein, Sonny Meiselman, Jack Prince, Herbie Schlussel, and Lenny Shapiro; Rabbi Moses Tendler, the spiritual leader, also encouraged us to move there. Both Sheila and I felt it was now time to put down some roots and achieve some stability—financial and psychological—for our growing family in an Orthodox Jewish neighborhood.

Aside from what we had saved from my year in Vietnam, we had almost no money. I managed to secure a loan from my Aunt Hannah, as well as receiving some money from my in-laws to help pay the down payment on the house. In addition, I had to take a bank loan in order to open my medical office, which I located in the community of Spring Valley, a few miles from Monsey. Things were really hand to mouth at the beginning. My cousin Melvin gave me a good deal on the furniture to decorate my office. I even had my father-in-law hang around the first few days to make it appear to passersby that I actually had some business. Of course, I could not afford a nurse, so for the first eighteen months in operation, Sheila served as my nurse/secretary/bookeeper.

Meanwhile, I was on surgical call at the emergency room at a local hospital, Ramapo General, in order to make a few dollars while waiting for my own practice to begin taking off. One day when I was at the hospital Sheila called in tears to tell me that a major leak had occurred in the ceiling of our house. It turned out that a pipe had burst and we were faced with serious water damage, which would cost more to repair than we had on hand. As I stood there pondering where I could possibly find the money to pay a painter to repair the damage, my reverie was broken when a man was wheeled into the emergency room with a serious scalp wound that required immediate attention. He looked like he had been scalped as in cowboy and Indian movies. The gruesome accident had occurred when his irate wife threw him out of a speeding car.

As I began preparations to operate, however, the man informed me that, unfortunately, he had no insurance coverage and no way to pay for his medical care. I asked him what he did for a living and he replied that he was a housepainter. Eureka! A little light bulb went on in my head, and I made him an offer he couldn't refuse; or at least was happy and relieved to accept. Sure enough, a few days after I sewed the man up, he came to our house and patched up the damage to our house in lieu of a medical bill.

One of my first patients was an African-American woman with a case of hemorrhoids who was referred to me by a general practitioner who had told me she needed extensive surgery. However, when I examined her, I realized that she didn't need surgery after all, and sent her on her way. When I spoke later to the other doctor, he seemed chagrined I hadn't performed the surgery even after I explained it would be unnecessary. He then asked how much I would give him if he referred further cases to me. I didn't understand what he meant at first, so he spelled it out; he wanted a fifty percent kickback for every case he referred to me. I told him I wouldn't do something that was both unethical and illegal, and he responded; 'Why not? Everyone around here does it.'

This sleazebag, who was ready to betray the Hippocratic Oath in search of extra income, was very angry that I wouldn't play ball. For my part, I was equally furious that he would try to tempt me into doing something illegal at my moment of maximum vulnerability. Over time, I learned that this guy was a rare case; that the great majority of doctors are ethical and straight.

I was on my own for about a year and a half, then joined a group of surgeons, consisting of Dr. Shelly Adler, chief of surgery at Good Samaritan Hospital and Dr. Mike Cavanagh, both of whom were general surgeons, and Dr. Al Moscarella, a thoracic and vascular surgeon. Initially, I was taking a considerable pay cut by joining a partnership, but I knew that in the medium to long term I would come out ahead since my partners were the premier surgical group in Rockland County with a large practice and impeccable reputation. Also, since two of the partners were non-Jews, I would now be able to take off three weekends a month and Jewish holidays, which was, of course, very important to me. Things were really beginning to look up.

What really put me on the map professionally, however, was my facility at performing two new medical procedures. The first involved applying rubber bands to treat hemorrhoids in lieu of surgery. This is an office procedure without anesthesia that essentially tied off the blood supply of internal hemorrhoids with great success and minimal discomfort. The second was a revolutionary new procedure called colonoscopy. I had read about the procedure in medical journals, and took the initiative to go to Manhattan and meet Dr. Jerome Waye at Mt. Sinai Hospital and Dr. Hiroshi Shinya at Beth Israel. I observed these pioneers in the procedure perform it in their offices and endoscopy suites on several occasions until I was confident I had mastered it. Then I began offering colonoscopies in Rockland County and for the next 5-6 years, I was the only physician in our area that performed the procedure. Given my expertise, and the fact that I was the only board-certified colon and rectal surgeon in Rockland, other surgeons would occasionally send me difficult cases they themselves didn't feel competent to undertake. Nor did I antagonize the many gastroenteologists who later started performing colonoscopies themselves, but sometimes referred other colon surgery procedures to me.

Shortly thereafter, U.S. Surgical Corp. developed a new instrument called the EEA (end-to-end anastamotic) gun, which allowed colorectal surgeons to save the rectum in certain cancer cases and avoid the patients having to live the rest of their lives with colostomy bags. As the EEA gun hit the market, I went to the U.S. Surgical's dog lab in Connecticut to learn the procedure and became proficient at it. Thereby, I enhanced my reputation as a cancer surgeon.

As my career began taking off, so did our family life in Monsey. We were blessed with good schools for our children, a wonderful synagogue, and friends who shared our dream for a vibrant and fulfilling way of life. The arrival of our third child, Elliot was a source of great happiness to Sheila and myself.

The Orthodox community has always distinguished itself by successfully creating a strong sense of community that provides satisfaction and support for adherents whether in times of joy or sorrow. Although our children grew up faster than Sheila and I would have liked, our lives and theirs have remained intertwined even as they have grown into adulthood. Whereas in the 1970's we celebrated a birth and bar and bat mitzvahs, all too soon we moved on to graduations and weddings.

We originally bought our dream house with a beautiful garden directly across the street from the synagogue. But as our family grew and we were able to afford it, we bought a one-acre lot and built a beautiful ranch house that we helped to design. A wonderful feature of the new house was an indoor sukkah with a retractable roof. One lesson I had learned from my Grand Rapids experience was that I did not want the trouble of putting up a "hut" every year.

We developed a taste for travel and today there are few countries around the world we have not visited at least once. After Israel, which we have visited sixty to eighty times, our favorite destination has been East Asia, especially Hong Kong. We have enjoyed cruises to Alaska and the Mediterranean, and occasionally I have served as scholar in residence on these trips.

As my medical practice grew, I was also able to devote increasing amounts of time and energy in service to the Jewish community. In 1974, I became president of the Community Synagogue of Monsey, which was my first official position as the leader of a Jewish institution. I took the presidency seriously instituting its first ever dinner, weekly mailed bulletins to each congregant, totally renovating the *bais medrash* (sanctuary) with the help of Shimon Sontag and the late Jerry Cobrin, and creating a Men's Club. The very first function held in the *Bais Medrash*, even before the furniture was installed was the *bris milah* (circumcision) of our son Elli. A few years later, I became president of the Adolph Schreiber Hebrew Academy of Rockland. ASHAR is a co-ed Zionist oriented institution with high academic standards both in Torah and secular studies. Max Thurm, a good friend, was chairman of the board and was a great partner in leading ASHAR. Rabbi Howard Gershon, our Executive Director was a delight to work with. As President of ASHAR I had the privilege of going with Rabbi Nachum Muschel, our Dean, to invite Rabbi Yakov Kaminetsky, a world-renowned Torah scholar and Aggudist, (since his family were my patients) to speak to our Yeshiva. He readily agreed and although a local delegation of right-wingers tried to dissuade him from speaking in our Zionist co-ed Yeshiva, he threw them out of his house.

He related to us a story. As a young rabbi in a small *shtetl* in Europe he was invited to give the Sabbath sermon in the adjacent major city on the condition that he share his sermon in advance with the synagogue Rabbi, which he did. The inviting Rabbi was satisfied and introduced him to the packed synagogue on the Sabbath wherein Rabbi Kaminetsky gave a totally different sermon. The Rabbi thanked him afterwards but asked, "this was fine but what happened to the sermon you delivered during the week?" "Oh that one" answered Kaminetsky "I heard that one already!"

As time went by I got involved in a fund-raising capacity in several national Jewish organizations—especially Israel Bonds. This was hardly earth-shaking stuff, but it allowed me to learn the Jewish organizational ropes so that later I was able to operate effectively thanks to many of the lessons I had absorbed as a neophyte community leader. I have always taken each position in which I have served extremely seriously with total personal commitment.

I believe it is fair to attribute some of my success in life—both as a surgeon and later as a communal leader—to always doing my homework and eschewing shortcuts. Not only did I attempt to be on the cutting edge of new technology and procedures, I also won't let anyone put anything over on me or pressure me into making a professional decision I don't concur in. I vividly recall that a couple of years after I began using the EEA gun, another prominent firm came out with a similar gun and one of their salesmen came to our hospital to urge me to try it. I said, "OK, give me one or two as samples and I'll give them a try," but the salesman replied, "Sorry, but if you want the gun, you will have to buy a gross." Since each gun cost a few hundred dollars, a gross would set our hospital back a bundle, and I wasn't going to ask them to put out all that money when I already had the EEA gun and was very happy with it. I declared in no uncertain terms that I wasn't interested. He came back the following year and offered me his gun but again stipulated that I had to order a gross. Whatever else one could say about him, he had no shortage of *chutzpah*. I told him to get lost.

Then the determined salesman did a very clever thing. He contacted the chief of surgery at our hospital and said that he wanted to pay for a lox and bagels spread at an upcoming doctors' breakfast at our hospital on the condition that he have the opportunity to show a film on his company's gun during the breakfast. The chief of surgery agreed and the salesman showed the film and then said to all the doctors enjoying the lox and bagels; "I want to make this machine available here, but your hospital refuses to buy it. Can all of you sign a petition urging your hospital to use this machine?" So most of the doctors signed the petition—it was no skin off their backs, since they were orthopedists, urologists and neurosurgeons and would never even use it. I was one of the few at our hospital who would potentially use the gun, but my partners and I did not sign the petition. So after getting everyone else to sign the petition, the salesman took it to the hospital's central supply department. Seeing that so many doctors had signed the petition, they relented and ordered a gross.

The triumphant salesman figured that once the hospital had ordered the guns, I would have to start using them to justify the outlay and then he would have a steady customer. But after a while when I didn't use even a single gun, he came to see me. He asked me why his guns were still unused in the closet. I informed him once again that I had no intention of using one until he supplied me with one or two free samples to see if I was satisfied with them. He was loath to do it, but in a last act of desperation, he took two guns out of his briefcase and presented them to me for my use. After using them with little satisfaction, I looked the salesman straight in the eye and said that no matter what he did and whose palm he greased, I would never ever use his machine again. To his embarrassment, he had to remove the guns from central supply and credit the hospital for the purchase.

I have always been tough with salespeople, especially ignorant ones. My attitude is, "Why are you trying to sell me this
drug, when you don't really know what you are talking about?"
I certainly don't like people thinking they can insult my intelligence, just because they can offer me a "freebie," whether it is a
pastrami sandwich, a pen or tickets to a Broadway show. Actually, I am opposed to "freebies" on principle; even when there is
no behind-the-scenes agenda. On one occasion, during the time
I was president of the OU, Sheila and I went to a restaurant with
another couple and, shortly after we had given our orders, the
waiter came over with a plate of hot delicacies that we hadn't
ordered. I asked what this was and he replied that the appetizers
were compliments of the owner.

It seemed to me that the owner, knowing that I was president
of the Orthodox Union, the organization in charge of enforcing
kashruth standards, had decided to try to endear himself to me.
I asked to see the owner and when he came out, I said to him;
"Thank you for the nice gesture. I really appreciate the thought,
but I ask you not to do it again."

Part of the dynamic of being a physician is being on call to
one's fellow men and women—even when we least expect or
welcome it. Several times while relaxing aboard transcontinental
flights, I have heard the telltale call of "Is there a doctor on
board?" and have thrown myself, however reluctantly, into service. Never, however, have I experienced a situation quite as
chaotic; replete with potential tragedy and real time farce, as the
one with which I came face to face one afternoon as I settled into
my seat in the business class section of a Tower Air 747 shortly
after takeoff from Tel Aviv to New York. After hearing the call,
I clambered down the stairs into the main body of the huge
aircraft to be informed that not one, but three people had become sick simultaneously. There was a pregnant woman who
had begun hemorrhaging, a man who was experiencing massive
chest pains and another with an irregular pulse and shortness of
breath. The captain of the plane asked me to examine the three
and make a quick determination as to whether we should return
to Tel Aviv, make an unscheduled landing in Athens or continue
with the flight.

After examining the first man, who had had a previous heart
attack and was on oxygen, it was clear to me after checking his
blood pressure and raising his oxygen intake level that he ur-

gently needed hospitalization. The second fellow was less seriously ill, but it would be good to hospitalize him as a precaution. As to the woman, an assertive religious Jewish woman sitting in the very back of tourist class, her seatmate claimed she was bleeding badly, but she told me firmly that she would not allow anyone to examine her except her obstetrician back in Borough Park. She also seemed less than thrilled about the idea of hospitalization in Athens, instead demanding that she should be bumped up to business class; arguing that her bleeding would subside if she could put her feet up in a less cramped environment. I suspected the airline would be less than thrilled with that request. I warned her in no uncertain terms of grave dangers she was incurring for her fetus and herself by leaving her hemorrhaging unattended, but she insisted she would be fine.

When I got back to the captain, he told me that they had already checked with Tower CEO and founder Morris Nachtomi back in New York and he had ordered the plane to touch down in Athens. When we landed, a Greek doctor immediately rushed aboard. He turned out not to speak a word of English. I communicated to him in sign language and universal medical terminology as best I could regarding my diagnoses. After he visited the three people he came back to say he agreed with me that all three should be taken off to a nearby hospital. The problem was that all three refused to get off, insisting that they were feeling better than before. The airline promised the three that they would leave a stewardess behind in Athens to look out for them, but their resistance to staying behind appeared set in stone.

Equally unyielding was Nachtomi who ordered the pilots not to take off with the three passengers on board. In the meantime, we sat for four hours on the runway as the rest of the passengers became more and more restive. I vividly remember one man banging on the window. Meanwhile, the pregnant woman was loudly denying to anyone who would listen that she was bleeding at all—claiming that the doctor (me) was a liar. I still cannot fathom her motive in the whole affair, unless, as I suspect, it was an elaborate effort on her part to get a free upgrade.

Finally, a group of Orthodox rabbis who were aboard the flight formed a *beit din* (rabbinic court) to try to find a formula for ending the impasse. The urgent need for such a solution became clear when the airport crew informed the airline that they would be charged $80,000 for landing rights and additional needed fuel, costs that would compound dramatically if the plane stayed longer on the ground. The three recalcitrant passengers were informed that they might have to bear the $80,000 charge. The rabbis eventually brokered a deal that if the plane took off and any of the three sick passengers died during the flight to New York, Tower Air would not be legally responsible. They put my name in the agreement as the attending physician. Would I have been liable if any of the passengers had died before the flight ended? I never knew for sure, but was much relieved when the remainder of the flight passed uneventfully.

Sheila and I have been blessed with two wonderful daughters-in-law and one terrific son-in-law about whom we feel no different than about our own children. The courtships of Ari and Banji, the daughter of Eita and Dr. Richard Latkin of Fairlawn, New Jersey and of Elliot and Brina, the daughter of Ellen and Sam Rausman of Woodmere, New York were almost textbook in nature. Both Banji and Brina are sweet Orthodox girls from warm and wholesome religious homes and everything just seemed to fall naturally into place.

Malkie's courtship took considerably longer before ending up happily ever after. Malkie fell in love with Paul Ratzker, a neighbor three doors down and a classmate from elementary school, starting in the sixth grade. Paul is the son of our good friends, Helen and Menno Ratzker. After a long courtship that extended through high school and college (Paul attended Yeshiva University and Malkie went to Stern College), they broke up while Paul was in medical school. For six years, Malkie went out on hundreds of blind dates—all to little avail—until she and Paul met again on a skiing trip for singles. They got back together and soon were headed to the chuppah.

Since I was often asked to deliver small sermonettes on the celebratory occasions of Shevah Brachot (the week following an Orthodox Jewish wedding), I decided it would be a great idea to put together a volume of Torah thoughts for brides and grooms based on the weekly Torah readings. The success of that volume, which was entitled *Sasson V'Simchah* and published by the Orthodox Union and Art Scroll Publications, encouraged me to publish a second volume on circumcision entitled *Entering the Covenant*. The two books contain essays by over 50 rabbis and friends. I have contributed all of the proceeds to the Union's youth organization, the National Council of Synagogue Youth (NCSY).

In addition to attending medical meetings in the U.S., I tried whenever possible to visit surgeons and hospitals in foreign countries to learn and observe new concepts and techniques. My visits to operating rooms in London, Amsterdam, Beersheva and Jerusalem were such examples.

On one occasion, I spent a day with a noted rectal surgeon near Antwerp, Belgium. He informed me that part of his routine post-operative regime was the use of six to eight bottles of beer per day. Belgium has the highest per capita beer consumption in the world. He claimed his patients had less pain, required less narcotics, and urinated faster without the need for catherization. They also had easier bowel movements.

Though unconvinced, I decided to try it at Good Samaritan Hospital. Despite a skeptical nursing staff, I was delighted with the results. An inspection team of the accrediting committee were shocked to find beer in the surgical ward's refrigerator. "Oh, they belong to Dr. Ganchrow" was the retort.

Before I concluded my medical career in 1994, I had written 19 surgical papers, served for two years as chief of surgery at Good Samaritan Hospital, had become an associate clinical professor of surgery at New York Medical College and had lectured in various countries around the world, including Singapore and Israel. I was board certified in general as well as colo-rectal surgery. I was a Fellow of the American College of Surgeons, The American College of Gastroenterology, The American Society of Colo-Rectal Surgeons and the Society of University Colo-Rectal Surgeons.

CHAPTER FIVE
HUVPAC

The late Sylvia Schreiber of blessed memory was a persistent woman. A resident of Monsey, and the mother of my close friend Elliot Schreiber, Sylvia pestered me nearly every time we ran into each other that I should join the American Israel Public Affairs Committee (AIPAC) the pro-Israel lobby in Washington. Eventually, no longer able to avoid her and having run out of excuses why I could not join, I enrolled as a member of AIPAC in the late 1970s and began contributing thirty five dollars a year to the organization. At the beginning I did not know even what AIPAC was. Yet after joining and receiving my first copy of AIPAC's weekly Near East Report, I immediately felt grateful to Sylvia for pursuing me. I resolved to go beyond paying dues and to become actively involved in the work of AIPAC.

Every spring, I trekked to Washington for three days for AIPAC's annual policy conference. I would arrange my schedule so that I could attend the Sunday and Monday sessions of the AIPAC conference and be back in my office early on Tuesday morning. Unfortunately, I was unable to attend the Tuesday sessions; in those days I was building up my medical practice and that had to be my first priority.

Those AIPAC policy conferences were like a breath of fresh air to thousands of individuals like myself; people who loved Israel and yet needed guidance as to how to strengthen the U.S.-Israel relationship within the American political system. 1500 or more pro-Israel activists from all over America joined together for three days of serious discussion, sharing of information, and a good deal of fun besides. New friendships were forged. A high point of the conference every year was the Monday evening dinner, which was attended by a majority of members of Congress and where one could hear a speech from a leading Republican and Democratic senator and, often, the prime minister of Israel as well.

For a political buff like myself, however, the opportunity to get acquainted and swap ideas with the AIPAC professional staff was equally as exciting. Each one of them was a repository of information and political sophistication. Most had worked on the Hill before coming to AIPAC. In addition, the organization's officers were superb role models for people like myself. Bright, politically sophisticated and dedicated, they seemed to come to the table without personal agendas. Their only goal, as individuals and as a collective group, was to strengthen the U.S.-Israel relationship.

Every year, as I left the AIPAC policy conference, my batteries were recharged and my motivational level came back up to one hundred and ten percent. Knowing that I belonged to a political community dedicated to an agenda I believed in and with the clout to make an impact on behalf of that agenda made all the difference in the world. By example and by osmosis the AIPAC lay leadership had a huge impact on me; providing me with a keen understanding of the full potential of citizen political power. I believed then and believe to this day that the single most important organization in the American Jewish community is AIPAC.

The 1981 AIPAC conference was especially memorable because it took place at the height of the political battle over President Reagan's plan to sell AWAC planes to Saudi Arabia. The keynote speaker at the convention was Senator Roger Jepson, Republican of Iowa. Jepsen, who was an unabashed evangelical christian and supporter of the Moral Majority, gave a tub-thumping address in which he bellowed that "G-d had spoken to me and we will not allow the AWACS to be sold to the Saudis." Only a few weeks later, however, after undergoing some arm-twisting from President Reagan, Jepson issued another statement in which he said that God had spoken to him a second time with a new message, and suddenly he became the leader of the floor fight in favor of the sale. In the end, the Administration's sale of AWACS to Saudi Arabia passed the Senate by only one vote.

The narrow loss of the battle to prevent the sale of AWACS to the Saudis, coming three years after another stinging loss; the

Senate's passage of a bill to sell F-15 planes to Saudi Arabia by a 54-44 vote, actually served to fire up the pro-Israel community rather than to deflate it. We realized that the rules of the game concerning how money and influence worked in Washington had changed radically in the wake of the Watergate scandal, and not to Israel's benefit. The ever-more successful efforts by the Saudi Arabian government to attain huge amounts of American arms, aided and abetted by their friends in big oil and big aerospace businesses through sophisticated political action committees, had been vividly documented by Steven Emerson, the noted anti-terrorism expert, in his book *The American House of Saud*. If the organized American Jewish community was to compete with these powerful pro-Saudi interests, we realized that we would have to become more sophisticated in our political activism.

The buzz in private discussions and at the luncheon tables at the 1982 AIPAC policy conference was that as critically important as AIPAC was to the defense of Israel, AIPAC could no longer do it alone. AIPAC did not endorse candidates and was forbidden by law from giving financial support to candidates for the House, Senate and the Presidency. It was obvious that in an era when the cost of political advertising—especially on television—was going through the roof, the pro-Israel community needed to be able to provide financial backing to candidates sympathetic to our issues. So despite the fact that the word "PAC" was never mentioned by a speaker at the conference or by any AIPAC official (since AIPAC had to avoid—and did manage to avoid—the appearance of collusion with PACs that donated money), there was a sense among many of the attendees that the success of the pro-Israel agenda in the future would also depend upon the financial support of candidates either by pro-Israel supporters of means, or for such supporters in local areas coming together to form a PAC.

While sitting in the lobby of the hotel in Washington where the conference was taking place, I happened to meet a well-spoken man in his twenties. He introduced himself to me as Dick Durbin. Durbin was running for Congress against Paul Findley of Illinois. Findley, a veteran Republican congressman, was often called "Arafat's man in Congress." Durbin, whose manner was extremely personable, told me that if people like myself would go home and form a PAC, he could win the election if we sent him sufficient money and volunteers. Durbin pointed out that whereas under federal law an individual can contribute only $1,000.00 to a candidate in a primary and another $1,000.00 in the general election, that same person can contribute $5,000.00 to a PAC and the PAC can contribute $5,000.00 to the candidate in the primary and another $5,000.00 in an election. The beauty of the PAC system is you can have many single issue PACs, all independent of one another, which can raise considerable sums for a candidate in a tough election. Back in 1982, there were also some tax benefits for individuals who contributed to a PAC, although these were later repealed.

I was so excited by the vision that Durbin had shared with me that when I saw my wife the following day, I immediately said to her, "Sit down. I am about to start a PAC." She looked at me like I was crazy. I have said jokingly over the years when I first informed her of my intentions she said, "I didn't know that you were interested in the Cub Scout movement." But truthfully she was quite upset since I was at the time still president of the Adolph Schreiber Hebrew Academy and would not finish my term for another year. She asked me to please put off this decision until the conclusion of my presidency. I told her that this could not wait since the 1982 election was in seven months and thus proceeded to organize the Hudson Valley Political Action Committee (HUVPAC).

During our first election cycle, we made Durbin's election to the House our top priority. His win over Findley turned out to be our first great victory. After his election Durbin was a guest speaker at a cocktail party in our home. He later went on to become a United States Senator. At a pro-Israel event years later at which he did not know that I was present, Durbin informed the audience; "Because of a few members of the pro-Israel community Mendy Ganchrow and some others, I am a United States Senator today." In May 2002, Durbin revisited our home in Monsey on behalf of his own reelection campaign and of a revitalized HUVPAC.

Durbin's unexpected victory in 1982 encouraged pro-Israel activists from around the country to form local pro-Israel PACs. Had Durbin lost to Findley at that early stage of pro-Israel activism, it might have discouraged many from seeing the potential for effective political activity on behalf of pro-Israel candidates. Yet because things came out so well, Durbin's election served as a signal to each of us that small amounts of funding, given independently by citizens throughout the United States, could dramatically make a difference in strengthening the relationship between the United States and Israel.

The PAC system has always exemplified in my mind the highest level of citizen participation in the political process. I am referring of course to PACs that promote a cause, rather than business PACs that are only interested in the profit motive. The election cycles of 1982 and 1984, the first two in which I had been directly involved, were the most exciting. Our earlier lost battles to prevent the sale of U.S. F-16's to the Saudis in 1978 and the AWACS in 1981 indicated that the organized Jewish community could no longer expect to win political battles in Congress based on the moral capital we had accumulated from the Holocaust. Falling back on moral relationships on behalf of a fellow democracy would not work forever. We needed to exercise the instruments of power.

We began to turn around that situation of temporary weakness with Durbin's win in 1982. But Durbin was not alone in benefiting from our support. That year, our brand new PAC supported sixteen other candidates and was victorious with eleven. Among them was Senator George Mitchell, who went on to fill the unexpired term of Senator Edwin Muskie and eventually became majority leader of the Senate. In the summer of 1982, Mitchell, who is of Lebanese descent, was far behind in the polls. Yet in his moment of maximum political peril, the pro-Israel community stood solidly behind him and stepped up our giving to his campaign. This was a fact that a grateful Mitchell never forgot for the remainder of his career in electoral politics.

Another important race for us was the election of Jeff Bingaman, then the attorney general of New Mexico. He defeated Harrison Schmidt, a former astronaut, who would not even meet with the pro-Israel community. In Nevada, Chic Hecht, a supporter of Israel and a Jew, was elected senator.

There was a certain magical formula that seemed to be the cohesive gel that allowed our PAC to grow. It was the excitement that comes over newcomers to the political process when they realize that our political system is open and accessible even to amateurs like themselves who are anxious to get involved. Whatever we were doing right, the results were impressive. Within a few years, 1,600 families joined HUVPAC. This was out of a total population in Rockland County, New York of 250,000 men, women, and children.

Not all of our members were Jewish. Among them were Monsignor Cox in Suffern, Vincent Monte, the Democratic Leader, and Sister Joan Regan, the director of the main Catholic hospital in the county. Local and state political leaders of both parties, regardless of religion, were eager to be associated with our group. They probably felt comfortable because HUVPAC did not stress Jewishness as our sine qua non. Rather, our credo was and remains that support for Israel is part and parcel of being a good American. During the 1980's with the Cold War at a peak of intensity, we made the case that a strong America needed faithful allies who would stand unconditionally with America in its rivalry with the Soviet Union, in the United Nations, and in the fight for human rights. In the key strategic area of the Middle East, only Israel fit that bill.

In our appeals to American policy makers, we reminded them that our country's moral relationship with Israel and commitment to ensuring her security went back to the formation of the Jewish state in 1948. We also sought to make the case for supporting Israel in hardheaded dollars and cents terms. We often used the "battleship argument," namely that the cost of one battleship was $3 billion dollars, and that in the absence of a strong ally in the Middle East, an area that is vital to American interests, we would need quite a few of them to patrol the Mediterranean Sea. Yet if we provided Israel with the same $3 billion a year, she could protect the region for us without the need for American troops.

HUVPAC organized community by community and developed a technique of holding parlor meetings in homes of prominent families choosing one or two couples to be "guests of honor" and then inviting a congressman or a senator as our guest speaker. At the end of such parlor meetings, we would ask participants to join our organization or our board. Our guest speaker would always receive a campaign contribution from HUVPAC.

Every year at Chanukah time, we had a large party for our major contributors and once a year had a dinner in which two United States senators, a Republican and a Democrat spoke. Those events usually attracted 500 to 600 people. For example, in 1987, we honored Monsignor Cox, and Senators Joseph Lieberman of Connecticut and William Cohen of Maine were our guest speakers. Cohen, of course, went on to become Secretary of Defense under Clinton. Within a few years, the HUVPAC dinner became the best-attended and most popular organizational dinner in Rockland County.

The highlight of the year was a mission to Washington, which allowed as many as 100 of our members who took part to get the feeling they were really interacting with power. We held a foreign policy briefing followed by a kosher luncheon that drew eighteen to twenty Senators. Then our members broke up into small groups of three to four people and visited as many as 120 members of the Congress. Each group had three or four thirty-minute appointments. We concluded the day with a cocktail party for members of Congress whom we had either supported or planned to support. Often we added a briefing at the White House or at the Pentagon.

How could it be possible that any individual who got up at 3AM and traveled to Washington for such an intensive day of politicking returning home to Rockland only at 9PM, would not be moved to feel that they were playing a 'hands on' role in impacting American foreign policy? In fact they could not, and those missions turned into marvelous recruiting tools.

Each year we grew in numbers and influence. It did not take long for us to become the largest local pro-Israel PAC in the country. Indeed, by 1989, HUVPAC was the hundredth largest PAC in the United States, regardless of cause. The other ninety-nine top PACs included major national groups such as the AMA, the realtors, and the National Educational Association. HUVPAC became even better known in the halls of Congress. For my part, I felt more confident every day about our ability to successfully make our case. I really loved being a part of the national scene. I felt similarly at ease in developing relationships with members of Congress and their staffs.

Earlier on in HUVPAC's ascent, in 1984, when we were still finding our way and feeling our oats, we successfully contributed to the defeat of Senator Charles Percy of Illinois, who had vocally criticized Israeli policy and had shown sympathy for Yasir Arafat and the PLO. During the campaign, Sheila and I had planned a parlor meeting for his opponent, Congressman Paul Simon, at our home, but at the last moment Simon could not attend and he asked Congresswoman Geraldine Ferraro to appear in his stead. Little did we know that in a few short weeks she would be selected as a candidate for the vice presidency.

Overall, the 1984 election was an unalloyed triumph for

HUVPAC. We were victorious in fourteen out of nineteen Senate races and fifty-three out of sixty-five House races. Not only did Simon defeat Percy in Illinois, in neighboring Iowa, Tom Harkin unseated Roger Jepsen, the Christian fundamentalist senator who had done that flagrant about face during the AWACS debate. Another person elected to the Senate that year we strongly supported was Al Gore of Tennessee. Still, we suffered a few losses as well. The big ones were the re-election of Senator Jesse Helms over Governor Jim Hunt in North Carolina and the defeat of Congressman Clarence Long for reelection in Maryland. Long was the Chairman of the House Appropriations Committee and a strong supporter of aid to Israel, but he was hurt with the voters in his last campaign by his evident advanced age.

One of the tokens of appreciation HUVPAC used to give to members of Congress who visited us was a *shofar*, (a ram's horn), of the kind blown on the Jewish New Year in synagogues throughout the world. Our shofar had a small plaque at the bottom to remind the Congressman of the clarion call of democracy that Israel represented in the Middle East. It also caused some very funny incidents. For example, one day when I was visiting with Senator Dan Coats (R-Ind), I saw one of our shofars in his closet. On a whim I decided to blow it for him, causing a shrill sound in the senator's high-ceilinged office. A moment later, several security men came rushing in to make sure nothing untoward was happening.

One day Congressman Tommy Robinson of Arkansas, a former sheriff, stopped me in the halls of Congress and said, "My dog ate the shofar." I thought he was referring to the driver of his car until I understood what he meant. The staff of Senator Tim Johnson (D-S.D.) reported to us that his shofar had been stolen and we happily replaced it. Senator Max Cleland's shofar was delivered to us with the wrong name attached, so we had to delay presenting it to him until we had another one made. His office called HUVPAC a few times, anxious about the whereabouts of their "horn."

As I noted previously, my personal history of service in Vietnam was extremely helpful in forging relationships with members of Congress who had served in that conflict such as Senator John McCain, Republican of Arizona and Senator Larry Pressler, Republican of South Dakota, as well as many other conservatives. On one occasion I had a few moments to relax and walked into a committee hearing simply to observe. Senator Pressler was sitting behind a desk and when he saw me walk in he ran out of the hearing room through the back entrance, came into the front to embrace me with a hug, "Mendy, my Vietnam buddy."

HUVPAC and the rest of the pro-Israel PAC community was confronted with a grave crisis on January 12, 1989, when a group of pro-Arabists filed suit with the Federal Election Commission against AIPAC and ten pro-Israel PACs including HUVPAC for violation of federal election law. The group consisted of Paul Findley, George Ball, Richard Hanks, James Akins, Richard Curtiss, Andrew Killgore, and Orin Parker. They charged that HUVPAC and the other major pro-Israel PACs were directed and coordinated by AIPAC.

Our antagonists argued that if, for example, Senator X received an average of $1,000.00 each from twenty-five pro-Israel PACs that was solid evidence that all of us had been in collusion in making a decision to support that senator and had done so under the direction of AIPAC. If they were correct, that meant that the twenty five PACs were essentially one PAC—in essence, AIPAC in disguise, and, in that case, were in violation of federal election law forbidding an organization to give more than $5,000 to any candidate during the primary campaign and an equal amount for the general election. Such a pattern, the litigants charged would constitute a violation of the law on the part of the giver and the receiver.

Specifically the complaint charged that HUVPAC and other pro-Israel PACs across the country had violated federal election law by making excessive contributions in 1984, 1986 and 1988. The thrust of the charge however, was really to prove that AIPAC was behaving like a PAC that gave money to candidates, something it was forbidden to do. The lawsuit represented a grave threat, which if it had succeeded, would have crippled the pro-Israel political action community as well as AIPAC.

When I learned the suit was pending I understood that we would have to defend ourselves against it without any help from a common source such as AIPAC and would have to eschew pooling of legal talent in our defense. Such gestures would clearly appear to be collusion and would strengthen the case of those suing us. Given that reality, I realized that defending ourselves against the suit could be an expensive proposition. I notified a number of friends of mine who were attorneys and extremely vocal in their support of Israel. Each chomped at the bit hoping that they would be the one to have the opportunity to be the counsel of our PAC and many offered to do so on a pro bono basis. For my part, I was thrilled and relieved that the legal costs, whatever they would be, would not be borne by HUVPAC.

Nevertheless, when I was finally served with the papers and showed them to my friends in the legal profession, each of them quickly realized that the project would be an enormous drain of time and resources for their firms. Despite their earlier expressions of interest, they now demurred to take the case. Luckily there was a young man in my synagogue named Joshua Levine, the son of longtime congregants Rebecca and Les Levine, who was a first or second year associate at the law firm of Wilkie Farr and Gallagher. Josh, whom I had seen grow up, went to his section chief, Lawrence Kamin and made a case that the firm should undertake the pro bono defense of HUVPAC. They agreed.

HUVPAC's response to the suit was to present evidence that we had made our decisions about which candidates to support in the election cycles in question independently of AIPAC or any other organization. We pointed out that only five of our twenty-two steering committee members had ever contributed to AIPAC. In 1989, for example, seventy HUVPAC members went to Washington and met with one hundred members of Congress in small groups. Each of our members filled out questionnaires on the candidates' views and made recommendations for our future support, demonstrating that we had come to our own decisions by our own investigations.

The complaint alleged that all of the pro-Israel PACs supported John Evans in his 1986 race against Senator Steve Symms (R-Ida). In fact HUVPAC contributed to Symms in the Idaho race. Similarly, opposition to Senators Jesse Helms and Byron Dorgan of North Dakota were inaccurately attributed to our PAC. As noted, we did oppose Helms in the 1984 race, but once we met and developed a relationship with him, we contributed funds.

We presented evidence that of the 177 candidates for the House and Senate that HUVPAC supported during the 1988 election cycle, over seventy five percent of the money we contributed went to candidates who received financial support from less than one-third of the pro-Israel PACs. Further, we were able to show that, as of 1989, fifty members of Congress had come to Rockland County to meet with members of HUVPAC, while thirty six senators and approximately eighty members of the House had come to our annual luncheons and cocktail parties in Washington. Clearly, then, HUVPAC operated as an independent force on the national political scene, and not as some sort of adjunct of AIPAC.

Our law firm, Wilkie Farr Gallagher, did a wonderful job in researching and then cogently laying out our case in court. They not only presented the facts concerning HUVPAC's record of contributions to Congressional candidates, but also in pointing out that my own right to serve simultaneously as president of the PAC and a member of the executive board of AIPAC was protected under the First Amendment and not proof of collusion between the two bodies.

One interesting and amusing event took place on the day that our brief was due to be delivered to the Federal Election Commission in Washington. I went to the offices of Wilkie Farr Gallagher in New York to read and reread the document to attest that it was true and then sign. The main theme of our brief, hammered home over and over again, was that AIPAC and HUVPAC were truly not related factually or in any other way other than that both were pro-Israel in our orientation. As I was about to sign the brief, Mr. Kamin abruptly stopped me. It seemed I had pulled an AIPAC pen out of my jacket. I quickly signed with his pen.

Our victory in this matter relieved us of a great potential legal burden. It was quite interesting that during that period the TV news magazine "60 Minutes" decided to do a story on AIPAC and the pro-Israel PACs. They started calling me everyday but I realized that there was a certain inequity to be questioned by Mike Wallace for a long period of time when he had the ability to edit the tape. Someone on the AIPAC staff thought I might be a suitable candidate to represent their organization on the show. However wiser heads came forward with the name of the late Rabbi Israel Miller, a vice president of AIPAC and Yeshiva University. He did a superb job not only because he was a wonderful soft-spoken person of obvious erudition and refinement, but also because he had nothing to do with the PAC movement at all. Thus, it was easier for Rabbi Miller to maintain believability answering hostile questions regarding AIPAC and its lack of connection to the pro-Israel PACs than it would have for someone like myself.

I met many outstanding leaders, Jewish and otherwise, during my years at HUVPAC. One was Seymour Zises, a well-known member of a distinguished financial and real estate family in New York. Zises was extremely knowledgeable in the minutia of American politics and accomplished in advocating on behalf of Israel and other causes that mattered to him. However, he taught me a great life lesson in another field; that of *menschlikeit*. I was sitting in Zises' office on the first occasion I met him when his secretary announced that a Mr. Schwartz was there. Zises asked his secretary to show him in and an elderly gentleman with a cardboard suitcase appeared in the doorway. Seymour asked him "What do you have to show?" "I have some beautiful ties that you might be interested in!" Schwartz responded.

Seymour said that he was going to buy a few and turned to me and asked me to pick a tie because he was going to buy me a present. I replied that I could not accept such a gift as I had only met him five minutes earlier. After picking out two or three ties for himself, Zises called his secretary and asked her to take Mr. Schwartz upstairs to see James Tisch, one of the owners of the Loew's Corporation, and very well known throughout the business world as a financial titan. "Make sure that Mr. Tisch sees to it that all of Mr. Schwartz's ties are bought by him and his employees," Zises instructed.

Seymour must have been able to tell from my expression that I was stunned that an important man like him would take the time to receive a "nobody" like Schwartz and then give him entrée to meet one of the wealthiest men in America. After Schwartz walked out, Zises turned to me and said, "This is the real meaning of *chesed* (loving kindness)." To give someone pride, to help them make a living is far more dignified and important and certainly more meaningful than giving him a handout." The willingness of such a wealthy and powerful man to perform such acts of loving-kindness was a lesson and an example that has always remained with me. Every time I see Seymour at a political event or social occasion, the astonishing act of *chesed* that I witnessed him perform that day in his office is uppermost in my thoughts.

HUVPAC became a labor of love, a full-time non-paying position that exposed me to men and women at the pinnacles of political life and of the business world from throughout the United States. They included owners of basketball and baseball teams who loved Israel. Several members of Congress from the class of 1982 who became personal friends of mine includedVin Weber of Minnesota, Larry Smith of Florida, Mel Levine of California, Ed Feighan of Ohio and Bob Torricelli of New Jersey.

I developed an extremely close relationship with a number of senators, including the late Quentin Burdick of North Dakota. He was a gentle patrician and chairman of a major committee. During one of his campaigns for re-election, Burdick chose me to be his point man in his relationship with the pro-Israel community. His chief of staff, David Strauss, later went on to become the deputy chief of staff to Vice President Gore, and my relationship with Strauss continued during his tenure there. Some of my friends on Capitol Hill became sources of inspiration to my sons as well. My son Ari served an internship for Senator Burdick, while my youngest son Elli spent a summer under Senator Helms' tutelage in the Foreign Relations Committee.

Though I remained involved in a full-time surgical practice, the excitement and fulfillment I received from my immersion in politics was heightened by my involvement in some memorable encounters in the corridors of power in Washington that I could never have anticipated in my wildest dreams before becoming involved in pro-Israel advocacy. Each of these experiences, which I document below, confirmed for me my deep love for America and our unique system of participatory democracy.

The Free Trade Legislation

I was in the operating room at my hospital in Rockland County conducting a major procedure when a voice came over the intercom "Dr. Ganchrow, you have an emergency call from Washington." I was surprised and more than a little irritated as I had never before received a political call during my workday. I had tried hard to keep the two parts of my professional life strictly separate. I had no idea who could be calling me. I asked our operator to inform the caller that I had at least two hours more to go in surgery and that I would call back as soon as I was through. One hour later the intercom again made the same announcement and I returned the same message.

When I finished surgery and returned the call, I learned it was regarding a free trade agreement between the United States and Israel, which was under discussion that day on the floor of the Senate. The agreement would basically allow Israel and the

United States to trade with each other without the imposition of certain duties. Senator Ernest Hollings of South Carolina however was filibustering because he wanted exemptions for some of South Carolina's agricultural products. Were he to get this exemption every United States Senator would stand up and demand the same exemptions for his or her state. The pro-Israel community felt strongly that it was important either that Hollings yield on this point, or the bill would be killed.

It turned out that I had been urgently contacted by a friend in the pro-Israel community in Washington because he was aware of the political relationship I had built with Hollings. Just a year before I received that call, Hollings had run for President of the United States as a Democratic candidate. Friends of Hollings were active in the pro-Israel community around the country on behalf of the Hollings presidential campaign. HUVPAC was happy to give financial support to this pro-Israel senator since we were aware that even if his presidential campaign were not to prove successful, he would still remain a senator.

Because of that connection, I was asked to call Hollings immediately and to tell him that the pro-Israel community was concerned about his "filibuster." I immediately called Hollings' office and asked to speak to him. I was informed that the senator was at that moment on the floor of the Senate. I then asked to speak to his Chief of Staff, who likewise was on the Senate floor. I therefore said to the secretary to whom I was speaking, "Please send the following message to Senator Hollings: "As a friend of Israel, you must realize that your filibuster could strengthen attempts to kill this bill." The staffer promised to deliver the message. One-half hour later I repeated the call with the same message. An hour later Hollings had ceased his filibuster and the bill passed unanimously. An hour and a half later I received a call from Hollings' chief of staff stating that the senator had not considered himself to be doing anything anti-Israel. On the contrary, he had been trying to strengthen the bill, and was happy that it had passed.

Some time later after the bill passed both Houses, a celebration took place in a large Congressional office. I was invited to the event that preceded the bill's signing. Congressman Sam Gibbons of Florida, the chairman of the House committee, presided. It was one of the few times that I had the personal satisfaction of feeling that just perhaps I had played a small but vital role in the passage of legislation benefiting both Israel and the United States.

Senator Jesse Helms

In 1984 Senator Jesse Helms of North Carolina was considered to be one of the most outspoken anti-Israel members of the United States Senate. He was the Senate's most tenacious opponent of U.S. foreign aid, the largest recipient of which was Israel. Helms was up for reelection and his opponent was Governor Jim Hunt. The pro-Israel community, feeling it had acquired political power in 1982 (with the election of Congressman Dick Durbin in defeating Paul Findley of Illinois,) turned their attention to Helms among other races.

The stationery for Governor Hunt was not entitled "The Committee to Elect Jim Hunt" but rather "The Committee to Defeat Jesse Helms." The stationery had about 150 names on the left column, seventy five to eighty percent were Jewish names primarily from New York, Chicago, and Los Angeles. It was almost a joke as to how many of Hunt's supporters were Jewish.

However, Senator Helms took great advantage of this. In a very spirited and tough race, he focused his fund raising, which included mass mailings, on the fact that most of his opponent's financial backers were from out of state. Eventually, Helms spent approximately twelve to fifteen million dollars in a successful campaign.

Helms made his first-ever trip to Israel a few months after his reelection together with Senator Steve Symms of Idaho and freshman Senator Chick Hecht of Nevada. On the senators' itinerary in Israel was a visit to the Hecht Synagogue, located on the grounds of the Hebrew University. Accompanying them during the trip was a good friend of mine, Robert Jacobs of Staten Island, who made me aware of the warm statements in support of the Jewish state that Helms made during his stay in Israel. Helms said,"I hope the American people will understand that Israel is the only reliable ally we have in the region."Seeking to take advantage of what I saw as a significant political opening, I told the White House liaison to the Jewish community, Marshall Breger, that I wanted to invite Helms to a HUVPAC luncheon in Washington, but was afraid he would turn me down because my name appeared on Jim Hunt for Senate stationery from the year before. Breger promised to call Senator Helms in the name of the White House and tell the Senator that the President would like him to attend our luncheon. After Breger spoke to Helms, I sent him an official invitation to the luncheon and he accepted.

When I informed pro-Israel advocates and other political professionals that Senator Helms would be coming to the HUVPAC luncheon, almost no one believed that he would actually show up. After all, he was considered an anathema by most of our community.

The room, which Senator Robert Kasten (R-Wis), a strong friend of Israel had obtained for us just off the floor of the Senate, filled early with disbelieving Washington insiders waiting to see if Helms would really come. Many in HUVPAC were quite upset with me because they were political liberals who felt that Helms was not only anti-Israel, but a racist to boot. They reminded me that we had worked hard for his defeat only a few months before. I responded that I understood their complaints, but was convinced that this was a historic opportunity that should not be lost. After all, Helms was likely to remain an influential voice in the Senate for many years to come.

Suddenly, a hush came over the room as Helms entered with a dignified bearing that almost felt military. One would not have thought from his demeanor that he was entering any sort of lion's den; on the contrary, his obvious self-confidence and sense of being "at home" sent the message that he considered himself to be our best and oldest friend in the Senate. When Helms stood up to speak, there was a palpable sense of apprehension on the part of the audience. Yet, within a few moments one sensed that a dramatic transformation of attitudes was taking place as Helms spoke eloquently and convincingly of his belief that Israel is a strong partner and strategic asset of the United States in the Middle East. He stressed how much he had learned during his trip to Israel, and how he had returned from the trip more committed to Israel than ever before.

The man long known as "Senator No" did not renounce his longstanding opposition to foreign aid. Rather, he explained that the reason for his opposition was not U.S. aid to Israel, but rather our sending hundreds of millions of dollars in support to other nations that often opposed U.S. interests in the United Nations and other international forums. Helms explained that were the

Reagan Administration to transfer foreign aid sent to Israel to the defense budget, he would have no problem voting for it. This was a recurring theme that he repeated to me many times over the subsequent years.

The response to Helms' speech from our group was overwhelmingly positive. It was difficult not to be impressed with his manner. Helms came across like a towering presence and looked and spoke like a classic southern Senator. Yet, more significantly, everyone in the room realized they were witnessing a highly unusual political realignment from Helms as well as from the pro-Israel community. In short, there was considerable electricity in the room, and Helms captured the imagination, if not the hearts, of most who heard him.

From that moment on, Senator Helms and I developed a warm personal relationship and I visited with him on many occasions. Indeed, I was sometimes the only member of the pro-Israel community who had entrée to him. His chief of staff for the Middle East was Danielle Pletka, an Australian woman who had lived on a kibbutz and spoke a perfect Hebrew. On a number of occasions when I invited Helms to subsequent HUVPAC events, Pletka came along to introduce her senator and charmed the assembled crowd by mixing some Hebrew into her remarks. As I noted, my son Elliot served one summer as an intern for the Foreign Relations Committee under the aegis of Senator Helms, and it was a wonderful experience for him.

When my son Ari was at Brooklyn Law School, I asked Helms to submit a scholarly piece for the spring 1994 Brooklyn Law School Journal of Law and Policy. Helms personally rewrote his article, which was entitled "Is It Art or Tax Paid Obscenity; The NEA Controversy" five or six times before submitting it.

In September 1995, President Clinton hosted Israeli and Palestinian leaders to mark Phase Two of the Oslo Peace Accords. Shimon Peres and Yasser Arafat came to visit President Clinton. One of the main wishes of the administration as part of the Oslo Accords was that America would supply economic aid to the Palestinians. However many partisans in the United States objected. The Administration introduced the Middle East Peace Facilitation Act (MEPFA) in order to get the aid approved.

On September 12, 1995 I returned from a trip to Israel as president of the Orthodox Union (OU). I met with many leaders of the settlement movement, as well as the heads of Ateret

Kohanim, who were in the forefront in the fight to preserve Jerusalem as the united, undivided capital of Israel. Most of those with whom I had met in Israel felt that America should not be funding the Palestinians.

The day following my return from Israel I went to Washington to meet with Senator Helms, by now chairman of the Senate Foreign Relations Committee and my congressman, Ben Gilman, chairman of the House International Relations Committee, to discuss U.S. funding for the Palestinian Authority (PA). I was the first member of the national pro-Israel community to discuss these matters directly with Helms. I expressed my extreme displeasure to Helms and Gilman concerning loopholes within the proposed legislation and the fact that there was no reciprocity required on the part of the Palestinians in return for the American funding. I argued that at a minimum, in exchange for U.S. aid, the PA should disarm Hamas and cease incitement on the part of Palestinian leaders against Israel's very existence.

On September 20, 1995 I testified before the House International Relations Committee; speaking not only on behalf of the OU, but rather in the name of all the Orthodox organizations, including the National Council of Young Israel, Rabbinical Council of America, Amit Women, Emunah Women, Religious Zionists of America, and Poala Aguda. In my testimony, I took a different approach than that of the Zionist Organization of America (ZOA) and other right-wing Zionist groups who demanded flatly that the U.S. cut off all funds to the Palestinians. Rather, I propounded a new idea; that the money for the Palestinians should be appropriated but placed in escrow until the PA had met certain criteria.

I took this tact not because I believed the PA should receive U.S. funding but rather because I could read the political tea leaves and understood that many members of Congress who were troubled by U.S. aid to a longtime terrorist body were nevertheless not prepared to go all out against the President on the issue. After testifying, I found a great deal of agreement and encouragement on the part of members of Congress for my compromise position.

On the evening of September 27 at a moment when very few members of the Senate were present, Senator Helms went to the floor of the Senate in his role as Chairman of the Foreign Relations Committee and introduced a series of five "stealth amendments" to the Middle East Aid Package. Those in the Senate chamber quickly passed the amendments unanimously after Helms explained reassuringly that his purpose was not to sabotage the Israeli-Palestinian agreement signed that very week by President Clinton, Prime Minister Peres and Chairman Arafat, but rather to strengthen it.

Two days later, *The Forward* hit the newsstands with a front page headline reading; "Helms, Ganchrow, Set Time Bomb on Funds Due to Explode in 1996." As the paper pointed out, the amendments Senator Helms had introduced that week at my request, and which had been passed unanimously by the Senate, would cut off American financial aid for the peace process on October 1, 1996, unless the PA met a stringent set of conditions to combat Palestinian terrorism. In addition the PA would have to officially disavow and cancel the clause in the Palestinian National Covenant calling for Israel's destruction, as well as to close its offices in Jerusalem, which Israel had long proclaimed to be its eternal undivided capital. The date of the deadline for compliance by the PA that Helms had selected at my suggestion was significant because it fell only a few weeks before both U.S. and Israeli voters were expected to go to the polls.

The article in *The Forward* asserted that; "Passage of the amendments by the Senate followed a one man lobbying blitz by the hawkish President of the Union of Orthodox Jewish Congregations of American, Dr. Mandell Ganchrow, who shuttled between New York and Washington. Trading on his long relationship with Mr. Helms, and his role as a fundraiser for the Carolinian, Dr. Ganchrow steered Mr. Helms to a more hard line stance on the Middle East after reports in *The Forward* and Insight magazine quoted critics as saying, "Jesse has gone soft " on the PLO.

In interviews with various media, I argued that we had actually helped to strengthen MEPFA by forcing full compliance upon the Palestinian authorities and removing other loopholes that in the past had allowed Mr. Arafat to be non-compliant and yet still receive full American aid. We had also been successful in changing the expiration date of MEPFA from 18 months hence, which would have carried it beyond the 1996 U.S. presidential election, to 12 months from October 1, 1995. This meant it would expire just before the election. In addition, the amendment would mandate the closing of Orient House, the PLO headquarters in Jerusalem, and dozens of other political offices within six months from the date of passage or all of the funding would dry up.

The amendments I proposed and Jesse Helms pushed into law were eventually endorsed both by AIPAC and the Conference of Presidents of Major American Jewish Organizations. The Forward wrote the following, "At least they weren't caught napping by the Orthodox Union's lobbying whirl, as dozens of American senators were. AIPAC and the Presidents Conference did not initiate the changes but were notified of the insertion of the amendments into the bill. Still they were cut out of the tete-a-tete between Dr. Ganchrow and Mr. Helms where these changes were first forged. Critics of the proposed legislation which they dubbed the 'Ganchrow amendments' accused the Senate of passing the measures by a voice vote at the moment where most senators didn't grasp the meaning of the measures they were in the process of passing—unanimously."

I had wanted the "stealth" amendments to be even tougher on the PA by including a stipulation that the declaration of a Palestinian state would trigger an automatic cutoff of American funds. Unfortunately, some of these changes were not written into the final bill because the Administration scurried around to take it out of the authority of the House International Relations Committee to write the House part of the bill. Overall, however, we had achieved an enormous victory against great odds by getting Helms into the process and showing that it was possible for the U.S. to force compliance on the Palestinians in exchange for aid.

Senator Steve Symms

In 1984 the pro-Israel PAC community was trying to see if we could repeat our election triumph of 1982 when we helped to defeat a number of prominent senators and congresspeople considered to be unfriendly. In the Senate, we focused our efforts on legislators such as Senator Steve Symms of Idaho, Senator Jesse Helms of North Carolina and Senator Charles Percy of Illinois. As it turned out, Senator Percy was defeated but Helms and Symms were not.

Not long after the election, it was suggested to me that on my next visit to Washington I should drop in for a meeting with Senator Symms. I cannot recall who made the suggestion and why, as it did not seem to make sense at the time, given Symms' perceived hostility to Israel. Still, I was granted an appointment with no difficulty. Upon my arrival, I was ushered into Symms' private office. The senator sat on a large black couch. I sat down on a chair across from him. He pointed to the black couch and asked me to sit down closer to him, which I did.

After a routine introduction Symms asked bluntly; "Why are the Jews after me"? I responded; "Can we be honest? Can we talk openly"? He answered, "One hundred percent. That is why you are here."

I proceeded to tell Symms that on every single issue of importance to the pro-Israel community whether it was foreign aid, arms sales to Arab countries that bordered Israel and were still at war with her, and various other concerns he had always voted against the interests of Israel. Indeed, our community felt that he was one of the most negative senators on Israel-related issues. Symms became agitated and wheeled on me sharply. He wagged his finger in my face and growled; "You people will have to decide whether you want someone in the Senate who is strong against Communism and is prepared to support the survival of Israel even if I don't vote for things you want, or someone like Solarz, who is not strong on Communism and does not believe in a strong America, but believes only in Israel."

My own temperature rose sharply. I was incensed that Symms was accusing Steven Solarz, a Jewish Democratic congressman from Brooklyn, and, by extension, the organized Jewish community, of dual loyalty. I turned to him and responded sternly in a voice of tightly controlled anger, "Senator, don't you dare talk to me that way. I served in Vietnam and have the medals to prove it. I am just as much an anti-Communist as you are whether it concerns Nicaragua, the Soviet Union, China, the United States, or in the Middle East. I don't have to make any excuses for my American citizenship or my loyalty. And I believe that you are doing a great disservice to America as well as to Israel by the way you vote."

In the face of my angry response, Symms' attitude changed completely. He became both apologetic and very friendly, and from that moment on, we developed a very warm relationship. Although Symms did not consistently vote with Israel on issues vital to the U.S.-Israel relationship, he became considerably more receptive to our community. An example was his vote against a proposed stinger weapons system by President Reagan to the Saudis, as described in my introduction.

Subsequently, our personal relationship grew closer, and six years later in 1990, when Symms was running for re-election, I brought him to Monsey to meet with a group of supporters of HUVPAC. Strangely, even though Symms understood he was speaking to a pro-Israel group, he proceeded to devote his entire speech to the 65-mile speed limit in Idaho and his conversations with President Reagan as to how the speed limit was against the interests of the citizens of Idaho. It was a perplexing speech and was totally out of place that evening. Symms won that election and served six more years.

Senator Harris Wofford

I first met Harris Wofford (D-Pa) when he came to the United States Senate to fill out the unexpired term of Senator John Heinz, Republican of Pennsylvania, who had been killed in a plane crash.

When Harris came to the Senate he was a political unknown outside of Pennsylvania. Certainly in the pro-Israel community, Wofford required the type of exposure that would allow him to raise money and national support for the upcoming election that would be held shortly for a full term as senator. Dr. Harvey Peck, a friend and colleague, asked me if I would stop by Harris's office on my next trip to Washington and offer my assistance. So when the Orthodox Union went to Washington on a mission shortly thereafter, I made an appointment to see the senator. On the way over I picked up Lawrence Burian, who had been our first IPA intern, and asked if he would join me. This would be my first meeting with Senator Wofford and I believed Lawrence, who is a brilliant young man, would benefit greatly by being present as I talked candidly with a senator about the politics of the pro-Israel community.

We walked into an office full of cartons, many of which had not been unpacked. Wofford had only been in office a few days. Despite the feverish activity all around us, the new senator greeted us warmly and focused his full attention upon us. I articulated my belief that a senator needed to master not only the issues but also the nuances of the Middle East. As a young man, Wofford had lived briefly in Palestine when it was still a British dependency, but he had been away from the issue for many years. I urged Wofford to meet with Senators Inouye (D-Hawaii) and Moynihan (D-NY), two Democratic senators who were especially well liked in the pro-Israel community, and suggested he ask them to allow him to take the lead on certain legislative issues in order to gain an immediate presence in our community. I also suggested to the senator the names of a few professional fund-raisers who had worked successfully in the pro-Israel community around the country on behalf of other senators and congressmen.

Finally the issue of loan guarantees arose. Harris's son, Dan Wofford—who was married to Harvey Peck's daughter, then chief of radiology at Good Samaritan Hospital and a founding member of HUVPAC—now interjected himself into the discussion. To our dismay, the younger Wofford proceeded to argue quite strongly to his father that he should oppose U.S. loan guarantees to Israel because of the country's policy of settling a small percentage of the hundreds of thousands of Russian Jews then pouring into the country in Jewish settlements in Judea and Samaria.

I responded with equal passion that the land in question was not per se Palestinian, but rather disputed between Israel and the Palestinians. I argued that despite the propaganda put forward by the Palestinians, the settlements were not really an impediment to peace, since the Arabs had never given Israel a day of peace during all the years before a single settlement was built. I spoke about the historic right of the Jewish people to its own homeland and pointed out forcefully that the loan guarantees were necessary to create the proper infrastructure for the huge wave of Russian emigrés pouring into Israel. My argument with Dan Wofford went back and forth and at times our voices rose sharply even though we continued to communicate in civil language. Finally Harris brought his hand down and said, "Enough. I've decided. I'll support the loan guarantees."

The senator then asked me to write an outline of a pro-Israel platform that summarized all the issues we had discussed. In the taxi on the way to the airport, I asked Burian if he would volunteer to write up the discussion, which I would subsequently edit. Lawrence, who later graduated from Yale Law School, did an outstanding job. As promised, I delivered the papers to Harris Wofford within a few days.

My relationship with Senator Wofford deepened and several years later I had the opportunity of joining him in Israel, where he visited with Prime Minister Rabin a few days after the announcement of the Oslo Accords.

Dan Wofford ran unsuccessfully for Congress in Pennsylvania in 2002 on a very pro-Israel platform.

Senator Chic Hecht

In the fall of 1983 there was an open senatorial seat in the state of Nevada. Chic Hecht, a businessman, entered a crowded Republican primary race. Shortly after he entered the race, Chic travelled to New York to meet the Lubavitcher Rebbe and receive a bracha (blessing). Chic told me that he was informed by the Rebbe that if he attended synagogue on the morning of the primary election he would win. Chic, who came from a traditional Jewish background, did so and came out the victor in the election. It was an election that the Hudson Valley PAC contributed to in support of Chic. His victory was an important milestone for our PAC.

Hecht looked to two other conservative senators for guidance; Jesse Helms and Steve Symms. In 1984, it was Chic who squired Helms and Symms on that trail-blazing trip to Israel during which they visited the Hecht Sanctuary at the Hebrew University, which Chic and the Hecht family had dedicated.

Surprisingly however, the relationship between Chic and AIPAC was spotty. Chic complained that AIPAC did not give him enough respect and did not coordinate legislative initiatives with him. Chic was very thin-skinned and was constantly concerned about how people viewed him. Nevertheless, I felt quite close to him during the early part of his tenure in Washington. Indeed, when HUVPAC held its first dinner in my honor, Chic Hecht was one of the guest speakers.

My falling out with Chic Hecht started with the Goldman case. Dr. Goldman was an Orthodox physician in the U.S. Army who insisted it was his religious duty to wear a skullcap. The Army forbade him to do so. Goldman took it to court, and lost. The case went all the way to the Supreme Court, which ruled in support of the military. Eventually, the issue came before the United States Senate. Supporters of Goldman, most of them adherents of Orthodox Judaism, strove to convince senators to pass a law allowing religious personnel in the military to wear head coverings while on active duty, provided it did not interfere with the carrying out of duty, whether in the battlefield or in the office.

During the course of the debate Chic Hecht took to the floor of the Senate and announced that even though he himself was an Orthodox Jew, he did not believe the bill had to be passed, since Jewish law does not require the wearing of a head covering.

When those of us who are truly Orthodox heard what Chic had said, we were furious. This was not because the bill did not pass, since the issue was not really one of the most important issues facing the Orthodox community. Rather we were deeply angered and offended because Hecht had gotten up on the floor and falsely portrayed himself as Orthodox, and had in effect ruined the possibility of winning the vote.

I went to see Chic and we had a harsh exchange. I told him that he had misrepresented himself in the debate since he did not conduct his personal life according to halacha. I told him that he should have been proud to back Captain Goldman.

Subsequently, the OU arranged with NCSY, our youth group (National Conference of Synagogue Youth) to crochet a skullcap for each member of the Senate, including the female members, and have it delivered to their offices. By doing so, we were hoping to demonstrate to the legislators that the skullcap was an unobtrusive garment. In view of the fact that the Israeli Army allows skullcaps and that other armies in the world allow turbans; we argued that wearing a skullcap would in no way interfere with U.S. military personnel carrying out their duties. On the second try, the skullcap bill passed.

My second clash with Chic Hecht took place following our meeting at the White House with President Reagan over the Saudi arms package. It was Senator Hecht who agreed to set up a meeting for Jewish leaders at the White House with the president in the hope that a personal appeal from Reagan himself would force the Jewish leaders to yield on the package. Chic arranged for his brother, Marty to be there. Also present among the so-called Jewish leaders taking part in the meeting was the soon-to-be disgraced financier Ivan Boesky. Both Boesky and Marty Hecht spoke out ardently at the meeting in favor of the Saudi arms package. This bit of political trickery was too much for me, and I vowed to do everything I could to help to defeat Chic in his next race for re-election in 1988.

When the primary season came along and Governor Richard Bryan of Nevada, a Democrat, decided to run for the Senate against Hecht, the Hudson Valley PAC became the very first pro-Israel PAC to support him. This contribution gave license to other pro-Israel PACs who were also dissatisfied with Hecht to support Bryan. Although some of the leadership of the pro-Israel community felt that we had to support an incumbent, I was quite vocal in my opposition to Hecht and was pleased when he was defeated. Hecht was later appointed ambassador to one of the Caribbean nations.

President Reagan and the Saudi Arms Sale

In May 1986, it became evident that President Reagan had promised Saudi Arabia 345 million dollars of sidewinder and harpoon missiles and had given a personal commitment to Prince Bandar, the Saudi Ambassador to Washington, that the deal would pass Congress. There were many rumors flying about this proposed deal. A common practice within the pro-Israel community was that once the rumors started to fly, we would begin to mobilize Congress in opposition to such initiatives well in advance of the formal announcement by the Administration. By doing so, we would have a fighting chance to succeed in a campaign to defeat any proposed U.S. arms package to any country still at war with Israel.

As chairman of the Community Relations Commission of the Orthodox Union, I had frequently invited United States Senators and Congressmen to come to New York and meet with our leaders. Immediately after the legislators met the OU leadership in Manhattan, I would drive them up to Rockland County for a HUVPAC meeting. In this way I had the opportunity of having them in my car for at least an hour to make our case in greater detail.

During the time when we were gearing up to fight the Administration's expected new arms sale to the Saudis, my guest for the day in Manhattan and Rockland was Senator Paul Trible (R-Va). I had been informed by AIPAC that the President would announce the arms package on the following day. I was determined to use the occasion of Trible's visit to try to get a commitment from him to vote against it.

Trible greeted me warmly when we met at Lou J. Siegel's kosher restaurant in midtown Manhattan, where I was hosting him for dinner. We already had developed a friendship in Washington. I immediately told him that before we moved inside to meet the delegation from the OU, I wanted to inform him that I had learned the Administration planned to announce the impending arms sale the following day. I then asked him if he would vote with us to defeat the arms package.

Trible replied that his own sources had told him that, contrary to my information, the arms sale would not, in fact, be introduced the following day. I responded that AIPAC had just assured me that it would happen. AIPAC was correct. Once again I asked him to commit himself to vote in our favor. To my relief, Trible agreed to do so. Whereupon I said, "I know that we can defeat this on the first vote but the President will surely veto the rejection. Can we count on you to stick with us on the veto override?" I asked. He answered unambiguously, "Yes you can."

I thanked Trible for his commitment, but then added, " Paul, our community remembers Senator Jepsen of Iowa, who promised to stick with us on the AWACS and then spoke to G-d, and changed his vote." Trible smiled and replied, "Mendy don't worry. G-d does not speak to me, nor do I speak to him." The two of us then went in to dinner, and afterwards drove up to Monsey.

As it turned out the Israeli government had made a deal with President Reagan. For reasons they never explained to us, the Israelis decided not to fight the Saudi arms sale. Left high and dry by the Israeli action, AIPAC decided not to publicly oppose the deal. Nevertheless, Senator Alan Cranston of California, one of the pro-Israel community's best friends on Capitol Hill, decided that the sale was not in the best interests of the United States and that he would lead a fight against it in the Senate despite the actions of the Israelis and of AIPAC. Heartened by Cranston's bold stand, a number of pro-Israel activists including myself, decided to join the battle against the arms sale.

Our decision to press ahead with our campaign against the arms sale upset the Israeli government. Despite this, we persevered in our effort, going from senator to senator to press them to oppose the bill. I myself secured three such commitments; from Senator Jesse Helms, Senator Steve Symms, and, as noted, Senator Paul Trible. Momentum began to build in our favor, and sensing the possibility of defeat, the Administration chose to bring the arms sale bill up for a vote on a day when President Reagan was in Japan. Still even we were stunned when after the votes were counted it turned out that, under Senator Cranston's skilled leadership, we had managed to narrowly defeat the arms sale. The result surely was a shock to the Israeli government, which had chosen to hoard political capital by acquiescing to the Saudi arms deal.

The administration's headcounters on the Hill may have anticipated the possibility of defeat, but that did not mean President Reagan manifested any less fury at Republican defectors to our side upon his return from Japan. After vetoing the bill as passed by Cranston, the President called in each of the GOP senators who voted against the sale to the Oval Office. He urged them to switch to the Administration's side on the veto-override vote. Reagan told the senators that he needed their help to maintain his promise to the Saudis and this was a critical component of the Administration's Middle East policy.

Several of the senators who had voted with us explained to the president that they were up for re-election that year and had made commitments to oppose the arms sale to pro-Israel activists who were financially backing their campaigns. Therefore they said to the president in effect, "If you will get us released from our commitments we will vote to support you."

The President asked the senators for the names of the people to whom they had given commitments to oppose the arms deal and a list was drawn up. The next thing I knew, I received a call from the White House that President Reagan would like to see me at a meeting he was calling at the White House just before Memorial Day. I felt quite nervous since I had never before been invited to the White House to meet with any President.

At least the setting of the meeting—the Roosevelt Room of the White House—was not unfamiliar to me. Only two or three weeks earlier when I had been attending the AIPAC Policy Conference in Washington, a White House aide came to me and invited me for a private tour of the White House quarters. This gesture was a way of thanking me for supporting the Administration's successful effort in Congress to secure funding for the Nicaraguan Contra rebels, a cause that was a top priority for President Reagan. I had volunteered to help the President because I have always been very anti-Communist and firmly believed that anything that can be done to defeat Communism anywhere in the world was an important objective. On that occasion, I had posed in front of the White House seal used by the press secretary.

I called Sandy Eisenstat, an old friend and pro-Israel activist from New York, to arrange to go together to Washington on the following day. Robert Jacobs, another friend of mine who was close to both Helms and Symms, and had also been invited to the meeting by the President, decided not to go after Senator Chic Hecht informed him that it was a "setup" and that he should avoid the meeting.

The night before the White House meeting I stayed up almost all night studying facts and figures about Saudi Arabia, as though I was cramming for a medical school exam. I took extensive notes and, by the end of that long night, felt confident I had most of the material at my fingertips. The following morning on May 20th, I met Sandy at LaGuardia airport and we flew together to Washington. Before heading for the White House, we met with friends in the pro-Israel community who put us through our paces in preparation for the meeting. Finally, with our hearts in our mouths, Sandy and I got into a taxi and rode to the White House.

We had no idea in advance who was going to be at the meeting. In the small reception room outside the Oval Office we found Malcolm Hoenlein, then executive director of the Jewish Community Relations Council of New York. Others, whose presence seemed more surprising, but turned out to have great significance, included Marty Hecht, the brother of Senator Chic Hecht and the billionaire financier Ivan Boesky, who had made his fortune in junk bonds. Also in attendance were Rabbi Shem Tov of Chabad-Lubavitch and a gentleman I had never met prior to this meeting, but subsequently became friendly with, Hart Hasten, of Indianapolis, the head of Herut America.

When we were ushered into the Roosevelt Room of the White House, numerous generals and other military men confronted us. I also noticed that there were many cameras. Each of us was given a predetermined seat. Secretary of State George Shultz was seated directly on the right of the president's seat, although Mr. Reagan had not yet arrived in the room. Admiral John Poindexter, the National Security Advisor, likewise was present at the table.

We commenced a general discussion about the arms sale until the President entered the room. He sat down and, unlike other presidents whom I have encountered in the White House, Reagan did not walk around the table to shake our hands. On this occasion, Reagan, so well known for his charm and bonhomie, was all business. Reading from cue cards, the President explained his rationale for the arms sales and then said something like the following; "I am not asking you to support this arms sale. What I am asking, however, is that you support the President of the United States, and, therefore, release the United States Senators from the commitments they have made to you; thereby freeing them to vote in favor of this sale."

I had gone into the meeting without the intention of speaking. Being in the presence of the President of the United States in a situation in which he was pressuring us to change our position was an overpowering experience. Although this meeting represented the first opportunity I had to speak my mind directly to any U.S. President, my feeling of awe at being part of a high stakes policy meeting in the Roosevelt room of the White House only added to my trepidation.

After the President finished his remarks, Malcolm Hoenlein was the first to take the floor. He thanked the President for inviting us and told him how much we appreciated his overall support of Israel. Malcolm's remarks were general in nature and contained no discussion whatsoever of the issue immediately at hand; the Saudi arms sale. In fact, to the best of my knowledge, Malcolm had not been involved in lobbying against the arms sale.

Seated directly to Malcolm's left was Ivan Boesky, who I had never met before. It was known that he had an association with the Jewish Theological Seminary, and was a major contributor to a variety of Jewish causes. Still, it was not clear to me why he had been invited to the meeting, since he had not been much involved previously in pro-Israel advocacy work and, as far as I was aware, no Senators had made any commitments to him on the arms sales issue. Boesky had a large manila envelope, on which he had a series of notes he had evidently jotted down on the way to the meeting, and began to speak. He stressed his belief that when the President of the United States asked for our support, it was critically important that we give it. Boesky asserted that although his gut reaction was to oppose the arms sale, as an American his first obligation was to support his country and his President. Therefore he had decided to support the arms sale.

As I listened to Boesky, I started to fume. My strong suspicion was that Boesky's performance had been coordinated with the White House in advance and, was, I suspected, related to personal interests of the financier that had nothing to do with the business at hand. I realized that under the circumstances I could no longer keep silent. I raised my hand and the President immediately recognized me. As I began my remarks, I was conscious that I was speaking face to face with the most powerful man on the planet. It was, indeed, time to step up to the plate and be a shtarker.

I opened my remarks by telling the President that I was proud to have gotten involved in support of the White House in its fight against Communism in Nicaragua. I had opposed the Sandinista regime and supported the fight against Communism in Central America, I exclaimed, "not because it was good for Israel but because it was good for the United States." I then argued to the President, quoting from a variety of sources, that Saudi Arabia did not need the advanced missiles he wanted to sell them, would not know how to use them, and that their presence in the desert kingdom would only escalate problems in the Middle East. In short, I repeated, "Even though I am convinced that this sale is bad for our friend Israel, I oppose it not because it is bad for Israel, but because it is bad for the United States." I concluded by saying that as a devout anti-Communist, and Vietnam veteran, I supported President Reagan and his policies generally, but that I could not agree with him on this particular policy.

Hart Hasten of Herut-America next raised his hand and stated; "Mr. President, I am your greatest friend in this room. I was treasurer of the Reagan for President campaign in Indiana during the 1984 election. Yet I cannot support you on this issue because of something that happened yesterday in the World's Fair in Vancouver." I was totally puzzled by what he was talking about and since I had never met Hart before, I was concerned that he was about to say something foolish that would detract from the case I had just made. He explained, "My daughter went into the Saudi Arabian exhibit at the World's Fair. Mr. President, there was a large map of the Middle East at that exhibit upon which Israel did not appear. She was angered by this and called me and asked, 'Daddy how can the Saudis display a map of the Middle East without Israel?' Mr. President, I have a question for you. How can you ask me to support you in selling sophisticated offensive weapons to a country that not only does not recognize Israel, but refuses even to acknowledge its presence on the map of the Middle East?"

The President looked perturbed, but basically just shrugged his shoulders in response to Hart's question. He evidently could not think of a retort. Administration insiders in the room winced because they knew that the President's inability to move either Hart or myself was extremely damaging to their cause since both of us were normally staunch Reaganites who had convinced several senators to oppose the Saudi arms sale.

Rabbi Shem Tov spoke next, but his remarks were general in nature. Since the rabbi had not lobbied senators on the arms sale issue, I, frankly, had no idea why he had been invited to the meeting.

The President was then informed by one of his handlers that he would have to leave the meeting as he had another engagement. Reagan apologized for leaving but informed us that Secretary of State Shultz would continue the discussion. As the President stood up to leave, Marty Hecht shot up his hand like a schoolboy and starting yelling, "Mr. President, Mr. President, I am Marty Hecht, Senator Chic Hecht's brother, and I would like to say something." So the President sat down again and said, "Please, Mr. Hecht, go ahead." Marty Hecht then proceeded to state vociferously, "We must support the President. He is our only President, and we must back him on this endeavor." The President thanked him and left the room. Subsequently, a few more comments were made and the meeting came to an end.

At the conclusion of the proceedings, those of us who had been invited to represent the pro-Israel community asked for time to caucus among ourselves. Yet it quickly became evident that we could not achieve unanimity. When we voted among ourselves there were two in favor of supporting the President, one or two abstentions, and the rest of us, approximately eight, against ceding to the President. At the end of our deliberation, upon hearing of the negative outcome, an Administration insider gave us electrifying news; the President had decided to reduce the arms sales and remove the 800 advanced portable anti-aircraft missiles from the package. These "stinger missiles" could reach targets five to six miles away. They did leave 1,066 air-to-air sidewinders and 100 harpoon missiles in the package. They then asked us to issue a public expression statement for this scaled-down arms sale.

Most of us felt deeply gratified at that moment that our staunch opposition had led President Reagan to abandon his plans to sell sophisticated offensive weapons to Saudi Arabia, and we understood that they desperately wanted the smaller sale as a kind of fig leaf. But we felt we needed time to study the ramifications of the new sale, so we told them we would remain noncommittal. Still, we did agree not to say anything against the administration to the reporters and television cameras waiting for us on the front lawn.

In retrospect our actions prevented Saudi Arabia from being

able to share the stingers with the most anti-American elements in the world, i.e. Al Qaeda.

On May 27th I wrote to Secretary of State George Shultz, expressing my appreciation for the "dignified, fair and open manner in which you and the President conducted the meeting." Despite disagreeing on the Saudi arms sale, I pledged my "continued support for this administration."

As soon as we walked outside, the full force of the national media confronted us. I vividly recall especially the aggressiveness and nastiness of Sam Donaldson of ABC. I was wearing my skullcap and during the media frenzy an Israeli reporter came over to me. Gesturing to some of the American media types, he said to me in Hebrew; "They're laughing at you." We went our way after a brief and innocuous press conference in which we said nothing against the Administration. The Senate soon passed the abbreviated bill. The following day the story of the meeting was in the *New York Times*.

A close friend and financial advisor called me shortly after I left the meeting to ask what had transpired. I recounted events to the best of my recollection. I mentioned Ivan Boesky's strange performance at the meeting, and told my friend that I thought I had heard somewhere that the financier might be in trouble with the Justice Department. I conjectured that Boesky had taken the position he did on the Saudi arms sale in an effort to curry favor with the Administration.

Though my friend was a serious and intelligent leader in the Orthodox community and the world of finance, he became irate and told me that I should never say such a thing about Ivan, whom, he characterized as an outstanding, upright citizen. One could agree or disagree with his opinion, but no one should ever accuse him of doing something dishonest. Unfortunately, history would shortly show that my friend was wrong.

Tom Dine

I first met Tom Dine, executive director of AIPAC, in 1980 while attending the organization's annual Policy Conference. In 1982, when I began to be more active in AIPAC, I became more familiar with him. Tom's most outstanding contributions to the pro-Israel cause were his leadership qualities as well as his great intellect. A tall, thin and rather elegant figure, Tom projected a demeanor and persona that commanded a great deal of respect in Washington and beyond.

Each year on the first evening of the Policy Conference, Dine would deliver a State of the Union-type address in which he covered the world as it related to the State of Israel and the Jewish people. Year after year, these speeches were well-thought-through and erudite analyses of the political situation and the challenges before the pro-Israel community that I found to be second to none. Certainly, these insightful analyses added immeasurably to Tom's growing stature.

During Tom's tenure as AIPAC's top professional, he transformed the pro-Israel lobby and enormously augmented its power and influence. During his tenure as the organization's top professional leader, AIPAC grew from 10,000 members to 55,000. During the same period the three billion dollars in U.S. foreign aid to Israel ceased being loans, and became grants. As Israel's cause prospered on Capitol Hill and in the White House, Tom Dine became known as the single most powerful lobbyist in Washington impacting on U.S. foreign policy.

After I became chairman of the Orthodox Union's Institute for Public Affairs in 1990, and decided that the OU should have a Washington internship program, I approached Tom and asked him if he would designate one of the then eighteen slots of the AIPAC summer internship specifically for an Orthodox Union student. The AIPAC summer internship was the only Washington-based Jewish political program available for college students at the time and its internships were much sought after plums. Tom assented to my request, even though it potentially opened up a Pandora's box for him, since every other Jewish organization might now request the same for its own interns. Yet I was not surprised that Tom agreed to what I had asked, since both of us knew that there was a chronic dearth of Orthodox involvement in AIPAC. One of the things most noticeable at meetings of the organization's executive board was that one saw very few skullcaps. As it turned out, our internship program proved to be a great success. The following year, I requested a second summer internship position, which Tom immediately granted to us.

Yet in 1993, AIPAC was under severe pressure due to self-inflicted wounds. Its president resigned after he was allegedly taped making "exaggerated claims" about the power of AIPAC to choose members of President Clinton's cabinet. Subsequently a vice president from Florida, was censored by the board for speaking his mind against the dovish policies of Israel's Prime Minister Yitzhak Rabin. It was in this background that an eruption occurred which quickly led to the resignation of Tom Dine.

David Landau, an Israeli journalist published a book entitled *Piety and Power: The World of Jewish Fundamentalism*, which contained some incendiary quotes from Tom Dine. Landau quoted Dine as saying, "I don't think mainstream Jews feel very comfortable with the ultra Orthodox. It is a class thing I suppose. Their image is 'smelly.' That's what I'd say now that you've got me thinking about it. Hasids and New York diamond dealers." He then went on to add the following, "United Jewish Appeal people have told me several times that they don't want to fly El Al because of 'those people,' but I fly El Al to Israel because it is direct. Yes, TWA flies direct too, but it is low class, like the Orthodox. Yes, that's still the image, still the poor immigrant image. That is the perception of a lot of people I mix with."

A story highlighting Dine's remarks soon appeared in the *New York Times*. Not surprisingly, there was an immediate outcry in the Orthodox community. Rabbi Moshe Sherer, the highly respected veteran leader of Agudath Israel of America, dispatched a blistering public letter to Tom in which he asserted that Tom's remarks showed he did not have the slightest understanding for or sensitivity toward the Orthodox community. Rabbi Sherer demanded that Tom make a public apology and a meaningful display of goodwill so as to restore a sense of mutual trust. He wrote to Tom, "Perhaps most importantly of all you owe yourself the opportunity to learn and to grow and to rise above your narrow stereotypes and destructive prejudices."

For my part, although I was shocked by the comments attributed to Tom, I did not believe that my long time friend was really anti-Orthodox. To the contrary I believed him then, and still do, to be a straight shooter who perhaps shot from the hip without thinking in an interview that was taken out of context.

I spoke to Tom a number of times during the days following the publication of the *Times* story. I expressed the belief that we could fight successfully at the board level to preserve Tom's job and that as a visibly Orthodox AIPAC leader I was prepared to help lead the battle. Tom decided to apologize to the national Orthodox community in the form of a public letter that he would address to me personally and which would be made available to

Parents, Rabbi Morris and Kate Ganchrow.

Paternal grandparents, Sarah and Mendel Ganchrow.

Age three with parents and maternal grandparents, Ann and Jacob Wallach.

Sheila's parents, Anna and Jack Weinreb.

Boyhood on Eastern Parkway in Brooklyn.

My bar mitzvah, 1950. My grandmother, Saul, Jacob, my mother, myself, and my father.

1954 Brooklyn Talmudical Academy Debating Team. L to R: 1st row, H. Burg, myself, Avi (Alan) Dershowitz, Steve (Shlomo) Riskin. Standing, J. Blau, J. Wohlberg, A. Cantor, E. Herschmann, H. Zuckerberg, T. Groner.

Busboy at the Hotel Fiurst, South Fallsburg, NY 1955. I am standing in the second row, sixth from left.

Yeshiva College 1958 graduation yearbook photo.

With my father, Rabbis Morris S. Ganchrow, during my early college days.

Dr. Isadore Snapper poses with the Beth-El Hospital house staff, June 1963. I am in first row, third from left.

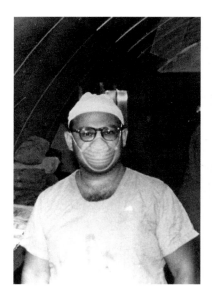

In the 45th Surgical Hosptial, Tay Ninh, Vietnam.

Our wedding day, June 26, 1962 at the Park Manor, Brooklyn.

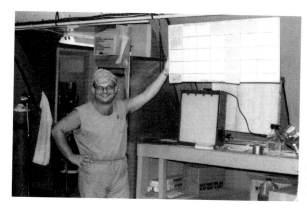

Getting ready for surgery at the 24th Evacuation Hospital, Long Binh, Vietnam.

Joining Rabbi Harold (Chico) Wasserman as we celebrate Succoth (Feast of Tabernacles) with an etrog (citrus) and Lulav (palm) at Long Binh.

Promoted to Major, I receive the Army Commendation Medal from Col. Hammond.

Rabbi Moses D. Tendler, myself, and the late Rabbis Yitzchak Isaac Tendler and Moshe Feinstein, of blessed memory, in the Tendler home circa 1974.

Presenting an award to Tom Dine at the Embassy of Israel in Washington, after he left AIPAC

After supporting President Reagan in his fight against the Contras, I was taken on a private tour of the White House that included the press room.

At our first
annual
HUVPAC
dinner.

Presenting a knitted
skullcap to Ehud
Barak in the Knesset

Jerusalem Mayor Ehud Olmert
at a dinner in Israel

With Prime Minister Shimon
Peres at the Orthodox Union
convention in Jerusalem

Rabbi Yisrael Meir Lau,
Chief Ashkenazi Rabbi of
Israel, and Rabbi Bakshi
Doron, Chief Sephardi
Rabbi of Israel, at a visit
to the Orthodox Union
Convention

Yossi Beilin and Gen-
eral Ariel Sharon
highlighted the 1994
OU Convention

With Israeli Prime Minister Bibi Netanyahu
at the OU convention in Jerusalem

the media. While I made suggestions regarding the wording of the letter, the sense of contrition it transmitted was purely Tom's.

The letter opened, "Dear Mendy: As a follow-up to our conversation today I want to express to you once again my deep regrets caused by my quotes . . .My entire life has been committed to promoting tolerance in ethnic, racial, and relgious relations." He then noted that during his thirteen years as AIPAC's executive director he had worked hard to bring members of the Orthodox community into the AIPAC fold by taking steps like making sure that only kosher meals would be served at AIPAC functions.

Tom explained in the letter that, four years earlier, he had spoken with Landau about the latter's research project on what he called "Jewish fundamentalism." Tom noted that he had spoken of his limited personal and professional experiences with Hasidim in the United States, Europe, and Israel. He had cited to Landau, in a highly positive manner, his interaction with Lubavitch, Satmar, Aguda and other Orthodox communities at the 1980 Democratic Presidential primary in New York and with Orthodox lobbyists on Capitol Hill over the years.

When Landau asked for examples of negative attitudes, perceptions, and stereotypes that he had encountered and heard, Dine went on to describe a variety of situations in which non-Orthodox Jews had expressed themselves negatively to him about the Orthodox. In relating these comments to Landau, Tom wrote, he was in no way describing or elaborating on his own feelings or views. Nevertheless, Dine noted, Landau had written his account of his remarks in a manner that made it appear as though Tom endorsed the offensive sentiments being expressed, when, in fact, he did not. "Frankly," Tom wrote to me in the open letter; ""I was stunned to see myself characterized in a way that is demeaning to the Hasidim, (ultra-Orthodox), etc." He then went on to assert that it remained his hope to attract larger segments of the Torah community, including the yeshiva and Hasidic worlds, to the cause and work of AIPAC. He concluded by taking full responsibility for his remarks and stating that he was deeply sorry for them.

Under normal circumstances I believe that, having offered a heartfelt apology, Tom would have survived this crisis. Certainly, I tried very hard to save his position, by speaking to other Orthodox leaders on his behalf. However, many members of the AIPAC Board of Directors wanted to get rid of Tom, and the truth was that I was not senior enough at AIPAC to have much impact. It seemed that the officers had concluded that Tom Dine had gotten too independent and too big for his britches, so to speak, and therefore had to go. The Landau incident smoothed the way for his departure. So, when it became clear that his open letter would not suffice to make amends, Tom submitted his resignation. AIPAC's managing director Howard Kohr became acting executive director, and a few years later, executive director. Howard has been outstanding as a leader and has grown in stature over the years.

Shortly after leaving AIPAC, Tom became a top executive at the U.S. Agency for International Development. The following year when the Orthodox Union came on one of its missions to Washington, we decided to honor Tom Dine at a dinner at the Israeli Embassy. Tom and his wife Joan were present, as was the Israeli Ambassador, Itamar Rabinovitch. As I spoke about Tom from the rostrum, describing him as a good human being and a warm personal friend, I noticed that there were tears in his eyes. I believe receiving that award from the Orthodox Union represented a vindication for him. For my part, it represented a statement that I never believed Tom Dine could have ever been involved in Orthodox bashing.

Humorous Incidents

HUVPAC's raison d'etre—ensuring the security of Israel—was a deadly serious one. Yet that did not mean there were not funny moments along the way. For example, at one of our dinners in Monsey, one of the United States senators who was scheduled to speak became noticeably inebriated. I had asked him to speak for ten or fifteen minutes. However, once at the podium, he rambled on and on, far beyond his allotted speaking time. Sitting by his side, I tugged at his suit, passing him notes asking that he wind up his remarks. Finally, he did so with an effort at a grand rhetorical flourish, proclaiming; "Therefore we must support the only friend we have in the Middle East—Egypt." For a moment, it was possible to hear a pin drop in the room and then the audience erupted in good-hearted laughter.

A few moments later it was time to introduce our second Senator, Wendell Ford of Kentucky. Ford realized that the crowd was quite tired of the long speech that his colleague had delivered. Therefore he stood up, discarded his speech and deadpanned with typical southern humor; "Ladies and Gentlemen, the doctor here came and asked me to make a good speech. I prepared one. Yet when I came to the hotel I couldn't find it. I looked in my room, in the lobby, in the men's room, but I still couldn't find it. When I came down here I realized that Senator X, who had just spoken, had taken my speech and delivered it. In any event, I want you to know that I will always be a friend of Israel; not because of any campaign contribution but because we have a moral commitment to help and preserve the only democracy in the Middle East." Ford sat down and the loud applause he received made clear that the audience appreciated the brevity of his remarks.

On another occasion that Senator Ford addressed HUVPAC, I remember him telling us a story about a hillbilly who had never been to a city before coming to town with his son. The two of them came into a building and saw an elevator, something neither had ever seen before. A fat and ugly woman walked into the elevator, the doors closed and she went up. The hillbilly was amazed by the whole procedure and stood in the lobby staring at the elevator. A few minutes later the elevator came back down to the lobby, the door opened and out came a slim and gorgeous young woman. The shocked hillbilly yelled to his son, "Jasper, go get your mama!"

There are no secrets in Washington. On one occasion, I was participating in a closed-door breakfast on the Hill, when the subject of the intellect of a senator who did not happen to be present came up. The chairman admonished the participants not to speak in derogatory terms about members of Congress. For my part, I was burning to express my opinion about this one member of the Senate whom I felt richly deserved criticism. But how could I make clear my distaste for that individual while honoring the admonition of the chairman not to use derogatory language? Eureka! I had an inspiration. Rising from my seat, I said, "Senator X is a perfect specimen in my field." The room erupted in laughter, as everyone knew that I was a proctologist. Four hours later, Senator Rudy Boschwitz (R-Minn), a good friend of mine, came over to me and said jovially, "Mendy, I hear that you called Senator X an a—hole." "I never used that term," I responded, with mock indignation.

One of the simple ways I often use to develop relationships with members of Congress is to give them a copy of a book such as *The Haj*, by Leon Uris. I would usually ask the senator or congressman if he or she had read the book, and usually the reply would be 'No'. Then I would say, "The next time you are on a plane, if you sit and read *The Haj*, you will understand the Arab mentality. I would like to send you a copy, if I may."

Often, I had difficulty getting hardcover copies of *The Haj*, so I would usually buy a paperback copy of the book and try to give it in person to the chief of staff of the congressman or senator in question. Many times, I would get a note or a call saying how much the senator or congressman loved the book. I recall once entering the subway of the United States Senate. Senator Harry Reid (D-Nevada) was coming out of the subway car, and upon glimpsing me, shouted as he rushed by, "Hey, Doc, I only read about thirty pages of the book, but it is wonderful. Thank you so much."

Senator Jay Rockefeller (D-W. Va.) is a scion of one of the wealthiest and best-known families in the United States. When the PAC decided to contribute funds to his re-election campaign, I felt a certain sense of euphoria. "I can't tell you how happy I am to be able to give a check to a Rockefeller," I said to him. Without pausing for a second, he responded, "I can't tell you how happy I am to take your money."

Senator Daniel Inouye (D.-Hawaii) has always been one of the most outspoken allies of the pro-Israel community on Capitol Hill. His empathy for our cause goes back a long way. As a young man, he had worked for a short time as a salesman for Israel Bonds. As is well known, Inouye lost his right arm in the U.S. Army during World War II. When I first met him, he told me that he had planned to be an orthopedic surgeon before entering the Army, but his injury during the war had, of necessity, changed his plans. Seeking to comfort him, I said: "You know, Senator, I always wanted to be a senator." He quickly answered, "But you can still be a senator. However, I can never be an orthopedic surgeon."

During the summer that Ari worked as an intern in Washington on the Senate committee under Senator Burdick, he sent daily letters to Elli in summer camp in Netanya, Israel. Besides brotherly chitchat, he enclosed major league baseball scores. Elli noticed that whenever the envelope might be from the committee it had been opened, inspected and re-sealed, assumedly by some security in Israel looking for who knows what.

The Beirut Marine Massacre

A tragic and poignant episode in which the medical imperative to do everything possible to save a life directly clashed with rather arcane foreign policy considerations in the aftermath of the appalling terrorist attack on the U.S. Marines base in Beirut. This terrorist attack occurred on a weekend in October 1983. In addition to the 243 Marines who were killed in the attack, hundreds more were injured, including many with severe burns. The Armed Forces immediately decided to evacuate all of the wounded to army hospitals in Germany. To carry out this intricate operation, the military mobilized transport planes with medical personnel from airbases in Germany and elsewhere and flew them to Beirut. It then moved the badly wounded soldiers, many of whom were in critical condition, on stretchers into the planes for the long flight back to Germany.

I was incensed. Why didn't the United States transfer these wounded to the closest well-equipped hospital that was available? Indeed there was one such medical facility only forty minutes away from Beirut by helicopter. The Rambam Hospital in Haifa, Israel, is not only a trauma center, which, unfortunately, has exhaustive experience dealing with war wounds, but it also has an excellent burn unit. Rambam was the obvious choice, if the armed forces were putting the highest priority on saving the lives of the brave servicemen. Unforgivably in my opinion, Washington's fear of the reaction of the Arab world to its sending wounded marines to Israel to be treated caused the State Department and the Defense Department to nix the Israeli offer to use their facilities.

On the Wednesday after the Beirut attack, I brought a HUVPAC delegation to Washington on a previously scheduled mission. During the course of that day, I made the same pitch to each and every senator and congressman with whom I spoke. As a surgeon in Vietnam I had written not only papers on colon injuries, but also an article that was published in the Armed Forces medical journal on emergency surgery in combat. In my paper, which was published in the Archives of Surgery on 240 colon injuries in Vietnam, I compared injuries from World War II, Korea and Vietnam and pointed out the sharp decrease in the number of GI's who died in surgery in Vietnam compared to the earlier conflicts. Aside from antibiotics and better anesthesia techniques the number one

factor resulting in decreased mortality in Vietnam was the short-
ened period of time from injury to proper treatment. The helicopter and front line hospitals made the difference and allowed greater
survival and less serious complications.

How many marines died unnecessarily because we insisted
on transferring critically wounded men to far off Germany instead of to nearby Haifa? How much increased pain and suffering did even those who survived endure due to that incompre-
hensible policy? There is no way to quantify those figures, yet in
my whole career as a political operator, I never saw such expressions of anger and frustration from members of Congress when
I laid out the facts to them. They became agitated and banged on
their desks, yelling to their assistants, "Get me the Pentagon/Get
me the Secretary of Defense!"

For my part, on that occasion, I felt that I was not there as a
lobbyist pleading a public policy issue. Rather, I was speaking as
an American who happened to be an expert on war wounds. I
took some consolation that quite evidently, the point I was trying
to make resonated so strongly in official Washington; namely
that there is no room for sensitivities concerning foreign policy
to get in the way of critically ill Americans receiving prompt
quality medical care. Not long after the Beirut massacre, the US
and Israel signed an agreement that should there ever be such a
future tragedy involving U.S. military forces in the Mideast the-
ater, all the medical facilities in Israel would be available and
would be utilized.

Leaving HUVPAC—And Coming Back Again

Among the most moving events for participants in HUVPAC
ocurred when members of Congress, came to our dinners and
cocktail parties and thanked HUVPAC for financial contributions they received for their election bids. On one such occasion,
freshman congressman John Lewis of Georgia arrived too late
for our party. He joined us on our bus just as we were about to
leave for Washington National Airport, to thank us with evident
deep conviction for our support. Over the years, many HUVPAC
members who were on the bus that evening have reminded me
emotionally of that event.

As the 1980's turned into the 90's, running HUVPAC as well
as becoming far more active in the work of the Orthodox Union

was beginning to take too much of my time. All of my political work was definitely impinging on my medical practice. Sometimes, I would be required to sit in the operating room between cases and call Washington. Similarly in my office I would use all the time in-between patients to handle PAC business. Yet there were occasions when my political activities stood me in good stead on the professional front. For example, on one occasion I was sitting in my office with a landlord and a lawyer negotiating a lease for a medical building that our group of doctors was considering moving into. By then I had become the senior partner. Given the importance of the meeting, I told the secretaries to please not disturb me. Nevertheless, midway in our deliberations, a secretary buzzed me and said apologetically, "Dr. Ganchrow, I know you told me not to disturb you, but the White House is on the telephone and would like to speak to you." I asked her to put the call through and excused myself. Someone in the White House was calling me about a meeting I had requested. I could see that the two gentlemen with whom I was sitting were quite impressed.

About three minutes into the phone conversation the intercom bellowed again, "Dr. Ganchrow I know you are on the phone with the White House but Senator Arlen Spector of Pennsylvania is on the telephone." I said, "Please tell him I am on the phone with the White House and will call him back." My visitors appeared incredulous.

I also had some embarrassing episodes as well, as a result of my HUVPAC activities. One involved an appointment that I had with Senator Connie Mack of Florida. HUVPAC had been a supporter of Mack's since his days in the House of Representatives. On a personal level, Connie, the grandson of the great Philadelphia A's owner-manager, was a true mensch. A few days after he assumed his Senate seat, I had made an appointment to see him in his new office. Upon arriving, I was told by his secretary that a scheduling mistake had been made. Evidently, a member of the diplomatic corps was sitting in Connie's office during the time allotted to me and she asked if I could come back in an hour or so. Just then Connie walked through the front door. When he found out what had happened, he apologized profusely and said that he would see me immediately. The diplomat could wait while he and I talked.

I was flattered, but asked him which country the diplomat

represented. Connie replied, "He is the ambassador to Israel." I was totally embarrassed and suggested that we cancel our meeting since I did not want to be the cause of a snub to the Israeli ambassador and, in any case, was confident that the ambassador would touch upon the same issues I was going to bring up. Nevertheless, Connie insisted on taking me in to introduce me to the ambassador and asking him to wait a few minutes while we spoke. He then forced me to go through the entire legislative agenda, which I hurried through as rapidly as possible, before he finally went out to his meeting with the ambassador.

The second incident also involved Connie Mack. On that particular occasion I had traveled to Washington on my own for a day to lobby as many senators as possible on behalf of the loan guarantees for Israel. I had made approximately ten appointments during the course of a long day that began at 9AM. To my chagrin, I found out that the dovish group, Americans for Peace Now (APN), had chosen that very day to bring their lay people to Washington to lobby against the loan guarantees because they opposed the settlement policy of the Israeli government.

Representatives of APN appeared to be all over the Capitol. I had never before encountered Jews lobbying against Israel. Every time I crossed their path in the corridors of Congress, my blood boiled. I was sitting alone in the waiting room at the end of the day, waiting for my appointment with Senator Connie Mack, when a member of Americans for Peace Now came into the room. His name card indicated he was a "Rabbi." Since he was not wearing a skullcap I assumed he was not Orthodox, but he was wearing a large APN pin. The rabbi was scheduled to see Saul Singer, then Connie Mack's chief of staff, during the same period of time that I was to see the Senator. Saul now lives in Israel and writes for the *Jerusalem Post*. He is married to Wendy Singer who is in charge of the AIPAC office in Jerusalem. Saul's brother had died in the service of the Israeli army in Lebanon.

I turned to the Peace Now rabbi and asked, "Do you, by chance, have an additional pin for me?"

He answered, "No, but why would you want one?"

I lost my cool: "When I go back to Monsey I would like to show my friends what a self-hating Jew wears."

He looked at me gravely but did not lose his temper. Then he said, "I see you are wearing a kippah serugah, a knitted skullcap, and I know you are extremely dedicated and believe in what you are advocating, but I want you to know that I served in the Israeli army in 1948, 1956, and 1967 and believe the settlements are an impediment. I do not want my children and grandchildren to die for them." Momentarily, I could not think of a proper response and deeply regretted my intemperate remark. That incident reminded me that American Jewry is not a monolithic community.

Another example of close mindedness comes to mind, although, in this case, it was not on my own part. One of the major projects that the United States and Israel were working on together was the development of the Lavi fighter plane. It was to be a state of the art aircraft but it was extremely expensive. A controversy arose as to whether Israel could afford the price of these planes. It appeared that the Jewish state would have to forego many armaments necessary for her survival in order to invest in the Lavi. I was fortunate that Sheila's cousin was an official of the Israel aircraft industry and thus we had an opportunity to see a prototype of the plane at the company's hangar outside its plant near Ben-Gurion Aiport.

A decision needed to be made by the Defense Department in Washington about whether or not to proceed together with Israel in building the plane. Secretary of Defense Casper Weinberger placed the entire controversy into the hands of Dov Zackheim, one of his deputy secretaries, who studied both sides and finally decided against green-lighting the project. A tremendous amount of pressure was placed on Zackheim. Even though he is Orthodox, some in our community went so far as to label him a self-hating Jew and harass him even in his own synagogue. When I took HUVPAC to Washington that year I arranged for Dov to give our members a briefing. I then received a call from friends who were upset with me for taking the PAC to listen to someone they considered "unfriendly." I explained that since we were going to have to lobby Congress on the issue of the Lavi, it was important we hear both points of view.

It was quite clear when he spoke to HUVPAC that Zackheim was not only sincere but extremely knowledgeable on the Lavi and about Israel's overall defense needs. I was quite upset the way he was being talked about, because it was evident he genuinely believed that his position against building the plane was best for Israel's security. It did not take too much longer for officials in the Defense establishment in Israel to agree publicly that Zackheim had made the right decision.

Today Zackheim is the Comptroller in the Defense Department under Secretary Donald Rumsfeld. Dov's son happens to be a friend of my son Elliot.

As my twelfth year in HUVPAC came to an end and it became obvious that I would soon become president of the Orthodox Union, I tried very hard to find other people to take over the leadership of the PAC. In truth, I was getting tired of doing the same routine over and over and I was concerned there might be a conflict between the workings of the PAC, including endorsing and giving money to candidates, and serving as president of the Orthodox Union. Unfortunately there were no takers and HUVPAC went into hibernation for six years until 2001, when I completed my presidency at the OU.

Not only did I come back to HUVPAC refreshed, but as we started calling some of our old friends in Congress and the many new people elected while the PAC was on hiatus, it became quite clear to me the need for our existence was as great, if not greater, than it ever had been. Certainly, it has become evident, especially since the eruption of the new Palestinian intifada that the issues that impelled HUVPAC in the 1980's and early 90's have not discernibly changed. Arafat still seeks to destroy Israel, and the Europeans and the U.N. quite evidently wish Israel would disappear. Although President Bush, his National Security Adviser Condaleeza Rice and the Defense Department have been wonderful, little appears to have changed in the Arabist attitudes at the State Department.

In May, 2002, HUVPAC returned to winning form; helping to win an election upset that brought back memories for many of us of the glory days of Dick Durbin twenty years earlier. Together with other pro-Israel PACs and activists, we helped to defeat Earl Hilliard, a black Democrat who was a five-term congressman in the primary in the ninth District of Alabama. We replaced him with Artur Davis, a black Harvard-educated lawyer who was supportive of our issues. For his part, Hilliard had voted against many pro-Israel resolutions and had visited with Muammar Kaddafi in Libya. Upon hearing the news of Davis' victory, a feeling of great joy encompassed me. We repeated that success soon after by defeating Congresswoman Cynthia McKinney in her primary and replaced her with Judge Denise Majette. To many young people who did not live through the 1982-84-86 years, the Davis and Majette races transformed them into true believers. I look forward in the coming years to rebuilding HUVPAC into a political force to be reckoned with on Capitol Hill. Hopefully a new generation of activists can be trained to lead the PAC in the future.

In the final analysis, the imperative for the pro-Israel community to support our friends in Congress remains an absolute necessity if we are to ensure continuing U.S. support of Israel. Given that enduring reality, pro-Israel PAC's will need to be around for a long time to come.

In the 2002 elections HUVPAC was involved in twenty two Senate races and was victorious in eighteen and won forty two of forty six House races.

CHAPTER SIX
My Presidency at the Orthodox Union

I t is estimated that from ten to fifteen percent of the six million American Jews in America are Orthodox. Of this population, fifty to sixty percent could be considered "modern Orthodox" or "centrist." Modern Orthodox Jews, unlike so-called ultra-Orthodox or Hasidic Jews, are characterized by a worldview that includes modern dress, a stress on obtaining secular education, involvement in the general community and support of the State of Israel, but intertwined with all of this is a strict adherence to Torah law—both oral and written.

The Orthodox community, like the overall Jewish community, is represented by a myriad of organizations of varying sizes and importance. None comes close in size and influence to the Union of Orthodox Jewish Congregations of America, which is more often referred to as the "Orthodox Union" (OU) or simply as "the Union."

In 1997, the late Saul Bernstein published a wonderful book in honor of the celebration of the 100th anniversary of the foundation of the Orthodox Union entitled *Centenary Portrayal*. Bernstein's commemorative volume contained compelling insights into the condition and outlook of American Orthodox Jewry in the early years of the 20th century and how they have evolved over the decades. He noted that many Jewish immigrants to the new land of America at the turn of the century thrust aside their traditional patterns of observance of Judaism because of economic pressure to work on the Sabbath or the lack of religious schools and other institutions. It was not uncommon in the first half of the 20th century for Orthodox synagogues to change their affiliation to the then-dominant Reform movement. Given these trends, many predicted that Orthodoxy would not be able to survive in America.

In 1877, one of the great heroes of American Orthodoxy arrived in the United States from Manchester, England. Dr. Henry Pereira Mendes, a rabbi and physician, was the single most important personality in sustaining Orthodoxy in America at the close of the old century and the first decades of the new one. Concerned that halachic Judaism was adrift in America and that its exacting standards were not being maintained, Dr. Mendes issued a call to Orthodox congregations around the country to join together in an umbrella organization. His goal was to buttress and reinforce each other in their common endeavor to sustain Orthodoxy in the strange new world of the *goldyne medina* (golden land). On June 8, 1898, forty seven congregations from eleven states joined together to form the Union of Orthodox Jewish Organizations, with a stated purpose "to defend the rights of Orthodox Jews" and "to speak with authority in the name of Orthodox Jews."

Dr. Mendes was elected as the Union's first president and served for sixteen years. By sheer determination and force of personality over the years he patiently built a solid organization with a compelling vision that was to spearhead the revival of American Orthodoxy in the 20th century. Although it took nearly 100 years for some of his ideas to be realized, everything we are about today as an organization and a community can be traced to Dr. Mendes' vision and perseverance.

In addition to founding the Orthodox Union, Dr. Mendes also served as the first rabbi of the Spanish-Portuguese Synagogue. He was also the founder of the Jewish Theological Seminary, which was originally an Orthodox rabbinic seminary dedicated to training English speaking Rabbis. Only after running into severe financial difficulties did it change into a Conservative institution.

Dr. Mendes spoke out with fervor against the growing Reform movement, which he contended was trampling the central tenets of Torah Judaism, as well as the Conservative movement, which he believed was following the footsteps of Reform in defiling the central tenets of the Jewish faith, albeit in a more gradual and less open way. That has remained our position on the "liberal" Jewish movements until today.

During the first decades of the 20th century, other centrist

Orthodox organizations came into being, but none were able to challenge the preeminence of the OU. The Union's growth paralleled that of Yeshiva University; many of whose graduates became the core supporters of the Union. Although, over the years, there were rare moments of tension or miscommunication between the Union and YU, the outlook, priorities and even the personnel of these institutions were largely the same.

After World War II, the portion of the Orthodox community that adhered to Agudath Israel and the Hasidic movements attained greater prominence than they had during the early decades of the 20th century. Although these groups manifested the same pious adherence to Torah and halacha as did the centrists, they discouraged their young people from receiving a secular education. Also, while they expressed undying love and devotion to the land and people of Israel, support for Zionism and the State of Israel was antithetical to their form of Judaism. For these reasons, a number of efforts through the early years to merge the OU with Aguda all failed to accomplish their goal.

In 1924, the Union inaugurated a service that was to become its most distinctive contribution to Orthodox Jewish life; a not-for-profit standard of kashruth supervision, free of corruption and the profit motive. The Heinz Corporation was the first company to place an OU label on its products, signifying that they are kosher according to the highest rabbinical standards. In the mid 1990's, close to 100,000 products produced by a panoply of firms in more than 3000 plants in over sixty countries carried the OU label. Thus observant Jews could be confident that they had a web of food stores, hotels and airlines throughout the world where they could feel confident to find kosher products under OU supervision. The OU kashruth department was a source of considerable revenue for the entire Union, and every penny made by the department over and above expenses was plowed back into the Orthodox community for social and religious projects.

Another key department of the Union, the famed National Conference of Synagogue Youth (NSCY), was created in 1954 and rapidly became a force leading thousands of teenagers to make a decision to return to Torah standards in their personal lives.

I personally knew very little of the Union and had an even lesser interest until 1984, when my former roommate in college, Shimmy Kwestel, decided to run for the presidency of the Union. Our friendship dated back to 1954 when we entered the freshman class of Brooklyn Talmudic Academy together, but the connection between our families goes back much further than that; our fathers were classmates at Yeshiva Chaim Berlin in Brooklyn. Shimmy, who became a partner in the top flight Manhattan law firm of Kaye Scholer, was and is a straight shooter and a person of warmth and compassion. So, given my close friendship with Shimmy, it was natural that I would become interested in the OU when he assumed its presidency.

I was not a novice at that point in organizational life; not only had I been president of my local synagogue and day school, but my reputation in the pro-Israel community was growing thanks to my almost instant success at HUVPAC. Therefore, although I had no previous connection with the Union I was elected as an associate vice president. At the same time, my two boys, Ari and Elli, were becoming NCSY leaders in our Monsey region. The involvement of my sons served as a further incentive to me to do what I could to improve the overall operation of the NCSY's parent body, the Orthodox Union.

Although I was impressed by all that NCSY was accomplishing in keeping young people faithful to Torah principles and was also proud of the work that two other arms of the OU, Yachad and Our Way, were doing with the developmentally disabled and deaf, my overall impression of the Union was of a sleeping giant. It seemed to me that the OU had enormous unrealized potential, not only within the Orthodox community, but also in society at large.

In line with my involvement with AIPAC and HUVPAC, it is not surprising that my primary interest in the OU in those years lay in raising its all-too-modest profile in the arena of public affairs. I began to work actively with the Union's Public Affairs Committee chaired by my good friend Sandy Eisenstat. Sandy, who has an outgoing personality and a terrific sense of humor, was one of the few OU leaders I knew at the time who was extremely sophisticated politically. Sandy was involved in the work of AIPAC as well as the OU, and knew his way around Washington very well. Under Sandy's guidance, the Union, which hitherto had a low political profile, began taking groups of lay leaders to Washington on a regular basis, for meetings with senators, congressmen, as well as members of the Reagan Administration. Our missions would invariably stop also at the Israeli Embassy for a session with the ambassador and other key officials.

When Sandy decided for personal reasons to leave his OU activities, I took up the chairmanship of the Public Affairs Committee. Within four years I had progressed to a vice presidency of the Union, a testament to my growing involvement in Union activities.

It was quickly apparent that the new burst of political energy in the Orthodox community was having an effect. In 1986, I wrote an op-ed piece in the *Jerusalem Post* in which I commented on the growing power and involvement of the Orthodox community in national politics. I noted, for example, that the OU had recently held a Congressional breakfast at which every member of the New York Congressional delegation had made an appearance. On *Yom Hashoah* (Holocaust Martyrs' and Heroes' Remembrance Day), we sent a mission to Washington for briefings in the White House and on the Hill. We had the pleasure that day of sitting in the Senate galleries to witness that body reject a U.S. arms package for Saudi Arabia. Another high point of that glorious day was that fourteen senators stopped by to make appearances during our glatt kosher luncheon in the Senate dining room. After that, we held a minyan for afternoon prayers. I could see that many participants appeared deeply moved to be reciting their prayers in that temple of American democracy; powerfully affirming for them the complete compatibility their dual role as committed Jews who were also deeply patriotic Americans.

During the luncheon, I noticed a man who looked familiar, but whose name I could not recall. It turned out he was an Israeli diplomat who happened to be in the Senate that afternoon to watch the debate over the Saudi arms package. He had been intrigued to see a large contingent of skullcapped individuals and had simply followed us to lunch. The Israeli told me he was amazed and gratified that so many senators would take time out from their busy day to join us in a luncheon—all for the sake of strengthening the U.S./Israel relationship. In May 1988, I asked two friends of mine, Congressman Richard Durbin (D.-IL) and Congressman Bill Schuette (R.-MI) to run mock lobbying sessions for the 200 members of our OU mission to Washington. These sessions were invaluable in training our activists in the art of meeting with members of Congress.

On September 25, 1990, the OU was welcomed by President George H.W. Bush into the Oval Office to present him with a resolution in honor of Yom Kippur. OU President Sidney Kwestel expressed our support for Bush's Persian Gulf policy. I thanked him for his key role in freeing and transferring Ethiopian Jews to Israel. The President responded that we should never rest until all Ethiopian Jews were safe in Israel.

After the Gulf War, we had the opportunity to meet with President Bush again. Although he was upset over pro-Israel lobbying for loan guarantees during Israeli settlement activity, he desired to highlight our support for his civil rights position against quotas (HR-1). The OU was the only Jewish group invited to the White House during this period. During our visit in the Roosevelt Room, we discussed our support for Israel and for loan guarantees in addition to civil rights issues.

After the President's statements, he opened the floor for questions. Responding to queries without notes, President Bush seemed well-prepared for all questions. There was but one exception. Rhoda Miller, sitting on my left, became emotional as she asked her question. The President, sitting on my right, leaned over and reassured her not to be nervous. She replied, "Mr. President, I am not nervous. Today on our way from the airport I saw the flag of Syria waving as part of the Gulf War Coalition. Mr. President, they are harboring the killers of my husband, Joseph Miller, [the Union's treasurer] who died on Pan-Am 103. When are we going to see justice done?"

The President was visibly moved, and gave her a hug before he left, assuring her that the perpetrators would be punished.

Sheila and I were always impressed with the warmth, dignity, and sincerity President Bush displayed during our brief meetings.

Despite the heightened profile of the Public Affairs Committee, I felt very strongly that we needed a full-time presence in Washington to press our agenda and heighten the OU's public policy profile. I made this case forcefully to President Kwestel and was eventually able to convince him to create an Institute for Public Affairs (IPA). Shimmy appointed Shelly Rudoff as the IPA's chairman. When Rudoff became president of the Union a year or so later, I was made both a senior vice president and chairman of the IPA.

I focused considerable energy during the next several years on the creation of an internship program at the IPA, in order to bring politically attuned orthodox college students more directly into the political process. During the first few summers, I arranged with Tom Dine's help for our interns to work at AIPAC in Washington. After the program showed its worth, we began placing interns in the offices of senators and congressmen with whom I and other OU leaders had developed personal relationships.

During the first few years, I did the interviewing and selection of the students myself. The students I met were extremely qualified; most had 3.8 to 4.0 grade averages and were very motivated to work on behalf of the Jewish community. Yet since there was only one position available during the first year and two positions during the second year, I found it difficult to choose the winning candidates and very frustrating to turn down so many superbly qualified people. By the fourth year the number of internships we could offer increased, but so did the number of applicants. No longer wanting this particular responsibility, I therefore created an academic admissions committee to make the selections. By the year 2000, the program had approximately fifty interns a year and was still growing. Perhaps my greatest contribution to the Union was conceiving and creating this internship program.

An episode during my chairmanship of the IPA that proved to many at the OU that an organization like ours could wield significant clout through a campaign of public advocacy was our success in convincing Baxter Labs to rescind plans they had already announced to build a plant in Syria. Critics claimed it might be used to produce chemical weapons (see Baxter Labs chapter). To realize that we had the power to force a major corporation like Baxter to reverse course and walk away from a business deal that would have netted it tens of millions of dollars was both exhilarating and confidence enhancing.

The more I became involved in the work of the OU, the more I realized that I hoped to eventually become president of the organization. However, since I was not a member of the tight coterie of leaders from the orthodox community of Queens who tended to dominate the OU lay leadership (although there were also many former presidents and other officers from Manhattan and elsewhere), I realized I could only become president if I worked hard on behalf of the OU for many years and produced results. To that end, I faithfully attended late afternoon meetings of OU committees in Manhattan, even though it required curtailing many of my afternoon surgical cases in Rockland County. I was prepared to make financial sacrifices to achieve my goal of heading the OU.

By 1990 Shelly Rudoff had become Kwestel's successor and I had risen to the position of senior vice president. Under our constitution a president cannot serve for more than three two-year terms. Rudoff decided for personal reasons that he would not seek a third two-year term in November 1994. I appeared to have the inside track for the presidency that year, but I had a very serious decision to make. If I was truly serious about becoming president of the OU, I would only be able to do it on a full-time basis. My predecessors as president had been lay people; mostly high-powered Manhattan lawyers who had left the day-to-day administration of the Union to the professional staff. Unlike them, however, I had no New York office or apartment and no New York secretary to manage my meetings. I realized that the demands of a high-pressure surgical practice like my own were simply incompatible with assuming the presidency of the Union on a full-time basis, but that without such a commitment I could not hope to be successful as president. I would have to make a choice.

I was fifty seven years old as I wrestled with this difficult decision. I was the senior partner in a four-man surgical group and my medical practice was thriving. On the other hand I wasn't enjoying medicine as much as I had in the past. I still relished being in the operating room and doing colonoscopies and other challenging surgical procedures, especially cancer cases, but I was frankly fed up with dealing with paperwork and insurance companies. I was also no longer enjoying my interaction with my partners. The convivial "us against the world" camaraderie of the original partners—Doctors Cavanaugh, Adler, Moscarella and I, was long gone, to be replaced by an often tense and contentious relationship between myself and some of my more recent partners.

The changed atmosphere between us had a lot to do with the advent of HMOs, which brought about a slow but steady decline in our income. Sometimes things would reach a breaking point and the partners would lock themselves in a room and ventilate their frustrations until they managed to work out an agreement. Still, every year there were more difficulties with insurance companies, which were making it ever more difficult for us to provide the highest quality medical treatment for every patient. For my part, I was beginning to feel life was too short and precious for this kind of aggravation.

I recall one case in particular that brought those feelings to a head. A patient was scheduled for major rectal cancer surgery and probable removal of a significant portion of his liver. I requested from the insurance company that the man be approved for a single-day pre-operative admission for testing and preparation. My nurse called the insurance company and reported back that they had denied our request. Stunned, I picked up the phone myself to speak with the physician reviewer. After keeping me on hold for twenty minutes, he got on the phone and informed me that, based on a single paper in a recent surgical journal, my request would not be honored. I responded that I could supply a much-larger list of recent papers, showing the need for greater testing and pre-op preparation. He refused to budge.

Furious that the insurance company was clearly risking a patient's medical well-being because of dollars and cents consider-ations, I shouted at the bean-counter on the other end of the line. If my patient were to develop an infection or be otherwise physically harmed due to the insurance company's policies and were to sue the company, I would certainly testify on his behalf, I yelled. The reviewer raised his voice in return, saying he con-sidered my words threatening and that I should be aware that the conversation was being recorded. Eventually, we both calmed down, and he said he wanted to give me a piece of friendly advice. Pointing out that he himself was not an accountant, but rather a surgeon in his mid-fifties like myself, he said that in his opinion the future would be with the HMO's. If I wanted to conclude my career in comfortable fashion, I should consider taking a position like he had done.

Over and above these insurance-related miseries, I was find-ing it increasingly difficult and ever more painful to close my fingers around medical instruments in the operating room. I was diagnosed with psoriatic arthritis, as well as tendonitis of the hand and carpel tunnel syndrome. As it turned out later, within six months or so of my leaving my practice, I developed Meniere's syndrome of my left ear with tinnitus and a progressive deafness which today has left me without most hearing on my left side.

These physical infirmities plus a melanoma removed in 1994 made me more aware of my mortality. I was always conscious of the fact that my father had passed away at the age of fifty seven and I had long believed that fifty seven years was my allotted time on this earth as well. As I got closer to that age, I began to believe that if G-d were to give me the blessing of additional time beyond that age, I would be honor bound to dedicate my time and energy to working on behalf of the Jewish community. Putting all these factors together, and especially in light of my physical condition, I decided that the best thing I could do with the remainder of my working life was to take on the challenge of the presidency of the Orthodox Union and to do that in a full-time capacity.

Of course, I was aware that the OU presidency was a non-paying position. Sheila and I examined our finances and thought long and hard about whether I could afford to interrupt the income stream my medical practice afforded us. We finally decided we could indeed do so without significantly changing our lifestyle. Only Elli, our youngest son, was still in school and we had already put aside the funds needed to cover his educational expenses. Yes, leaving my medical practice years before I had originally expected would mean that Sheila and I would perhaps have a less lavish retirement than we could have if I were to grit my teeth and stay with my medical practice. Yet both my dear wife and I concurred that service to the community and my own peace of mind mattered far more to us than our bank account balance. Having finally reached a decision and feeling that I was taking the weight of the world off my shoulders, I happily informed my partners that I would soon be retiring from the practice.

Now that I had decided to go for the OU presidency, I had to deal with the reality that not everyone at the Union was thrilled about the prospect of my becoming president in November 1994. As mentioned, I was not a member of the inner circle that had dominated the Union leadership for so long. Many Union old timers—both professionals and lay leaders—were anxious about what having me in the office as a full-time, hands-on president would portend for the organization—and for their own positions as well. Other officers complained that I was too focused on pro-Israel political activism and would not give enough time and energy to other Union programs.

More than a year before I was selected as president, secret meetings were being held by OU insiders to consider how they might block my looming ascendancy. The theme of these efforts was clearly ABG or "Anyone but Ganchrow." During the spring of 1993, when I served as chairman of the national dinner, a senior lay leader was overheard by a friend of mine telling the Union president in a forceful tone that he had "made a great mistake in highlighting Ganchrow," since it was obvious that my serving as the chairman of a successful dinner would give me a major boost toward becoming president. One close friend confided in me that highly placed people in the national office told him he should work for my defeat as president because I was not "religious enough." That seemed a particularly cheap shot, given that I had devoted my life to upholding kashruth and Yiddishkeit, and indeed that I was sometimes criticized for being too rigid in upholding traditions.

Despite this grumbling, I was never seriously worried that I would be denied the presidency. As the old adage says, "You can't beat somebody with nobody," and those who objected to my candidacy had no credible candidate to run against me. In the end, despite the objections to my candidacy, I ran unopposed. A former president was asked to run, but he declined. Other key lay leaders could not or would not take the time from their practice or business.

As in any organization, large or small, there are often clashes of personalities and interests. Nevertheless other than some minor glitches I looked forward with excitement to assuming my new position, and outlining and implementing a vision to revitalize the OU. I was not interested in winning a popularity contest, but rather being an effective president who would provide strong leadership for the Union and American orthodoxy.

Some of the problems I faced included an aborted attempt to divide the presidency into two components, one for domestic and the other for international issues. This attempt to dilute the office during the pre-convention period was defeated quickly. During this time a new Executive Vice President, Rabbi Raphael Butler was promoted from his position as National Director of NCSY. Although I had little or no consultative imput in this choice, I vowed to work with him once I would take office.

Perhaps if I had been given a greater voice in the 1994 convention, I would have made some suggestions regarding the scheduling of my inaugural address, which took place after midnight.

I was determined to appoint new chairmen for the various commissions based upon competency, my relationship with them and their commitment to working with me to carry out the extensive agenda that I enunciated in my inaugural address. I resisted attempts to either clear my appointments with the outoing administration or to announce their appointments until after the convention.

I had previously asked Marcel Weber to become chairman of the board of directors. Much later, that was proven to have been a very wise move on my part as Marcel's loyalty, intellect, and calm, analytic mind proved an enormous support for me during the Lanner affair.

For the chairmanship of NCSY, I turned to Tzvi Friedman of Baltimore, a close friend and a young dynamo with experience in the leadership of AIPAC and Federation. I chose another friend long active in the Jewish community, Professor Richard Stone of Columbia Law School, as chairman of the IPA. Many were surprised at the appointment of Shimmy Kwestel as the chairman of kashruth; a position he fulfilled with great integrity and dedication.

For the first five and one-half years the relationship between Rabbi Butler and myself deepened and our mutual trust and respect grew. As time went along, I developed considerable affection for Rafi and invited him to Ganchrow family *simchas* (celebrations). In a certain way, we were symbiotically connected. Our offices were next to each other. We spent hours together every workday and, in the end, much of what I was able to achieve as president, was due to the fact that Rafi and I learned how to work together effectively.

As is well known, in the wake of the revelations of the Lanner affair in 2000, I came to the reluctant conclusion that as the scandal increased in scope at the end of the day there would need to be major changes in the top professional positions at the OU if the organization was to regain its credibility. Some of Rafi's supporters accused me of undermining him for personal reasons, but that was completely untrue. As noted, over the years I had come to like and respect Rafi Butler and to positively evaluate the job he had done as executive vice president. Nevertheless, Rafi was the Union's top professional leader at the time of the Lanner debacle, and, sadly but unavoidably, he and other top professionals would have to be held accountable as those events took place on their watch. There was nothing personal in that judgment.

To return for a moment to my installation as president of the Union at the 1994 convention, my inaugural speech may have been delayed until after midnight, yet I still managed to make it a substantive one. I outlined a series of plans during that address which I believed would be necessary if the OU was to be revitalized, and which, in fact, I largely managed to bring to realization during my three terms as president. Among the priorities I articulated from the podium that night were the opening of a permanent OU office in Washington, the creation of a public relations department and a wholesale revamping of the synagogue services department. Overall, I made it unmistakably clear that I wanted the Union to become a more aggressive and proactive political voice for the Orthodox community.

Some were less than enthusiastic at what they no doubt considered to be an overly optimistic agenda. Yet many of my staunchest critics would change their tune over the next few years as they came to acknowledge the positive impact of the reforms I instituted. They would give me a sustained standing ovation for my success in changing the face of the Union when I was honored with the Keter Shem Tov award at the annual dinner in May 2000, just over a month before the Lanner story exploded in the *Jewish Week*.

For example, I vividly remember the expressions of incredulity on the faces of many in our kashruth department at the 1994 convention when I proposed the creation of a kashruth internship program for rabbinical students to address what I portrayed as a chronic "need to inspire a new generation of rabbanim to consider a career in kashruth." It took two years to implement my internship program, which has since become a magnet for rabbinical students from throughout the world.

I also realized the skepticism when I intoned in my inaugural address; "Public relations must be a significant element in our future plans," and promised that under my presidency the OU would set up a top flight PR department headed by a savvy professional. I had been aware of the importance of message and image ever since the day when Dr. Jim Ferguson of the Ferguson Clinic explained to me that I would have to "sell Ganchrow" if I was going to succeed in creating a successful medical practice. Now my goal was to "sell the OU." But many in the Orthodox world had traditionally been contemptuous of the whole field of public relations; feeling that everything would come out all right if we remained faithful to "Torah true" values. Perhaps so, but that approach had not prevented many Americans—and many Jews as well—from forming totally false conceptions of what

Orthodoxy and the Orthodox lifestyle are all about. It was time we came into the modern world in terms of our approach to PR.

Unbelievably, the Orthodox Union, with a multi-million dollar budget the year I took over, did not have a single staff person dedicated to public relations. By the time I finished my presidency six years later, our budget had more than doubled and we had created a first-rate public relations department under the chairmanship of Stan Steinreich—himself director of public relations for a major nationwide firm. In addition, we had put in place a dedicated and highly competent three-person professional department, headed by Sharyn Perlman, a savvy wordsmith with a deep personal dedication to *yiddishkeit*.

Mike Cohen, a sports writer who initially signed on as an assistant public relations director, led us into the modern world of the Internet. Our new website with the URL http://www.ou.org was launched in August 1996 and quickly became the premier website for the Orthodox world. Thousands of organizations and synagogues from over sixty countries made use of the offerings available on our website—including books, tapes and programs—within a few months of its launch. A state of the art communications center was established for our NCSY advisors and rabbis, as well as for the kashruth department. In addition, by the end of my presidency, I instituted periodic e-mail newsletters, which we sent to tens of thousands of subscribers. Sadly, after I left the Union, the Department of Public Relations soon had no employees.

My modus operandi as president was to be actively and intimately involved in every aspect of the Union's growth. I resisted the temptation to micromanage, but every day toured the Union's office and acted as a cheerleader and coach, greeting the staff, asking questions and making suggestions. I would often write ideas on little slips of paper, which I just as often managed to lose. Still, my mind is well organized and, fixated as I am on programs and goals, I rarely forgot what I had written on those lost pieces of paper.

I am also a nudge, and when I conceive a plan, I like to see it executed immediately. If, during my time at the OU I suggested that we get out a press release on a certain topic and it was not done promptly, I would be quite vocal in making my displeasure known. But I never engaged in yelling or cursing. I could be exacting, but I also made it a point to thank every staff person for even the smallest task done properly and to treat every employee, without regard to rank, with courtesy and dignity. Overall, I think I was a good executive who brought out the best in our people.

I approached the building of the Union methodically. From the beginning, public relations was a central preoccupation of mine, because I realized that if the world does not know that you accomplished something, then, in effect it did not really occur. I visited the Public Relations Department of Yeshiva University to see first hand my old friend Sam Hartstein, a real pro and the individual responsible for Yeshiva's positive image. By talking to Sam and others I quickly came to the conclusion that the methods traditionally used by the OU, namely to outsource with a consultant on a particular story, was neither efficient nor effective. So I perservered for the creation of our own PR department and soon we were showing up a lot more in both the Anglo-Jewish media, the *New York Times* and on television.

I always believed we could not present ourselves as a force on the international Jewish scene until we held a convention in Israel. Not everyone agreed, but I pushed hard for it and our first-ever Orthodox Union convention in Israel was held in January 1996—attracting 335 delegates from twenty states. In addition to arranging for our delegates to tour the usual tourist sites, we spent a great deal of time in Judea and Samaria, including the Jewish community of Hebron, as well as visiting the newly opened tunnel alongside the *Kotel* (Western Wall). We had meetings with a coterie of top Israeli officials including Prime Minister Shimon Peres, opposition leader Bibi Netanyahu, President Ezer Weizman and Jerusalem Mayor Ehud Olmert. The highlight of our convention was our observance of Shabbat at the Plaza Hotel in Jerusalem, at which time we were blessed with the presence of both Chief Rabbis Yisrael Lau and Rav Bakshi Doron. The culmination was a celebration marking the end of the Sabbath known as a *melava malka* to which 450 people were invited. At that time, Prime Minister Peres addressed us and his remarks were broadcast live on Israeli television.

We also held our 1998 convention in Jerusalem to be part of the celebration of the 3000th anniversary of the Holy City's creation. For those in our community who were unable to travel to Israel to celebrate the official event, we created a traveling museum to build awareness of the magnificent history of Jerusalem and on the need to stand up to worldwide pressure on Israel to divide it with the Palestinians. Two interactive multi-media exhibits on this theme traversed fifty four cities in the United States and Canada, and introduced tens of thousands of children and adults to the rich history of Jerusalem. Unfortunately the officers chose not to hold our 2000 convention in Israel, because of the costs involved. I felt then, and still do today, that this was a great error.

Other OU programs kicked into high gear during the first years of my presidency. Our rapidly growing programs in Israel were operating at near capacity; our kashruth program was growing at a phenomenal rate and NCSY worked to revitalize a national Jewish youth sports league. Our Synagogue Services department under Rabbi Moshe Krupka and headed by chairman Steve Savitsky began providing a higher level of much needed services to the hundreds of synagogues affiliated with the OU.

The IPA, which I had played the lead role in creating and which remained my first love now that I was president, began to realize its full potential with my appointment of Nathan Diament as director. The selection of Nathan allowed the talented Betty Ehrenberg to concentrate on international affairs and community relations. A brilliant young lawyer with a passion for public service, Nathan walked away from a litigation association at a prestigious law firm to come to work for the Union. Nathan's desire to move our IPA headquarters to Washington complemented my dream to accomplish that, and despite opposition from the old timers, it came to pass. That was one of the most important innovations of my presidency and thanks to Nathan's superb leadership, has allowed the OU to project its values into the national political discussion in a way it was unable to do before. Today Nathan is a bright star in the Union's post-Lanner inertia.

I had the honor to be president of the Orthodox Union on the occasion of the Union's centennial celebration in 1998. It was a year marked by special programs and thanksgivings. During those unforgettable days, I thought many times about our first president Dr. Mendes. Though I never met him, I felt that I knew him well and always felt inspired by his vision of an Orthodox Jewry in America scrupulous about maintaining and upholding Torah-true Judaism. From his presidency until mine, no other physician had served as president. Dr. Mendes died in 1937, the year I was born. The opening celebrations of our centennial were held at the Spanish-Portuguese Synagogue, where Dr. Mendes had once been the pulpit rabbi. Centennial symposiums were also held in Washington.

At the 1998 convention in Jerusalem, I came to the decision that our NCSY program, which had been so phenomenally successful in keeping tens of thousands of American Jewish youngsters committed to living according to halacha, should be offered to Israeli youngsters as well. With the support of Rabbi Butler, but without prior notification of the executive board, I announced at our farewell dinner in Israel the formation of an NCSY Israel initiative and made a public appeal to raise over $150 thousand to get us off the ground. I turned to my close friend Avi Blumenfeld for the first major contribution, and then, together with Avi and Rabbi Butler, we worked hard to solicit a number of other advance contributions.

Though I had anticipated there might be trouble, no one on the Board raised any objections concerning NCSY Israel. It seemed that they had begun to see that there was a method behind the Ganchrow madness—and a track record of impressive success. Fred Ehrman similarly made a major contribution towards the new program and agreed to serve as NCSY Israel chairman as a result of his commitment to the project. Seymour Abrams of Chicago donated $1 million for the purchase of a building for the program in Jerusalem, which we moved into in the year 2000. Naomi and Harvey Wolinetz dedicated the synagogue at the new NCSY Israel Center, and Sheila and I the *Beit Medrash*. The creation of the Israel Center served as an added impetus for our programs in Israel both NCSY and adult oriented.

Every year during my presidency I traveled two or three times to Los Angeles to speak at the dinners and conventions of our West Coast division. We had only a small office there, and were constantly beset with problems regarding our lease. I was frequently prodding our west coast leaders to go out and buy a building, but their wheels were grinding slowly. In 1999, I was the guest speaker at the west coast dinner and without informing any of the leadership what I was about to do, I made an appeal from the rostrum for a new building. I complimented the wonderful people sitting before me on the magnificent work they had done in raising funds for other institutions to buy permanent homes, but told them that it was time to do the same for the Union. Fortunately, my efforts at getting them fired up were successful, and I was proud that before the end of my presidency, I was able to take part in the dedication of a brand new building directly across the street from the Wiesenthal Center.

Overall, there was a sense of momentum, a new energy, and a buzz at the Union during those boom years of the late 1990's. It seemed that wherever I traveled, people in the Jewish world and beyond were commenting on the new surge of activism at an organization many had seen as stodgy and unimaginative. The Kashruth department when I left the Union was certifying more than 250,000 products of 2,500 corporations in over 5,000 factories and plants, in 68 countries, a significant increase over the period prior to 1994. High profile companies such as Nabisco and M & M Mars were turning to the Union for certification. In 1997 with the help of Rabbi Butler a department of video and broadcasting was created. Our first video was "The Kosher Video" which explained how a 3,500-year-old tradition of dietary laws was maintained by the OU in today's complex, highly automated food industry.

The IPA political internship, which I had started in the late 1980's, had grown beyond anything we could have imagined a decade later. The kashruth internship likewise was growing rapidly. As a corollary to this program, we created a refresher course for practicing rabbis known as "Ask OU."

Despite all the problems that would emerge at NCSY in 2000 with the shocking revelations of the Lanner Affair, NCSY nevertheless remains the crown jewel of the Orthodox Union. The organization grew rapidly during my tenure as president and today reaches 40,000 high school aged youths annually, with chapters in 39 states and 215 communities. NCSY offers 750 major educational programs, and offers twelve different summer experiences. All of this is in addition to the summer programs we offer to Jewish children in the Ukraine and Israel.

From the moment that I assumed the OU presidency, the challenges of the Orthodox community became all encompassing for me. Although I was the sixteenth president in the Union's hundred-year history, I happened to be the first full-time lay leader. I took the title and position of president extremely seriously. I came in to the office three full days a week and was in constant contact with the office from home or when I was traveling abroad.

I nurtured a very close relationship with the media. Monday afternoons and Tuesdays are very important days for dealing with the Anglo-Jewish press, as their deadline is Tuesday evening. The high profile of the Union in recent years has changed our relationship with the press. In the early years of my presidency

I was called by reporters to comment only when a specific issue that the Union was involved in. Starting in 1996-1997 I routinely received five or more calls on Tuesdays, most frequently from reporters for the *Forward*, but from the *Jewish Week* and the *Long Island Jewish World* as well.

By way of illustration, let us examine my phone logs for the afternoon of November 9th, 1999, a fairly typical Tuesday in the frenetic world of the Jewish media. I came into the office at 1PM and spent the ensuing three hours on the phone with reporters. Adam Dichter of the *Jewish Week* called to discuss Hillary Clinton's upcoming trip to the Middle East, as well as some recent issues involving Jonathan Pollard. Adam also tried to trap me into condemning Assembly Speaker Shelly Silver concerning a story in that day's *New York Post* that I hadn't even seen. Nice try, Adam, but I know better than shooting from the hip until I have all the facts.

Seth Mnookin, the metropolitan editor of the *Forward*, spoke to me about Hillary's change of heart concerning visiting the Western Wall in Jerusalem and spoke about the Pollard case with me as well. Eve Kessler of the *Forward* called to discuss a story that had been in the preceding week's *Jewish Week* about Mendy's restaurant and its plans for a millennium New Year's Eve celebration slated for six week's hence. I was excited that Nadine Brozan of the *New York Times* called to inform me that she had read that same story and was interested in finding out whether this was worthy of a *New York Times* feature. I had to spend a great deal of time with her to bring her up to speed on the "aleph bet" (ABC's) of kashruth and Shabbas. Although she is Jewish, it was clear from her questions at the beginning that she hadn't understood where we were coming from. So, it appeared that we had a good shot at getting a story in the religion section of the *New York Times*, though, alas, it never came to pass.

Elissa Gootman, the Israel correspondent of the Forward also called that day from Jerusalem, as she did almost every week. She wanted my opinion on a session of the upcoming General Assembly on secular humanists as well as recent events at the Union's Israel Center. It just happens that I knew that Rabbi Butler, who was finishing his trip in Israel, had spoken to her and therefore the discussion was not as long as usual. A reporter from MSNBC called because he was monitoring the Jonathan Pollard website and Jonathan put up something about Hillary Clinton and her visit to Israel. I spent about twenty minutes explaining the Union's position on the Clinton trip, as well my own position on Jonathan Pollard.

Yes, I loved talking to reporters. I was gratified to have a bully pulpit—the OU presidency—from which I could expound the mainstream Orthodox political perspective, with just a bit of Ganchrow spin.

My relationship with the Rabbinical Council of America was excellent. I instituted the first annual all rabbinic dinner which honored Rabbis throughout the U.S. We also developed a relationship with the RCA Beth Din (rabbinical court) of America, giving them funding and placing our officers on their Board. My travels around the country helped cement this relationship.

The two areas of operation at the OU in which I rarely got involved in hands-on fashion were the kashruth department and NCSY. This was partly due to my lack of abiding personal interest in the activities of these departments and partly to the prickly sensitivities of the insiders. I was careful not to get involved in halachic questions vis a vis the kashruth department, since I did not have the expertise, even though I followed up every single complaint that I received and there were quite a few.

On one occasion a restaurant had been denied certification because it played music on a Saturday night while serving liquor. The Union follows the proscription that has been followed ever since the destruction of the Second Temple in Jerusalem, except for meals that are dedicated to a *mitzvah*—such as a wedding, circumcision, or completion of a text of the Torah—music at a meat meal where alcohol is served should be avoided due to our constant bereavement over the destruction of the Temple. Using common sense and the power of persuasion I was able to convince the restaurant to construct their night program to mark the end of the Shabbas as a religious event known as a *melave malka*.

As for NCSY, it has a group of dedicated and highly motivated professionals who have always looked with suspicion on lay interference, even though they have paid lip service to the concept. This was a trait that was rightly criticized in harsh terms by the Joel Commission in its report on the Lanner affair. I myself was reminded of the great power of the NCSY professionals on one occasion when I desired to name a new head of NCSY. Though the lay leadership supported my choice, I ran into strong opposition from Butler, the national professional staff of NCSY, and Lanner himself. I contemplated going to the wall on behalf of my designated choice, but finally decided it would not be worth beginning an all-out civil war within the OU in order to carry the day. Given the horrible scandal that would descend on us only about a year later, that was clearly a tragically wrong decision on my part.

One of the reasons I so enjoyed being president of the Union was the opportunity it afforded me to visit synagogues around the country as a scholar in residence. I played this role in synagogues in forty five cities during my six-year tenure. During the course of a twenty five hour Shabbat stay, I would usually speak to a particular congregation three to four times on such topics as tikkun olam, the meaning of the Jewish belief in trying to repair the world in our own era; the future of Orthodoxy in the United States; why the Reform and Conservative push for "religious pluralism" represented a grave danger to the future of Jewry, and the perils to the future of Israel by the so-called "peace process." I would always weave into my speeches an overview of the role of the OU in Jewish life so that I could emphasize the story of the revival of the OU in the 1990's and the need for the entire modern Orthodox community, including people like themselves, to become involved in our activities.

No Union president before me had ever traveled as much as I did. The showing of the Union banner in cities from Savannah to Houston, Kansas City to Detroit, among many others, helped to amplify awareness of the Union and its work in places where we traditionally had only a token presence. During those visits, I was always available to speak to reporters or editors from the local Jewish newspaper. To the same end, I instituted an ongoing series of telephone conference calls with Orthodox rabbis and community leaders around the country.

Nothing gave me more satisfaction than attending on-site meetings of our youth programs. On one occasion, as Sheila and I arrived in Israel, we were picked up at the airport in Tel Aviv and driven directly to an NCSY Center in the city of Lod, where recently arrived Ethiopian and Russian immigrant teens were interacting with Israeli-born peers. In less than one year, this program had brought amazing changes to Lod, which had long been a deprived community. Prior to the involvement of NCSY, the local elementary religious school had about thirteen classes for girls, but the religious high school had only one or two classes because the vast majority of religious girls opted for secular high school. Within a few months of NCSY's initial involvement in Lod, the religious high school was able to add another two or three classes for the upcoming semester because so many of the girls had been influenced by their NCSY experience to continue with their religious education.

Sheila and I were also privileged on that trip to witness children from a secular school in Beersheva participating in a one-day NCSY outing to the Yeshiva in Gush Etzion. On the trip the children learned biblical history via hands-on geography lessons and were given a much more vivid sense than they usually receive of the deep connection of the Jewish people to the land they inhabit.

One of the programs of which I am proudest is our youth program in Kharkov, Ukraine. We all owe enormous gratitude to Debbie and Shimmy Kwestel for their selfless and tireless efforts in conceiving this project and then raising the funds and overseeing the construction of a boys' and girls' school, dormitories, camps, and a community center in that city. Often they worked alone against great odds in their advocacy for the Kharkov project, yet they always succeeded. Ironically, our greatest problem in Kharkov has been the very success of the NCSY program in stimulating feelings of Jewish identity and pride in Jewish youngsters there, leading a large percentage of them to leave on aliyah to Israel and depleting our student body in the process. We have maintained close contact with our Kharkov alumni in Israel and are gratified that they have remained Torah-true.

These fantastic results are a tribute to the inspirational leadership of Rabbi Shlomo Asaraf, an Israeli-born paratrooper and graduate of a hesder yeshiva. Rabbi Asaraf did not allow himself to be deterred by the experience of being held for a number of weeks by the KGB in Kiev; but instead redoubled his dedication to the children of our Kharkov program—and to the OU as well.

Occasionally, during my years as OU president, I would become depressed because I was working so hard for no financial compensation. I suppose that was the effect of being told frequently by so many friends and acquaintances that I must have lost my marbles to be dedicating myself so totally to a religious cause on a volunteer basis. I was able to recharge my spiritual batteries, however, by attending NCSY or Yachad events. Those shabbatonim—large or small—are special gatherings. It was extremely inspiring for example to meet youngsters who had given up a week of holiday vacation to come together and learn Torah with dedication and purity of purpose. I reminded myself that many of those young people could have been skiing during those days, but instead sat from early morning to late at night absorbing Jewish learning.

During one NCSY convention I attended, I dropped in on a beginner's prayer service for teenagers who had not grown up in the Orthodox community. I walked into a room of boys dressed in jeans. Many had their baseball hats on backward, and some wore earrings. Certainly these beginning students were dressed markedly different than the yeshiva students in the room who wore suits and ties and special Sabbath clothing. I wondered how our rabbis would manage to have an impact on these overtly secular youngsters.

The rabbi who was leading the discussion said something about "higher feelings and emotions," whereupon a 14-year–old student blurted out, "Like good sex!" The other students laughed. I was shocked at the effrontery of the child and had I been the lecturer, I would have immediately thrown the young man out of the class for disturbing the session. Instead, the rabbi took up the challenge and said, "O.K., let's discuss that point." He then launched into a discussion in which he spoke with passion and eloquence about the sanctity of marriage in Judaism; the beauty of sex between husband and wife; the laws of mikvah (ritual purity) and the shortsightedness and self-destructiveness of a lifestyle devoted to hedonistic pleasure without commitment and purpose in life. It was evident that by not shying away from the subject of sex, but addressing it head on, the rabbi completely won over the participating students who crowded around him to express their agreement with what he had said. The youngster who had shouted out so rudely came over to the rabbi to publicly apologize.

The following day I approached the rabbi to congratulate him on a brilliant pedagogic exercise and asked how he had such an intuitive grasp of how to connect with kids who came from cultures remote from Orthodoxy. The rabbi smiled, opened his wallet and showed me an old photograph of a hippie with a headband and beard. He said, "That was me before I connected with NCSY and became a ba'al teshuvah. Believe me, I've been in their world and understand exactly what those kids are going through."

I was proud also of the success of our Yachad program in helping young Jews with developmental disabilities to connect with their heritage. I remember the life-changing impact of Yachad on a son of a dear friend of mine in Monsey. Thanks to the program, the boy became integrated into the community, found a job and learned to read Hebrew. When Yachad took a group of developmentally disabled kids to Israel, he met a young Yachad girl, fell in love, and got married. I remember many of us crying unrestrainedly at the wedding as we watched the other Yachad youngsters dancing joyfully around the radiant bride and groom. What nachas we felt to see that these developmentally challenged young people had been able to progress to this wonderful stage of life.

It was moments like that one, repeated many times over my six years in office that reassured me day in and day out that the work I was doing was making a positive difference in thousands of lives and was therefore enormously worthwhile, despite the political backbiting I had to endure and the great financial sacrifice I was making. That was the point I made during my farewell speech to the 2000 convention at which I said that despite the disillusionment we all felt at the seamy revelations of the Lanner affair, it would be a terrible mistake to destroy the Union because of the transgressions of a few individuals. I reminded the delegates that it had taken one hundred years to develop the apparatus we call the Orthodox Union, and there is no organization available to take its place.

Indeed, despite the Lanner affair, which made my last six months in the top position at the Union an extremely difficult one, I left the presidency of the OU with my head up, knowing that what I had accomplished in strengthening the organization over six years would endure. It will likely take the OU a few years to fully overcome the impact of the Lanner mess, but when it does, the structures that I helped to put into place in so many parts of the Union will still be up and running and enriching the lives of countless individuals. I feel humble that I was given the opportunity to serve the Orthodox Union for six years as its highest official, and proud that I have left a living legacy that will serve the cause of tikkun olam decades after I am gone. Of the many things I have accomplished in Jewish life, I am perhaps proudest of my contribution to revitalizing the OU, and thereby helping to ensure a vibrant future for the American Orthodox community. My fondest dream is that this revitalization and vision will soon get back on track.

CHAPTER SEVEN

The Bully Pulpit of the OU

After I attained high office at the Orthdox Union and especially after I was elected president in 1994, I managed to use the platform to take a series of controversial stands on widely varied issues that resonated far beyond the organization itself.

For those who thought that the primary purpose of the Orthodox Union was to watch over kashruth issues, my ascendancy to the Union presidency reinforced the fact that Orthodox Jews are full participants in American life and interested in much more than dietary laws. The issues upon which I had a concerted impact while speaking on behalf of the Orthodox Union were eclectic in nature, both before and during my presidency.

The Baxter Laboratory Affair

It was January 1988, when the Syrian army opened discussions with the Swiss affiliate of Baxter, a well-known international pharmaceutical firm, about building an intravenous-solution plant in that militant Arab state.

A month later, in an action that was clearly not coincidental, Baxter sold its profitable hospital supply base in Israel to Teva Pharmaceuticals. Three days after that sale was announced, Baxter submitted documents to the Syrian army attesting that the company's divestiture of its Israeli division deal had been completed. Throughout the remainder of 1988, leading executives of Baxter held meetings with officials from the Syrian Ministry of Defense during which they offered documentation to prove that they had recently sold off their operations in Israel.

In January 1989, the Arab League informed Baxter that it had been dropped from its blacklist of companies doing business with Israel. Three months later, Baxter and another corporate giant Nestle, formed a fifty-fifty partnership known as Clintech International to develop and market clinical nutritional products worldwide. Finally, in late 1989, Baxter reached an agreement with the Syrian army on a joint venture to build the much-discussed intravenous fluid plant.

The U.S. Commerce Department launched an investigation in February 1990 into whether Baxter violated American anti-boycott laws by closing its operations in Israel in order to qualify for a larger deal with Syria.

Yet there seemed no evident way to prove that such a quid pro quo had actually transpired until a former Baxter executive, Dr. Richard Fuinsz, released a series of internal Baxter documents covering the period of 1988-89. These documents—correspondence between Baxter executives and Syrian officials—offered hard evidence in support of Fuinsz's charge that the company had agreed to meet Syria's condition that it end its activities in Israel in order to gain access to Arab markets.

Opponents of the Baxter-Syrian agreement, primarily members of the American-Jewish community, were concerned about Baxter's apparent accession to the notorious Arab economic boycott of Israel. Some Jewish groups also accused the company of agreeing to build a plant whose technology could later be converted by the Syrians into laboratories for the production of chemical and biological weapons for use against Israel. This charge was hotly denied by Baxter, which hired an outside counsel who supposedly investigated the charges and released a report denying that its planned intravenous-solution plant could be altered to produce such weapons of mass destruction. However, Baxter refused to make the report public and instead released only a one-page summary of its findings, a statement that failed to quell the growing controversy over its dealings with Syria.

Many Jewish groups joined the fight against the project. We had a staunch ally in New York Comptroller Elizabeth Holzman, principal trustee of the $17.4 million of Baxter stocks in the city's portfolio. Holtzman put together a proposal on behalf of New

York City stockholders that Baxter provide a full accounting of its dealings with the Syrians. The Orthodox Union, like many other organizations, sent out letters to synagogues across the country, urging them to write to company executives and U.S. government officials. We also appointed an ad hoc committee to mobilize physicians associated with the Union in the campaign to pressure Baxter to reverse course.

On January 15, 1991, Dr. William Schwartz, a close friend and neighbor whom I had appointed as the chairman of the Physicians Anti-Boycott Campaign and myself as chairman of the Orthodox Union's Institute for Public Affairs (IPA), sent a joint letter to the members of our organizations. We urged recipients of the letter to contact members of Congress and institutions that purchased Baxter products, such as hospitals and nursing homes, and ask them to join in a nationwide protest directed at Baxter over its deal with Syria and apparent decision to adhere to the economic boycott of Israel.

Meanwhile, as I roamed the halls and the operating rooms of Good Samaritan Hospital in Suffern, NY going about my professional duties, the idea of starting a boycott of Baxter products came into my mind. While serving at the hospital, I noted that all the IV solutions used by Good Samaritan came from Baxter. It occurred to me it might be possible to achieve a multiple-doctor or hospital boycott of Baxter products at Good Samaritan and beyond. It is no secret that there are a large number of Jewish doctors in the metropolitan New York area. I myself was involved in a network of Orthodox doctors who could be mobilized even though they had never undertaken such a project in the past. I was certain that such a campaign would have a real impact on Baxter's bottom line.

I inquired with the central supply office at Good Samaritan if there was an alternate supplier of IV solutions. Yes, I was informed, there was indeed another company that could easily supply the hospital's needs for IV fluids and other medical products. I then invited Sam Colman, a neighbor of mine in Monsey who was also a New York State Assemblyman, to join me in a meeting with the administrator of Good Samaritan Hospital, Sister Joan Regan. We informed her about what was happening with Baxter, and asked a hypothetical question. If we were able to get other hospitals, private doctors, and others in the medical establishment to join a boycott of Baxter, would Good Samaritan

Hospital be willing to announce publicly that it was participating in such a boycott? Sister Regan informed us that she would do so. Yet she went even further, promising to try to convince a consortium of forty Catholic hospitals in which Good Samaritan participated, which bought medical supplies as a unit for all participating hospitals, to take part in the boycott.

Such an action would have serious consequences for Baxter, a company with annual sales of about eight billion dollars a year, considering that in 1990, Good Samaritan Hospital alone purchased three and half million dollars a year of Baxter products. Within days Sister Regan informed me that the buying group's administrator likewise was prepared to cooperate in a joint effort to send a message to Baxter regarding its treatment of Israel. It was now clear that we had the economic clout to make Baxter think twice about whether it was really worthwhile to go ahead with its deal with Syria.

We decided to focus on organizing the "boycott Baxter" campaign first in the New York metropolitan area, and eventually, if that effort was successful, throughout the United States. A central purpose of our campaign was to educate physicians regarding Baxter's activities in the Middle East and thereby, hopefully, convince them to participate in our effort.

I began the campaign by calling friends of mine who were attending physicians in various hospitals throughout metropolitan New York. They all were quite enthusiastic and eager to start. Marty Gotel, a Monsey resident who worked in the purchasing department of the New York City Board of Hospitals, promised to mobilize the Board of Hospitals to join the boycott.

As this effort got under way, someone in the central supply room in Good Samaritan inadvertently informed the local Baxter sales representative of our conversations and plans. Immediately I received a call from the Baxter representative. He told me, "Don't worry. Everything is under control." I responded that from where I sat, things were not under control. I explained to him why we were undertaking our action and that I expected that our planned campaign would have highly negative implications for Baxter.

It didn't take long for a regional manager to call me. He seemed convinced of the correctness of Baxter's decision to build the plant in Syria and end its activities in Israel. He also appeared to me to be quite unconcerned about the deep disquiet in the American Jewish community about what Baxter was doing.

I told him that, in my opinion, he was underestimating the likely damage that our boycott of Baxter products could cause the company; pointing out that I represented not only a local group, but a nationwide network of Jewish communities as well. I stressed that our committee had access to doctors throughout the country who were prepared to take action that could severely hurt Baxter Laboratories.

After hearing me out, the manager told me he would get back to me within a few days. The news of our planned boycott obviously quickly raced up the chain of command at Baxter, because, within a week, I received a call from the highest corporate level of the company, asking for a meeting. I informed the Baxter official that I had scheduled a meeting of New York physicians under the auspices of the OU's Institute for Public Affairs (IPA), of which I was chairman, for the day after the Jewish holiday of *Shavouth*, in May 1991, about two weeks hence. We were expecting 100 physicians, representing most area hospitals, at the IPA meeting to discuss the Baxter case. Participants in the meeting were to be educated as to the "economic opportunities available to those who wished to protest Baxter's actions in a meaningful way"—another way of saying "those prepared to boycott Baxter" without using the word "boycott."

Nevertheless, I informed the Baxter executive, if the company's corporate leadership was prepared to meet with us in the near future to discuss our charges, I was ready to postpone the IPA meeting. The Baxter representative responded that the company would agree to such a meeting with us. Indeed, within a matter of hours, they invited us to meet them at the Loews Hotel in New York and informed me that they had secured a kosher caterer for the event.

A senior delegation from Baxter, including the company's European and Middle East representatives, arrived at the meeting to present their point of view. Once the meeting began, Marvin Jacob, a lawyer and member of our Board who had previous experience in Washington in the Securities and Exchange Commission, proved quite persuasive in demonstrating to the Baxter officials that we meant business. Our principle demand was that Baxter agree to turn over to us the full report of the internal probe conducted by the company. Heretofore they had released only the executive summary.

I stressed to the Baxter executives that the reason the Jewish community felt so passionately about this issue was because it evoked the Holocaust for us. We feared that the plant Baxter wanted to build in Syria and turn over to the Syrians might eventually produce poison gas, which, as in the Nazi gas chambers, could bring instant death to many thousands of Jews. I told them that in order to prevent the possibility of such a murderous scenario, we as a community were prepared to flex our economic muscles. I was gratified that we managed to present our case forcefully and that by the conclusion of the meeting the representatives of Baxter understood the full danger that a national boycott of Baxter products by the Jewish community represented to the company.

The Baxter executives responded to our presentation in strikingly conciliatory language. They promised to investigate the points we had raised and get back to us in a few weeks. For the time being, they declined to accede to our request that they turn over to us their full internal report, but asked for a grace period before giving us a definitive answer.

In response to the positive attitude the Baxter executives evinced at the meeting, we agreed to hold off on launching any action against the company for the time being. We also chose not to talk to the press about the meeting, as our goal was not publicity, but rather getting Baxter to understand that we were serious and to respond accordingly. We waited to see what would be the results of Baxter's internal consultations on the issue.

It turned out that we did not have to wait very long. On the morning of June 10, 1991, I received a call at my medical office from one of the senior vice-presidents of Baxter. He informed me that the company had made the decision not to proceed with its plans to build the intravenous-solution plant in Syria and would so announce by 1PM that day. I immediately called the Orthodox Union office, and our IPA Executive Director Willie Rapfogel. We had a statement drawn up in which we congratulated Baxter for its responsible decision and announced our role in impacting upon its decision.

In the statement, I was quoted as saying that the Orthodox Union was gratified that "Baxter had been sensitive to the ongoing discussion of the IPA's Law and Legislation Commission chaired by Marvin Jacob and the position taken by our organization and many others on this issue." On June 10, the very day that Baxter announced its decision to pull out of Syria, one of the national Jewish community's main umbrella bodies, officials of NJCRAC–the National Jewish Committee Relations Council–were holding a previously scheduled meeting in a city in mid-America. As soon as I got off the phone with the Baxter executive, I called David Luchins, who was representing the Union at the NJCRAC meeting, and informed him of Baxter's impending announcement. Luchins returned to the NJCRAC deliberations and immediately told the group of our success with Baxter.

As is all too typically the case in the publicity-hungry organized Jewish community, the representative of every organization at the NJCRAC conclave immediately ran out to the telephone to issue statements and to contact the media. The following day, the statements of other major Jewish organizations hailing Baxter's about face appeared in the national newspapers. Yet not a single paper picked up the OU statement. In effect, the other Jewish organizations were claiming credit for Baxter's capitulation, when, in reality, that credit belonged squarely in the hands of the OU, which had done almost all of the work in organizing the threatened boycott.

Unfortunately, the Union did not yet have a department of public relations, and that absence vividly showed that day. I never forgot the lesson of that event, which was that in matters of taking credit in the Jewish community, it is every organization for itself. Not one Jewish organization even mentioned our efforts in forcing Baxter to pull out of Syria. It was only on July 28, 1991, after the successful conclusion of our campaign, that we published an op-ed piece in the *Jerusalem Post*. We explained how the Union had spearheaded the effort to force Baxter to reverse course, as well as the reasoning behind our call on private doctors, as well as hospitals, to join with us. "Physicians are free to act in accordance with their own moral interests," we wrote. "American law permits an individual to boycott a product for reasons such as participation by a major corporation in an illegal boycott of a U.S. ally. Such was the case when American Jews acted against Mexico after it voted in favor of the U.N. Zionism is Racism resolution."

Though Baxter had acceded to our demands, the company's travails in the matter were not over. In 1993, Baxter would plead guilty to U.S. Commerce Department charges of having provided information to an Arab boycott authority. Baxter agreed to pay $6.5 million to settle the matter and to restrict exports of

U.S. products and technology to Syria and Saudi Arabia for two years.

In a follow up letter to the Orthodox Union on March 25, 1993, Vernon R. Loucks Jr., Chairman and CEO of Baxter, summing up the three year investigation by the government, claimed that the company had never boycotted Israel, but, rather, had supported medical research in that country for more than twenty years. The company asserted that the U.S. Government had concluded that Baxter improperly shared with Arab officials information about its business operations in Israel in violation of anti-boycott laws. However "we made a mistake and we regret it, but I assure you that our mistake was unintentional and we certainly never intended to work against the interests of Israel." The company noted that sales to Israel had grown consistently, and in 1992 these sales reached approximately six million dollars— double those to any other nation in the Middle East. Baxter also said it was planning to widen its relationship in Israel in the field of medical research. One can surmise what might have happened if we had not intervened after Baxter announced three years earlier that it was ending its operations in Israel and building an intravenous solution plant for the Syrian Army.

Thus ended a significant chapter of implementation of the law to combat the Arab economic boycott of Israel. Our humbling of a multinational pharmaceutical giant like Baxter showed the power of committed individuals to band together under the banner of a national organization like the Orthodox Union in order to achieve positive results beyond what many of us had believed were remotely possible at the beginning of our anti-boycott boycott.

L'Oreal

Fundraising—whether it is accomplished through collecting dues, carrying out special projects, or holding dinners—is the mainstay of all nonprofit organizations. And in the pressure-cooker world of fundraising, successfully soliciting a corporate sponsor is the equivalent of hitting a home run. When that corporation actually agrees to solicit its suppliers and customers to give funds for your charity, then you have truly connected for a grand-slam.

Thus, when Shelly Fliegelman, my good friend, confidante

and director of development, was able to convince the L'Oreal Company to accept a major award at the 1997 Orthodox Union dinner, we were extremely gratified. L'Oreal had promised not only to make a major contribution to the OU, but also to work diligently in order to fill many tables at the event with suppliers and friends.

Yet we were also concerned. We knew there was a definite downside to the award—a long-running controversy regarding L'Oreal's history vis a vis the Jews, going back to France in the late 1930s.

The charges against L'Oreal were many and had been passionately enunciated in recent years. L'Oreal's late founder, Eugene Schuller,was said to have been an open anti-semite and to have supported far-right wing causes during the late 1930's. In addition, Andre Bettencourt, who eventually took over the company from his father-in-law Schuller, admitted writing anti-semitic articles in 1940-42. Bettencourt later renounced and apologized for these pieces after joining the French resistance to the Nazis. Bettencourt himself was succeeded at the helm of L'Oreal by his son-in-law Jean Pierre Meyers, who is Jewish. Yet the company also had a long period of cooperation with the Arab boycott of Israel.

These matters had come to the surface not long before our dinner in a book entitled *Bitter Scent* by an Israeli, Ben Zohar. Although it was not a new book, it had only recently been translated into English. While detailing these unsavory moments in L'Oreal's history, the author also acknowledged that L'Oreal was a significant participant in Israel's economy, and had also contributed to her cultural life.

Before deciding whether or not to honor L'Oreal, we contacted the Israeli government—at the consulate in New York and the embassy in Washington as well as in Jerusalem—in order to get their take on the matter. We also consulted the Anti-Defamation League, the World Jewish Congress and the Presidents Conference. The answer came back to us loud, clear and unanimous— there was no reason we should not go ahead with our plans to honor L'Oreal.

Unfortunately, a small slice of the Jewish public, especially in the "activist" wing of the Orthodox community, saw the matter quite differently. When you are "Number One"— as is the OU in the Orthodox world—all types of so-called leaders come out of the woodwork to attack you, especially on small community radio stations and via the Internet. Suddenly, I found myself being confronted by longtime friends who unbelievably asked me whether it was really true that I had decided to accept Nazi money.

Amidst the growing controversy, L'Oreal and the Union decided to stand up to the pressure and not allow the company's record to be distorted. The OU turned to Israeli Prime Minister Binyamin (Bibi) Netanyahu for help and he came through wonderfully; dispatching to me a "Dear Mendy" letter in which he stated that he was "pleased to learn" that the Orthodox Union would be "honoring the L'Oreal corporation for its contribution to the economy of Israel." Netanyahu also wrote: "We appreciate the efforts of the OU in strengthening both Jewish identity and the link between the Jewish people and the State of Israel."

In the months before the dinner, we also received a letter of support for L'Oreal from Natan Sharansky, Israel Minister of Industry and Trade, as well as statements on behalf of the company from such world Jewish leaders as Avrum Burg, chairman of the Jewish Agency, Leon Levy, chairman of the President's Conference, Abe Foxman of the ADL, and leaders of Hadassah. All of these testimonials helped quell the furor. If the Prime Minister of Israel and Natan Sharansky saw our honoring L'Oreal as legitimate, then the company's critics had a severe credibility problem in arguing that the company was somehow anti-semitic. In addition L'Oreal issued a White Paper that refuted every charge. All of this convinced most of our critics to cease and desist from their attacks on the OU and L'Oreal.

What gave us an additional feeling of confidence that we could go ahead with the dinner without serious negative consequences was the fact that another honoree at the event was to be Rabbi Marvin Hier of the Simon Wiesenthal Center, who has a sterling reputation as a hunter of Nazis throughout the world. When the question of L'Oreal arose, I called Rabbi Hier, a longtime close friend, and asked him forthrightly if he had any problem either with our honoring L'Oreal or concerning his being a co-honoree together with the cosmetics firm. Rabbi Hier replied that he had neither. When I told people who had expressed disquiet about our honoring L'Oreal that Rabbi Hier had no problem appearing with the top executives of the firm as a co-honoree that certainly helped to calm the concerns of many of them and soothe the overall situation.

Though we expected a substantial demonstration on the sidewalk outside the Manhattan hotel where we were holding the dinner, in fact only a few pickets actually showed up and the dinner itself was a major success for the Union. Attempts by some of the agitators to interest representatives of the Anglo-Jewish press to write critically about the Union's award to L'Oreal came to naught in part because reporters who attended the event witnessed a beautifully documented film that clearly defined the large and varied role of L'Oreal in Israel. Not only is L'Oreal Israel's leading cosmetics company, but the company's leadership consists of many Jews in both France and Israel. These men and women support research and education efforts in Israel, bolster the economy of the Jewish State, and nurture relationships between Israel and world Jewry.

In short, although, L'Oreal may have played a less than savory role in the 1930's, it is a strong supporter of Israel today. I am gratified that we at the OU stood strong in our determination to honor L'Oreal and declined to be cowed by those who sought to pressure us to back away from a firm that has been a good friend of the Jewish state.

New Year's Controversies

American Jews celebrate two New Years—the general one, on January 1st, and the first and second days of the Hebrew month of Tishrei, which falls either in September or early October. Known as Rosh Hashanah, the Jewish New Year also marks the beginning of the Ten Days of Penitence, which culminate in the fast day of Yom Kippur—the holiest day of the Jewish calendar.

The difference between the solemn observance of Rosh Hashanah and the celebratory nature of the secular New Year was dramatically brought home to me in 1998. In that year, Rosh Hashanah began on September twentieth. That was also the day the House Judiciary Committee released its videotape of President Clinton's grand jury testimony in the Monica Lewinsky scandal.

It was a great surprise to me that some Jews objected to the release of the tape on our holy day. For example, the *New York Times* reported that Joseph Weinberg, senior rabbi of the Washington Hebrew Congregation, led a group of rabbis who phoned members of the Judiciary Committee urging them to postpone the release of the tape for two days—till after Rosh Hashanah. "Releasing it on Rosh Hashanah is such a mean-spirited thing to do," Rabbi Weinberg was quoted as saying. Other Jewish religious and secular groups likewise expressed dismay that Jews would be left out of one part of the judicial process surrounding the Lewinsky scandal. A few even implied that the timing of the release of the Clinton testimony was in some way discriminatory against the Jewish community.

I looked at the matter entirely differently "I think it is good for the soul of the Jews not to be looking at these tapes for 48 hours," I told the *New York Times*. "It actually gives us a chance to be concentrating on our atonement, on our souls, and not upon looking at salacious material. So let us not look for anti-semites behind every videotape. In truth, it is a blessing in disguise." Looking back, I think I was right. There is no evidence that the involvement of the Jewish community in our country's political process was diluted by that forty eight-hour Rosh Hashanah hiatus.

There has also been some controversy of a different sort within the Orthodox Jewish community concerning Jews who celebrate the secular New Year's Eve. To true Christian believers, New Year's is not secular at all. The holiday's origins are purely christological. Therefore, while Orthodox Jews acknowledge the end of the calendar and financial year, they generally refrain from holding New Year's Eve celebrations. When I was growing up, it was common for Jewish day schools to emphasize this point by scheduling half-day class sessions on the morning of January 1st, even though teachers of secular subjects usually took the day off.

An unprecedented issue concerning Jewish observance of New Year's Eve arose on December 31, 1999, the last day of the 20th century and the advent of the third millennium according to the secular calendar. For starters, that particular New Year's Eve fell on a Friday night. Despite the fact that kosher restaurants are normally closed on the Sabbath from just prior to sundown on Friday to after dark on Saturday, they may remain open on special occasions under certain conditions: the food must be precooked and all payments made in advance. A rabbinic supervisor must be present to ascertain that no Sabbath violations occur.

Many of us were troubled by the evident desire of Jews to take part in worldwide celebrations of the advent of the third millennium, even though that chronological milestone had no meaning for our people. For example, sixty of the one hundred and twenty Conservative synagogues in metropolitan New York had planned celebratory events to mark this once-in-a-lifetime occasion. Several young Orthodox entrepreneurs, sensing an opportunity to make a bundle by sponsoring a New Year's Eve event for the celebrants under strict rabbinic supervision, rented out an Upper West Side restaurant at 150 dollars a person for a sit-down Sabbath meal. The kashruth supervision was under the OU, with the assumption being that the event would be a classical "shabbat meal."

Those arrangements had been perfectly acceptable to the Orthodox Union until we learned that the restaurant would be offering an open bar until 1AM. The kashruth department then revoked its approval, arguing that the event was nothing but a subterfuge for a secular New Year's Eve party. Amidst mutual barbs between the Orthodox and Conservative movements and considerable coverage in the *New York Times* and other media, it fell to me to defend the OU's decision to revoke its certification of the event. "We'd like to remind people that it may be the new millennium now, but shabbos has been around for 3500 years and will be here indefinitely. The future of your children, family, and people depends on shabbos," was my response.

The idea that American Jews should join the rest of the nation in celebrating holidays with Christian roots like Halloween or even St. Valentines Day is foreign to our teachings. On the other hand, Thanksgiving Day, which had its origins among the devoutly Christian Pilgrim fathers of Massachusetts, is extremely popular in Orthodox Jewish circles. For us, it is an occasion to celebrate our love of America and to give thanks for the freedom we enjoy here. On the other hand, the secular New Year, while a day we look forward to because it starts a new fiscal year, will never be an occasion that observant Jews should celebrate.

Rudy Guiliani and the Brooklyn Museum

American Jews have been among the prime beneficiaries of living in an open and pluralistic society. Allowing full freedom of expression, including obnoxious presentations that hold up individuals or groups to sharp criticism or even ridicule—is one price we pay for the free way of life we so enjoy and under which the Jews of America have so prospered.

Given that we as a community have always ardently upheld the principle of freedom of expression, it may have seemed like an unlikely move for the Orthodox Union to become so publicly involved in a controversy between Mayor Rudolph Giuliani and the Brooklyn Museum, in which the mayor accused the museum of exhibiting obscene and sacrilegious art. He removed city funding from the museum as a result. Yet in upholding the position taken by the mayor, namely, that government funds should not go to a museum displaying works that are obscene or profoundly offensive to religious sensibilities, we were not denying the principle of freedom of expression, but rather upholding other profound moral values at the core of the Jewish tradition.

The controversy over the Brooklyn Museum exploded in September 1999, when an exhibition of avant-garde art entitled "Sensation" opened at that city government funded and supported art institution, a place that I visited many times in my youth. The exhibition featured a painting called "The Holy Virgin Mary" by the British artist Chris Ofili that had a clump of elephant dung smearing one of the Virgin Mary's breasts. Mayor Giuliani and the Catholic Church were infuriated by the painting, which they cited as an example of a growing phenomenon known as "Catholic bashing." For its part, the Brooklyn Museum defended the painting as a legitimate work of art. They argued that continuing the display despite the criticism represented the upholding of freedom of expression against attempts at censorship by Guiliani and the Church. Others, including some who defended the right of the Brooklyn Museum to exhibit The Holy Virgin Mary and the other controversial works in the "Sensation" exhibition, took a more jaundiced view of the museum's motives; contending that it had intentionally manufactured the controversy in order to raise the price of the paintings in question after the exhibition had ended.

For my part, I came to the conclusion that the primary issue at play in the Brooklyn Museum controversy was not that of censorship. Though I believed that the painting itself had no discernable redeeming social importance, I had no problem with the artist creating it for exhibition at a private gallery that did not receive government financial support. Yet the board of the Brooklyn Museum accepted money from the city to create a cultural institution for the entire community. Therefore, in my opinion, the museum had no right to exhibit works that were deeply insulting to large segments of the New York community.

I believed the Orthodox Union should issue a statement supporting the mayor's position for a number of reasons. Throughout his tenure, Cardinal John O'Connor of New York had been extremely sensitive to the needs of the Jewish community in general and the Orthodox community in particular. It seemed to me that it was time for a major Jewish organization to take a stand against such an insult to the Catholic Church. It was clear to me as well that had the painting in question been one of a Torah covered with dung instead of the Virgin Mary, not only would we be screaming and yelling but would also be seeking the backing of the Catholic Church. I realized that if the Torah were portrayed in that way, it would be quite difficult to control elements of our community who would respond violently to such an insult to our holiest religious object.

Still, while I strongly criticized the museum for exhibiting "The Holy Virgin Mary," I did not advocate that the city should close it down. Rather, I believed that Guiliani should press the museum to appoint a more responsible and civic-minded board of directors.

Because we were the only Jewish group to issue a statement in support of the mayor's position in the Brooklyn Museum controversy, our position was well covered by the media. During one talk radio program on which I was a guest, I remarked, "Just as public funds should not subsidize the pollution of our air, river, and earth, the Orthodox Union believes that taxpayer monies should assiduously avoid supporting cultural pollution. The right of free expression enjoyed by the 'artist' is not a right to a government check."

The position taken by the Orthodox Union during the Brooklyn Museum controversy is very much in line with the outspoken support we gave to Senator Joseph Lieberman (D-Conn) and other prominent figures who, while opposing censorship, have condemned excess violence and sex in the media, in entertainment, and on the Internet. I believe leaders of our community need to continue speaking out on these moral issues in the years ahead.

CHAPTER EIGHT

The OU and Other
Orthodox Organizations

The Orthodox Union is by far the largest and most influential organization within American Orthodoxy, but it has long had complicated and sometimes acrimonious relations with other national Orthodox bodies such as Agudath Israel and Young Israel. When I became president of the OU in 1994, I made it a priority to reach out to these groups to see if we could work more closely and harmoniously together and in the case of Young Israel, to explore the idea of a merger. As it soon became clear, despite our sustained efforts at reconciliation, both Agudath Israel and Young Israel remained too invested in their real or imagined ideological differences with the Union to build a common agenda or to effect a merger. Later in my term, we were confronted by the creation of Edah, which positioned itself to the left of the Union, just as Aguda and Young Israel stood to the right. Here again, our efforts to prevent further Orthodox schism were frustrated by the Edah leadership's insistence on focusing on the relatively little that divided us as opposed to the broad consensus that we shared.

Relations With Agudath Israel

The relationship between the Orthodox Union and Agudath Israel of America—the principle organization representing right wing Orthodoxy—has never been particularly warm.

Aguda has never encouraged its rabbis and teachers to speak or teach at Orthodox Union events. The organization does not consider itself "Zionist," and, therefore, does not lobby on behalf of Israel. It also does not participate in the main national Jewish umbrella organizations such as AIPAC, the President's Conference, NJCRAC, the Jewish Agency or the Jewish Community Relations Council of New York.

For the most part Aguda does not belong to or participate in organizations that interact with Reform or Conservative Jews. Thus, Aguda was extremely vocal in its opposition to the membership of the Orthodox Union in the now-defunct Synagogue Council of America, since that organization included representatives from Reform and Conservative lay and rabbinic groups as well as Orthodox ones. On an international level, however, the World Aguda Movement does belong to the Memorial Foundation for Jewish Culture, which has a large number of Reform and Conservative participants. Rabbi Menachem Porush, a former member of the Knesset and leader of World Aguda, is a widely respected participant in the work of the Memorial Foundation and has been extremely successful in pushing for greater funding for scholarships and projects sponsored by the Orthodox community. I deeply respect Rabbi Porush for his leadership.

While there are physicians, lawyers, and other professionals who are either members of Aguda or philosophically support the organization, a majority of the yeshiva heads—those who constitute the Moetset, the theological leadership of Aguda—do not encourage their young people to obtain a university education. There are a few who take a more tolerant position, such as the leadership of the Ner Israel Yeshiva in Baltimore.

In 1988, I was one of ten vice-presidents of the Orthodox Union and chairman of the Institute of Public Affairs (IPA). The IPA was planning a Washington mission on March 4, 1989 in conjunction with its principle partners in Orthodoxy—the Rabbinical Council of America (RCA), Amit, Emunah, Religious Zionists and Poalei Aguda. The goal of the mission was to build support for the Orthodox agenda in Congress as well as to promote the U.S.-Israel relationship.

The controversy over "Who Is a Jew" was again erupting in Israel and Reform Jews were reportedly approaching members of Congress asking that support for Israel be withheld if the Knesset passed any change in the Law of Return. The Reform Movement, which has a high percentage of members who are intermarried, viewed such changes in the Law of Return as a delegitimization of those of their rabbis who conduct such marriages and "conversions."

I proposed that in view of the bitterness of the debate and the broad attack on Orthodoxy being undertaken by the Reform movement that we should expand our mission beyond the modern Orthodox groups to include Aguda and the Young Israel movement. The national leadership of Young Israel had, in recent years, quietly removed itself from the orbit of Yeshiva University and the Orthodox Union and moved slowly toward the Aguda world without really consulting their branches if they supported that shift. Actually most of their local branches, including those who were members of the OU and those who were not, were never even aware of this subtle, but significant, shift by the leaders of the Young Israel leadership. For example, for years, the Young Israel leadership refused to attend meetings at Yeshiva University with other modern Orthodox groups, an unofficial boycott that is clearly a reflection of Young Israel's rightward turn, as well as a desire not to hear urgings for them to merge with the Union.

My goal in pressing for a unified Orthodox mission to Washington was to demonstrate to the world that though we are a diverse community, Orthodoxy is nevertheless united in its commitment to the survival of the State of Israel. Moreover, I wanted to make clear that the Orthodox Union and the larger Orthodox community had never threatened to withhold that support from Israel if we did not get our way legislatively—and we expected others to do the same.

Baruch Kohn, a friend of mine from Monsey and a lay leader of Aguda, arranged a luncheon meeting at the Aguda office with the late Rabbi Moshe Sherer, its president. One could not help but be impressed with Rabbi Sherer. Articulate, extremely intelligent, charming and modern—unlike nearly all other Aguda rabbis, he was clean-shaven—Sherer was widely acclaimed to be the most-outstanding and influential Orthodox Jewish professional in the United States. Despite my ideological differences with him, I happened to agree with that assessment. Sherer always projected a quality of simplicity and humbleness. He claimed, against all evidence to the contrary, that he was simply a professional servant of the Moetzet who faithfully implemented their decisions. In fact, it was Sherer, with his impressive knowledge of Torah and keen political acumen, who often, but not always, guided the decision-making of the rabbis of the Moetzet.

During our meeting, I promised Sherer that if Aguda and the other right-wing Orthodox groups would join our mission, I would see to it that the mission would be led by three co-equal chairmen—from Aguda, Young Israel, and the Orthodox Union. I also gave him my commitment that the word "Zionist," which would be objectionable to Aguda, would not be used in any public statements. We would lobby for an agreed-upon Orthodox agenda. I asked for Aguda's support on only two issues regarding Israel— support for U.S. foreign aid to the Jewish State, and opposition to the sale of sophisticated weapons to Saudi Arabia and other countries at war with Israel.

Our discussion lasted about three-and-a-half hours. At first Sherer appeared totally opposed to the concept of a unified Orthodox mission to Washington, stating that lobbying on behalf of Israel was a function of AIPAC and not of denominational bodies like ours. However, after a while, he called David Zweibel, the Aguda legal counsel, and asked him to join the meeting. After Zweibel expressed support for my idea, Sherer himself became positive. I left the meeting with a promise from Rabbi Sherer that in January of 1989 he would present my proposal to the Moetzet with the recommendation that Aguda support the idea. He cautioned me, however, not to be overly optimistic.

Unfortunately, Sherer was correct. A few weeks later he called to inform me that the Moetzet had rejected my proposal. The National Council of Young Israel likewise refused to join the mission. It was evident to me from that experience that the leadership of the Moetzet would never work together with the OU, except, perhaps, to recite psalms.

When I became president of the Union in 1994, Sherer invited me to lunch. As usual, he was an affable and sophisticated host. Still, I was hardly a neophyte myself in the ways of Jewish organizational politics and I was vividly aware that if Sherer could have his way, the Orthodox Union would restrict itself to matters of kashruth and *kiruv* (spiritual outreach to non-religious Jews) and leave public-policy issues involving the Orthodox community to be handled by Aguda. However, Sherer well knew that my own reputation had been built on my political acumen and success as a Washington "lobbyist," and that I was committed to opening an OU office in Washington and to project a more robust influence in the capital through the IPA and our new internship program. He must have understood that Aguda's goal would not sit well with me.

During our luncheon conversation, I pressed Sherer on the issue of why Aguda had not given an expression of respect and recognition to Rabbi Joseph B. Soloveitchik OBM, when he had recently passed away. Rabbi Soloveitchik had been the outstanding scholar and rabbinical leader of American Orthodoxy over the past generation. Yet Sherer did not respond directly to my question, citing political concerns inside Aguda as the reason for his reticence. Noting that a number of other rabbinical luminaries had passed away around the same time, I suggested that Aguda should dedicate a subsequent issue of its magazine to all of them, including Rabbi Soloveitchik. I could see, however, that my appeal was falling upon deaf ears. Indeed, shortly thereafter such an issue did come out with a feature on the rabbis who had passed away in the past few years, which, incredibly enough, contained not a word about Rabbi Soloveitchik, who was truly the titan of our generation of Orthodoxy.

In late 1997 the debate over the contentious issue of "pluralism" within Judaism heated up again. Rabbi Sherer arranged a meeting of Orthodox leaders with Prime Minister Binyamin Netanyahu in New York and graciously invited the Orthodox Union, the Rabbinical Council, and Young Israel to join in the meeting. Independently of each other, both the modern Orthodox camp headed by the OU and Aguda had begun the process of putting together a consortium to sponsor public ads in Israel and the United States combating the claims of the Reform and Conservative movements. The group put together by Aguda, which called itself "Am Echod," (One Nation), was successful in gaining the backing not only of their members but some of ours as well. Overall, our advertising campaign was not nearly as successful as that of the Aguda camp.

Sensing his advantage, Rabbi Sherer called me to invite the Orthodox Union to join the "Am Echod" group. I responded that we would certainly consider such a move, provided that all of our partners, not only the RCA (Rabbinical Council of America), but also the Religious Zionists of America and the two modern Orthodox women's groups— Emunah and Amit—were invited to join Am Echod as well. Sherer was adamant that those conditions were not acceptable to Aguda; pointing out that their organization had affiliated women's groups, which were not part of *Am Echod*. He insisted that *Am Echod* should be composed of American Orthodoxy's three major synagogue organizations — Agudath Israel, the Orthodox Union and Young Israel—and all other groups should have a subsidiary role. Only the three main groups should be listed on the stationery of *Am Echod*.

We were attempting to sort out that issue when, during the national convention of Agudath Israel of America over the Thanksgiving Weekend, 1997, Rabbi Elya Svei of the Philadelphia yeshiva made a speech in which he chose to characterize Rabbi Dr. Norman Lamm, the president of Yeshiva University and the titular head of our movement, as a *"soneh Hashem"* (a hater of G-d). Although Svei had apparently not informed the Aguda leadership in advance of what he intended to say, sadly not one person at the Aguda convention stood up to defend Rabbi Lamm or to tell Svei that he was out of line. Certainly no one chose to walk off the podium or out of the hall to protest such a disgraceful and hateful remark. Nor was there any subsequent pronouncement by Aguda of organizational regret offered either publicly or privately.

The Orthodox Union, together with several other modern Orthodox groups, happened to be holding a Thanksgiving convention at the Homowack Hotel in the Catskills at the same time as the Aguda conclave. Ironically, at just about the time that Rabbi Svei made his ugly slur, Rabbi Lamm was giving a keynote address. In it he congratulated Aguda for its outstanding success in organizing a worldwide event at Madison Square Garden a few months earlier to celebrate the *"Siyum Ha-Shas"*—the seven-year cycle of completing the Talmud. Many from the modern Orthodox world, including Rabbi Lamm and myself, had taken part in that wonderful event, which featured the enthusiastic participation of Jews from across Orthodox ideological boundary lines.

Naturally, we at the OU and our counterparts in the other main modern Orthodox organizations were infuriated by Rabbi Svei's comments. The attack on Dr. Lamm was personally hurtful for two reasons. Firstly Dr. Lamm is the titular head of our movement. His teachings and weltanschauung represent a way of life that is extremely meaningful to me. To delegitimize him is to, in effect, make null and void all that I believe in. Secondly, he is one of my two role models. The other being Malcolm Hoenlein, Executive Vice-President of the Conference of Presidents of Major American Jewish Organizations.

On a personal level, especially in my second and third terms of office, I was able to interact with Dr. Lamm without an intermediary and thus we have had a warm and excellent relationship.

Malcolm, who is a close personal friend, is the sine qua non of a dedicated public servant on behalf of the Jewish people. His knowledge, skill, drive, perserverance and political wisdom are second to none in our broad Jewish community. Having had the opportunity to vacation with him and Fraydie on a cruise to Alaska where we both served as "scholars-in-residence," I observed that he is always involved in solving the major problems in the greater Jewish world, even on vacation. On that occasion it was the imprisoned Jews in Iran, which is an untold story that one day will become public knowledge, bringing great deserved honor for Malcolm.

On December 4, after a meeting of all of its former presidents, the Rabbinical Council of America sent Rabbi Sherer a letter expressing its outrage and calling on Aguda to formally disassociate itself from Rabbi Svei's "degrading and extreme remarks." The RCA statement concluded that if Aguda failed to take that step, it would be impossible for the Rabbinical Council henceforth "to have any sort of meaningful relationship with Aguda."

For my part, I had sent Rabbi Sherer a letter along the same lines on behalf of the OU. On December 10, I spoke with him on the phone. Sherer was decidedly in an unapologetic mood and from his questions and remarks made clear to me that he knew exactly what had taken place at a private meeting of the presidents of our various modern Orthodox organizations at the Homowack event. In a reference to the RCA letter, he asked me rhetorically how it could be that the RCA would have relationships with the Reform and Conservative movements, but not with Aguda?

Sherer noted that Rabbi Svei had never previously spoken out at a convention against Dr. Lamm, and that furthermore, when any Rosh Yeshiva (head of a yeshiva) speaks at a convention, he is never speaking on behalf of Aguda as a whole, but only on his own behalf. Sherer also urged that we not rush to judgment until we saw what the full text of Svei's remarks were. As a matter of policy, Rabbi Sherer said, when someone" is *marbitz* (a disseminator of) Torah and speaks at an Aguda convention it "would not be *Kovod Ha'Torah* (respectful of the Torah) to repudiate him." (Years later, at an Aguda dinner in 2002, Rabbi Svei attacked Rabbi Joshua

Fishman of Torah Umesorah in personal terms. He called for Fishman's resignation with the same ferocity that he had exhibited against Rabbi Lamm. Rabbi Svei subsequently resigned from the Moetzet after Rabbi Fishman remained in his post.)

I countered by asking Rabbi Sherer about the mitzvah of admonishing someone who does something wrong, such as publicly embarrassing an individual. He responded that that commandment is not a public one, and people had already spoken to Svei privately. Sherer also said that the Aguda operates on the principle of great respect for its *gedolim* (Torah scholars) and would never publicly express disagreement with any of them. The public understands that whatever any individual says at the convention is not the official policy of the organization. Such a stated policy, he added, comes out only from the office of Agudath Israel of America or in the name of the Moetset.

Rabbi Sherer argued that despite the controversy concerning Rabbi Svei, we should continue to work together. In an obvious effort to sound conciliatory, he said that thanks to my letter he had attained a better understanding of the close relationship between the OU and our sister organizations such as the RCA, Amit and Emunah.

Yet since Sherer had refused to make a public statement condemning Rabbi Svei's remarks, I challenged him to come up with some other way to make it understandable that Rabbi Svei does not speak for Aguda. Sherer answered, "You know Svei says what he says. It has happened before and it will happen again. Going back over the fifty years of Aguda, we have never violated the policy of publicly admonishing one of our gedolim for remarks he had made."

He then read to me the letter the RCA had sent to Agudah, focusing particularly on the following sentence: "We write this letter for indeed a deep cloud has appeared—one which, if it is not dispelled, can abrogate any relationships that the RCA has with Aguda." Sherer asked me; "How could one justify contemplating violating a policy of fifty years especially at a time when we are in the presence of a fire?" He explained that the "fire" he was referring to was the growing influence of the Reform and Conservative movements.

I responded that the board of the Orthodox Union had met the night before, and we had unanimously agreed that we would fully support the RCA letter. I added sternly that we remained "appalled" at Svei's remarks and were quite unmollified by his explanations about Aguda's "policy of not admonishing" its rabbinical gedolim—even when they make slanderous statements that endanger the unity of the Orthodox community.

In response, Rabbi Sherer continued to refer to the perilous "fire in our community." I responded that since there was such a fire, perhaps it was time for Aguda to begin fighting fire with fire by changing its policies toward the rest of the Orthodox community. Perhaps it was time to realize that one man, Rabbi Svei, was standing in the way of unity among all the forces of Orthodoxy, and that Sherer should therefore suggest forcefully to the Moetzet that they change certain policies so that they would disassociate Aguda from the Svei remarks.

Turning to our sources for an analogy that fit the circumstances, I pointed to the Talmudic law which dictates that if marauders surround a town and demand that one specific individual be sent out as a sacrifice in order to spare everyone else, it is permitted for the community to give up that individual. Sherer repeated adamantly that that Aguda's fifty-year old policy would not be changed.

After the death of Rabbi Sherer several years after these events, Rav Perlow, the Novominsker Rebbe, was elected president of Aguda. I tried on a number of occasions to obtain an appointment with him, but was turned down. Although the chairman of the board of the Orthodox Union, Marcel Weber, did meet with Rav Perlow personally, the latter rebuffed Weber when he asked that I be invited. He replied he was not yet ready to meet with the President of the Union. I did meet with the Rosh Yeshiva of Chaim Berlin, Rabbi Aaron Schechter, in the hope that he might use his good offices to help arrange a meeting between Rav Perlow and myself. That meeting never materialized.

I wrote in my final column of *Jewish Action*, the Orthodox Union's magazine, that although our relationship with the senior professional staff of Aguda was excellent, until the titular heads of the OU and Aguda meet and until Aguda encourages their rabbis and scholars to attend our conventions and participate in lectures, the OU and Aguda will never have the kind of relationship that we should have.

I wrote; "Since the death of Rabbi Moshe Sherer of blessed memory our relationship with Agudath Israel has been proper even to the point of cooperating on certain political and public-policy issues. However, true cooperation will not develop until there are meetings and discussions of substantive issues between the titular head of Aguda and the President of the Orthodox Union which, until now, has not occurred."

Rabbi Chaim Dovid (David) Zwiebel, counsel of Aguda and one of its current leaders, wrote to me complaining that my above comments were so obtuse that a number of people in Aguda had been angered that I appeared to be criticizing Rabbi Sherer, whereas others thought I was criticizing the Novaminsker Rebbe and the current leadership. Actually, as I informed Zwiebel, I was neither praising nor criticizing Rabbi Sherer, for whom I had great admiration. Unfortunately, however, like his successors, Sherer was compelled to carry out a policy vis-à-vis the OU that was dictated by the most rabid elements of the anti-Yeshiva University, Rabbinical Council of America, and OU position. So far, neither the Aguda moetzet nor the organization's usually more moderate professional leadership, exemplified for so many years by Rabbi Sherer, has demonstrated the requisite determination to reach out to the modern Orthodox community. Their unwillingness to do so has been profoundly to the detriment of the entire Torah community.

Aguda's non-cooperative attitude has continued up to the present day. On April 7, 2002, representatives of major Orthodox organizations met in an emergency session to discuss plans for participation in a pro-Israel rally. It was the height of Israel's Operation Defensive Shield against Palestinian terrorism and Israel was under intense international criticism.

The representative of Aguda at the meeting, informed me that his organization could not join the other Orthodox groups at a rally. The absence of Aguda from the massive, highly successful 250,000-person rally on the Mall in Washington on April 15 was noted and criticized even by some of Aguda's own supporters, many of whom attended. Rumor had it that objections from Rabbi Svei was one of the reasons Aguda declined to take part. Even at a rally with the OU and the Rabbinical Council of America, Aguda would not agree to have rabbis of either group lead in the recitation of the Psalms or to say the prayer for the State of Israel. Sadly the Union and RCA went along with this.

Efforts At Merger With Young Israel

I was raised in the Young Israel movement. My father was a product of the Young Israel of Brownsville (Brooklyn). When I moved to Monsey, one of the first suggestions I made to our synagogue was that we become an affiliate of the National Council of Young Israel. That suggestion was not followed.

During my medical internship and residency days, I had been an officer in the Young Israel of East Flatbush. As I have noted, my youth was full of pleasant experiences in the Young Israel of Eastern Parkway. I fervently believe in the motto of Yeshiva University—*Torah U'madah* (Torah and secular learning combined)—which represents a weltaunschauung of modernity combined with an unswerving commitment to the Torah and its halachic process. As a young person, I believed the Young Israel philosophy to be totally in sync with that approach. Only years later did its national leadership veer to the right.

The Young Israel of my youth was associated with joy and spirituality. This was especially the case with our Sabbath services, which were filled with spiritually uplifting group singing, and with the soaring Torah sermons delivered by Rabbi Harold Kanatopsky OBM. The rabbi's sermons were on such a high intellectual level that they often left me literally gasping for breath as I listened to him explore the profound depth of the wisdom of our Torah and its traditions.

I was also deeply impressed by the policy of the Young Israel movement of encouraging young people of high school and college age to lead the services as cantors or Torah readers. In these roles, youngsters like myself often had the opportunity to deliver mini-sermons. We had our own youth services that trained us not only in a religious sense, but for leadership roles as well. In addition, our program of gym and social clubs helped forge bonds with friends outside the formal classroom scene. This entire approach of Young Israel was to help our young people attain a feeling of genuine closeness to G-d.

It was not easy being Orthodox in the 1940s and 1950s, although for us it appeared quite natural to observe Sabbath and kashruth. There was a Conservative temple in our neighborhood, but its ideology was completely foreign to my way of thinking, which allowed no room for compromise in man-G-d relations. If my memory serves me, I recall that in my youth more people seemed to be interested in serious discussion about atheism than about Orthodoxy, which they considered irrelevant and doomed to disappear.

In my own case it was an experience with a personal G-d that cemented my underlying faith. My father was critically ill with pneumonia. I recall that Charlie the barber came over to our house to apply boiling cups to his back (bankus) to no avail prior to his entering Unity Hospital in Brooklyn. With tears and deep distress, I prayed to the Almighty and recited the Book of Psalms. When my father recovered, words could not express my gratitude to G-d. My level of belief and devotion has never wavered. From that day forward and even today, more than fifty years later, I look upon that episode as the seminal event in my spiritual growth.

My subsequent struggles in life, whether in medical school or Vietnam, have never been a challenge to my faith, even when I have been in situations where I have been isolated from other Torah Jews for sustained periods. I have always been conscious of living in a wonderful country blessed with religious freedom where no one laughs at a nun in her habit, a devout Catholic with ashes on his forehead on Ash Wednesday, or a devout Hindu or Muslim wearing a turban or veil.

In such a country, why should I have any misgivings about wearing a skullcap or eating only kosher? I have found that Americans judge a person on sincerity, fairness, and talent. While anti-Semitism clearly exists in this country, it has, thankfully, never tainted my own life, nor, honestly, have I even been conscious of its existence around me.

Thus, modernity and the Young Israel movement were synonymous for me when I was growing up. It was only later, when I became involved in the Orthodox Union, that I realized that bad blood existed between the Union and the Young Israel. Even so, I believed those differences were mainly about personalities and that with good will, we could move together in the direction of merger. Both organizations, despite sporadic rhetorical clashes, were appealing to very much the same slice of modern Orthodox Jewry and both appeared to have very similar beliefs and organizational goals. Indeed, almost forty of the 130 Young Israel synagogues across the United States, were also members of the Orthodox Union. In the 1980's, during the presidency of Sidney Kwestel, secret negotiations took place between our two organizations on a possible merger. Marcel Weber and I represented the Union in these discussions, while Young Israel was represented by its executive vice president, Rabbi Frank Sturm. Although Sturm promised Marcel and I that lay leaders of the Young Israel would eventually join the discussions, that never transpired. It happens that Sturm is the father of my brother-in-law, Ira, and I have a very special feeling of friendship for him, even though we often strongly disagreed on how to bring about the merger between our two organizations.

It turned out that despite the obvious similarities between the two organizations, their respective goals and the problems each encountered were significantly different. The Union far dwarfed Young Israel in budget, the size of its staff and the extent of its programming. Whereas Young Israel then had a staff of 10-15, the Union staff—including part time kashruth employees—numbered between 750 and 1000 with its commensurate budgets.

Aside from the avoidance of duplication of dinners, magazines, and fundraising—the question was obvious: Why would we at the OU desire a merger with Young Israel? The Union's strength lay in its national office—with outstanding programs and professional leaders and a sophisticated lay leadership. Our weak point lay in the failure of many of our synagogues and their memberships to identify themselves as members of the Orthodox Union. Indeed, our "brand identity" was basically limited to two areas—kashruth certification and our youth group, the National Council of Synagogue Youth (NCSY).

Young Israel, on the other hand, had a much smaller and weaker central operation but a strong brand identity. To its credit, the organization was able—by concentrating on issuing statements against the peace process and other policies of the Israeli government—to appear larger and stronger than it actually was. I often had the feeling that they accomplished their outsized national reputation with smoke and mirrors and a very deft mastery of public relations. All of this was to the credit of Rabbi Sturm and his successor as executive director, Rabbi Pesach Lerner.

When a young Orthodox couple wished to invite other couples to move to a new area in the suburbs and create an Orthodox synagogue, they would speak of their desire to create a "Young Israel synagogue." In using that name, they made a statement that spoke for itself, since everyone in the Orthodox world had a clear picture of what a Young Israel shul was about. On the other hand our synagogues had names such as the Community Synagogue of Monsey, or Beth Aaron; names that gave no hint of the synagogue's affiliation with the OU. Orthodox people from Monsey to Miami and Scarsdale to Seattle will say, "I went to Young Israel last Shabbos." No one says, "I went to the OU synagogue last Shabbos."

I believed that from the perspective of the OU, it would be worth it for us to merge with Young Israel simply to acquire the Young Israel brand name alone. Motivated as we were in that direction, we worked hard to achieve a merger and were as conciliatory as possible in the terms we offered them. For example, we offered job security and guarantees to the entire Young Israel professional staff. We agreed to keep the Young Israel name above the name of the Orthodox Union in any merger, and promised that the most senior executive of the newly merged organization would be Rabbi Sturm, rather than Rabbis Butler or Stolper.

Nevertheless, despite the deference we showed to Young Israel's sensitivities, when the two organizations got to the point of exchanging employee rosters, the Young Israel leadership went into shock at how much larger we were than them. Clearly, that exchange of rosters left them with a feeling that if the two organizations moved forward toward a merger, the effect would be that Young Israel and its staff would be submerged by the OU rather than merging with us on an equal basis.

In addition to disparity in size between the two organizations, there were three substantive issues that were problematic and prevented us from reaching an agreement on merger back in the '80's. The first was our participation in the Synagogue Council of America, an umbrella group of Orthodox, Conservative and Reform rabbinical and lay bodies that Young Israel opposed on ideological grounds. Then there was the fact that there were a number of old time member Orthodox Union synagogues without a mechitzah (the required separation between men and women in the synagogue), an anathema to the rigorously traditional Young Israel. Finally, Young Israel took an even more militantly right wing approach to the peace process in Israel than did the OU.

As the years dragged on, our two organizations became ever more intertwined despite efforts by Young Israel to oppose this tendency. As more Young Israel synagogues around the country made the decision to affiliate with the Orthodox Union, the Young

Israel leadership became increasingly agitated if an OU leader made a public statement, as I often did, that appeared to suggest that merger was the wave of the future.

At the same time, there was a new factor that was causing increasing friction between the two organizations. During the 1980's and 1990's, there was a proliferation of small Orthodox synagogues in communities around the country. When these congregations reached a certain critical size, they naturally desired a spiritual leader, but often could not afford the cost of hiring a full-time rabbi. To meet this challenge the National Council of Young Israel set up a placement bureau that was often able to find these synagogues relatively inexperienced individuals with *smicha* (ordination) from right-wing "yeshiva" backgrounds who could serve as part-time rabbis.

The creation of this bureau placed the Young Israel parent body in competition with the OU's main sister organizations; Yeshiva University and the Rabbinical Council of America, which ran a placement service for YU-ordained rabbis. It also helped to create a cadre of rabbis who were extremely loyal to Young Israel as well as being strongly opposed to a merger with the OU, which they saw as being opposed to their interests.

At that time, Young Israel also ran two nursing homes. Our request to examine the books of these homes as part of a merger agreement was greeted with less-than-enthusiastic response from the Young Israel leadership. Certainly, the nursing homes issue was one more reason why our merger talks eventually came to naught. The Young Israel approach was that, if there ever was to be a merger, we should tackle one specific project first to see if we could actually work together effectively. Our approach was that we should work out as many problems as we could and then plan a merger that would come into effect within a given period—such as two or three years. We viewed their approach as a way to stymie a merger while making it look as though their intentions were pure and they were making a good faith effort to achieve one.

These differences remained despite the fact that we seemed to be surmounting the three ideological issues that had previously divided us; the Synagogue Council of America (SCA), *mechitzot* and the peace process in Israel. Concerning the issue of the SCA, I found myself actually in agreement with the position of Young Israel. I had long argued within the councils of the OU that we should leave the Synagogue Council—an umbrella group consisting of Reform, Conservative and Orthodox rabbinic and synagogue groups. At one time such a group might have been necessary, in order to enable the organized Jewish community to speak with one voice. Yet with the advent of the Presidents Conference, AIPAC, and other umbrella bodies, the SCA no longer served a useful function. In addition, because the Reform and Conservative constituents took the existence of the Synagogue Council very seriously, they pushed the umbrella body into playing a prominent role in ecumenical discussions with the Vatican and the Catholic Church in America, something which we, the Orthodox, could not be a part of.

More than twenty years earlier, our ultimate rabbinical authority, the revered Rabbi Joseph Soloveichik zt'l, had ruled that it was halchically permissible for the OU and the RCA to belong to the Synagogue Council provided that no theological discussions were undertaken with the Christian Church. As far as engagement with the other streams of American Jewry, Rav Soloveichik had ruled that our work together with the Reform and Conservative movements was to be limited to issues such as Israel and Jewish poverty in America, but not to touch on matters of theology. In my own opinion, the Synagogue Council had repeatedly crossed the red lines laid out by Rav Soloveichik and therefore participation in its activities by Orthodox groups had become counterproductive.

As it turned out, in the first year of my presidency of the Orthodox Union, the Synagogue Council became bankrupt and soon closed its doors. That might have seemed a useful denouement to our long-running dispute over our membership in the organization with Young Israel, except that during our drawn-out negotiations over the issue, my intent had been to use our membership in the SCA as a bargaining chip, and agree to leave the organization at a given future time upon our merger. Unfortunately, our merger negotiations with Young Israel had never reached a level of seriousness whereby I could have offered to pull the OU out of the SCA in exchange for a concession from the Young Israel side.

In certain OU-affiliated synagogues, the difficulty lay in the fact that, decades earlier, the 100-year-old Union had accepted as affiliates about twenty venerable synagogues that did not have kosher mechizot. In the early part of the 20th century standards in some sections of modern Orthodoxy were less strict than they are today. In any event, during the past twenty years we had admitted no new synagogues which did not meet our now more exacting criteria in this area. In addition, we started a process, during the presidency of Sidney Kwestel, of cutting our ties with all non-mechitzah synagogues. This process was basically completed by the end of my term.

This move was necessitated not only by our determination to maintain proper religious standards, but also by a new factor in American life; the advent of the Internet. Since many individuals had begun to check the Orthodox Union website on the World Wide Web when searching for an Orthodox Union-affiliated synagogue where they could daven when on the road and away from home, we realized that we had to insist that a basic standard of adherence to halacha be maintained in all of our synagogues.

In the post-Oslo agreement period after 1993, the OU feared that the agreement endangered Israel's security and that safeguards needed to be built into it. We did not always agree with Young Israel on tactics in terms of how best to manifest opposition to Oslo, but we were very close on the essentials.

Still, throughout the years that the Israeli government was headed by Labor and pressing ahead with the Oslo peace process, Young Israel initiated large-scale demonstrations against the Israeli government, while we opposed doing so. After the assassination of Prime Minister Yitzhak Rabin, Young Israel chose to boycott the memorial event at Madison Square Garden one month after his death, whereas I worked successfully behind the scenes to make it non-political in nature, so that Orthodox Jews who opposed Rabin's peace policies could feel comfortable to attend. On one occasion, Young Israel chose to boycott a meeting in Jerusalem between Foreign Minister Shimon Peres and representatives of American Orthodox Jewish organizations, whereas I eagerly went to the meeting to communicate our feelings of opposition to the policy the Israeli government was pursuing.

Despite the virtual disappearance of ideological differences between Young Israel and the OU during the 1990's—the period during which I served as President of the Union—we were unable to broker a merger. Indeed, discussion barely progressed beyond the stage of preliminary talks. This failure has been due to a Young Israel leadership that clings ever-more fiercely to its separate identity even as there is less and less reason to do so.

Still, I believe strongly that a merger would be in the best interests of the Orthodox community. Combining the respective strengths of both organizations would provide American Orthodoxy with a quantum leap forward into the much-transformed world of the early 21st century and would greatly augment its political power in the process. The problem is that it is much easier to create an organization than to summon the necessary vision and leadership to close the doors of that organization when it has clearly outlived its usefulness. The quite unnecessary duplication of function and the mutually destructive competition between the OU and Young Israel is symptomatic of a problem that is rife throughout American Jewry today; that there are far too many organizations competing for the same stable or even declining base of membership and funding. This is a distraction that the organized Jewish community can ill afford, if it is to hold its own in the ever more efficient, streamlined and inter-connected world of the 21st Century.

Edah

During the late 1990's, a national Orthodox organization known as Edah was founded and, almost immediately, began to cause considerable controversy within the Orthodox community.

Created by a group of left leaning Orthodox individuals, the new organization ran several meetings and conventions during its first few years that were extremely well-advertised and well-attended. During this time, another much-hyped "progressive" Orthodox group was founded, the Jewish Orthodox Feminist Alliance, and they also held national conferences.

As president of the OU, I was very concerned by the portrait these liberal groups were successfully painting of themselves. In their advertising and statements to the media they asserted that they were "modern Orthodox and proud of it." The clear implication of this kind of rhetoric was that those of us in the OU, were neither truly modern Orthodox nor proud of it.

To be sure, neither Edah nor the Jewish Orthodox Feminist Alliance showed signs of developing a significant national following. In truth these organizations were basically kept alive by a small number of very wealthy lay leaders and the encouragement of New York based liberal activists. Still, although minute in size, Edah, especially, captured the imagination of the Anglo-Jewish media, especially the *Jewish Week*. My concern was that in time, with the kind of free publicity it was receiving, Edah might grow from a fringe group to a genuine national movement.

Determined to make my unhappiness known at what I viewed as Edah's none-too-subtle OU-bashing, I had several conversations with Union officers and board members who were close friends of Edah. I explained to them that it was not in the interests of the Orthodox community to countenance the development of a new organization that would compete with established ones like the OU.

At the same time, I held several meetings with the board of *Jewish Action*, our intellectual magazine, to discuss editorial policy. The point of these discussions was to take issue with concerns that had been expressed by some Union officers and assiduously fanned by Edah that we had tilted too far to the right both politically and religiously. I also took vigorous issue with that picture of the OU in meetings with the leadership of the Rabbinical Council and Yeshiva University.

On March 18, 1999, I invited Rabbi Berman to the Orthodox Union office for a meeting. It was a cordial, warm, and open discussion that lasted for two hours. We spoke to each other on a first name basis, which was hardly surprising since I had known Saul Berman since our days at Yeshiva College where I had been one year ahead of him. Nevertheless, I pulled no punches in presenting my concerns. I and many other leaders of the mainstream of American Orthodoxy were concerned that some prominent supporters of Edah might desire to start a new national movement. We perceived this as a danger that they might pass over the *halachic* (Jewish law) red line in doctrinal matters.

I told Berman that I felt Edah's evolving ideological line on certain issues seemed to place them more closely in line with the thinking of Conservative Jewry rather than with the Orthodox version of halacha. I also expressed our consternation that Edah seemed to be implying that theirs was the true face of modern Orthodoxy and that institutions like the Orthodox Union, Yeshiva University, and the Rabbinical Council of America were somehow closet ultra-Orthodox.

I argued to Rabbi Berman that American Orthodoxy was too small for yet another organization, which, if came into being, would further fragment our community and weaken the efforts of groups like the OU to advance the interests of Orthodoxy. Noting that many of the leaders of Edah were already involved in the activities of the Orthodox Union and Yeshiva University, I asked Berman why none of their leaders had come forward within the confines of the OU and YU to argue that these flagship institutions of modern Orthodoxy were moving too far to the right. I then asked Berman directly; "Why haven't you or (other Edah) leaders become more active in the Union and raised the relevant issues with us?"

In response, Berman denied that Edah had any intention of becoming a national movement. Nevertheless, he stressed, there was a need for an organization like Edah to highlight certain issues—including that of the role of women in Judaism—that he believed the Orthodox community was not adequately addressing. Arguing that modern Orthodoxy is in retreat in the face of more right-wing manifestations, Rabbi Berman contended that there were approximately 600,000 Orthodox Jews in the United States—of whom only half can be called "modern."

When, I asked Berman for his definition of "modern Orthodox" he replied that in addition to supporting the State of Israel and sending their children to secular universities and graduate schools and into the professions, adherents of modern Orthodoxy should have a more tolerant and accepting attitude toward the legitimacy of non-Orthodox expressions of Judaism than do the ultra-Orthodox. Yet it was exactly such expressions of tolerance, he argued, that are in retreat in the modern Orthodox movement. He pointed to the demise of the Synagogue Council of America as an example of the rightward trend of Orthodoxy which he and other "modern Orthodox" groups and individuals opposed.

In that context, many critics cited with strong disapproval a much-discussed *bracha* (blessing) of Rabbi Pinchas Stolper, Senior Executive Director of the Orthodox Union, who thanked G-d for the disappearance of the Synagogue Council. I always responded that this was a personal statement by Rabbi Stolper and did not represent the OU as a whole. I also pointed out that despite the demise of the SCA, the Union remains involved in many joint activities with the Conservative and Reform movements and also worked in cooperation with non-religious Jews in many non-theological areas of concern.

I pointed to our active membership in AIPAC, the Presidents' Conference, NJCRAC, JCRC, Memorial Foundation for Jewish Culture and the Jewish Agency to name a few. I noted that Rabbi Butler and I had met privately with Rabbi Erich Yoffie, executive director of the Union of American Hebrew Congregations, the most prominent leader of Reform Jewry, and together with Yoffie and the leaders of the Conservative movement, had initiated letters to President Clinton on behalf of Jonathan Pollard. Therefore, I said, it is ridiculous to suggest we do not engage and work with the non-Orthodox movements. Perhaps, I said, Rabbi Berman was not fully aware of the extent of our outreach in this respect.

We also discussed the issue of religious Zionism. I took strong exception to the assertion that the OU is anything but a strongly Zionist organization; pointed to our unswerving commitment to religious Zionism as well as many public pronouncements and actions we had taken in support of Israel. Indeed, I pointed out, I myself had written and spoken extensively on the subject.

Another charge was that the OU had failed to support the Ne'eman Commission (an Israeli Commission that had focused on solving the contentious "Who Is A Jew" issue), and that we had supposedly co-signed a unity statement with Agudath Israel, an Orthodox organization well to the right of us ideologically. I responded that neither of these charges had any validity. I had been President of the OU for five years and I could recall no such unity statement with Agudath Israel. In addition, I had spent considerable time and effort trying to convince members of the Chief Rabbinical Council in Israel to support the findings of the Ne'eman Commission; pointing out to them that conversions would ultimately be supervised by an Orthodox Beth Din.

Finally, we turned to a discussion of the OU's attitude toward women. Berman argued that there was no organized voice within the Orthodox community on women's issues, and Edah had been created to fill the void. When I asked him why these efforts could not be made within the rubric of the RCA, his reply was that the organization had previously failed in this matter.

Berman dismissed as window dressing the women's organizations the Orthodox Union had set up. He said he found it telling that the OU had no women officers, even though, as I immediately pointed out, we did have female Board members. Berman concluded by noting that Rav Hershel Schachter, head of the Yeshiva University Kollel and our spiritual mentor, had recently stated that women should not be allowed to serve as presidents of synagogues, a stand that Berman himself found unacceptable.

While my meeting with Rabbi Berman was pleasant and we promised to keep our lines of communication open, there was no meeting of the minds and nothing of long-term consequence was accomplished. The decision by supporters of the movement, to open a new rabbinic seminary, appeared to validate my concern that the Edah community desired to break away from Yeshiva University, the Orthodox Union and the RCA. The threat of a disastrous schism within modern Orthodoxy remains very much alive.

Indeed, in November 2002, the Jewish Orthodox Feminist Alliance was discussing female Torah readers at mixed (men and women) services. Unlike the other streams that are clearly identified as conservative, reform, etc., the fact that this group labels itself as "orthodox," "modern orthodox," and "proud modern orthodox" potentially represents a schism in the making which should have been nipped in the bud years ago by our leadership who did not respond to the challenges raised.

My basic question that I have frequently asked of rabbinic and lay leaders of Edah still stands. Why not bring your considerable influence and power to bear within the mainstream organizations (YU, OU, RCA) to make the changes you desire instead of creating a potentially divisive competing organization?

CHAPTER NINE

From Oslo to the Rabin Assassination

I n the summer of 1993 Israel and the PLO stunned the world, announcing that they had reached a historic agreement they hoped would lead to peace after decades of conflict. The PLO recognized Israel's right to exist in peace and security. They committed themselves to renouncing acts of terrorism and violence. The PLO covenant, which called for Israel's destruction, would become inoperative and the PLO leadership would work for its final repeal. Israel, for its part, recognized the PLO as the legitimate representative of the Palestinian people, and affirmed that the United Nation resolutions 242 and 338—recognizing the principle of land for peace—applied to the Palestinians as well as the Arab states.

As a first step toward implementing the agreement, Israel promised to allow the PLO to set up shop in Gaza and the West Bank town of Jericho, with the understanding that if the PLO carried out their side of the agreement, more territory would be turned over to them. Both sides pledged to reach a final peace settlement by 1999.

Although there had been direct bilateral talks between Israel and a Palestinian delegation that did not officially include the PLO at the Madrid Peace Conference in November 1991, no one realized until the Oslo Agreements were announced that secret talks had been going on for months in Norway between high level Israeli and PLO delegations. We later found out that Deputy Foreign Minister Yossi Beilin was the architect of the peace agreement, which he and his mentor, Foreign Minister Shimon Peres, then convinced Prime Minister Yitzhak Rabin to endorse.

The United States government, which for decades had acted as an intermediary between Israel and its Arab enemies, had been kept out of the loop during the secret negotiations, and only found out about the Oslo Agreements hours before they were revealed to the rest of the world. Yet President Clinton chose to overlook that snub and invited Rabin and PLO Chairman Yasir Arafat to a signing ceremony on the White House lawn; thus managing to capture some of the reflected glory from this momentous event.

Sheila and I were in our apartment in Netanya on vacation when the announcement was made on Israeli television and radio of the agreement in Oslo. As someone who had fought for many years on behalf of a secure Israel at peace with its neighbors, and who had bitterly opposed the PLO, I had very mixed feelings upon hearing of a peace agreement that would apparently force Israel to make painful territorial concessions in the heart of Eretz Yisrael, and incredibly enough, would establish murderous Yasir Arafat, with so much Jewish blood dripping from his hands, as the governing authority in much of Gaza, Judea and Samaria. Still, upon reflection, I took some solace from the possibility that we were witnessing a true miracle that would actually result in lasting peace.

Before I even had time to absorb the news, I received an unexpected call from Senator Harris Wofford who happened to be in Israel on a fact- finding mission. Wofford informed me that on the following day he was going to meet with Prime Minister Rabin and invited Sheila and I to join him and his small group at the meeting. I thanked Harris profusely and told him that Sheila and I would meet him early the following morning at the King David Hotel in Jerusalem.

Thus, the next day, my wife and I found ourselves together with Senator Wofford in the Prime Minister's office face to face with Yitzhak Rabin. The Prime Minister opened the meeting by expressing his delight that Israel had reached an agreement with the PLO, long its most inflexible enemy. Rabin said that Israel had no choice but to make certain difficult concessions, like abandoning its longtime quest for the concept of the "Greater Land of Israel" because of the danger she confronted from "Khomeinism without Khomeini;" the growing peril that fundamentalism and rejectionism, as typified by Iran and Iraq, represented the wave of the future in the Arab and Islamic worlds.

Given that grave danger, the Prime Minister said, it was imperative that Israel reach peace with its immediate neighbors, including the Palestinians, so as to keep these hard-line states away from the conflict. Only if Israel accomplished that goal, Rabin argued, could it protect itself against the onslaught of Islamic fundamentalism.

I had met Rabin many times before, but always as part of delegations from the Presidents'Conference, AIPAC or other American Jewish groups. On those occasions, he had always seemed stiff, reserved and even taciturn. The fact that a U.S. senator was leading our small delegation, rather than Jewish leaders, seemed to make a major difference in Rabin's demeanor; this time he was warm, friendly, and even mildly gregarious. Evidently he saw someone like Wofford as being a fellow political professional and therefore more on his level.

When Rabin completed his presentation, I challenged the Prime Minister's analysis of the political situation that had led him to reach an accommodation with the PLO. Wasn't it the case, I asked Rabin, that after the PLO was chased out of Lebanon by the IDF, it became an increasingly moribund organization? Why had he decided to resuscitate the PLO by signing an agreement that allowed Yasir Arafat and his gang to return from exile in far-off Tunis to rule a "Palestinian entity" in the heart of Eretz Israel? If he was convinced of the need to reach an agreement with the Palestinians, I asked, why had he not waited for another three years until the PLO was totally defunct? In that case, he could have made a deal with indigenous Palestinian leaders, such as Hanan Ashrawi and Feisel Husseini, rather than the murderous Arafat.

Rabin responded by saying, "We can't afford to wait for three years. "In three years, Hamas will take over from the PLO. We can deal with the PLO; we cannot deal with Hamas, who are fundamentalists. In three years Hezbollah will take over Lebanon. We can deal with the Lebanese government, not with Hezbollah, who are fundamentalists." Finally, Rabin said candidly that he was getting on in years, and wanted to go out as the prime minister who had brought peace to the people of Israel.

I couldn't have imagined when I left Rabin's office that day that in only two weeks I would witness him sign the Oslo agreement on the White House lawn and then awkwardly extend his hand to Israel's bitterest enemy, Yasir Arafat. It was surreal enough

that late August day to sit in the office of the prime minister of
Israel and listen to him talk about making peace with the PLO.
As he spoke, I wondered to myself; 'Could such a thing really be
happening in my lifetime? Had I been wrong all along in my
political analysis. Perhaps it was possible, after all, to reach a just
and lasting peace with the Arabs, including the PLO that would
allow Israelis to live in peace and security.

From our meeting with the Prime Minister, those of us in
Senator Wofford's delegation taxied to the American Consulate
opposite the Sheraton Plaza Hotel for a meeting with a delegation of Palestinian leaders. Many times before and since that visit
I have walked or driven by the consulate with a deep sense of
resentment that the U.S. diplomats inside deal primarily with
Palestinian Arabs, rather than Israelis and remains almost independent of the U.S. Embassy in Tel Aviv. No other country in the
world has an American Consulate which functions in such a
manner, more in harmony with the Arabs than with the Israelis,
although located in the heart of the capital of the Jewish state.

On that day in August 1993, one could feel the euphoria in
the corridors of the Consulate as its diplomats sniffed the heady
smell of peace and fraternity around the corner. During our
meeting with the Palestinian delegation, whose names I unfortunately did not write down and have since forgotten, one Palestinian made one of the most outrageous statements I have ever
heard. He said in a matter of fact tone that since the Palestinians
did not yet constitute a state and were therefore not subject to
intense scrutiny by civil or human rights organizations as was
Israel, they had it in their power to wipe out Hamas and other
terrorist organizations by simply massacring all of their members. All of the U.S. officials in the meeting simply smiled without raising their voices in protest at this bloodthirsty scenario.

As it turned out, of course, not only did the massacre scenario not occur, but the Palestinian Authority would soon become partners in terrorism with Hamas and Islamic Jihad. At
that time, however this official delegation was proposing to us
that they would carry out a policy of massacring many of their
own people and expressing the opinion that this would be necessary to achieve peace in the region. Certainly, based on the
response in the room, there seemed little doubt that if they
embarked upon such a course, the world would not say, "boo"
in response.

Flash forward two weeks later to the ceremony on the White House lawn on the beautiful sunny afternoon of September 13, 1993. I looked around at the crowd, and saw so many people I had met during my intense involvement in pro-Israel activism for more than a decade. There were many members of Congress present—some of whom had become my friends during my many lobbying forays to Capitol Hill. There were the leaders of the organized Jewish community and representatives of the Anglo-Jewish press, as well as diplomats from the Israeli Embassy in Washington and the Consulate in New York. Hundreds of machers (big shots) had been clamoring for tickets and only those with first-rate connections managed to get them. A few right-wingers had denounced every Jewish leader who attended the event, which they considered a sellout to Arafat and the PLO.

What were my innermost feelings on that historic day? I was torn between a hope against hope that the Israeli-PLO agreements would really work and we would finally see an end to many decades of Arab-Israeli warfare, and a contrasting conviction that we could never really trust either the PLO or the Arab nations surrounding Israel. One of the reasons I always gave copies of Leon Uris' *The Haj* to Senators and Congressmen was to acquaint them with the "Arab mentality," of which exaggeration and lying naturally form a part. I could never forget that the Koran calls on Muslims to make temporary peace with their enemies, so they can strengthen themselves in preparation for a final battle. Mohammed himself had successfully employed this tactic against his enemies, including the Jews of Medina.

As I sat there in the warm sunshine, I pondered whether the Arab countries were truly prepared to say to their people in Arabic that it was time for peace with Israel. Would they say it explicitly via radio and television? Would they teach it in their schools? Based on what I had read in *The Haj* and in other books on the Arab world like Joan Peters' *From Time Immemorial*, I was extremely skeptical they would do so.

The signing ceremony was an electric, highly emotional occasion. President Clinton was followed at the speaker's podium by Foreign Minister Shimon Peres, who was followed in turn by Mahmoud Abbas, a member of the executive committee of the PLO. Then the historic signing of the Oslo agreement by Rabin and Arafat took place. The crowd was on its feet. And in that memorable photograph we have seen many times over the years, the youthful-looking U.S. President seemed to wrap his arms around all of the participants—thereby seemingly coaxing Mr. Rabin to grit his teeth and extend his hand to his archenemy, Yasir Arafat. The entire audience stood as one and cheered this spectacle. I stood like everyone else. Tears were pouring down from my eyes. I did not know if these were tears of sadness or joy. Were we being tricked? At that moment, I prayed my grave doubts would prove unfounded. I prayed that I was having the privilege at that moment of being not simply a witness to a unique moment in modern history but also to the fulfillment of generations of hopes and prayers for peace for the Jewish people. Was this the millennial moment in history when we would see the fulfillment of the Prophet Isaiah's words; that at last we would beat swords into plowshares and spears into pruning hooks?

Upon leaving the signing ceremony, I, like many of the other guests, headed over to the Israeli Embassy, where a large party was underway. In normal times, the Israel Embassy in Washington is a serene place on a secluded block with strict security. Yet on that historic day, the embassy was the scene of almost complete bedlam. It seemed that the embassy had invited almost everyone at the signing to come over to celebrate. There was no program and no decorum; but rather what seemed like a thousand people milling around in a space meant for about 200. Many guests were trying to hug or kiss Mr. Rabin or Mr. Peres or to get them to autograph the White House program. It was too crowded to even consider taking photos. I was fortunate enough to have both men sign my program. Neither Peres nor Rabin were normally gregarious individuals, but they put up well with the joviality of the day. Indeed, they seemed almost euphoric themselves.

One month later, on October 18, during an interview with a Rockland County newspaper, I was asked if I supported the peace plan. I answered by noting that while the Orthodox community supported the concept of peace, it was important to remember that despite the signing on the White House lawn "Peace has not broken out. This is just the beginning of stages. We have concerns about the PLO and its motives—economically, politically and militarily."

I then made two contrasting points; one that we in the Orthodox community would support the Government of Israel even when we disagreed with it, and two, that we would continue our political efforts on behalf of Israel in Washington in spite of voices which were already saying that with the advent of peace that support would soon no longer be needed. I told the interviewer; "We support the right of the Israeli government to do what it thinks is best, even if we do not always agree with it. Israel is a democracy. Who are we in America to make these decisions? (The Israelis) put their lives on the line." Nevertheless, I commented: "This is not the time for the American Jewish community to cease its political activism." Whatever lay ahead, I said, Israel would need the assistance of its American friends for a long period of time.

The agreement signed in 1993 gave the new Palestinian Authority physical control only over the Gaza Strip and the West Bank town of Jericho. It also contained numerous provisions for the early empowerment of the Palestinian Authority, which gained administrative control throughout the Palestinian areas in fields like education, culture, taxation, and tourism. The agreement created a large and well-armed Palestinian police force. This move ultimately would have severe negative implications for Israel; as this force grew into an offensive army—double and even quadruple the size projected for it. Incidentally, even as Israel was encouraging the creation of an armed Palestinian force, only fifty percent of the PLO Council voted in favor of the Oslo Accords, with many denouncing it as a sell-out to Israel.

Thus, despite the warm sentiments expressed at the 1993 White House signing ceremony, peace, clearly, was not just around the corner. Nevertheless the left wing in the American Jewish community constantly urged the Clinton Administration to put ever-greater pressure on Israel for escalating concessions to the Palestinians that even the dovish Rabin government was often unable to accept.

As the months went by, the Orthodox community became ever more apprehensive about the direction the peace process was moving, despite the good intentions manifested at Oslo and at the White House signing ceremony. At the Union's convention in November 1994, at which time I was installed as president, we responded to the growing external pressure on the Israeli government to give up the Golan Heights to Syria by passing a resolution affirming that Israeli foreign policy should be decided by the people of Israel. In my inaugural address to the convention, I expressed concern about the grave dangers American troops would encounter were they to be stationed on the Golan between Israel and Syria as part of a peace agreement with the latter country: "As long as Syria continues to occupy Lebanon and is involved in narcotics and terrorist activities, it is not a worthy partner for peace."

I also took the occasion to express grave concern about the failure of the PLO to renounce the thirty two articles in its infamous charter calling for the destruction of Israel. As long as that remained the case, I said, the U.S. should not be giving financial aid to the Palestinians.

There were those who criticized me for what they characterized as the militant tone of my speech and theorized that my goal was to transform the OU into a political action committee similar to HUVPAC. Actually, I was determined to create an OU office in Washington in order to create a leadership role for the Union in Jewish life and to better spread the word of Torah. Taking clear positions on public policy issues seemed to me very much in line with my overall goals for the Union.

Given that the Rabin government considered the OU to be hostile to its position, the only member of that government who would consent to address our 1994 convention was Yossi Beilin, the ultra-dovish deputy foreign minister, who evinced a refreshing willingness to appear before groups who did not agree with him. In order to present a balanced point of view, we asked Dr. Marcos Katz, chairman of our board of governors and a close friend of General Ariel Sharon, to invite him as well. Thus, on the final day of our convention, over 1000 delegates were treated to a Beilin-Sharon debate.

Despite the fact that my personal political leanings were obviously much closer to those of Sharon, I found that on a human level it was much easier to deal with Beilin. The latter placed no conditions on his appearance at the convention, except to be given the chance to make the government's case. One had to admire his willingness to step into the lion's den before an audience that was certain to be hostile. Concerned that things could get out of hand, I took the time at the breakfast preceding the debate to remind convention delegates that they should behave with civility. Beilin and Sharon were our honored guests and should be treated as such. Our people should feel free to ask tough questions, but should also abstain from undignified behavior. Our rank and file responded as they should have, and the debate took place in a dignified atmosphere. I believe that most of our people appreciated Beilin's intellect, if not his political positions. He received polite applause but, of course, the audience favored Sharon.

Before the meeting I divided the OU officer corps into two groups for concurrent private meetings with each of our distinguished guests. Since Beilin was in the government, I attended that meeting, which was the larger of the two. During that session, Beilin focused on his idea of bringing young diaspora Jews on a visit to Israel at no cost to themselves; a kernel of an idea that would develop into the Birthright Israel program. Beilin argued that every Jewish child in the world should receive a voucher for travel to Israel; something that would prevent many of them from giving way to assimilation and intermarriage.

For our part, we informed Beilin that his idea was a superb one but that a major deficiency in the plan as he outlined it was the lack of a set program for the young people once they arrived in Israel. Beilin felt that even sitting on the beaches of Tel Aviv would accomplish his goal. Our point of view was that the success of this type of program depended upon proper planning and educational substance. Where would you send these young people? Who would supervise a formal-informal program? Beilin responded that none of the above was necessary. All the visitors would need was the opportunity to come into contact with the electric atmosphere that Israel provides, especially for young people.

Sidney (Shimmy) Kwestel, the OU's immediate past president, asked Beilin whether, as a general principle, one ought not to conduct a serious market survey before undertaking a multi-million dollar enterprise. Why not give organizations like the OU, which has enormous experience in bringing American youth to Israel for summer and yearlong programs, the opportunity to undertake such a market survey for the government of Israel? Shimmy added that the OU would be in the position to develop some pilot projects. Beilin responded that he appreciated the ideas, but made no commitment. Clearly, he had a much more secular perception of what draws diaspora Jewish kids to Israel than we did.

Nevertheless, once the Birthright Israel program got off the ground a few years later, funded by philanthropists Michael Steinhardt and Charles Bronfman, the OU's youth organization, NCSY, became a full partner in the program, which brought

American college students to Israel without cost to themselves. Beilin deserves considerable credit for coming up with the idea and selling it to the American Jewish leadership.

The Sharon-Beilin debate took place at the closing session of the convention. The weathermen forecast a heavy snowstorm for that day. I knew that our delegates would be apprehensive, as they had to drive home not only to New York but also to Philadelphia, Baltimore, Washington and places in South Jersey. Sharon demanded that he should speak first and answer questions first as well. Beilin readily agreed to those conditions.

Throughout the debate that followed, Sharon spoke of security as a prerequisite for peace and emphasized that the Arabs were still committed to destroying Israel, while Beilin stressed the cardinal importance of the peace process for Israel's future. Beilin accused Sharon of endangering the prospects for peace with the Palestinians by insisting that no settlements should be dismantled, even though he himself had carried out the destruction of Yamit while defense minister in 1982. Sharon acknowledged the precedent, but stressed that there was no comparison between the distant Sinai and Judea and Samaria in the heart of Eretz Israel and at the heart of Jewish history. He won ardent applause when he told the audience, "Yerushalyim, Har Habayit, Hebron, Beit El and Shiloh are yours no less than ours."

In his turn, Beilin retorted, "I subscribe totally to the Orthodox Union resolution that Jews have the right to live wherever they want in the land of Israel, no matter what political solution is made."

The debate was on a high level and the audience clearly relished it. It started to snow just as the kitchen was preparing to bring out the food. It was obvious that, given the inclement weather, we would have to end the debate if we were to have lunch. I asked the delegates if they preferred to skip the food and allow Beilin and Sharon to continue. There was wild applause and agreement. When it came time for the question and answer period, Beilin turned to me and said that since Sharon had gone first in answering questions, he felt it would be fair if they now reversed the order. I agreed, even though Sharon was not pleased by what he saw as a reversal of the agreement made at the beginning. In any case, I was pleased to be able to show that despite my own ideological position, I had treated Beilin with the respect he deserved as a minister in the government of Israel.

It turned out that the 1993 Oslo agreements were only the beginning. After a meeting at Taba in the spring of 1995, the so-called "Oslo 2" agreements were consummated. This agreement called for the redeployment of Israeli forces from the main cities of the West Bank (Jenin, Nablus, Ramallah, Bethlehem, Hebron, Tulkarm and Qaqaliya); to be followed by elections of a Palestinian president and a Palestinian Council. There were to be three zones of control. The first was Area A—the Palestinian cities, which constituted only three to five percent of the land but one-third of the Arab population, where the Palestinians were to be in charge of both administration and security. Area B, which consisted of 400 villages and surrounding areas were to be under Palestinian civilian control, but the IDF would remain in charge of security. Area C—which consisted of uninhabited areas as well as Israeli settlements and military posts, would remain under Israeli control. No settlements were to be dismantled, and Israel was to maintain control of the water supply.

In a major concession, Israel would allow Arabs from Jerusalem to run for the Palestinian Council in elections set for January 1996 as long as they had a second address outside of Jerusalem. In addition, East Jerusalem residents with a second address could vote in the Palestinian elections at the main East Jerusalem post office. Israel also promised to release 1500 Palestinian prisoners.

With the signing of Oslo 2, Israel's "red lines," the parameters beyond which it had repeatedly proclaimed it would not go in terms of making concessions to the Palestinians, suddenly appeared to have became inoperative. In August of 1995, after the signing of the new agreements, Rabin's red lines appeared to be Jerusalem and retention of the Jordan Valley. Yet even the new red lines looked less than solid, given an informal understanding reached between Yossi Beilin and Arafat's top aide, Abu Mazen, which would have given nearly all of the West Bank to the Palestinians and allowed them to establish their capital in Abu Dis, a suburb of Jerusalem. Meanwhile, as Israel's leaders continued to make concessions, Arafat's own "red lines" remained unchanged; namely Jerusalem as the capital of the Palestinian state and the "right of return" to all of Israel for all Palestinian refugees from 1948 and their descendants.

As 1995 progressed, the internal divisions in Israel over Oslo 2 grew exponentially, causing great anguish for the people of Israel. The threat of civil strife between those backing Prime

Minister Rabin and the peace process on one side, and the settlers and Likudniks opposing the peace process on the other, appeared to be increasing daily. The settlers pointed out that Rabin himself had been among the politicians who had previously encouraged them to build their homes and futures in Judea and Samaria. Yet, now he was prepared to tear the country apart by making life untenable in the settlements. Acts of civil disobedience were talked about and occasionally acted out.

American Jewry was likewise divided. Most of the Orthodox community was on the hawkish side of the debate, but the Orthodox leadership felt limited in taking issue with the dovish Rabin government because of our longstanding policy of not challenging Israeli government policy on security-related issues. Yet what the Rabin government was doing seemed to us to be endangering Israel's very future, and it felt increasingly frustrating to sit quietly by as Israeli society drifted toward civil war.

While we tended toward the right-wing side of the ledger, in fact the leadership of the Orthodox Union cut across all shades of political opinion. Union leaders were not "knee-jerk anything." Yet overall, our leaders were deeply concerned about what was happening in Israel. Many had children and family living and studying there. At the same time, we were being accused by people both inside and outside our organization of straddling the issues and not being outspoken enough in defending the "Land of Israel" and the "settlers," many of whom came from our own movement in Israel.

We were constantly struggling with the dilemma of how to make it clear that we were horrified with the PLO and Arafat, and supported Judea and Samaria as an integral part of biblical Israel, but still backed the government of Israel in its search for peace. As noted, we were constrained by our unwillingness to publicly criticize the Israeli government. After all, who were we as people living 6000 miles away in the comfort of America who did not send our children to the Israeli army and did not vote or pay taxes in Israel to tell the democratic government of Israel how it should decide on security issues? It seemed to me that too many Americans were prepared to fight "to the last Israeli."

I am certainly not a pacifist. I believe a country must be willing to go to war, if necessary, to protect its security and ensure its survival. Still, I have an intimate understanding of the destructive impact of war on both soldiers and civilians. It is for

this reason more than any other that I have always been convinced that it is unconscionable for outsiders to tell Israelis what
to do on life or death issues of war and peace. Those of us on the
outside may feel that certain decisions Israel makes are ill-con-
cerned, yet if we love and support Israel, we should support
their right as a democracy to determine the course they think is
best for the security of their own people. It is not our own lives
that are on the line, but those of Israelis. They are the ones who
vote in elections to choose the government of Israel. All of that
seemed self-evident, but as things came undone in Israel in the
years after the signing of the Oslo Accords, not everyone in the
American Orthodox community was ready to accept that logic
and lower their voices.

Realizing that in the aftermath of Oslo 2 our community needed
to express its views in a way that would not challenge the right
of Israelis to make their own security decisions, I appointed a blue
ribbon panel composed of a cross-section of our leadership to
craft a statement concerning the situation in Israel that we could
all subscribe to. Chaired by Julius Berman, a distinguished former
OU president, the panel spent twenty five hours preparing the
document, which even our critics agreed was a well thought
through and eloquent statement.

On August 28th 1995, we sent our statement to Prime Minister
Rabin. It didn't take long for us to receive a response. Concerned
that the statement would undercut the perception of American
Jewish support for the Israeli-Palestinian peace process, Israel's
Ambassador to the United States, Itamar Rabinovich, and Israeli
Consul General in New York, Colette Avital, each phoned me within
hours and tried to dissuade the Orthodox Union from issuing the
letter as a public statement. Nevertheless, we decided to do so and
went ahead with plans to run public service ads containing the
statement in both the Anglo-Jewish papers and the *New York Times*.

The OU statement, which strongly urged American Jews to
stand together in solidarity with our brethren in Israel, contained
no direct criticism of Israeli government policies. Nevertheless, we
tackled head on issues that the Rabin government had chosen to
play down and expressed agreement with the position of then-
Israeli President Ezer Weizmann that in light of continued suicide
bombing attacks on Israeli civilians by groups like Hamas and
Islamic Jihad, Israel should take a "time out" to re-assess the impact of the ongoing peace process.

The statement expressed our displeasure with the burgeoning Palestinian governmental presence in the city of Jerusalem. It affirmed our belief that Jerusalem, the City of Gold and the center of our daily prayers and aspirations, belongs to the entire Jewish people, and therefore every Jew around the world has as much of a right to comment on the city's fate as do Israeli citizens or even Israeli cabinet members.

We also expressed alarm over the growing civil strife among Israeli Jews and about the escalating dangers to the security of 150,000 residents of the Jewish settlements. They had acted upon the advice of a string of Israeli governments, including that of Mr. Rabin during the 1970's, to settle beyond the green line.

In a direct reference to President Weizmann, formerly a peacenik who had lately been calling for a pause in and a reevaluation of the peace process (which he had taken to calling a "bloody process"), we urged him to "heal the wounds of a fractured nation as you continue your search for peace. Bring your people alongside you in your quest. Slow the process as you reach out to a nation in despair. In the name of Jewish unity and destiny we plead with you to use your resolve to unite our nation through a dialogue with all elements of Israeli society in order to bring about a sense of unity that the Jewish people so desperately require before proceeding further."

At the end of August, Sheila and I were again vacationing in Netanya while our son Ari and new daughter-in-law Banji were celebrating their honeymoon in Jerusalem. I received a call from them informing me that the *Jewish Press*, a New York-based Orthodox weekly, had attacked the OU with a headline on page one to underline its importance. It was the beginning of a series of such attacks on myself and the OU that ceased only after the assassination of Prime Minister Rabin.

I was quite upset after reading the editorial and my initial reaction was to prepare a blistering response. However, as I have done often before and since, I relied on the wisdom of Sheila— who advised me not to respond. I was also attacked on the Internet by far right wing groups.

Being publicly attacked from the left is something I fully expect and even thrive upon. Such attacks get my juices going. Being attacked from the right, on the other hand, was a shock that left me somewhat disoriented. I have always considered myself a moderate right-winger, both in domestic and international politics. But I have learned from bitter experience that those holding extreme positions on either the left or right cannot tolerate someone who agrees with their position seventy or eighty percent of the time. Either you are with them 100 percent of the time and endorse their extreme positions as *Torah me Sinai* (Torah given on Sinai), or they consider you an enemy.

I similarly ran into some very vocal criticism from people who are normally my allies when I testified on September 20, 1995 before the House Committee on International Relations on the issue of U.S. funding for the Palestinian Authority. During my testimony, I cited the AIPAC policy statement of 1995 in order to point out that the nation's main pro-Israel lobby supports the Spector-Shelby-Lowey amendments. This links the funding of the Palestinian Authority to compliance with PLO commitments. I urged that U.S. funds already appropriated to the PA but not yet delivered be placed into escrow until the PA fully met obligations it had agreed to under the Oslo Accords. However, top professionals at AIPAC, under pressure from both the Israeli and U.S. governments to support U.S. funding for the PA, let me know that they were not entirely pleased with my interpretation of their policy statement. On the other hand the harder-line Zionist Organization of America, testified at the hearings against granting any U.S. funds at all to the PA. Despite my stance, there were some who took me to task for being too soft.

During my presentation to the Committee, which since the beginning of 1995, had been chaired by my old friend and congressman from Rockland County, Benjamin Gilman, I stressed the failure of the Palestinian Authority to carry out its obligations under the Oslo Accords. These included its unwillingness to renounce and revoke the PLO Covenant, disarm Hamas and other Palestinian terror groups still committed to war against Israel, and turn over terrorists to Israel— as well as the continuation of anti-Israel incitement in the Palestinian media and its use of Orient House as a quasi diplomatic mission in East Jerusalem. These were proof positive that the PA was in flagrant violation of the accords.

I pointed to reports in the British media that Arafat had accumulated at least twelve billion dollars in Swiss and other European banks instead of spending these funds for the betterment of his people. The U.S. General Accounting Office was refusing to give Congress its findings on this question, since they considered it to be highly classified. Indeed, to this date we do not know the full amount of Arafat's investments in Swiss and other banks. Given the PA's failure to keep its word on critically important commitments to Israel under the Oslo Accords and given its own very considerable funds, I argued that its behavior could be considered as a cause to put appropriations in escrow as a matter of "law" and not merely "a sense of Congress." Thus, we would give real teeth to the bill.

I had come up with the idea of putting U.S. funds for the PA into escrow during a previous meeting with Gilman and his staff. Gilman took to the idea immediately, but as I learned the day I testified on Capitol Hill, it was difficult to build support for the concept among normally pro-Israel senators and congresspeople. The problem was that both the Clinton Administration and the Israeli Embassy were supporting full funding for the PA. Making the rounds of Congress, I realized that although many of its members agreed philosophically that the PLO deserved no funding, they naturally had no stomach to fight the Administration without an explicit statement and request from the Israeli government itself. The Israeli position, as articulated on the Hill, was that as bad as Arafat was, any potential successor would be worse. Only American funding could entice him to be a serious partner, preventing his collapse, which would lead to anarchy in the Palestinian territories.

Before I went up to the Hill that day, I had secured the permission of the mainstream Orthodox organizations—AMIT, Emunah, Young Israel, Poale Agudah, Rabbinical Council of America, and the Religious Zionists of America—to allow me to testify on their behalf in support of the escrow concept. But Ambassador Itamar Rabinovich called me a number of times and pressed me not to testify. Although our conversations were always civil and correct, I knew he was very angry when I insisted on pressing ahead. The AIPAC leadership was, likewise, quite upset, and during the hearings, many of my old friends at AIPAC refused to acknowledge me. I found this gratuitous and very hurtful.

Needless to say, I was not happy to break with AIPAC, where I had begun my career as a pro-Israel activist and which was still by far the most important pro-Israel organization in America. Yet I believed that the position I was advocating on behalf of the modern Orthodox groups was more in line with AIPAC's own policy statement adopted unanimously by its policy conference than the approach they were following on the Hill that day.

Luckily this break in our relationship was short lived. A few months later, a number of the AIPAC senior staff privately acknowledged to me the correctness of my position while still arguing that I had been unwise to testify for them on the Hill. Thus my mini-estrangement from AIPAC came to a reasonable conclusion.

On September 8, in an op-ed piece in the *Jewish Press*, entitled "A Questionable OU Certification," a member of the OU Board, blasted us for not consulting rabbinical authorities, before issuing our statement. Despite this and other complaints against me, I remained the only member of the pro-Israel community who was able to get directly to Senator Jesse Helms. As noted, Helms and I later came up with a formula to punish the PA by withholding funding, a coup which was breathlessly documented in the *Forward*. Subsequently in 2001 when Senator Jesse Helms announced he would retire in 2002, Doug Bloomfield who long ago left his position at AIPAC, and now writes a political column for Jewish newspapers described my role in the "conversion of Jesse Helms" to a pro-Israel position. I hope some of my critics took note.

In an open letter to me dated October 20, 1995, the same Board member purported to show how I had betrayed the settlers and the national camp in Israel.

I strongly disagreed with many of the article's suppositions. For example, he claimed that the OU had supported Oslo 2, when in fact we had never discussed or taken a position on it. The article castigated my testimony before Congress; condemning me for having only demanded that the U.S. put its funding of the PA into escrow rather than cutting it off completely. The latter goal was in my opinion politically impossible at the time. He apparently wanted the symbolism of advocating an ending to all U.S. support of the PA, even if the effort failed rather than a substantive political initiative that might take us a long way in that direction.

The article also condemned the OU leadership's refusal to support civil disobedience in Israel as a means of protests against government policy. On the last point, I must admit that the author was correct. I have always believed that civil disobedience is counterproductive. Even if it would have been a wise strategy for the Israeli right in 1995, I believed strongly that it was not appropriate for American Jews to advocate that it be used against any elected government of Israel, even one that we disagreed with.

The letter further charged that the Union's board had not spoken in opposition to police brutality in Israel against settlers during anti-government demonstrations. In fact, I had spoken many times privately to government officials about our concerns regarding a series of such incidents. But I also believed that for a major Jewish organization to criticize Israel publicly on such an issue would only have played into the hands of anti-Semites—especially in view of public comments by anti-Israel groups or human rights organizations and the State Department regarding supposed human rights violations by Israel in its treatment of Palestinians.

Finally, he also attacked the OU Board for failing to endorse a call for a referendum by Israelis to decide whether to endorse the Oslo 2 Accords. Here again, I viewed this is an internal matter for the Israeli populace to decide without pressure from American Jewry.

Of course I had other detractors. Dr. James Zogby, President of the Arab American Institute was quoted as calling me "one of those people" who twist the minds of Congress with distorted facts and play off stereotypes of the past.

There was every indication at that point in late October 1995 that the attacks on me would continue and that the hard-liners would make an issue of my supposed dovishness at the 1996 OU convention or even attempt to run a right-winger against me for the presidency in the fall of 1996. I was heartened that many members of my synagogue in Monsey made a point of coming up to me and saying that they thought the attacks on me were highly unfair. Still, it looked like there were stormy days ahead.

All of that came to an end on November 4, 1995, when we received the shocking news that Yitzhak Rabin had been assassinated by an Orthodox Jewish assailant while speaking at a peace rally in Tel Aviv. In the wake of the assassination, the entire community right and left joined in a period of introspection and mourning.

Soon thereafter, I had an opportunity to meet with Rabbi Sholom Klass, the publisher of the *Jewish Press*, and its lay leaders to try to defuse the tensions and find a way to work together on our common goals. The meeting seemed to clear the air. Since then, our relationship has improved so much that in 2002 the newspaper publicly lauded me for spearheading the successful campaign by the Religious Zionists of America coalition to the World Zionist Congress. They have been extremely helpful in my campaign to re-energize and revitalize the Religious Zionists of America. On this point I am deeply appreciative of Jerry Greenwald's leadership.

I was deeply grieved by the killing of Rabin. While I strongly disagreed with his "peace policies," he was a great leader of Israel and the entire Jewish people. He was a warrior and a diplomat, who strove for peace and security for his people. No one could doubt his sincerity or his ultimate goal of a real and lasting peace. In addition, the murder of any elected leader is a dagger in the very heart of a democracy. No society can allow such things to occur without risking a dictatorship.

I was privileged to meet with Rabin several times during the final months of his life. This was a period of great stress and escalating cultural and political conflict between the Torah community and secular groups in Israel. The most memorable meeting came as a result of an invitation from the Prime Minister to myself and other presidents of American Orthodox organizations to come to Jerusalem to discuss ways to try to calm the atmosphere. The prime minister listened carefully and respectfully to what we had to say and we left that meeting feeling we had been at least partially successful in impressing upon Rabin the need to avoid the kind of harsh rhetoric that could increase the danger of a kulturkampf between the opposing camps.

The last time I saw Rabin was immediately prior to his death at a breakfast at the Regency Hotel in Manhattan where he was briefing the Presidents Conference. I asked him if he could lay out his vision for how the Palestinians would govern themselves. He replied simply, "an entity, not a state." I countered that there is no such animal on the world political stage or in international law. He retorted, "We'll make one." It seemed to me that he either purposely avoided giving a full and candid answer to my question or he couldn't visualize where Oslo was leading. Since Rabin was a man of keen intelligence, I suspect he was just playing it safe and planned to wait until he was re-elected in 1996 before announcing his support for a Palestinian state.

In the aftermath of Rabin's assassination, the atmosphere in the American Jewish community, like that in Israel, seemed perilously close to civil war. Pointing to the fact that the assassin, Yigal Amir, was Orthodox and a student at Bar-Ilan University, the only Orthodox institution of higher education in Israel, the non-Orthodox groups and left wingers in the Jewish and general media took the opportunity to demagogically brand all Orthodox Jews as being co-conspirators. Admittedly, a few extreme nuts gave them plenty of material to work with. One crazy individual allegedly announced the creation of a 1-800 number to collect funds for Amir's defense. The media and the Jewish left had a field day with the fact that a few Orthodox rabbis in Israel and the U.S. had publicly stated in the months before the killing that Jewish law stipulated that it was right and just to kill a "pursuer;" that is, someone who seeks to kill his fellow Jew. Some interpret this to mean Rabin and other Israeli government leaders, since their giving away of land would cause the deaths of innocent Jews." For example, Rabbi Abraham Hecht of Brooklyn had been quoted in New York magazine as having said: "Any one person who. . . hands over human bodies or human property or the human wealth of the Jewish people to an alien people is guilty of the sin for which the penalty is death."

Amidst this maelstrom, I saw it as my task to calm the atmosphere and to make clear to the larger community that 99.9 percent of Orthodox Jews abhorred and were revolted by the assassination. I made a series of public statements, published newspaper ads on behalf of the OU and reached out to members of the media to make the point that the Orthodox community mourned for Rabin and was determined to avoid further bloodletting.

On November 7, only three days after the assassination, I wrote to the acting Prime Minister of Israel, Shimon Peres, to express our feeling of loss and devastation. I pledged to Peres; "We look to you as the leader of our beloved nation to help heal the terrible wounds and bridge the great divide within our people. In this endeavor, we pledge to you our whole hearted support." I also wrote an op-ed piece for the *Jewish Telegraphic Agency* in which I noted that during the months preceding the shooting of Rabin, the OU had issued repeated calls to lower the tone of the inflammatory rhetoric on both sides of the inter-Jewish divide, and to do everything to avoid a kulturkampf that would split our people.

In the JTA piece, I strongly condemned the inflammatory statements of Rabbi Hecht and noted that in personal discussions with the Prime Minister a few months preceding his death, I and other Orthodox leaders had assured him that that the overwhelming majority of Orthodox Jews were not in any way associated with the extremists who had labeled him a traitor. In fact, as I pointed out, only two days before the assassination, the OU leadership met with Gideon Meir, assistant to the Foreign Minister, to discuss methods to create a fruitful and affective dialogue.

Just over a month after Rabin's death, on December 10, 1995, the leaders of American Jewry held a memorial rally in New York in honor of the slain prime minister. Among the speakers were Prime Minister Peres, Vice President Al Gore, Mrs. Leah Rabin and Yisrael Lau, the Askenazic Chief Rabbi of Israel. The event drew a standing room crowd of close to 16,000 at Madison Square Garden, including people from all sections of the Jewish community.

The Rabin memorial rally was not an easy event to arrange, given the deep bitterness the dovish and secular groups felt toward the Orthodox community. Since many of these groups wanted to use the rally to issue a full-throated endorsement of Oslo 2 rather than simply to honor the fallen leader. For our part, the Orthodox community was determined to resist a politicization of the occasion in support of a peace deal we were convinced was dangerous for Israel. The organizers wanted the participation of a united Jewish community and we were anxious to participate as well—but made clear we would take a pass rather than sign on to a theme counter to our deeply held beliefs.

I was the principle representative of the Orthodox groups in the planning for this event. Looking back, I believe that my success in negotiating a formula that allowed the mainstream Orthodox groups to take part in that cathartic event as an essential element of a Jewish community united in grief was perhaps my finest hour in communal leadership. As Marilyn Henry reported in the *Jerusalem Post*, after intense negotiations the theme of the event shifted from a memorial rally in support of the "peace process" to one of "support for the government of Israel, the people of Israel and the pursuit of peace." A major sticking point in those discussions was over the article to insert in front of the word "pursuit." Henry wrote, "Some of the government's stalwart supporters wanted to specifically refer to the government and its pursuit. The Orthodox groups, whose participation in the rally was ensured only by strict adherences to the nuances of language," insisted on simply saying "the pursuit."

As I pointed out to Henry, we at the OU and other modern

Orthodox groups did not bargain hard in this instance because we were obsessed with inconsequential "hairsplitting." Rather we were concerned that the statement should reflect the desire for peace on the part of all Israelis and Jews and not only those who backed the peace policies of the government headed by Shimon Peres, who stood even further to the left than the late Prime Minister Rabin. Nevertheless, we very much wanted to take part in the rally if the right formula could be found. The key thing from our point of view was to manifest Jewish unity at a moment when virtual civil war seemed to threaten.

"They'll say it's a peace rally, we'll say it's a unity rally and then we will go about our business. We have to work together. As long as there is no Orthodox bashing or it doesn't become a political rally, they can say whatever they want."

Despite my best efforts, to convince Orthodox and hawkish groups to take part in the rally, the ZOA and National Council of Young Israel finally decided to boycott the event. The National Council is reported to have demanded as a condition for their participation that a prominent Likud leader, like the party's leader Benjamin Netanyahu, be invited to speak at the memorial rally along with Peres and other supporters of Oslo 2. This was rejected by the Presidents' Conference, no doubt because the Peres government insisted on it.

Yet despite the boycott by the National Council, quite a few Young Israel synagogues and their rabbis and congregants decided to take part in the rally. One was Rabbi Steven Weil, rabbi of the Young Israel of Greenfield/Oak Park, Michigan, who traveled all the way to New York to participate. Weil told the *Detroit Jewish News*, "Now is the time for unity. If we can't come together for a memorial rally then for what can we work together?"

I was sorry about Young Israel, but pleased that the OU and the other principle mainstream Orthodox groups took part in the Rabin memorial rally. By doing so, our community sent a message in strong support of Jewish unity and reconciliation. Nor can it be credibly claimed that we took part in that event mainly for PR reasons and didn't really care about Rabin. A week earlier, on December 4, the thirtieth day after the prime minister's passing, (the shloshim), the mainstream Orthodox groups had already held a memorial service at Congregation Kehilla Jeshurun in Manhattan at which Dr. Norman Lamm, was the keynote speaker.

Gradually as the weeks went by, the hostile atmosphere between the Orthodox and non-Orthodox groups began to dissipate. In the umbrella organizations like the Presidents' Conference where all the Jewish groups interacted, the non-Orthodox leaders eased up on their hostile rhetoric and displays of coldness and resumed normal collegial relations. Nevertheless, profound differences remained on issues of security, settlements and the larger question of whether the continuing implementation of the Oslo Accords were moving the people of Israel toward peace, or exposing them to increasingly deadly peril. The events of the ensuing seven years would prove that those of us who had doubted Oslo had been more correct than even we understood at the time.

CHAPTER TEN

The Decline and Fall of Oslo

T he six month long period that Shimon Peres served as prime minister in the wake of the assassination of Yitzhak Rabin was a time of extreme trepidation for those of us who were not in the "peace camp." Peres and his young protégés like Yossi Beilin and Uri Savir had all along been the prime movers behind the Oslo peace process, and now, without the restraining hand of the security-oriented Yitzhak Rabin, the Peres team seemed primed to push ahead full steam with a plethora of dangerous concessions to the Palestinians.

During his premiership, Rabin had repeatedly stated firmly that, at the end of the peace process, Jerusalem would remain undivided under Israeli sovereignty. Although Peres also promised to maintain a united Jerusalem, his true position on the issue was suspect given that Beilin, who always consulted closely with Peres, had reached an informal agreement with PLO leader Abu Abbas to make Abu Dis, an eastern suburb of Jerusalem, the capital of the future Palestinian state.

Thus, when I had the opportunity to introduce Prime Minister Peres on live Israeli television at our Jerusalem convention in early 1996, I publicly called upon him to reaffirm the principle articulated so emphatically by Rabin of a united Jerusalem forever under Israeli sovereignty. Peres did so, but in a manner that left the distinct impression that those were not his true beliefs. In contrast, when I introduced Prime Minister Binyamin Netanyahu to our convention two years later, I felt no such assurance had to be requested, because, even more vociferously than Rabin, he had made clear that he was committed to preserving a united

Jerusalem. I did push Netanyahu, however, on the related issues of following through on his promise to press ahead with two controversial Israeli housing projects at two sites in Jerusalem; Har Homa and Ras-Al-Amoud. Netanyahu promised us that the projects would, in fact, be built despite intense pressure against them from the international community, and, as it turned out, he proved to be as good as his word.

I had known Bibi Netanyahu since his days as Israel's ambassador to the U.N. during the mid-1980's, but I met with him the first time on a one on one basis during his run for prime minister in the spring of 1996. I found him to be a charismatic and a dynamic political leader who, with his fluent unaccented English and supreme self-confidence, was a terrific salesman for the ideological beliefs to which we both subscribed. I was to learn first hand, however, that as charming and persuasive as Bibi could be when he needed something, he could also be arrogant and dismissive of people, even of those who supported and worked for him. This high handedness and lack of loyalty to members of his own government and party eventually came back to haunt him and caused a premature end to his tenure as prime minister.

During Passover of 1996, about a month before the day Prime Minister Peres had scheduled for the elections, Sheila and I were vacationing at our apartment in Netanya. Yoram Ettinger, one of the '"Gang of Three" who had lobbied in Washington against the peacenik policies of the Rabin government, dropped by to say that Netanyahu wanted to meet me. (The three were Ettinger, a former liason from the Israeli Embassy in Washington to Congress, Yigal Carmon, an anti-terrorist expert for three Prime Ministers, and Yossi Ben Aharon, a foreign policy specialist who also served a number of Prime Ministers.)

Ettinger explained that a few days hence Netanyahu was going to lead a five plus kilometer march from Bet Lid on the green line to the oceanfront in Netanya and he wanted me to march with him. Bet Lid had been the site of a massive terrorist bombing at a bus stop in which many Israeli soldiers had been killed. The point of the march was to not only denounce the Peres' government's weakness in the face of ongoing Palestinian terror attacks but also to emphasize that Israel would only be nine miles across its narrow waist between Bet Lid and Netanya if it were to return to the 'green line'—the pre-1967 boundary.

I agreed to take part, and drove to the starting point of the march in Ettinger's car. Unfortunately, the rest of the day was not nearly as enjoyable. I had not anticipated just how punishing such a hike can be on a middle-aged body. I ought to have worn sneakers and comfortable loose fitting pants, but instead had put on slacks and formal Shabbat shoes, which made it difficult for me to walk at a fast pace.

As I quickly discovered, I was too out of shape to do such a long walk comfortably, and Netanyahu, who is a decade younger than I, walked much faster. He was surrounded by a vanguard of young people from Likud Youth who were in a fired-up mood that created a sense of confidence and excitement around Bibi and probably caused him to walk even faster. We spoke for a few minutes at the beginning of the march, but because of the noise and my inability to maintain his pace, Netanyahu told me we would talk when we got to Netanya. The problem was that by the time I finally arrived in town—quite a while after Bibi did, a planned pro-Likud rally was already starting in the kikar (town square). Netanyahu asked if I would join him on the stage so we could chat while he waited to speak. I was somewhat concerned about appearing on stage, because this was a partisan rally and I was a high-ranking official in the OU, a non-partisan and non-Israeli organization. Oh well, I assured myself, who would recognize me in Netanya? It was only after I had taken my seat in a prominent position on the stage that I learned that a reporter for the New York *Jewish Week* was there to cover the event. Fortunately, my presence as a guest of honor at the Likud rally was never reported.

I sat two seats away from General Ariel Sharon, who glowered at me when I greeted him. Clearly, he was still angry at me for having allowed Yossi Beilin to answer questions before him at the debate the two had held at the Orthodox Union convention the year before. In any event, my focus that day was on his young rival, Netanyahu, who had been elected Likud leader in 1993. Bibi looked me straight in the eye and said that the upcoming election was one of critical importance for the future of Israel and that, the opinions of the pollsters and pundits to the contrary, he could and would win.

Speaking as though he were already prime minister, Bibi told me that the pro-Israel forces in the U.S. should focus on two issues. The first was to maintain the unity of Jerusalem; the second to prevent U.S. pressure on Israel for a deal with Syria on the Golan Heights from becoming too intense. To that end, he said that we should intensify our efforts in Washington to oppose the growing push from the think tanks and foreign policy establishment in favor of stationing U.S. troops on the Golan. Bibi said that we should emphasize that Israel was accustomed to defending itself against enemies many times its size, and did not want American troops to risk casualties in its defense.

I told Netanyahu I would try to help as much as possible. I was already working in close coordination with his "Gang of 3" allies, because I believed in a strong Israel and was convinced Peres was on the wrong track. Overall, I was extremely impressed with Netanyahu's dynamism and left that rally believing for the first time that he had a very good shot at victory.

Several weeks later, just prior to the election, I returned to Israel for our Orthodox Union convention. Netanyahu, who was the talk of the country after having bested Peres in a televised debate, was the featured speaker at a morning session at the Sheraton Plaza Hotel, where I introduced him to some 350 ardently cheering delegates. That afternoon, I had been invited to be a speaker at a convention of the World Jewish Congress at the cavernous Binyanei Ha'oomah Convention Center at the invitation of WJC General Secretary Israel Singer.

When I arrived at Binyanei Ha'oomah, I found out that I was part of a two-person panel representing the opposition to Oslo and that the other speaker on my panel was none other than Netanyahu himself. I was not at all pleased by this arrangement. First, I did not consider it my role to fight against the peace process, but rather to assure that Israel remained strong, independent and free of American pressure to make dangerous concessions. In addition, most of the 800 or so delegates from around the world who had packed the hall had surely come to hear Bibi Netanyahu and not Mendy Ganchrow. Indeed, most of them did not even know who I was. Why had I been put on the platform together with Netanyahu? I believe it was done intentionally to cut into the amount of time that Bibi would be allowed to speak and to reduce him from a highlighted speaker to a panel member. It was well known that WJC President Edgar Bronfman was a longtime friend and ardent backer of Shimon Peres, who would be speaking later that day and had been given star billing.

When Netanyahu arrived with his entourage and saw that I was to be onstage with him, he became visibly upset. He barely acknowledged my presence except to ask me in a brisk manner if the people at this meeting were the same he had spoken to at the OU event a few hours earlier. I assured him that was not the case.

Netanyahu was introduced to the audience by Jacques Kahn, a French Jewish leader and informed that he had twenty minutes for his remarks. The plan was for me to speak for ten minutes after him, followed by questions for both of us from the audience. Netanyahu proceeded to speak for thirty five to forty minutes. Instead of then sitting down to allow me to speak, he invited the audience to ask questions. A woman posed a question, which he answered in excruciating detail. Kahn was clearly peeved that Netanyahu had not stayed within the guidelines, but was clearly loath to challenge him directly. I just sat there very calmly.

As Bibi's endless answer seemed to segue into a filibuster, Kahn finally stood up. Netanyahu said, "I see my time is up. Let me just make one more statement." Then, touting his degree from MIT, he proceeded to give a fifteen-minute lecture on the need to re-order Israel's economy on a free-market basis, which was indeed a badly needed reform, but had nothing to do with the question at hand. When Netanyahu finally finished speaking, he did not sit down and listen to my remarks as Kahn had stipulated he would do. Instead, he immediately climbed down off the stage, shook a few hands and then marched out of the hall with his entourage.

My wife, Sheila, who was sitting in the fifth or sixth row, was furious at the way Netanyahu had treated me. I felt like a nonperson. During the last twenty minutes of Netanyahu's remarks, she was making hand signs to me and mouthing, "Don't speak! Don't speak! Don't speak!" Sheila became even angrier when the head of the Jewish community of Gibraltar, who was sitting next to her, whispered in her ear, "Who is that guy sitting up there with Bibi?"

I was less upset than Sheila, knowing politics and politicians. Still, despite my many years of public speaking, I was at a loss as to how to successfully speak after Netanyahu. I considered telling the audience that I felt like Elizabeth Taylor's eighth husband on their wedding night. He must have been thinking; "I know what I have to do, but how do I make it interesting?" However I changed my mind about telling a mildly risqué joke when I saw some rabbis in the audience. Therefore, when I stood up, I told the audience that I realized Prime Minister Shimon Peres was going to be speaking to the conference in forty five minutes, and since they had just heard Netanyahu, many of them might desire to go to their rooms and freshen up. I therefore asked for a show of hands as to how many people thought I should just say thank you and sit down. About half a dozen raised their hands. I announced that I would allow a few minutes for those who wanted to leave the room to do so, but that if anyone wanted to remain and hear me, I would limit my talk to seven minutes.

About 200 members of the audience left. I spoke for exactly seven minutes to the remaining 600. Realizing that it would be pointless to try to talk politics during my brief interregnum between Netanyahu and Peres, I decided instead to offer some perspective from our sacred texts. I noted that during the course of the day the audience had heard different points of view from government officials; including Netanyahu and Yossi Beilin and that they would hear shortly from the Prime Minister himself. Yet as talented as these individuals were, they could only speak from the limited perspective of their own beliefs and judgments. I noted that even the wisest human beings are frequently mistaken in assessing the future. However, I contended, that there is one thing we could confidently predict; that if we were to bring up the children of Israel without Torah and Jewish tradition, we would lose the battle for Jewish survival—in fact we would suffer a greater defeat than from any invading army.

To my surprise and gratification, the audience stood up and gave me a standing ovation. Edgar Bronfman walked across the stage and embraced me. I had turned around a difficult situation by suppressing my anger and speaking the truth as I knew it.

Several days later, after Sheila and I had already returned to the States, Netanyahu confounded expectations and the exit polls by defeating Peres in a squeaker. The election result shocked nearly everyone in the Jewish community and the foreign policy establishment in Washington. It was especially galling for the old guard at the Israeli embassy, nearly all of whom were Peres supporters.

Naturally, I was ecstatic by the surprising turn of events, which promised an early end to the Oslo appeasement policies. In the immediate aftermath of the election, I phoned my old friend David Bar-Ilan, who was serving as Netanyahu's director of communications, to put in a good word for Yoram Ettinger, who I believed, would have been an excellent candidate for the post of Consul-General in New York. But after the election, Netanyahu conveniently forgot many of his old friends and supporters. To my knowledge he never spoke to the "Gang of 3" again. For my part, I found it ironic that I had been able to obtain appointments with Prime Minister Rabin and Peres, who were on the other side of the ideological spectrum, yet was never able to see Netanyahu privately once he was elected.

Actually, I did have a tentative appointment to meet Bibi during the first several days of his administration. Yet while waiting in David Bar-Ilan's office I was chagrined to be informed that my appointment had been abruptly cancelled because either U.S. Special Ambassador Dennis Ross or U.S. Ambassador to Israel, Martin Indyk, was coming unexpectedly for a meeting. It seemed ridiculous to me that the brand new Netanyahu government did not even have a foreign policy team in place—in fact, they probably didn't even know where the toilet paper was kept—and yet the Americans were already sending emissaries to put pressure on them. Well, I reflected with satisfaction, the Netanyahu crew would resist that pressure with a lot more tenacity than had the last bunch.

Even though Netanyahu could hardly be said to have treated me with consideration, I was determined not to bear a grudge. There were larger issues at play. I was determined to help make Bibi's upcoming first visit to Washington as prime minister a success, despite the Clinton Administration's chagrin that he had upended Peres, whom they openly favored. One way would be to have the new prime minister acclaimed on Capitol Hill, which would force the Administration to treat him with greater respect.

I cannot recall who came up with the original idea but before long I was in the middle of confidential discussions with Presidents' Conference Executive Vice President Malcolm Hoenlein and a few other pro-Bibi American Jewish leaders about how we might arrange for Netanyahu to be invited to address a joint session of Congress. It is very rare for a foreign head of state to be accorded such an honor, and even rarer for a newly elected one. To think we could convince the Senate and House of Representatives to tender such an invitation without the encouragement of the White House or of the Israeli Embassy—neither of whom were happy with Bibi's ascension—seemed faintly ludicrous. Still, I have always relished a tough challenge and figured it was worth the try. Thus a small group of us began the effort.

I called my own congressman, Ben Gilman, who was chairman of the International Relations Committee, to ask him to use his influence to convince the Republican and Democratic leaders to invite Bibi to address a joint session of Congress. Gilman, who had felt almost from the advent of Oslo that Rabin and Peres were too weak in their approach to Arafat and the Palestinians, agreed to do whatever he could. Meanwhile, I also called friends in the office of House Speaker Newt Gingrich, and started enlisting the aid of friends of mine around the country such as Tsvi Friedman who had close relationships with congressmen and senators. Incidentally, it was Gingrich who through his chief of staff, Arnie Christianson, called me in Israel asking me if I would like to be nominated as a member of the U.S. Commission for the Preservation of America's Heritage Abroad. I was honored and became one of his nominees whom President Clinton approved.

Yet when I met with the Israeli Ambassador in Washington, Itamar Rabinovich, and gently asked him what he thought of the idea of inviting Netanyahu to address Congress, he laughed at me as though it was an impossible idea. We had not taken Rabinovich into our confidence, so he had no idea of the efforts already underway. By the time he did find out, AIPAC had gotten involved, and soon I was receiving calls from friends who were unaware of my role in initiating the operation, asking me to contact friends in Congress. Thus, a true-grass roots effort was brought to fruition when the Prime Minister visited Washington less than a month after his inauguration, and was invited to address a joint session of Congress. Bibi's appearance was a huge success and cemented a warm relationship between the Netanyahu government and the U.S. Congress.

Unfortunately that friendship contrasted sharply with the increasingly chilly relationship Bibi had with the Clinton Administration. Concerned that Israel would be unfairly blamed by the Administration and by American public opinion if the Oslo Agreements collapsed completely, I worked publicly and behind the scenes to point out that the Palestinians were not fulfilling the promises they made at Oslo. I asserted that under the circumstances it was inappropriate for the Clintonites to pressure Netanyahu.

For example, when the Palestinian Authority condemned to death a number of Palestinians who sold land to Jews in June

1997, I immediately dispatched a letter to Secretary of State Madeline Albright stressing how disturbed we at the OU were that the State Department did not issue a condemnation of this policy, which was certainly a great leap backward into the dark ages of hatred and discrimination. I never received a meaningful response.

Albright's career at State was a complete disappointment to me, and belied the myth that the Clinton Administration was pro-Israel through and through. The Secretary's evident lack of sympathy for the Jewish state was especially ironic given that the Arabs began speaking of Albright as part of a Zionist cabal at the top of the Administration even before the secret of her Jewish heritage was revealed. Whatever the nature of her Jewish identity, or lack thereof, Albright manifested none of the evident warmth or friendship always shown toward Israel and the American Jewish community by her gentile predecessor, Warren Christopher. As he was leaving office, Christopher hosted a delegation of the Presidents' Conference at a party at the State Department in his honor. Yet only a few weeks after attending that party, I was back at the State Department as part of a small Presidents' Conference delegation to express our concern that in the short time since Albright had taken over, the signals from Foggy Bottom appeared to have become considerably less friendly.

Our meeting with Albright was less than satisfactory, and afterwards, as our delegation stood in a knot in the lobby of the State Department discussing the nature of our public statement to the waiting press, we noticed a delegation of Arab-American leaders on their way up to see Albright. In fact, much of our session with Albright and that of the Arab-American group as well, was taken up with a discussion of the controversial Israeli housing projects in Jerusalem at Har Homa and on the Mt. of Olives. When Albright met with us she used the Hebrew names for those hilltops, but we learned later that when meeting with the Arab-American group, she had used the Arabic names for them. Clearly, the new Secretary of State was striving for a policy of "evenhandedness," a concept that had not been evident when Christopher was at the helm.

In the last week of November 1997, I was invited to an ecumenical breakfast of religious leaders at the White House, and was assigned to sit to the immediate left of Vice President Al Gore. I tried to make small talk with the Vice President, but found him to be more "stiff" and formal than on previous occasions. When I informed him that his daughter Karenna and my son Elliot were classmates at Columbia Law School, Gore replied blandly, "That's nice." Seeing that it was the wrong day for small talk, I switched to business and engaged the vice president on the subject of convicted Israeli spy Jonathan Pollard. I informed Gore that, on that very day, Yuli Edelstein, a Knesset member from the Yisrael B'Aliyah party, was visiting Pollard in jail.

By mentioning the role of Edelstein, whom Gore knew as a former Russian refusnik, in advocating for Pollard, I was signaling to Gore that our community believed that Pollard, although guilty of spying, had served an adequate sentence and was now, like the refuseniks, being kept in prison for unjust political reasons. The Vice President thanked me for the heads up, but made no further comment on Pollard's situation. Clearly, there were strong forces within the intelligence community and the Defense Department that were dead-set against a commutation of Pollard's life sentence despite the fact that he had already served more than a decade in prison and did his spying for an ally of the U.S. Indeed, a number of Americans convicted of spying for the Soviet Union had received much less onerous sentences.

Before leaving the event, Gore, who would certainly be running for president in 2000, invited me to contact his offices with issues of concern. I did so less than two weeks later, sending him a letter in which I charged that some in the administration were trying to make a linkage between the Iraqi crisis and the Middle East negotiations; advocating stepped up U.S. pressure on Israel to strengthen Arab support for U.S. action in Iraq. I wrote that "Pressure on Israel prejudices the negotiations and deprives the Palestinians of the need to negotiate in good faith," and informed the vice president that our community was distressed that Israel was being set up to be the sacrificial lamb on behalf of better U.S.-Arab relations.

On December 19th, I received a personal response from Gore in which he affirmed that the United States "cannot, should not, and will not impose solutions on the parties" in the Middle East. He added, however: "Unilateral actions which undermine confidence must be avoided. Settlement construction and Israeli confiscation of land damaged the credibility of the negotiating process."

Shortly after the New Year 1998, I responded to Gore with a tough letter asserting that his comments about Israeli settlement expansion and land confiscation were signs of a significant change for the worse in U.S. attitudes toward Israel. I pointed out that nothing in the Oslo Accords negated Israel's right to facilitate natural growth in the settlements. In fact, I wrote, Prime Minister Netanyahu had refrained from new settlement construction, even as the Palestinians increased their settlements in Judea and Samaria at a rate that exceeded their natural growth. I reminded Gore that Har Homa, which was being presented in the U.S. media as evidence of Israel's determination to build new West Bank settlements, was in fact not a settlement at all, but a new neighborhood within the municipal boundaries of Jerusalem, the eternal, undivided capital of Israel. I concluded that letter by stating emphatically; "We need not evenhandedness, but a continuation of the special U.S.-Israel relationship."

Early in 1998, President Clinton held a private dinner at the White House for a small group of Jewish leaders on the occasion of a state visit by Israeli President Ezer Weizmann. I learned from well-placed sources that I had been on the original invitation list but was removed at the last moment, presumably by Sandy Berger, the National Security Advisor, who prior to joining the Administration had been on the board of Americans for Peace Now. I gathered that Berger considered me to be too hostile to the Administration to risk inviting. The fact that neither of the two most prominent right wing Jewish leaders, Mort Klein, president of the ZOA and myself were not invited to the dinner was commented upon by the *Forward*. Robert Greenberg pointed out in the *Wall Street Journal* that some of the so-called Jewish leaders at the dinner suggested to Administration officials with winks and nods that most American Jews wouldn't be unduly upset if the United States stepped up its pressure on Netanyahu to make concessions to the Palestinians. It is no wonder they did not want me at the dinner.

We now had a government in power in Israel that would not go forward with Oslo without solid evidence that the Palestinians were meeting their commitments under the treaty. Thus I felt no compunction about public criticism by proclaiming my beliefs that the Oslo Accords had been fatally flawed from their inception and should on no accounts be forced down Israel's throat. On the occasion of the 50th anniversary of Israel in 1998,

I wrote an article entitled "Shame on Us," in which I criticized the American Jewish community for sitting on the sidelines and allowing President Clinton to pressure Israel to cede territory it believed critical to its security under the terms of Oslo. Why should Israel observe the terms of a moribund and dangerous treaty when the PA had ignored the obligations it had committed itself to under the terms of Oslo? It was time for the long-running Oslo charade to end.

I noted in the article that I took that position not because peace was unimportant for Israel, but rather, because a secure and meaningful peace was so vital for the future of the Jewish state. To those who might believe that I reveled in conflict and war, I pointed out that I keep a plaque on my desk with grenade fragments that I removed from critically wounded GIs and captured Viet Cong, in order to remind myself of the horrors of war. I believe that even a cold peace is superior to a hot war. Nevertheless, I affirmed, I would not support the sham of a peace agreement that would actually lead Israel into a war sooner rather than later.

I wrote that useful models for an Israeli-Palestinian peace could be seen in recent treaties involving Hong Kong, Macau, and the Panama Canal. In each of these cases, the parties negotiated slowly and carefully. Once an agreement was reached, a firm date was set for its implementation. Preliminary steps for confidence building were agreed-upon and faithfully executed. When it was clear that there would be no impediment, the transfers took place–the British from Hong Kong, the Portuguese from Macau, and the Americans from the Panama Canal Zone.

By contrast, under the Oslo process, an agreement in the morning yielded a statement of intent by the Palestinian Authority in the afternoon and a withdrawal by the Israelis in the evening. Agreements were carried out in the breach or not at all; there were no confidence-building measures and the climate between the two sides was becoming increasingly shrill and hostile. As a result, negotiations were becoming characterized by mutual recriminations and abiding mistrust and miscommunication. Eventually, outbreaks of violence became all but inevitable. Once that happened, as during the Palestinian "tunnel riots" of late 1996, relations between the two sides were essentially back to the pre-Oslo status quo ante, except that the Israelis had given up strategically valuable land and allowed the creation of an armed Palestinian entity. And with all of that, the Palestinians still cried "foul."

I recall sometime in early 1998 speaking privately with Martin Indyk after the-then U.S. Ambassador to Israel made a speech to AIPAC. He had received a rather hostile reception from his onetime place of employment. Martin's abiding ardor for Oslo appeared undiminished despite all of the setbacks the peace process had endured. As always, Martin, who had retained his distinctive Australian accent despite his many years in Washington, was soft spoken and gentlemanly in style. I tried to cut through the diplomatic fog that often characterized such sessions, and asked, "Martin, can you give me one example of PLO compliance with the Oslo accord?" "I know you won't like my answer," he retorted. "But they have declared their support for peace and recognition of Israel." Indyk didn't say whether they had made those declarations in Arabic as well as in English. I give him credit for being able to look me in the eye and repeat such nonsense, but then he is a trained diplomat and I'm not.

In an op-ed piece I published in the *Jerusalem Post* in August 1998, I recounted the following story as a way of illustrating my own attitude toward the Oslo peace process. A congregation's new rabbi gave an impassioned sermon on his first Shabbat. On his second Shabbat, he repeated the exact same sermon. The membership, though confused, attributed this repetition to the rabbi's inexperience. But when on the third, fourth and fifth week he repeated the same sermon again, a committee visited him to discuss the matter. The rabbi's answer was simple: "Until you act on the issues I raised in the first sermon, what is the point of going on to the second?"

Indeed, I asked rhetorically, why should Israel move to the next step stipulated by Oslo and withdraw from 13.1% of precious land, if there was no Palestinian compliance on matters already agreed upon and if the issues of Jerusalem, Palestinian statehood, and the Palestinian "right of return" seemed intractable. I noted too that in the long run American pressure on Israel was not sustainable. Israel would have to risk saying "no" to its only friend in the world, if the latter kept pressing the Jewish state to make concessions that put its very survival at risk.

In the first week of May 1998, First Lady Hillary Rodham Clinton set off fireworks when she declared her support for a Palestinian state. The immediate suspicion of many in the pro-

Israel community was that this was a trial balloon for her husband, the President of the United States. After all, Hillary's remarks came at a time when both the United States and Israel officially opposed such a move. At that very same moment, President Clinton announced that Prime Minister Netanyahu would be invited to Washington only if he accepted the United States' terms for a round of pullbacks in the West Bank. U.S.-Israel relations were obviously spiraling downward.

Several days later, at a closed-door meeting of the President's Conference, Israel's Ambassador to the U.N., Dore Gold, spoke passionately about the undue pressures being placed on Israel by Clinton. Sadly, but predictably, the left–wing organizations inside the Conference, consisting of the Reform movement, Americans for Peace Now (APN), some old Socialist groups, and a portion of the Conservative movement – made clear they were unmoved by Gold's presentation and, in fact, were sympathetic to the Administration's position. I had long believed that the admission of APN to the Presidents' Conference in the early 90's was a mistake; changing the internal atmosphere and dynamics and allowing the Reform Movement to move more publicly to the left. Still, the rebuke of Dore Gold by many members of the Presidents' Conference was deeply upsetting even by the standards of the time. It was almost unheard of for American Jewish groups to sit in a room and hear the pleadings of a representative of the State of Israel in clear analytic tones and not only remain unmoved, but to try to substitute their own agenda.

Even some normally levelheaded American Jewish leaders tried to play down the growing rift between the Clinton and Netanyahu governments and denied there was inordinate U.S. pressure on Israel to make concessions. "I don't think this is a crisis," said Abe Foxman of the ADL to the *Washington Post* in the aftermath of the Gold meeting. "The administration's tactics were more a factor of frustration than of conscious deliberate bullying."

Angered by the reception Gold's message had received, I rose toward the end of the meeting and made a motion at the Conference that we issue a public statement critical of the Clinton Administration for pressuring Israel. I believed that despite the vocal objections of the left, an overwhelming majority of the Conference members would support such a resolution. However, Mel Salberg, the Conference chairman, who was clearly lukewarm to my resolution, quickly stepped in to remind delegates that the Presidents'Conference does not take formal votes, but instead rules by consensus. In effect, Salberg was ruling me out of order, but I chose not to press the argument for the moment.

Apparently, some members of the left-wing groups, leaked the story of the results of the meeting to the *Washington Post* despite the fact that the meeting was supposed to be strictly off-the-record. The paper ran a page one article specifying that a motion to issue a public criticism of the Clinton Administration for its treatment of Israel had been voted down by the Presidents' Conference by a wide margin. This was, of course, a complete distortion; Salberg had prevented my motion from ever being voted on. The Post referred to me by name as the "author of a failed motion." Needless to say, I was quite upset and was also miffed at myself for not having been more aggressive by challenging Salberg's right to rule my motion out of order.

The negative reaction of most Presidents' Conference members to the *Washington Post* story, in the context of continuing pressure on Netanyahu by the Administration and Mrs. Clinton's expressed support for a Palestinian state, soon backfired on the liberals who leaked the story. At an emergency meeting soon after, the Conference went squarely on public record against U.S. pressure on Israel. After the Conference took that position, the Clinton Administration, by then deeply immersed in the Monica Lewinsky Affair, appeared to ease up on Bibi for the moment. No Administration wants to have a public quarrel with the American Jewish leadership, especially at moments when it feels politically vulnerable.

Several months later, in the fall of 1998, President Clinton hosted Netanyahu, Arafat and their respective delegations at the Wye River Conference in Maryland. At the height of the conference, after several days of non-stop bargaining, Netanyahu sent out word to the American Jewish leadership that he would hold a phone conference with them to report on the results of the summit so far. I had been in Queens when the call came in and stopped at a gas station on the Palisades Parkway on my way home to Monsey to call in from a public phone booth.

The Prime Minister sounded so exhausted and his voice was so low that a number of people asked if he could speak louder or move closer to the telephone. He told us, in essence, that the Wye conference was hopelessly deadlocked and he had decided to walk out. The American side, which was almost certainly monitoring the call, knew this threat was almost certainly a bluff, and indeed, later that day, Netanyahu gave in to American pressure. I believe his mental exhaustion gave rise to some of the excess concessions made by the Israelis at Wye.

During the course of Netanyahu's three year stint as Prime Minister, he made numersous appearances at OU and Mizrachi dinners and conventions. He was almost never without his wife, Sara, at his side. Often, at these events, the Prime Minister would recall the walk he and I had made together from Bet Lid to Netanya and joke that I had outlasted him, which of course, was not true. Even once on the reception line at a State Department event, he turned to his wife and said, "Mendy walked with me from Bet Lid, and I couldn't keep up with him."

Several years later, after he was out of office, I ran into Netanyahu during a visit he was making to Cardozo Law School in Manhattan. I happened, at the time, to be recovering from arthoscopic surgery on my knee. When he saw me limping, he asked whether this was a result of our walk in Netanya.

As I noted, while Bibi was extremely charming and charismatic, he was not always loyal to close friends and staunch supporters. Also on the negative side of his ledger was that with Netanyahu, rhetoric often outpaced *tachlis*. While he spoke publicly with a tough demeanor and confident manner, the results of his negotiations with the United States, at Wye and on other occasions, appeared to belie that toughness and confidence.

I first met Ehud Barak, Netanyahu's successor, at a private luncheon in the opulent offices of World Jewish Congress President Edgar Bronfman in the Seagram's Building on Park Avenue. Barak had just left his position as Chief of Staff of the Israel Defense Forces and was planning shortly to enter politics. A protégé of Yitzhak Rabin, and like him, a Labor hawk, Barak was already being spoken about by knowledgeable Israeli political analysts as a future Prime Minister.

During that first encounter and in subsequent meetings, I found Barak to be an extremely bright, highly cultured and evidently talented individual. During those occasions, he certainly did not display any of the haughtiness and cockiness so publically evident a few years later during his prime ministership. Unfortunately, as with Bibi, access to high power, seemed to bring out many of Barak's worst characteristics; including a tendency to think he was the smartest person in the room and that he could afford to forego efforts to reach out to problematic constituencies.

All of that, however, was far in the future on the occasion of the Bronfman luncheon. After an hour of cocktails in the sitting room, we proceeded to a full two-hour meal, peppered with an enjoyable "no holds barred" discussion of religion and the Middle East crisis. Barak's affection for and allegiance to his mentor, Prime Minister Rabin, was clear. I left the meeting quite impressed with him.

Later, after Rabin's assassination, and Barak's appointment by Peres as Foreign Minister, I visited him in his office in Jerusalem. I was startled to see that he seemed to be talking to a huge picture of the late Prime Minister on the wall above his desk.

On that occasion, we discussed Bibi Netanyahu, who was then enmeshed in a tight election battle with Prime Minister Peres. Barak said that he knew Bibi well, but left the distinct impression he was less than impressed with Netanyahu's personal qualities and political acumen. Barak said that, in his opinion, there was only one individual in Israeli politics who actually said what he believed, and that was Benny Begin, son of the late Prime Minister, Menachem Begin. Yet it was Benny's very honesty and unwillingness to bend, Barak said, that made him a terrible politician. In fact, Begin would abandon politics for good after being crushed in the first round of the 1999 elections for prime minister by both Barak and Bibi.

I next visited Barak in his Knesset office soon after Peres lost the 1996 campaign to Netanyahu—a campaign in which Barak had served as Peres' campaign manager. Barak confided to me that, in his opinion, Peres had made several serious tactical political errors. Barak said he had begged Peres to use the term "*shalom u'bitachon*" (peace with security) during his campaign appearances, but Peres could barely get the word "security" out of his mouth. Barak had me in stitches as he mimicked Peres supposedly stuttering "b,b,b,b" as he tried to get "u'bitachon" out of his mouth. Barak also maintained that Peres had made a tragic error in alienating the religious portion of the electorate. Making clear that he intended to become the Labor Party leader and run someday for prime minister himself, Barak declared that he himself would never get into bed with the left-wing Meretz party, as had Peres. It is too bad I did not have a tape recorder for that portion of his conversation, because Barak's overwhelming defeat in the 2001 election against Sharon was in part a repudiation of his call in late 2000 for a secular revolution in Israeli life. Ehud evidently did not learn the lessons he himself had confidently pronounced five years earlier.

On the occasion of my visit to his office, Barak reached into his desk and took out a *kippah* in an evident effort to dramatize to me that he was sensitive to the feelings of the religious segment of Israel's population. Actually, what he showed me at that moment was exactly the opposite. Orthodox Jews tend to judge a politician's awareness of the subtleties of our community by the look and composition of the *kippah* he chooses. We judge by whether it is large, small, or mini or whether it is velvet, silk, leather, or crocheted. The color of the *kippah* – be it black, white, blue and white, or a combination of colors, also speak volumes about one's political, religious, and nationalistic feelings. The skullcap Ehud Barak pulled out of the drawer that day was a complete joke. In New York, when you go to a Jewish funeral and don't have a hat or a skullcap, they hand you a throwaway pointy skullcap. It is as if a sign were placed above your head saying: "I am getting this silly beanie off my head as soon as I walk out of the door." The skullcap Barak took out of the drawer was the equivalent of that funeral throwaway skullcap, thin and crumpled.

I told Barak I couldn't believe that someone who wished to run for prime minister of Israel and wanted to reach out to the observant community would wear such a lame skullcap. I asked Ehud to allow me to invite an NCSY girl to crochet one for him with his name on it. He agreed, provided his name would be on the inside. A month or two later I presented Barak with the skullcap. Unfortunately, the girl had written the word "Ehud" in the front and "NCSY" on the inside. Aside from posing for a picture with me, I doubt that he ever wore it. That incident became for me symbolic of the reality that Barak, like many Labor Party leaders before him, never figured out how to reach out to Orthodox Jews, whether in Israel or the diaspora.

During Barak's twenty-month tenure as prime minister I saw him in person on several occasions when he addressed the Presidents' Conference. It was painfully obvious on each of those occasions that he wanted to be there about as much as most people long to sit in a dentist's chair having root canal surgery. During a question and answer session at one such meeting, I rose from my seat and reminded Barak that as a minister in

Rabin's government he had signed permissions on several occasions for construction companies to proceed with controversial housing projects in and around Jerusalem. Did that mean, I asked, that he would approve a permit that was needed for a major Jerusalem residential project that was then under consideration? He favored me with a dismissive wave of the hand, and asked in an impatient tone, "Why do you bring up the past?" Barak seemed to imply that consistency has no place in politics.

In their own days as prime ministers of the Labor Party, Rabin or Peres each went to the trouble to meet with the leadership of the American Orthodox community to discuss ways to ameliorate strife between religious and secular Jews in Israel and the diaspora. Barak never held a similar meeting, even though I begged Yitzhak Herzog, his aide and cabinet secretary, to arrange such an event. I suspect Herzog spoke to Barak about the idea but that the prime minister nixed the meeting. Why should he do something that he didn't need to do, that might yield no immediate political benefit?

Even at the gala dinner given for Barak by Clinton under a tent on the White House lawn in July, 1999, just after his installment as prime minister, the Israeli leader could not summon forth even a modicum of the warmth and charm that Clinton effortlessly displayed to each and every guest who approached him. On that occasion, as so often in the past, Clinton looked each guest right in the eye and made each of them feel that there was no one else in the world who mattered to him at that moment. That was, of course, an illusion, yet being able to conjure and maintain that illusion was Clinton's greatest asset throughout his tumultuous political career. Barak's demeanor on that night, by contrast, was stiff and military in style. That was a shame, because, as I had learned by chatting with him in his office, Barak could be quite informal and engaging when not performing in an official capacity. In this respect, Barak somewhat resembled Al Gore, who was often personable and funny when "off the record" but came across as wooden, boring and an overbearing stuffed shirt when trying to "act presidential."

During Barak's last several months in office, after the failure of the Camp David Summit and the eruption of the intifada, he found himself more and more at odds with the mainstream of the American Jewish community, and more and more reduced for political support here to his allies in Americans for Peace

Now and the Israel Policy Forum. Like a great majority of Israelis, most American Jews had come to realize they had been bamboozled by Yasir Arafat at Oslo. By late 2000, they recognized the truth of what I and other once lonely voices on the right had been saying for years; that Arafat never really wanted peace with Israel, but rather a short truce that would allow him and his cohorts to establish themselves in the heart of Judea, Samaria and Gaza where they would be better positioned to make an attempt on the life of the Jewish state.

Unfortunately, Barak and his leftist allies didn't get it. Even after Arafat's strident rejection of Barak's offer of ninety four percent of the West Bank and much of East Jerusalem, the Israeli prime minister continued his shameful appeasement of the murderous PLO chieftain; offering him more and more territorial concessions at the very moment when top leaders of Arafat's own Fatah organization were calling for an intensification of the violence of the Intifada and glorifying suicide bombers as *shaheeds* (martyrs).

By the beginning of January, 2001, most observers that the Likud candidate Ariel Sharon would handily defeat Barak for prime minister in the elections that Barak had foolishly called for February 4. This was about three months before he was required to have elections. He originally calculated that it would be better for him to run against Sharon earlier than Bibi later. Barak had calculated that however unhappy Israeli voters might be with him, they would not turn to Sharon, who was widely perceived as being too old and too extreme. Sharon had been weighed down for nearly twenty years after having been found by the Israeli Supreme Court to be "indirectly responsible" for having caused the Sabra and Shatilla massacre in September, 1982 (In reality the massacre was carried out by Christian Phalangist Lebanese militias against Palestinian civilians and Sharon neither encouraged it or had any idea it was happening until too late.)

As it turned out, Barak was completely misreading the political map. The Israeli people no longer cared about a twenty-year-old massacre of Arabs by Arabs. Instead, they were concerned about getting a leader who would crack down hard in order to put an end to escalating Palestinian violence against Israelis, including suicide bombings. These were taking an ever-increasing toll in lives and making daily life inside Israel almost unbearable. Ariel Sharon looked like just the man for the job.

In fact, Arik Sharon was a lion in winter, who much like Winston Churchill in the late 1930's, had rejuvenated himself and come back determined to put an end to Barak's dangerous appeasement policies and put Israel's house in order. I had seen something of this transformation myself in my dealings with Sharon over the preceding few years. I didn't hear anything from Sharon for about a year after our misunderstanding at the 1994 OU Convention. Then, shortly after he became Minister of Infrastructure in the Likud government that came to power in June 1996, I received a call during a visit to Israel from his secretary inviting me to come to his office in the Knesset. She told me if that was inconvenient for me, Sharon would be happy to meet me either in Tel Aviv or at his ranch in the Negev.

I was unsure as to what precipitated this sudden interest in seeing me. Sharon was sweet as pie, and it was clear to me from the outset that bygones were bygones. He asked me, "Do you know why I help the Haredim (the ultra-Orthodox) even though I am personally not religious?" Seeing that I had no answer, Sharon explained, "I look at my children, and I cannot guarantee that in two or three generations my grandchildren or great-grand-children will be Jewish. I look at the Haredim, and know for sure that theirs will be. If there is anything I can do to help the Orthodox Union in your educational work here in Israel, I will gladly respond."

In the ensuing years, Sharon was a frequent visitor to the United States, especially to the Presidents' Conference. On those occasions, he was often his old combative self on behalf of those causes in which we both believed so deeply. Yet in the months after his beloved wife, Lilly, passed away from lung cancer in March 2000, Sharon looked old and tired and did not seem to be the same person. He certainly did not answer questions with the same feistiness and intensity that he had long been known for. Some people wondered out loud if he was the right person to run against Barak if (as was becoming increasingly likely) the prime minister's governing coalition fell apart.

Then, in November 2000, when I was elected President of the Orthodox General Assembly (OGA) in Jerusalem, Sharon came to address our closing session. I could see immediately that the old Arik was back. He had lost weight and was vibrant and full of energy. No doubt the intensity of the crisis facing his beloved

Israel and the shortening odds that he could defeat Barak in the coming elections had gotten his juices flowing. I was able to exchange a few words with him when he came into the audience and was impressed by his energy and evident zest for the fight. I was excited by the prospect that we might soon have a prime minister who had denounced Oslo from the very beginning as a tragic mistake and would finally put an end, once and for all, to the mindset of making concessions to an implacable enemy that was determined to destroy Israel.

Prime Minister Sharon's government responded decisively to the scourge of Palestinian suicide bombings, sending the IDF into the principle Palestinian cities of Judea and Samaria to smash the terrorist infrastructure built up painstakingly by Yasir Arafat's Palestinian Administration. The master terrorist himself was "isolated" in his compound in Ramallah, although U.S. pressure deterred Sharon from carrying through on his clear desire of expelling Arafat from the land. Arafat may survive as titular leader of the Palestinians, but it was now clear to all that the accursed Oslo peace process was dead and was a fraud on the people of Israel. For the foreseeable future, Israelis will no longer risk their security on wishful thinking concerning a Palestinian leadership that clearly has never given up its hope of expelling Israel from the area.

The Israeli peace camp and the Labor Party have at the moment almost completely imploded, as even their staunchest supporters have woken up to the reality that they were terribly deluded.

So we can finally breathe easy again, right? Wrong. Israel is under tremendous pressure from the rest of the world, including its best friend, the United States to make concessions to the Palestinians. President Bush has proven himself to be the most pro-Israel president since Ronald Reagan, but he is being pushed, not only by the Arab and Muslim worlds, but by China, Russia, our weak-kneed European allies and large sections of the American establishment, to adopt the so-called "Road Map" by the quartet in order to ensure Arab support.

It was easy to see this danger as early as the fall of 2001, when after the attack on America by Osama bin-Laden and his Al-Queda terrorist network, Secretary of State Powell began to mobilize a world response against terrorism and invited Yasir Arafat's PA and states like Syria and Libya to join. The pressure

has only intensified recently. President Bush is to be congratulated for standing firm in his formulation of standing together
with all states that confront terrorism—including Israel.

Yet the pressure on Bush to appease the Arab world will only
intensify. The only meaningful counter-pressure to the worldwide anti-Israel coalition is the American Jewish community in
coalition with our allies in the conservative movement and in
pro-Israel Christian groups. We must redouble our efforts to
remind the Administration that Israel remains the only democracy in the Middle East and one of America's few reliable allies
in the war against terror.

The odds against Israel may seem long given the disparity in
size between the broad coalition badgering her for concessions
and the much more modest group supporting her. Yet now that
Americans have themselves been directly attacked by terrorism,
they are likely to be much more sympathetic to the horrors of
violence Israelis endure on a daily basis. We will win this battle
with the Saudis and Europeans for the ear of the Bush Administration because we must. *Ein breirah* (we have no alternative).
The very survival of Israel hangs in the balance. Because of Oslo,
we lost a decade and hundreds of Israelis lost their lives to Palestinian terror. By November 2002, 15,000 terrorist attacks against
Israel had occurred in the last two years. Yet if the folly of Oslo
serves as a warning to Israelis and Jews that they must never
again imperil their security because of wishful thinking and
wooly-headed visions of a "new Middle East" then it may be
said to have served a salutary purpose.

CHAPTER ELEVEN

If I Forget Thee, O Jerusalem

Our first trip to Israel in 1964 was memorable on a number of counts beyond seeing the land. As we departed from the train station in Jerusalem we were told, as we observed the barbed wire which divided the city, not to look up at the tower of the adjacent building. The Jordanian soldiers had been known to fire at inquisitive eyes.

A story is told about the Chofetz Chaim, a saintly Torah scholar from the beginning of the twentieth century. He received a letter from a Jewish soldier who had been drafted into the Polish army. The soldier explained that he had been assigned to a remote base where there were no other Jewish soldiers, no minyan and no facilities for kashruth; making it impossible for him to keep Shabbat. How then, the soldier asked the Chofetz Chaim, would he be able to survive as an observant Jew? The Chofetz Chaim responded to the soldier in words that I find inspirational and as valid today as they were then. He said, "If it is impossible for you to keep Shabbat, kashruth, to daven (pray), or to keep the mitzvoth (commandments), don't be discouraged. There is one thing you must do. Whenever you have a moment, you should speak to G-d and when you speak to G-d, face east. Why should you face east? Because you will be directing your thoughts to Jerusalem, and in doing so you will unite yourself with the Jewish people, with its holy temple and with G-d."

I relate deeply to this story because it represents the cornerstone of my political activism. While I have always agreed with the oft-articulated premise that when it comes to Israeli foreign policy or defense issues, the American Jewish community does not have a right to interject its own positions into the public debate with the Israeli body politic, I feel entirely differently on the subject of Jerusalem. Prime minister after prime minister and foreign minister after foreign minister, both within Labor and Likud, have insisted both to the Israeli people and to American Jewry that Jerusalem belongs to the entire Jewish people, not only to those who live and vote in Israel. Therefore, these Israeli leaders have asserted, it is part of the responsibility of world Jewry to stand together with Israel in protecting the sanctity of Jerusalem, the eternal and undivided capital of the State of Israel.

To that end, I have always taken a very special interest in the long-running effort to convince the U.S. government to move our embassy in Israel from Tel Aviv to Jerusalem. Israel is the only country in the world with which the United States has diplomatic relations in which the U.S. embassy is not located in the host country's capital city. This peculiar situation has been maintained since the U.S. recognized Israel's existence back in 1948 because of fear of how the surrounding Arab countries would react if the embassy were moved to Jerusalem. In fact, the site chosen by the U.S. on which to build its embassy, if and when authorization comes from Washington, is in west Jerusalem, which is not part of the city that is under dispute.

Throughout my career as a pro-Israel activist, I have personally lobbied long and intensively in Congress on behalf of moving the U.S. Embassy in Israel to Jerusalem. This issue has come up in practically every conversation I have held with members of both Houses of Congress over the past 20 years. I have also raised the issue with every candidate for President of the United States I have ever met.

My reputation among members of Congress as a staunch advocate of a united Jerusalem and of moving the U.S. Embassy to Israel's declared capital grew during the 1980's when I made a mark as the maestro of HUVPAC. Once during those years, Tom Dine, the longtime executive director of AIPAC approached me during an AIPAC dinner in New York and said, "I heard your name mentioned today." I asked him by whom, and his reply was "Ambassador Max Kampelman." Though I had heard of the ambassador—during those years Kampelman headed the American delegation to the landmark Arms Control Negotiations with the Soviet Union—I had never personally met him. I therefore asked Dine in what context my name had come up.

Tom's answer made me smile. At the time, the Administration had released a trial balloon to Congress with a potential solution to the "embassy" issue. They hoped it would satisfy partisans on both sides, namely, to have two embassies, one in Tel Aviv and another in Jerusalem. Ambassador Kampelman had called Congressman Ben Gilman, then the ranking Republican on the House International Relations Committee, to gauge his reaction to the idea. Gilman, who represented Rockland County in Congress and is a close friend of mine, replied to Kampelman, "I could never support this because Mendy Ganchrow would never accept it." According to Dine, the Ambassador then asked him, "Who the hell is Mendy Ganchrow?"

At a White House meeting with President Clinton that I attended together with a number of other Jewish leaders in late 2000, I brought with me a statement that President Clinton had made when he was "Candidate Clinton" in which he had expressed support for moving the embassy. From my seat across from the President, I looked him directly in the eye and read the statement he had made on the Jerusalem issue as a candidate in 1992. I then asked, "Mr. President, do you still believe in that statement and do you intend to act on it?" He responded by affirming that he still believed that the embassy should be moved but as President he had global concerns that prevented him from doing so at that moment.

I believe it is the obligation of any pro-Israel leader worth his or her salt to press every candidate for Congress or for the presidency or vice-presidency for the kind of response I got from Clinton that day. That is how we keep the pressure on for an eventual change in U.S. policy on the embassy issue. Yet we need to be aware that the position of a candidate is different from that of a sitting president. Once elected, Clinton came under immense pressure from the unelected officials that make U.S. foreign policy not to move the embassy to Jerusalem for fear of damaging U.S. interests in the Arab world.

It must be said also that as we have sought to counter these entrenched interests, we sometimes have not had the sincere support of the government of Israel. Certainly, during the Rabin era, and under later prime ministers as well, we were frequently informed by U.S. officials on a not-for-attribution basis that they were aware that the Israeli government did not place as high a priority on moving the embassy, as did the American Jewish community. Thus the Israelis undercut our efforts.

During that particular meeting in the White House, I cited to President Clinton an op-ed article from the English edition of the Israeli newspaper *Ha'aretz*, which focused on the incitement against Jews and the State of Israel being perpetuated in Palestinian schools, camps and on television. I asked the President how we could ever hope for peace if the next generation of Palestinians never hears the word "peace" but rather is inoculated with cries of jihad and calls for the blood of the Jewish invader and infidel. I reached across the table and gave him a copy of the two-page article from *Ha'aretz*, which I had placed in a plastic cover. The President stopped the meeting and read the first page. Appearing quite upset by the content of the article, he turned to Secretary of State Madeline Albright and asked her if she would please make a copy and give it back to him.

During the 2000 presidential race I was in Washington for an AIPAC executive board meeting, when Condaleeza Rice, then foreign policy advisor to Governor Bush and now National Security Advisor to the President, arrived at the event. She was invited to deliver some impromptu remarks on foreign policy. Her brilliance was immediately evident, as was her pleasing smile and charm.

In the question and answer period that followed, I asked Rice: "If Governor Bush is elected president, will he move the embassy to Jerusalem? And if your answer is yes, why should I believe you?" I explained to her that I had heard too many presidential candidates over the years making the same promise and not delivering once elected. Rice responded flatly that Governor Bush would "definitely" carry through with his embassy pledge because in her experience, "He always carries out what he promises." After Rice completed her remarks, she walked over to me and thanked me for raising the question.

In fact, upon Bush's election and inauguration, he did begin the paperwork necessary to move the embassy. In addition, President Bush showed splendid leadership in refusing to send an official U.S. delegation to the UN Conference on Racism in Durban, South Africa, which became an orgy of anti-Zionism and anti-Semitism, as well as in vetoing several flagrantly anti-Israel resolutions at the U.N. Unlike President Clinton, he refused to meet with Arafat as long as Palestinian violence continued. All of this clearly demonstrated that President Bush did indeed have warm feelings toward Israel, and would support the Jewish state in its conflict with the Palestinians in a more forthright manner than had President Clinton.

The cataclysm of September 11 and Bush's need to put together a coalition that would include Arab countries in America's war against Iraq has caused the Administration to zig-zag from its earlier instinctively pro-Israel path. The Mideast policy sometimes set by Secretary of State Colin Powell is worrisome to pro-Israel activists like me. These indeed are dangerous times for Israel.

Although I personally feel strongly about a number of issues relating to Israel's diplomatic and military policies, I believe that these issues must be addressed by the people of Israel alone.

Yet on the sanctity and indivisibility of Jerusalem, I cannot and will not still my voice. If the Bush Administration ever proposes dividing Jerusalem between Israel and a Palestinian state and placing the Temple Mount—the holiest place in Judaism—under the control of the Palestinians—they can be sure they will be hearing loud and clear from our community.

CHAPTER TWELVE

Relations with Bill Clinton

I am probably the only living American who ran as a Clinton delegate to the Democratic National Convention in 1992 but ended up voting for George Bush.

I first met Bill Clinton at an AIPAC cocktail party in Washington during the time that he was governor of Arkansas, well before he became a candidate for President. Clinton approached me genially and struck up a conversation that lasted for a couple of minutes. Three days later he sent me a personal thank you note, which quite surprised me since I had neither identified myself to him by name nor given him my card. Unfortunately, Sheila, who had become jaded by the sheer volume of mail we received at home from political VIPs, discarded Clinton's note.

Then in the winter of 1992, the late David Ifshin, a close friend and attorney for Clinton, who also happened to be a pro-Israel activist who had helped me to set up HUVPAC, called to say that Governor Clinton wanted me to run as a Clinton delegate in the New York Democratic primary in Rockland County. Ifshin added that Clinton needed an answer within 72 hours. Without much time to make a considered judgment of Clinton's offer, I told him that I would agree to serve as a Clinton delegate on the condition that I could present to the governor through Ifshin a list of questions regarding his stand on the U.S.-Israel relationship. If I felt comfortable with Clinton's responses to my questions, I would go out and campaign on his behalf. If I did not, I would allow my name to be used but would not actively campaign. I looked upon Clinton as being in the mold of Senator Henry "Scoop" Jackson.

In a January 24, 1992 memo to Ifshin, I wrote that Orthodox

and traditional Jews would like their favored candidate to say that settlements "are not an obstacle to peace... They would like the candidate to say they approve of the ten billion dollars absorption loan guarantees without political strings or conditions" and, of course, no U.S. pressure on Israel.

I then drew up eight to ten questions for Clinton that focused quite specifically on issues like U.S. recognition of Jerusalem as Israel's capital and the fate of the settlements. To my disappointment the answers I received from the candidate were full of innocuous "I love Israel," type of rhetoric that did not directly address the issues I had raised.

Feeling that I had been burned, I did not campaign on behalf of Clinton in the New York primary even though I was listed as a Clinton delegate. In the primary, Clinton carried Rockland County in the balloting but I came in last in the list of Clinton delegates and therefore was not selected to attend the convention.

I subsequently voted for Bush and shortly afterwards changed my party affiliation back to the Republican Party, which I had joined as a young man. I had returned to the Democrats in the mid-1970's so that I could campaign on behalf of my hero Senator Henry (Scoop) Jackson (D-Wash) in the 1976 election. I had stayed a Democrat after that losing campaign not out of ideological conviction but as a personal favor to my close friend and neighbor Ken Gribetz, the Democratic District Attorney of Rockland County.

Flash forward six years to September 1998 at the height of the Monica Lewinsky scandal. The Orthodox Union received a call from the White House on the Thursday preceding Labor Day inviting us to come to the White House the following Tuesday for a ceremony that we had requested. In fact, for many years, we had an outstanding request to the White House to have the opportunity to present a scroll or tribute to the President in honor of the United States of America prior to the High Holy Days. We had previously made such a presentation to President Bush and then to President Clinton on one occasion during his first term. However we had been unable to obtain such an invitation from the White House in 1997. In addition, the Union had invited the President to be our guest speaker at our national dinner, but he was out of the country and could not attend (About the same time, however, Vice President Gore was our honoree at the Orthodox Union's 100th Annual Dinner).

Needless to say, under normal circumstances we would have

been gratified to receive an invitation to take part in a ceremony with the President of the United States. A visit to the White House and Oval Office is a thrilling moment for most individuals, and neither our OU lay leaders nor I are exceptions in that respect. Nevertheless, that particular week in September 1998 was hardly a normal time. Only three weeks before, President Clinton had finally acknowledged having an inappropriate sexual relationship with Monica Lewinsky, after more than six months of steadfast denial. There was enormous moral outrage across the country over Clinton's conduct that transcended party lines. Most stirring in this respect was a speech by Senator Joe Lieberman of Connecticut, a prominent Democrat and an Orthodox Jew, expressing stern approbation for the President's "immoral" behavior.

After Lieberman made his electrifying speech, I sent him a note congratulating him on his political courage, which Lieberman acknowledged in a note to me. For many in our community Lieberman was a role model. He also happened to be a member of our board of directors and belongs to two OU synagogues, in Washington and Connecticut.

When the invitation reached our office from the White House, I knew that the timing was not coincidental. I felt that the purpose of the White House was to show the American people that Orthodox Jews were, in effect, endorsing the veracity and moral stature of the President despite his admission of adultery. Surely we would have liked to take part in a ceremony signaling the respect shown to the Orthodox Jewish community by the highest official in the land. However, the last thing we wanted was to be manipulated by the Clinton White House in a way that would make it appear that we were endorsing the President's conduct.

I consulted with our senior officers about how to respond. I then arranged for a teleconference with former presidents and senior vice presidents of the OU as well as other prominent lay leaders who, under normal circumstances, would have been among those invited to take part in our delegation to the White House. The feeling among all of the participants in the teleconference was unanimous. The Orthodox Union should not accept the invitation to participate in the ceremonial encounter with President Clinton.

I called the White House the following morning and informed them that because of the shortness of time, (this already being the Friday before the onset of the Labor Day weekend), we did not have sufficient time to have a scroll designed and allow members of our delegation to clear their schedule and come to the White House the following Tuesday.

I am not sure whether the White House believed our explanation or not, but they responded cordially and, at least publicly, did not challenge it. One prominent OU member, Rabbi Menachem Genack, who had a close personal relationship with Bill Clinton, asked me a few days later why we did not arrange our schedules so as to meet the President of the United States in a ceremony in the White House. I told Rabbi Genack the truth.

As I noted, it was not easy for me to say no to President Clinton, in part because I have always relished the perk that my pro-Israel advocacy has afforded me of visiting the White House and rubbing shoulders with the American political elite.

I have been to the White House many times; including three visits to the Oval Office and a number of times in the Cabinet Room and Roosevelt Room. I have visited Blair House twice and have attended a large number of meetings and events in the old Executive Office Building.

I have also been gratified to have had the opportunity to make frequent visits to the office of the Prime Minister of Israel, as well as the Israeli government cabinet room. In comparison to the White House, there is nothing regal about the office of the Prime Minister. Many of the people who work there dress quite informally, as is also the case in the halls of the Knesset (suits and ties are still the exception and not the rule in Israel).

To be sure, the White House itself is fairly modest compared to, say, the majestic flavor of the palace in Amman, Jordan. As one enters the waiting room of the White House that leads to the oval office a Marine guard opens the door to allow you to enter the waiting room where a secretary greets you. The formal areas of the White House where state dinners are held transmit an aura of American history with paintings, historic china and outstanding furniture from all periods.

In stark contrast, the entrance to the Prime Minister's building in Jerusalem has posters for movies and concerts posted on a bulletin board. Unlike the large and modern edifices of the United States government, cabinet ministers in Israel often have their departments and offices in antiquated buildings spread around Jerusalem.

Our visit to the White House during President Clinton's first term took place under trying circumstances. Early that morning before I had even left Monsey to fly to Washington, a single engine plane crashed into the wall of the White House, killing the pilot in what was an apparent suicide. When I left for La Guardia to catch the shuttle, I had no information as to whether the White House would, under the circumstances, go ahead with our appointment.

Things remained confused once I arrived in Washington. Because of the closure of Pennsylvania Avenue and the security checkpoints everywhere in the vicinity of the White House, my taxi inched along so slowly that eventually I got out of the cab and walked. When I finally reached the White House I found that only one entrance was open and I had to walk around Lafayette Park in order to be admitted.

Security at the White House was unbelievably tight and some security personnel were wearing what appeared to be black combat uniforms with boots and visible firearms. Although the plane crash had occurred many hours earlier, no one inside the building was allowed to approach any window facing the downed plane. A secretary allowed me to take a fleeting glance of the plane as she opened the door. All the other doors facing the downed plane were closed.

The White House staff appeared to be in a state of disarray. To a casual observer like myself, it looked like they were running back and forth in a state of disorganization. There were certainly many more security people visible than I had noticed on prior White House visits and they appeared nervous and edgy. When we finally entered the Oval Office to meet the President it appeared to me that he had not slept well the previous night. I believe he couldn't wait until we left. However, his politeness combined with our desire for additional small talk and photographs allowed us to prolong our visit beyond the ten minutes we were allotted.

Another encounter with President Clinton in the White House was more enjoyable. On July 18, 1999, just over a year after we had declined to visit the White House during the Lewinsky fiasco and several months after he survived the effort to impeach him, President and Mrs. Clinton invited Sheila and I to join them at the White House at a dinner honoring the Prime Minister of Israel and Mrs. Barak. The dinner was to be held on the south

Prime Minister Ariel Sharon, congratulates me on being elected the first President of the Orthodox General Assembly (OGA) a world wide group of Orthodox leaders.

With the late King Hussein of Jordan at his palace in Amman

In the great hall of the president's home with President Moshe Katzav of Israel

King Abdullah of Jordan visits the Presidents Conference. Mel Salberg, conference chairman, makes the introductions

Israeli President and Mrs. Ezer Weitzman in his private office in Jerusalem.

With the late Prime Minister of Israel, Yitzhak Rabin, in his office a few days after the Oslo announcement.

With Rabbi Dr. Norman Lamm, President, Yeshiva University. I was proud to serve a number of years on the Board of the Rabbi Isaac Elchanan Theological Seminary of Yeshiva.

Malcolm Hoenlein, Executive Vice President of the Conference of Presidents, before a Mizrachi convention.

With Senator John McCain (R-Ariz.), a fellow Vietnam veteran.

With then-Defense Secretary Dick Cheney at the OU dinner.

Hadassah and Senator Joseph Lieberman (D-Conn.) at the 1996 OU convention where he inducted me into my second term as President.

Sheila and I
with President
Ronald Reagan.

Sheila and I were impressed
with the sincerity and
warmth of President George
Bush.

President George Bush
meets with the OU
leadership in the
Roosevelt Room of the
White House. OU Presi-
dent Sheldon Rudoff is
at President Bush's right.

With President
Bill Clinton in
the Cabinet
Room of the
White House,
August 1999 at
a meeting of
Jewish leaders.

Vice-President
Dan Quayle
joins us as a
guest speaker at
a Union dinner.

Elli upon completing
his summer internship
with Senator Jesse
Helms

With Vice President Al
Gore, special guest at the
OU's 100th anniversary
dinner June 7, 1998,
surprising him with a 1988
Gore for President poster.

With First Lady Hillary Clinton
at the OU office during her
campaign for the U.S. Senate.

With former New
York Mayor
Rudolph Guiliani at
a City Hall recep-
tion in honor of the
OU's centennial.

Ari and I visit
Senator Kent Conrad
(D-N. Dak.) At the
time, Ari served as
an intern to Senator
Quentin Burdick.
(D-N. Dak.)

Sheila with the
Grand Mufti,
Absattar Derbisali,
the highest cleric
in Kazakhstan.

President Bill Clinton with Sheila at the dinner for Prime Minister Ehud Barak.

Malkie joins me on a visit with Senator Alan Cranston (D-Calif.)

My mother, Kate Ganchrow, at age 91 in 2002.

Ari, Banji, myself, Sheila, Paul, Malkie, Brina, and Elli at an OU dinner.

Standing on the lawn of the White House we are on our way to dinner. It was held in a tent and honored Prime Minister and Mrs. Ehud Barak, and was hosted by President and Mrs. Bill Clinton.

Our children and grandchildren at my mother's 90th birthday (this predated Rachel and Tamara's birth -insert).

lawn of the White House under a great tent. As was subsequently reported in the media, many people tried to wangle invitations without success. It was not considered a large dinner by diplomatic standards. I believe the reason we were invited was that Mrs. Clinton had decided to go ahead with her race for a Senate seat in New York and was seeking to neutralize the strong criticism I had expressed, as president of the Orthodox Union, of her statement the year before in support of a Palestinian state.

As we left for Washington, Sheila made a most uncharacteristic remark, "You know I don't have a picture of myself with President Clinton." On what we call the Presidential wall in our dining room are pictures of Sheila and myself with Presidents Reagan and Bush as well as numerous photos of myself with Presidents Clinton, Bush and Reagan and with Vice Presidents Quayle and Gore. Normally I never carry a camera with me to such events, but I replied to Sheila that I would bring along a camera. If they allowed me to carry it into the event I would try to arrange a picture of her with the President.

When we arrived at the dinner event, we entered a long formal reception line that allowed each guest to greet and shake hands with President and Mrs. Clinton and Prime Minister and Mrs. Barak. Normally such reception lines take forty to sixty minutes. That evening it lasted for over two hours. In a style for which he is well known, President Clinton spoke extensively to each and every guest with such warmth and charm that every individual felt they were the only person in the room that counted.

When I came up to Hillary, it was immediately evident that she was well aware that in a few months she would be visiting me at the Orthodox Union as part of her planned senatorial campaign. She informed me that she was looking forward to the visit. No one could have guessed from Hillary's cordial manner to Sheila and me that she was still reeling from the enormous brouhaha that her recent visit to Israel and controversial kiss of Mrs. Suha Arafat had caused in the New York Jewish community. If the First Lady was stung by the sharply critical comments I had made in the media concerning her decision to meet Mrs. Arafat and her failure to immediately denounce the comments made by the latter charging Israelis with using poison gas against Palestinians, she gave no indication of it. Nor did she publicly acknowledge extensive media reports that Mayor Giuliani, her expected opponent, would be appearing at a parlor meeting in our home—albeit one sponsored by Sheila, not by me.

As usual during such visits, I recited the special blessing a religious Jew is enjoined to make when meeting a head of state or royalty. After the receiving line was complete, the entire crowd was shuttled from the White House to the dinner tent in open trolleys. It was a gorgeous night for an outdoor event, without a cloud in the starry sky. Inside the huge air-conditioned tent, the Marine band entertained. As is the custom at the White House, husbands and wives were seated at separate tables. I sat with Senator Patrick Leahy of Vermont, and James Rubin, the State Department spokesman as well as with the official hostess of the White House.

Since the Secret Service had allowed me to bring my camera to the dinner, I took numerous photos at the event, including Sheila with General Colin Powell and other dignitaries. The kosher food, doubly wrapped in cellophane with new dishes and silverware, served to the guests who could not eat the regular dinner, was first-rate.

The speeches were relatively short and innocuous and the event seemed to be winding to a conclusion much quicker than was normally the case at the Clinton White House. Yet the President, in full loquacious and gregarious form, appeared to be having such a wonderful time that he did not desire to leave. Numerous guests approached him, to shake his hand and ask him to sign autographs or take pictures. Eager to please Sheila, I asked both the President and Prime Minister Barak to sign my dinner menu, which they did. Despite the gentle urging of his security people that he should end the event, the President, with Barak by his side, just kept schmoozing. Even as some guests started to leave the President did not move for the exit, which is hardly the accepted protocol.

Sheila turned to me and asked; "Do you think I can ask the President to pose with me? I checked my camera and saw that I had only one exposure left. Sheila walked over to the President and said, "Mr. President, my husband has one picture left, could I impose upon you to pose for a picture?" Instantaneously the President said yes and spontaneously planted a kiss on her cheek. Sheila was totally surprised and flustered and, she turned red.

Unfortunately I had not been ready with my camera so I was not able to record the kiss. Then Sheila and the President assumed a more conventional pose and I snapped the picture. On the following day I had the roll of film developed at a Wall Street camera store, but was deeply disappointed that Sheila's eyes and that of President Clinton came out red. There was also a woman standing immediately behind the President who appeared in the middle of the photo. Chagrined that I had not done a better job of taking the photo, I asked the owner of the store if he could remove the intruding woman from the picture. He glanced at it and said in surprise, "Hey, that is the President of the United States." I replied, "Yes, and that's my wife."

Thanks to the wonders of modern computer technology, he was not only able to get rid of the woman, but to remove the red glare from the eyes of Sheila and the President. A few weeks later, I was invited to the Cabinet Room of the White House along with other Jewish leaders to meet the President and the Secretary of State on issues of concern to our community. I brought the picture of Sheila and the President along with me and he graciously autographed it and wrote a message to Sheila. While I often did not agree with President Clinton's politics and policies and, of course, was quite disappointed in his behavior in the Lewinsky Affair, I must acknowledge that he set a standard of warmth and spontaneity in the presidency that was quite captivating.

CHAPTER THIRTEEN

My Minuet with Hillary Clinton

W hen First Lady Hillary Rodham Clinton addressed a group of Israeli and Arab teenagers in May 1998 she expressed the opinion that a Palestinian state should eventually emerge from Palestinian self-rule in the West Bank and Gaza. The White House press secretary was quick to say that Mrs. Clinton had been speaking for herself and not articulating policy on behalf of her husband's administration.

A year later, Mrs. Clinton confirmed rumors that had been around for months that she was considering a race for the New York Senate seat that was being vacated by Senator Daniel Patrick Moynihan, who had announced he would retire in 2000. Needless to say, I and many other pro-Israel activists were less than thrilled by this development.

Over the years, the Union had a very special relationship with Moynihan, a brilliant intellect with a long history as a diplomatic and political leader. Moynihan served as the U.S. Ambassador to India and later U.S. Ambassador to the United Nations. He was in the latter post in 1975 when the infamous "Zionism is Racism" resolution was passed by the General Assembly despite Moynihan's brilliant oration against it. Once elected to the Senate in 1977, Moynihan became its foremost voice in favor of moving the U.S. Embassy in Israel from Tel Aviv to Jerusalem. It was to Moynihan's credit that the Senate voted almost unanimously to endorse moving the American embassy from Tel Aviv and declaring Jerusalem to be Israel's eternal capital.

Given Moynihan's forceful advocacy on the Jerusalem issue and for Israel in general, I wanted to make sure that his successor would also be a strong supporter of the Jewish state who would champion the cause of Jerusalem. Therefore, on June 8, 1999, I dispatched a very polite public letter to Mrs. Clinton in which I asked five questions: Do you consider Jerusalem to be the indivisible capital of Israel? Do you favor moving the American Embassy there from Tel Aviv? Are you concerned that the Administration is not following the law of the land by not moving the Embassy? If you were in the Senate, would you vote to remove the President's ability to waive the law's requirement and thereby postpone legislative funding sanctions for delaying the transfer of the Embassy to Jerusalem? In summation, if you were a Senator, would you be prepared to assure New Yorkers that you would take Senator Moynihan's place as the leader on the issues of the Embassy and 'Jerusalem as Israel's capital'?

On July 2, Mrs. Clinton responded to me in a warm letter in which she reminisced about her memorable trip to Jerusalem and Masada the previous Hanukkah. She wrote that she was looking forward shortly to hosting Prime Minister and Mrs. Ehud Barak on their first official visit to the United States. She then stated, "I personally consider Jerusalem the eternal and indivisible capital of Israel, and I admire the leadership shown by Senator Moynihan on this issue." Mrs. Clinton concluded by saying she planned to spend considerable time in New York in the next few months, and would welcome an opportunity to meet with the representatives of the Orthodox Union.

I responded with a note of appreciation for her expression of support of Israel and for her pledge regarding Jerusalem. I stated that her position that the U.S. Embassy should be relocated to Jerusalem, Israel's capital, represented "a meaningful public statement," adding, "The timing of such a move is an issue that we look forward to discussing with you." I pointed out that five years had passed since the United States Congress passed a law about relocating the Embassy, and that the law, as written, did not link the move with the completion of the peace process (President Clinton had declined to implement the law, stipulating that to do so could harm the peace process). Therefore, I noted, the way Mrs. Clinton would vote as senator on removing the President's power to waive such a move of the embassy based on concern over the impact on the peace process was a question in which we as a community had a keen interest. I concluded by inviting Mrs. Clinton to meet with us at her earliest convenience at the Orthodox Union's New York headquarters.

Meanwhile, my exchanges with Mrs. Clinton were garnering considerable press attention for the OU; more than the organization had ever received.

Mrs. Clinton's response to my first letter made news throughout the world. The headline of New York's *Jewish Forward* read: "Hillary breaks with Bill over Issue of Jerusalem, Vowing Fight for Capital; First Lady Sends Letter to Ganchrow calling City 'Eternal and Indivisible.'" The State Department's deputy spokesman James Foley, evidently chagrined by Mrs. Clinton's sudden endorsement of a Jewish Jerusalem, declared that Mrs. Clinton had "expressed her own views and that Israel and the Palestinians had agreed to take up Jerusalem in negotiations." James Zogby, president of the Arab-American Institute, said he was "shocked to hear of the First Lady's disregard for the U.S.-brokered peace process . . ." and that to take such a step on Jerusalem so as "to win 'points' in a possible Senate bid is reprehensible."

Perhaps miffed by the headlines our exchange of letters had generated, Mrs. Clinton dragged her heels over actually making her visit to the OU. Also, she decided to leave the visit until after her much-heralded trip to Israel in November, which she no doubt expected would generate good public relations for her in the New York Jewish community. It was actually after she had embarked on that ill-fated expedition in mid-November 1999 that her office contacted us and agreed that she would make her long promised visit to the Orthodox Union for a luncheon on December 14. Perhaps looking for protection for Mrs. Clinton before venturing into what she feared might be less-than-friendly territory, her office contacted David Luchins, a top aide to Senator Moynihan and a longtime Vice President of the OU, to ask that he accompany her to the luncheon. Luchins, who was known to be advising Mrs. Clinton on Jewish issues, responded that since he was an officer of the Union, she would be better served on this occasion to invite Senator Lieberman to accompany her. Lieberman of course, was a member of the OU board of directors.

The Clinton campaign called Lieberman's office and asked him to join her. Even before Lieberman had a chance to respond, Mrs. Clinton put in a call to the senator from Israel to thank him for accepting her invitation. Thus, Lieberman was trapped.

The next day, however, everything went haywire. While holding a joint press conference in Ramallah with Mrs. Suha Arafat, wife of PLO chairman Yasir Arafat, Mrs. Clinton sat silently by and did not offer a public response when Mrs. Arafat accused Israelis of intentionally poisoning the air, water, and food supply of the Palestinians. Instead, at the end of the press conference, Mrs. Clinton kissed Mrs. Arafat warmly on the cheek. Pressed later by U.S. reporters traveling with her as to how she could have embraced Mrs. Arafat after the latter had charged Israel with attempted mass murder, Mrs. Clinton claimed that she had neither heard Mrs. Arafat's words nor had been able to listen to a translation into English of what she had said. It was only the following day, when Mrs. Clinton traveled to Jordan and was informed by her advisors about the sharply negative reaction to the incident in the United States, that she issued a disclaimer. Even then, however, she focused her criticism more against those seeking to destroy the peace process rather than against Mrs. Arafat and her blood libel against the Jewish people.

Shocked and infuriated by the Clinton-Arafat affair, the OU leadership held an internal discussion in our office on November 19 to decide how to respond. Some of our officers argued that, given what had occurred, we should withdraw our invitation. After a very animated discussion, Rabbi Butler and I put in a call to Senator Lieberman. He called us back a few minutes later, and after much discussion he recommended that we go ahead with the invitation to Mrs. Clinton; arguing that while holding the meeting under these circumstances might be uncomfortable, it would look worse for the OU if we cancelled. I asked Lieberman whether he would feel ill at ease participating in the meeting if our questions to Mrs. Clinton were sharp and pointed. "Definitely not," he responded, quipping that if Mrs. Clinton were still a candidate by the end of the campaign, she would have had so much interaction with the Jewish community, he believed that she would become a *ba'alat teshuvah* (a person who returns to religion).

I informed Joe that he should be aware that Sheila was supporting Giuliani and would be running a fundraiser for him in our home. He good-naturedly reminded me that he would be the last person to criticize Sheila in view of the fact that she supported him when he made his first run for the Senate in 1984, while I had supported his incumbent rival, Senator Lowell Weicker.

Based on Senator Lieberman's recommendation, we decided to go ahead with our December 14 meeting with Mrs. Clinton. Still, I faced an embarrassing situation; Sheila had scheduled a fundraiser for Mayor Rudy Giuliani—Mrs. Clinton's likely Republican rival in the 2000 Senate race— at our home in Monsey on December 8. The fund-raiser had been long in the works, and we had no way of knowing when we scheduled it that it would fall a few days before the scheduled Hillary Clinton event at the Union. The newspapers jumped on the striking juxtaposition of the two events. Marsha Kramer of WCBS-TV wrote in her Internet column: "It probably came as a blow to Clinton to learn that Dr. Mandell Ganchrow, head of the Orthodox Union, was to hold a fundraiser for Giuliani at his home in Monsey." To her credit, Mrs. Clinton never responded to the media reports and carried on with her plans to come to the OU as though Sheila's Giuliani fundraiser was not happening.

On Monday, November 22, 1999, I received a call from Mark Allen of CNN requesting me to appear on "Inside Politics" with reporter Judy Woodruff the following day to discuss Hillary Clinton and the Jewish community. After a great deal of discussion with such OU leaders as Rabbi Butler, Nathan Diament, Betty Ehrenberg and public relations director Sharyn Perlman, I decided that such an appearance would be a no-win situation. To criticize Hillary and her policies on CNN would put the Union in a partisan light, while we claimed to be a nonpartisan organization. On the other hand, if I came across as being too soft on her, I would antagonize her presumed opponent, Mayor Rudy Giuliani—not to mention many of our own officers who were strongly anti-Hillary. Therefore, we decided it would be better not to accept the invitation.

On Sunday, December 5, I received a call from Mayor Ehud Olmert of Jerusalem concerning an article in that week's *Forward*, in which I had criticized Israeli politicians for becoming involved in the senatorial race in New York. On the one hand I had criticized Olmert, who had strongly endorsed Giuliani, and on the other, Prime Minister Barak, who had expressed support for the First Lady. Olmert told me that he understood my concerns, but wanted me to know his statements arose out of a debt of gratitude to Giuliani. He intended to come to New York during the campaign and inform Jewish audiences that he was not there to tell them who to vote for, but to express gratitude to Mayor Giuliani for the strong support he had shown to Israel over the years.

I told Olmert that while I personally was more comfortable with his own motivation to express support for Giuliani than I was with Barak's clearly opportunistic expression of support for Hillary, I believed in general that Americans should stay out of Israeli elections and Israelis should stay out of American elections. Nevertheless, I told Olmert that given Barak's endorsement of Hillary, I would offer no further public criticisms of Olmert's approach nor publicly criticize his plans to come to New York on behalf of Giuliani.

As we prepared for our meeting with Hillary Clinton, we solicited input from both Union officers and outsiders in order to prepare the toughest questions we could—feeling that if she answered those questions satisfactorily, that would clear the air. Even so, we were roundly attacked by some prominent people in the Orthodox community who felt our meeting with Hillary Clinton meant that we were endorsing her. That was nonsense since we already had entertained Mayor Rudy Giuliani at a similar event. Not only that, but we had given him the honor of dedicating our new office and helping us place a mezuzah on our front offices only a few months earlier.

The political atmosphere surrounding the event continued to be stormy. On December 13, one day before our scheduled meeting with Mrs. Clinton, I received a call from a national television news reporter I had never met before. The reporter, who insisted that she not be identified, told me she had been present in Ramallah when Mrs. Arafat made her accusations against Israel in Hillary Clinton's presence. "Do not listen to Mrs. Clinton's denial that she did not hear or understand what was being said," the reporter said adamantly, affirming to me that Mrs. Clinton, like the reporter herself "had her earphones on and surely could understand the English translation of the Arabic."

Meanwhile, Senator Lieberman and I were fine-tuning our approach to the meeting. Once he had agreed to escort Mrs. Clinton to the luncheon, Lieberman made it clear that he wanted to introduce her to those we had invited to the event. I insisted that this was my prerogative, but agreed he certainly could say a few words about her.

Finally, the day of Hillary Clinton's long-awaited visit to the OU arrived. Late on the morning of December 14, Mrs. Clinton arrived at our office with a small group of staffers. She seemed friendly and relaxed despite her large Secret Service contingent, warmly greeting and shaking hands with everyone around her. In deference to Orthodox sensitivities she was clad in a modest skirt instead of her usual pants suit.

Prior to the public luncheon event, to which 100 officers and Union leaders had been invited, Rabbi Butler, Marcel Weber, chairman of our Board, and I met privately for half an hour with Mrs. Clinton. We focused on two issues of particular importance to us; the fallout from Mrs. Clinton's session with Mrs. Arafat and the continuing imprisonment by the U.S. of convicted spy for Israel Jonathan Pollard, which we considered deeply unjust. We also asked Mrs. Clinton to clarify her statements on Palestinian statehood. We found her answers to be less than satisfactory. On the Arafat meeting, she stuck to her story that she did not understand what Mrs. Arafat was saying and, in any case, did not want to create a diplomatic brouhaha. As in the past, she refused to support clemency for Pollard—pointing out that Moynihan and Lieberman, two of Israel and the OU's closest allies, were also opposed.

When we escorted Mrs. Clinton into the luncheon event, she was greeted by over 100 OU leaders and guests. There was, needless to say, not an empty seat in the house. In introducing Mrs. Clinton, I noted the unique circumstances surrounding her visit in that she was both First Lady, representing the nation, as well as a candidate for the United States Senate. Turning to Mrs. Clinton, I added: "Unlike conventional candidates who visit with us, you do not come with a background of legislative accomplishments—but you are highly regarded for your advocacy on issues to which you feel passionately connected." I expressed the hope that the discussions would help those attending the meeting understand who Hillary Clinton was and what she believed in. I concluded; "While we will certainly agree and disagree on specifics, we trust that through our dialogue we will all gain."

After my introduction, Senator Lieberman rose and spoke glowingly of Hillary Clinton; lauding her as a superb First Lady and a staunch supporter of the State of Israel. Mrs. Clinton then gave a speech, which was followed by a question-and-answer period. During her speech, Mrs. Clinton said she considered Mrs. Arafat's comments in Ramallah "offensive and baseless" and promised that she herself would "continue to speak out against anti-Semitism and any accusation against the Israelis." She said she would support U.S. aid to the Palestinians only if they ceased circulating anti-Semitic propaganda through their media and school textbooks. Although she said she favored moving the U.S. Embassy in Israel to Jerusalem, Mrs. Clinton cautioned that actually implementing such a move "depended on the timing of the peace process."

I opened the question and answer period by asking Mrs. Clinton whether she would support changing the current rule whereby children of American citizens born in Jerusalem have their passports stamped "Jerusalem, West Bank," rather than "Jerusalem, Israel," Mrs. Clinton seemed totally baffled by the question. She noted that she had never studied the issue, and would have to look into it. She raised a few eyebrows by saying jokingly that my question sounded "Talmudic." In any case, she did not answer it. In retrospect, it seemed that she had prepared well for every question except that one.

We then went on to cover questions of interest to our community on the domestic front—the foremost of which was tuition tax credits. Mrs. Clinton said she was in favor of examining the issue and expressed the opinion that the country "must find constitutional ways to help those schools at the elementary- and high-school level, particularly with children at risk and those with special needs." This position appeared quite at variance with her husband's administration's staunch opposition to tuition tax credits and was a pleasant surprise to many in the crowd. Mrs. Clinton said further she would like to make all college tuition deductible and that she favors "federal aid for computers, transportation, and special education."

Also discussed was the Flatow legislation, which had been introduced in Congress to make it possible for American citizens whose loved ones had died at the hands of terrorists to sue to collect compensatory damages from countries supporting the terrorists. Specifically, the bill would allow Dr. Steven Flatow, a friend and OU member, to sue Iran to collect money for the loss of his daughter, Aliza, who was killed in Israel by Palestinian terrorists. The White House had prevented him from collecting the money. In a break with the administration, Mrs. Clinton said she strongly supported this legislation, which subsequently passed both Houses of Congress and was signed into law by President Clinton despite his earlier opposition to it. Subsequently, in 2001, Flatow was able to collect what was owed to him.

When asked about a bill by Senators Don Nickles and Joseph Lieberman supported by the OU banning assisted suicides, Mrs. Clinton noted that this was the first time she had been asked about this issue, and that her first reaction was to oppose it.

During the news conference that followed, reporters pressed me as to whether I believed Mrs. Clinton's account of what transpired during her ill-starred encounter with Mrs. Arafat and whether the OU was satisfied with her explanation of the affair. I responded carefully that in view of the tax-exempt status of the Union, I felt it would be inappropriate for its president to make political statements. Therefore, I said, "Our community will have to decide whether these things make sense to them." As a number of reporters noted at the time, my statement was hardly a ringing endorsement of Mrs. Clinton's position.

Mrs. Clinton called the meeting "a very useful exchange" and said our exchanges had been "frank and honest." For my part, I told the reporters; "I think we had a constructive dialogue," adding, "she was well prepared" and had "complete command of the issues." I reminded the reporters that the OU neither endorses nor raises funds for candidates and thus was supporting neither Clinton nor Giuliani. "Our job, "I explained, "is to meet with people, meet with candidates, to have them appreciate our point of view on the issues" and "to bridge the differences."

Press accounts of the event varied widely, some were replete with misinformation. In a story entitled, "Hillary Panders" in the *New York Post*, columnist Jimmy Breslin sneered that Mrs. Clinton had prostrated herself before "Mandell Ganchrow, president of a large right-wing Jewish organization, the Union of Jewish Orthodox Congregations of America. He is located on Seventh Avenue in Manhattan." Of course, we are not a right-wing organization, and we are not located on Seventh Avenue.

The *Forward* reported that after hearing about what Mrs. Clinton had said to us about tuition tax credits, the United Federation of Teachers called her campaign headquarters to express its concern. So what exactly was Mrs. Clinton's position on the issue? Her spokesman, Howard Wolfson, told the paper; "On the narrow question of whether she supports tax credits for grade K-12, the answer is no.'" In its typically witty style, The *Forward* commented in an editorial; "Or to put it in another way, when

Mrs. Clinton says she is in favor of examining tuition tax credits, the question seems to turn on what the meaning of is is."

Nevertheless, at the end of the day, the meeting with Hillary Clinton was very useful for the Orthodox Union and the overall Orthodox community. Our leadership had a chance to meet and get to know Mrs. Clinton and she received a thorough education of the positions she would need to take in order to capture a majority of the Jewish vote—an absolute requirement if she were to win the election. That seemed like a dubious proposition at the time; yet as the campaign progressed, and Giuliani dropped out as the GOP nominee to be replaced by Congressman Rick Lazio, Mrs. Clinton did achieve that comfort level with the community and indeed went on to win the election with a majority in the Jewish community—although less of a majority than she had hoped for.

How Mrs. Clinton performs in office on a sustained basis on Israel and other issues of concern to the Jewish community remains to be seen. However, in my opinion, she has done quite well so far. Senator Clinton has followed the lead of New York's senior Senator Charles Schumer on Middle Eastern issues, and has been a vocal pro-Israel advocate. I would like to believe that the education we provided her with during the run-up to her election campaign had something to do with that positive record.

In February 2002, I spoke with Senator Clinton in Jerusalem after an appearance she made before the Presidents' Conference during that organization's annual mission to Israel. During her presentation, she appeared self-confident and totally in command of the nuances of U.S. Middle East policy. No senator could have delivered a more impeccably pro-Israel presentation. Afterwards, I expressed to Mrs. Clinton my pleasure at her record on Israel during her first year in the Senate. I got the distinct impression that she was quite happy to hear that.

Indeed I was quite pleasantly surprised at the warmth and spontaneity of her greetings to me on the occasion of the wedding of Malcolm Hoenlein's youngest daughter in December 2002. Up to the present her pro-Israel record is flawless.

CHAPTER FOURTEEN
A Jewish Candidate For Vice-President

I first met Al Gore in 1984 when he was a congressman running for the Senate. On that occasion, during which I led
a four-member HUVPAC delegation to Gore's congressional
office to discuss issues related to U.S. Middle East policy, I found
the young congressman from Tennessee to be earnest and well
spoken, but quite stiff and formal. Yet as it turned out, Gore was
not nearly as stiff and formal on that occasion as he became later
in his role as Vice President of the United States.

I concluded that initial meeting by telling Gore I hoped that
the next time we met it would be on the other side of the Capitol
building, meaning the Senate, for which he was ardently cam-
paigning. I then informed the Congressman that I wanted to
leave him with a campaign check from the PAC for his Senate
campaign. The check was in an envelope in my jacket pocket.
Gore responded in a huffy and starchy tone; "I hope you realize
it is against the law for a Congressman or candidate to accept
money on federal property." He then asked me where I was
proceeding next and if he might accompany me a short distance
down the street. The two of us walked down the long Congressional hallways, out of the building and off the portico of the
Congressional Office Building. Only then did Gore say, "I can
now accept your contribution." Years later when questions regarding the Buddhist nuns and illegal fundraising calls from the
White House were raised it brought a smile to my face.

I next saw Gore when he was a United States Senator. Despite
his stuffy persona, I was impressed by his evident leadership
skills, his "moderate Democrat" stance on domestic and interna-

tional issues and by the strong pro-Israel record he built up in the Senate. In 1988, when Gore ran for the Democratic nomination for the Presidency, I became co-chairman of the Rockland County Gore for President Committee. Gore did reasonably well in Rockland, but he lost badly in the overall New York primary to Michael Dukakis and soon withdrew from the race. It was a similar story to what happened in 1976 when I served as co-chairman of the Henry Jackson for President campaign. On that occasion, Jackson actually carried Rockland, but, like Gore after him, was defeated in the statewide race.

After Senator Gore became Vice President in 1993, I was able to meet with him on a number of occasions, thanks in part to the help of his deputy chief of staff, David Strauss, an old friend of mine from the days when he worked for Senator Quentin Burdick. I became extremely close to Senator Burdick and for a while was active in raising funds for him on a national scale for his re-election campaign. I acted in a similar vein for the "leadership PAC" of Congressman Vin Weber, who was number three or four in the Republican Congressional hierarchy. Unfortunately, Gore remained stiff and difficult to connect with on a personal level.

Sometimes, however, Gore seemed to try to over-compensate for his normal stiffness with displays of obviously contrived over-exuberance. During the 1996 Presidential campaign, I took a small group to meet with him at the New York Sheraton Hotel. As we walked into his suite, the Vice President enveloped me in a bear hug and cried out with faux enthusiasm; "Mendy, my Vietnam comrade." That was stunning enough, but in his opening remarks to our group, he strained credulity by saying that whenever he and I got together, we would sit back and swap Vietnam War stories. I searched my memory, but could not recall having discussed Vietnam with Gore on even one occasion. Thus it hardly came as a surprise to me that he got into trouble stretching the truth on a number of occasions during the 2000 campaign. His press secretary Arlie Schardt had warned him as early as 1988 that "Your main pitfall is exaggeration."

Subsequently, through the efforts of David Strauss and the White House, Gore agreed to be the guest speaker at the 1998 OU national dinner. Upon their request, I supplied to his office an advance copy of the speech I intended to deliver at the event. The night before the dinner I could not sleep because I felt that

I had a moral obligation to speak out publicly on two vital issues, which I had raised with Gore and the President privately. Thus I chose to raise these two issues extemporaneously from the podium. First, I asked the Vice President in the name of our community to speak to President Clinton in support of releasing Jonathan Pollard on humanitarian grounds. Secondly, I noted that we supported not only the principle of a united Jerusalem, but also that two Jewish housing projects across the old green line, Har Homa and the Mount of Olives Development Project in Ras Al-Amud, should be considered a part of Jerusalem and of Israel. The *Jewish Week*, which covered the event, noted that Gore looked decidedly peeved by these remarks and demonstratively failed to applaud when I mentioned Pollard and Har Homa.

Gore was the guest speaker at the Columbia Law School graduation ceremony in June 2000 at which both Karenna and Elli were among the graduates. Sheila and I sat in the second row and when Gore entered the room and saw me, he gave me a "thumbs up." Unfortunately, that kind of natural human gesture came a little late in the game for me. As it turned out, I could not bring myself to vote for him for president even though he would put our close friend, Joe Lieberman on the ticket. After the cataclysm of September 11, 2001, I was even more pleased that the nation had chosen George W. Bush as president and not the talented, but decidedly uninspirational, Al Gore.

Not surprisingly, I developed a much warmer relationship with Gore's exuberant and very heimeshe 2000 vice presidential running mate than I did with the presidential candidate himself. I first met Joe Lieberman during the 1980's when he was the Attorney General of the State of Connecticut. The Orthodox Union was honoring a friend of his at a major dinner and Joe attended the event. I was aware that Lieberman would be the Democratic candidate in the upcoming election for the United States Senate seat held by eighteen-year incumbent Lowell Weicker, considered one of the most dependable and loyal friends of the pro-Israel community.

Those of us who raise funds for political candidates live by a set of simple rules. The first rule is never to abandon close and loyal friends of the pro-Israel community; even when, as was the case of Weicker in 1988, they are facing a Jewish challenger who might be even more knowledgeable concerning Israel and even more empathetic to her needs.

Joe knew who I was and introduced himself to me. I explained to him the nature of our commitment to his incumbent opponent in the Connecticut senatorial race. I stressed that were he to be successful in that race, we would show him that same loyalty that we had shown Weicker. As a political professional, Joe knew the score, and he accepted what I had to say without too much difficulty.

Sheila, who also attended the dinner and took part in my chat with Lieberman, told me afterwards that she had been enormously impressed with him. Shortly thereafter, she began to urge me to reverse my decision in the Weicker-Lieberman race. She not only thought Joe was the better candidate, but also that he would be victorious. I responded to her that if she felt so strongly about Lieberman that she should begin fund-raising for Joe on her own. She did so, and proved quite successful in raising money for him in the Orthodox community. Henceforth, whenever Sheila and I met Joe publicly or privately, he always took the occasion to needle me ever so gently by reminding me of the greater wisdom Sheila had shown in backing him from the beginning while I had stuck with Weicker.

With Joe Lieberman's election to the United States Senate in 1988 he not only quickly became a hero to the general Jewish community, but also a role model for the traditional and Orthodox faithful. He was, after all, the first United States Senator who was a Sabbath observer in addition to keeping the laws of kashruth. During his first election campaign, he received considerable attention in the media when he refused to hold election rallies on Saturdays in order to avoid desecrating the Sabbath. On the first Friday night that he had to attend a session of the United States Senate, Senator Albert Gore of Tennessee walked him across the street and allowed him to use his parent's apartment on Capitol Hill so that Lieberman would not have to walk several miles at night to his own home. In addition Gore turned on the lights for Lieberman as Jewish law prohibits turning on electricity on the Sabbath.

In 1996, I convinced Senator Lieberman to be the installing officer at the ceremony during which I was sworn in to my second term as president of the Union. I felt honored to have the man who is the most prominent role model of a modern Orthodox Jew in America today preside at such a milestone in my own life. On this occasion I was moved that Joe spoke from the heart about his own connection to our common faith. As he spoke, I reflected that his life was indeed a storybook tale that could only occur in the United States. Needless to say in his subsequent re-election campaigns I worked hard to raise funds for Joe in our community.

Given that Joe happened to be a longtime member of the Board of Directors of the Orthodox Union, it seemed appropriate to me to name a program of young high school scholars in his honor. I convinced him to allow us to do that and the Senator Joseph Lieberman Scholars Program became one of our finest programs for gifted young people with the potential to become future leaders of the Orthodox community.

When Vice President Al Gore electrified the political world by announcing that he was choosing Joe Lieberman as his running mate, I received 58 phone calls in a 48-hour period from the media focusing on Lieberman's Jewishness and the implications of having an Orthodox Jewish candidate for the second highest political office in the United States. I responded with great enthusiasm about Lieberman as a person and a political leader, adding that I believed his observance of Torah Judaism and commitment to our way of life would serve to educate both non-Orthodox Jews and the broader American public about the Orthodox way of life.

During the 2000 election campaign, Lieberman spoke eloquently on several occasions regarding the need for an enhanced role for religion in public life. Some in the Jewish community, including the leadership of the ADL, openly questioned Lieberman's premise and suggested that he was blurring the separation between church and state in this country. UPI asked me to write an op-ed piece responding to Lieberman's remarks and the controversy they were engendering in the Jewish community. In my piece, I affirmed my belief in the need for continued separation of church and state, yet nevertheless expressed strong support for Lieberman's position that Americans are a religious people and this is a country based on avowals of faith.

I contended that it is not by accident that our coins are inscribed "In G-d We Trust" and that the Congress of the United States has a chaplain whose role it is to begin each session with a prayer. I argued that what Lieberman was saying was not only healthy, but long overdue and we should not be frightened by public servants who openly avow their faith. After the UPI article appeared, Joe took time off from his frenetic campaign schedule to send me a note, which read, "Your statement for the UPI was superb. Thank you."

Nevertheless, Lieberman's nomination was not all hearts and flowers for our community. Whereas prior to his nomination he was among the leaders in the Senate urging the transfer of the U.S. Embassy to Jerusalem, after receiving Gore's nod he suddenly backed away from advocating that as an immediate step. In addition, Lieberman toned down his longstanding principled opposition to affirmative action; evidently because of the political necessity of not angering the Democratic Party's core African-American constituency. To our dismay, Lieberman also watered down his attacks on violence and sex emanating from Hollywood.

However, it was remarks that Joe made in response to questions from radio host Don Imus on his syndicated program "Imus In The Morning" during the campaign that most angered the Orthodox Jewish community. Asked about a blessing that Jewish males make at the beginning of their daily morning service in which they thank G-d for not creating them as women, Lieberman responded glibly that the prayer is optional and added, "I skip it anyway."

That, of course, was not the answer that Joe should have given. He ought to have said something like, "I am running for the vice presidency of the United States not for the chaplain or rabbi of this country. If you have theologic questions I'll be happy to refer you to a rabbi or expert in this field."

Lieberman's interview with Imus went downhill from there. Asked whether Jews oppose interfaith and interracial marriages, Joe answered uncategorically that they do not. He was only partially correct. To be sure, Jews are not interested in the color of one's skin. Thus an Ethiopian Jew can easily marry a Caucasian one and a dark-skinned Sephardi can marry an Ashkenazi. However, the operative factor is that both parents must be Jewish. Any non-Jew must be converted according to Jewish law before being allowed to marry a Jew in a Jewish wedding performed by a rabbi. Joe failed to point that out.

Lieberman's disastrous appearance on "Imus In The Morning" proved to be a source of embarrassment to him for many months thereafter. It also caused a problem for me when someone sent out a forged letter in my name to Orthodox rabbis and synagogues across the United States asserting that a special meeting was being called to place Lieberman into religious isolation known as a *cherem*. This was totally removed from reality and I had to call Joe to assure him that was not the case.

Part of Joe's problem, of course, was that during his long years of service as Connecticut Attorney General and as United States Senator his faith and religious activities had been a given. Never until he accepted the vice presidential nomination had his every comment and every aspect of his Judaic observance been placed under a microscope.

Lieberman's fellow Orthodox Jews showed particular interest in reports that seemed to cast doubt on his commitment to living according to true halachic standards. Lieberman found himself beset by questions as to whether he had worn sneakers on Tisha B'Av, the annual day of grieving for the destruction of the Temple in Jerusalem, when observant Jews fast for 25 hours and wear non-leather shoes. Others asked why he had prayed in a conservative temple during a campaign swing. Was he trying to reach out beyond his Orthodox image?

Despite the mistakes he made during the 2000 campaign, Joe Lieberman will continue to be a major source of inspiration to untold thousands of Jews, especially Jewish youth. We are aware that he may make future attempts at national political office, including running for president in 2004. I am certain that the lessons of the 2000 election have not been lost on this bright, articulate, and gifted public servant, proud Jew and quality human being. We will be watching closely.

CHAPTER FIFTEEN

Meetings with Presidents and Kings

King Hussein

Visiting with King Hussein in Amman in the spring of 1995 as part of a delegation from the Conference of Presidents of Major American Jewish Organizations was at once more and less impressive than I had anticipated.

We thought that the king would receive us in his main palace in the center of the city, but instead he invited us to one of his minor palaces, which was less grandiose than I had expected. To be sure, the lush palace grounds were truly regal and Hussein's security detail extremely impressive. Yet I must acknowledge that one of the highlights of the afternoon was a visit to the wildly opulent lavatory, which had pure gold fixtures and other lavish amenities. It seemed that every member of the delegation had to make a "pit stop" in the rest room and leave with such souvenirs as fancy soaps and colognes bearing the name and insignia of the palace.

During the meeting, King Hussein was friendly, relaxed and reasonably open; very much as he had been on the other two occasions that the Presidents' Conference met with him. Unfortunately, he spoke very softly and one had to strain to hear every word, even though he was using a microphone. At the conclusion of the King's remarks and a question-and-answer period, he posed individually with each member of the Presidents' Conference. Sheila, who had joined me on the trip to Amman, posed together with the King and myself. That took a considerable amount of time, but Hussein was exceptionally patient and his message was certainly conciliatory. He spoke about peace and cooperation with Israel with the same fervor he expressed on television.

A few months later, when King Hussein came to a luncheon meeting at the Presidents' Conference in New York City, I brought along the picture I had taken with him at his palace and asked him to autograph it. Queen Noor, who was present at this meeting, pointed out that although Sheila was in the photograph, she was not present at our luncheon meeting. Noor graciously invited me to return to Amman together with Sheila, so that she would again have the chance to meet the king and queen.

In addition to King Hussein and Queen Noor, other members of the royal family and members of Hussein's diplomatic team also attended the luncheon meeting in New York. I found them, as a group, to be intelligent, articulate and sophisticated. After King Hussein passed away, his son King Abdullah visited with the Presidents' Conference in New York and exhibited the same type of friendliness to our community that had become his father's trademark.

President Hosni Mubarak

One Arab leader who turned out to be more open than expected was President Hosni Mubarak, whom we met at Blair House in Washington. The members of a small Presidents' Conference delegation sat around the president in a semicircle, with his foreign minister at his side. After a brief statement Mubarak answered all of our questions with startling candor, and made, in the process, some less than complimentary comments about King Hussein.

On only two issues did Mubarak deviate from that openness and affability. Asked by one of our members about the rise of Islamic fundamentalism in Egypt, he looked us straight in the eye and claimed implausibly that there was no such thing as fundamentalism in Egypt. Mubarak ought to have realized that we were quite knowledgeable about the Middle East and even knew the names of the various Islamic groups his government had sought to wipe out because of the danger they presented to his regime. We also pressed the Egyptian President as to why he had not come to Jerusalem to speak before the Knesset, as had his predecessor Anwar Sadat. Mubarak responded airily; "What's so important about Jerusalem?" We were quite incredulous at that non-answer and it appeared difficult even for Mubarak to hold back a smile.

King Mohammed VI of Morocco

Our meeting with King Mohammed VI of Morocco took place at Blair House on the very day in June 2000 that the *Jewish Week* broke the story of the Baruch Lanner scandal at the Orthodox Union. I had received word of the story on my cell phone as I was going to the meeting with the Moroccan king, thus I found myself a bit distracted during the encounter. To make things even more stressful, upon arrival at Blair House I discovered that my name had somehow been left off the Secret Service list of participants. After a number of frantic phone calls to the Moroccan Embassy and efforts on the part of my colleagues in the Presidents Conference, I was finally admitted to the meeting.

I was intrigued to observe upon entering the meeting that one of the king's principal advisers at the event was Andre Azoulay, a member of the Jewish community of Morocco. Of course, we were pleased by that symbolism. We had high hopes that our meeting with the king, who had recently come to power upon the death of his long-serving father, King Hassan II, was going to be a productive one. The new king was being counted upon to play a positive role in the Middle East. There were hopes he would soon take decisive steps such as opening a Moroccan embassy in Israel and initiating direct flights from Morocco to Ben Gurion.

However, as we were soon to find out, the new Moroccan king appeared to be significantly less conciliatory toward Israel than his father had been. During our meeting, he kept bringing up ancient Israeli-Arab history, speaking repeatedly about the supposed injustices done to the Arabs in 1948 and 1967. To my dismay, he spoke emphatically about the so-called "right of return" of Palestinian refugees, which if ever carried out, would mean the demise of Israel as a Jewish state.

The king kept referring to the need for "religious freedom" for all in Israel, as though that right did not exist in Israel. In asserting the Arab connection to Jerusalem, King Mohammed did not mention that the Koran contains not even one reference to Jerusalem. During the twenty years that Jordan controlled East Jerusalem prior to 1967, the top religious figures in the Islamic world, such as the king of Saudi Arabia, never came even once to Jerusalem to visit the Muslim holy sites there.

Overall, our meeting with the Moroccan king was bitterly disappointing. Given the king's negative attitude, I was not surprised when, not long afterwards, 500,000 Moroccans took to the streets to demonstrate against Israel. Shortly thereafter, when sustained Palestinian violence erupted against Israel, King Muhammed VI cut off the less-than-full diplomatic relationships between Morocco and Israel his father had established during the honeymoon period after the Oslo Accords.

President Islam Karimov of Uzbekistan

Who would have imagined in 1997 that four years in the future Uzbekistan, a newly independent state that had been a republic of the Soviet Union until 1991, would become a base of operations for United States military forces. These forces would be used in the war against terrorism that erupted following the deadly attack on the World Trade Center. Uzbekistan, the most populous of the five former Soviet Central Asian republics with 24 million inhabitants, is a highly strategic Moslem country the size of California.

Certainly the extreme solicitude that President Islam Karimov showed toward the President's Conference when he invited us to his country as his guests for four days was a tipoff that Uzbekistan was moving in a pro-western direction. Karimov sent a private jet to pick us up in Tel Aviv and flew us to his capital of Tashkent and treated us like royalty throughout the entire visit. Not only were we given the opportunity to see storied cities like Samarkand and Bukhara, but were also given the chance to meet with members of the Jewish community. They told us moving stories about how Uzbekistan had served as a haven for many thousands of Jews from Russia and the Ukraine who fled there to escape the Nazi armies during World War II. At a warm reception in our honor, President Karimov announced that, as a tribute to our group, he had decided to open an Uzbek embassy in Tel Aviv.

The Uzbek government provided extremely tight security for us as we traveled around the country during those four fascinating and frenetic days, something that was especially evident when we walked to synagogue on the Sabbath. Traveling with us throughout the four-day visit was Congressman Jerry Nadler,

Democrat of New York, whose presence added prestige to our group. Prior to our leaving, the president presented each of us with a set of coins of his country; a souvenir of that fascinating trip that I have kept on my desk ever since.

Unlike President Mubarak of Egypt, Karimov did not seek to play down Islamic fundamentalism, but told us bluntly during our visit that fundamentalist terrorists represented a growing danger to the independence of Uzbekistan. Since his country borders on Afghanistan, he was extremely concerned about infiltration of terrorists from that country into Uzbekistan and asked us to convey his fears in that regard to the Clinton Administration and the U.S. Congress.

Although we understood what Karimov was referring to, it wasn't until Osama Bin Ladin's attack on the World Trade Center that the true significance of President Karamov's concerns became clear. In the interim between our visit and that event, his troops had been training jointly with American Special Forces and, as already noted, Karimov quickly green-lighted a U.S. request to base troops in Uzbekistan during operations to overthrow the Taliban regime in Afghanistan.

Why Are They So Good To Us?

The extraordinary solicitude shown to the Presidents' Conference by presidents and kings seemed a modern day confirmation that much of the world continues to believe in the reality of the concept articulated in the notorious anti-Semitic tract from the last years of the 19th Century "The Protocols of the Elders of Zion." This forgery proclaims that world Jewry dominates the power centers of the world from behind the scenes. Apparently, people like Mubarak and Karimov believe we as a community have unlimited power and influence over U.S. foreign policy. Their understanding of participatory democracy is nil.

I am reminded of a book entitled the *Fuji Plan* written by my friend, Rabbi Marvin Tokayer, a classmate from my Yeshiva days. Tokayer explains that the Japanese gave refuge to a large group of European Jews during World War II, both in Japan itself and in Japanese-occupied Shanghai, with the idea of opening doors to the American Jewish community, which might then intercede with Washington on Tokyo's behalf in case they lost the war. The extreme solicitude these leaders showed to us makes traveling

around the world as an American Jewish leader a deeply grati-
fying experience. It also allowed us to use our influence to increase their appreciation of the American Jewish community, our
commitment to Israel, and the usefulness to themselves of
strengthening their ties with the Jewish state. It is not necessary
for us to examine their inner motives.

Two of the most fascinating trips I ever took were missions to
two nations, South Africa and the Soviet Union, that were in
their last days before undergoing dramatic transformations. In
my guise as chairman of the Orthodox Union's Institute of Public Affairs, I was part of a small delegation of American Orthodox leaders who embarked on a memorable trip to South Africa
in 1989 four years before the official end of apartheid. The following year we headed to Moscow and Leningrad. It was just a
year before the failed coup against Mikhail Gorbachev that caused
the breakup of the Soviet Union and its replacement by Russia
and 14 other republics.

South Africa

At the end of 1988, the turbulent political situation in South
Africa seemed to be in a state of rapid transformation. The reform minded president, F.W. DeClerk, had taken his first tentative steps toward abolishing the structure of apartheid, although
Nelson Mandela, the leading anti-apartheid symbol and future
president remained behind bars. The South African business
community, desperate to bring about a relaxation of worldwide
sanctions against South Africa that were badly damaging the
economy, launched an outreach campaign. The purpose was to
bring opinion makers from important constituencies to South
Africa to make clear that the sanctions were hurting that country's
black majority more than the upholders of apartheid.

Among those the South African business community reached
out to during that period were leaders of the U.S. Orthodox Jewish community. Because we tended to be more politically conservative than other factions of the American Jewish community and
had opposed anti-South African sanctions in the past, we were
seen by the South Africans as a natural constituency for outreach.
For my part, I welcomed the opportunity to gain a first-hand view
of the situation in South Africa, particularly in terms of how the
anti-apartheid struggle might impact South African Jewry.

In January, 1989, a delegation consisting of Sidney Kwestel, then-president of the Orthodox Union, Rabbi Ephraim Sturm, executive vice president of the National Council of Young Israel and myself, then chairman of the OU's Institute for Public Affairs, flew to South Africa for an intensive week of fact-finding. We were allowed to go everywhere we wanted and meet whomever we wanted. This included the leaders of the 100,000 plus strong South African Jewish community, high government spokesmen, representatives of Chief Buthaleizi's Zulu movement and of the still illegal African National Congress and the South African Communist Party. We visited virtually every synagogue and Jewish school in the country as well as hospitals, universities and trade schools that served the general population. We stopped people on the street at random to get their opinions and insights. Overall, it was one of the most stimulating, as well as exhausting, overseas visits I made during my long career as a Jewish leader.

The trip did not change my political perspective on South Africa; I went home as opposed to the continuation of sanctions as I had been when I arrived. I must acknowledge in retrospect that I was wrong in taking that position. As subsequent events proved, the sanctions finally worked in convincing the white supremacist government to dismantle apartheid and allow black majority rule. Also, few of us would have anticipated in 1989 how Nelson Mandela would rise to the occasion and show greatness by putting aside any bitterness over having been imprisoned for nearly thirty years and instead focus on ensuring that whites would continue to have a place in a post-apartheid multiracial South Africa.

At the time however, my week in South Africa gave me plenty of evidence to support my belief that the sanctions were costing black workers far more than white owners, while squeezing the South African Jewish community to the point of threatening its viability. That might have been a tolerable prospect if there was reason to believe that the dissolution of South African Jewry would have led to a massive torrent of aliyah to Israel by members of this well-educated, highly skilled community. Unfortunately, the vast majority of Jews leaving the country during those years of the first intifada were headed for places like Australia, Canada and the U.S., rather than to the Jewish state.

What stays with me today about that trip, however, has little to do with political issues that have long since been rendered dated and irrelevant. It was my face-to-face encounter with the reality of the overwhelming poverty and squalor that black South Africans endured in their urban shantytowns. After our tour of Soweto, the giant black township adjoining the affluence of white Johannesburg, I was too overcome by the enormity of the human misery I had witnessed to concentrate on the issues of "sanctions-no sanctions." I had only one thought that evening and it was quite elemental, namely, "No human being should be forced to live under such conditions." No human being should be forced to live under terribly crowded and unsanitary conditions in a tin roofed shack without running water or electricity. I couldn't help but imagine what it would be like for my own loved ones to have to endure such conditions. The old expression "There but for the good graces of G-d go I" never seemed so apt.

To be sure, I was well acquainted with Harlem and the South Bronx and other slum areas in the U.S. Still, as miserable as American urban ghettoes are, they could be Scarsdale and Grosse Pointe in comparison with the horror of Soweto or Alexandria. I asked myself who was responsible for the horrors I had witnessed in Soweto. I suppose there was plenty of blame to go around and, for once in my life, I was not prone to play the political blame game. I couldn't help wondering, however, why American blacks were not doing more to help improve the conditions their African brothers were enduring. Certainly, African-American leaders like Jesse Jackson had been extremely voluble in denouncing apartheid. But even while Jackson and other black leaders fought that battle, why hadn't they launched a parallel effort to raise tens and hundreds of millions of dollars to improve intolerable living conditions that millions of African blacks endured in the townships on a daily basis?

When I asked myself that question, it made me realize that the apparatus that organized American Jewry has created to give comfort and support not only to Israel, but to Jews in every corner of the world, was very much the exception and not the rule. When, for example, Christians are enslaved or butchered in Sudan or Indonesia, does the Christian world rise up to defend them? No, it does not, though it is vastly larger and more powerful than world Jewry. It seems that only the Jews, whether in New York, Jerusalem, Buenos Aires or Cape Town retain that elemental sense of "We Are One" and the commitment to help our brothers and sisters whether they are mired in poverty in Moscow or threatened by terrorist bus bombings in Beersheva.

I do not write this to glorify the Jewish community at the expense of other communities, but only to point out an important difference, one in which I believe we can be proud of. In any event, what I saw and experienced during my visit to South Africa strengthened my belief in the common humanity of all people. I believe that all of us have a responsibility to work toward ending forever the terrible poverty, suffering and waste of human potential I witnessed vividly during my sojourn in the black townships of South Africa.

A Trail-Blazing OU Mission To The Soviet Union

Another memorable trip I took part in happened in August 1990, when the Orthodox Union, under the leadership of President Sidney Kwestel, brought 110 members on a mission to visit Jews in the Soviet Union. The Soviet Union still had a year to run, but the Berlin Wall had already fallen and Soviet Jews were enjoying unprecedented freedom both to emigrate to Israel and to manifest their Jewishness at home. Our delegation traveled with a scribe and an unfinished Torah scroll. We held huge public events in Moscow, Leningrad, Kiev, and Berdichev where we brought together thousands of Soviet Jews. Our scribe assisted hundreds of Jews who had never before seen a Torah "pen in" letters to our ancient Torah at each event.

We were amazed that the Soviet authorities allowed us to advertise in newspapers and on television wherever we traveled. In fact, we had no problems with the authorities at all, except once in Moscow, when we were compelled by the KGB to remove the Israeli flag from the stage at the hall where we were holding a large event. That was an unpleasant experience. When one compared our relative freedom to function unmolested in the heart of Russia compared with the situation of brutal repression of all manifestations of Jewishness that had existed only a few years before, the situation seemed astounding, almost surreal.

Our delegation included the late Rabbi Shlomo Carlebach, probably the most famous Jewish folksinger of his day. He traveled together with an accompanist and a choir composed of a group of NCSY students who were spending the summer in Poland. Thus, we were able to sponsor concert events that featured speeches filled with soaring rhetoric and joyous singing and dancing. We gave each of the thousands of Soviet Jews who flocked to these events—men, women and children—a *Magen David* (Star of David) to wear around their neck, as well as prayer books and portable radios. We were also able to smuggle in syringes and other medical supplies for circumcisions to be done on Jewish infants, children and adults who wished to fully acknowledge their Jewishness. Each of these events was an overwhelming emotional experience.

The youthful and wildly enthusiastic crowd we drew to our Shabbat service and concert event at the Moscow Chorale Synagogue on our first night in the USSR, contrasted sharply with the crowds of senior citizens who usually gather there for prayer. Gathered inside the main hall of the synagogue to hear Shlomo Carlebach, and spilling out onto the steps and the narrow street in front of the shul were hundreds of animated young people who did not have the faintest idea how to *daven*. They were, however, joyously manifesting fierce pride in their Jewish identities that many had felt forced to play down or actually to hide their entire lives. Though many of us were jet-lagged that first evening, our spirits soared on the wings of the spiritual energy and shared pride in Jewishness being shown by Soviet and American Jews dancing ecstatically with the Torah through the aisles of a synagogue. Here we were in the very heart of the Soviet Empire; a militantly atheist state in which such expressions of Jewish commitment and connection had been banned for so many decades.

At the service the following morning at the Chorale Synagogue, I was given the honor of leading the service as cantor. In the Orthodox synagogues which I attended throughout my life and in my upbringing, I have always been taught "skarbowe" which is a term that originates in Poland and represents authentic tunes and melodies which I learned from my father. I went to the *bimah* (altar) and before I could even start, there was some noise in the back. The sexton banged with a wooden paddle from behind my position and yelled in Yiddish, "Jews, give attention to Cantor Menachem Mendel from America." I turned around to see what was going on. When I looked again to the front, I was amazed to find myself surrounded by eight or nine elderly gentlemen from the community. They were, they informed me, "my choir." Someone had told them I was a real cantor and they wanted to take part in singing beautiful melodies of hazzonis (cantorial music) that they had not heard sung in public since their youth many decades before. One member of the "choir" kept repeating in Yiddish, "Ich vill zingen solo" (I want to sing a solo). Amidst all of the emotion, I tried to maintain my focus and proceeded to do the best I could, including allowing this gentleman to sing his "solo."

We spent the week following the Moscow events learning about the difficult conditions facing Jews in those last chaotic days of the unraveling Soviet Union. Nearly everyone we talked to was dealing with chronic food shortages and endless lines at food stores to procure the few scraps that were available. We saw that the only way to obtain basic services in the Soviet Union was through bribery; whether of shopkeepers, government officials, taxi drivers, and even tour boat operators. For our own part, we had to keep the pilot of our plane well-supplied with cartons of Marlboro cigarettes in order to make sure that he would continue to ferry us from city to city.

We spent our second Shabbat in the Soviet Union at the beautiful old synagogue of Leningrad. The designated leader of the musaf or additional service on Saturday morning was to be a retired cantor from Kew Gardens Hills, Queens, who had been born in the Soviet Union and had been rescued from a Nazi concentration camp by the Soviet Army. This was his first time back in Russia since leaving over four decades earlier. It surely was an overwhelmingly emotional experience for him. When it was time for him to lead the service in Leningrad, he stood up and tried to utter words of prayer – but nothing came out. Not a word, not a whimper. He tried again, a second, third and fourth time. Sheer emotion had overcome him and he could not continue. "Mendy!" came the cry "Get in there." Like a relief pitcher in a baseball game, I stepped up to the *bimah* and carried on.

By the following Shabbat we had left the Soviet Union and had traveled on through Poland, with emotionally searing visits to the death camps of Treblinka and Auschwitz-Birkenau, and on to Budapest, Hungary, which has one of the most beautiful and ornate synagogues in the world. We were welcomed to participate in the Orthodox service. When I asked for the privilege of serving as cantor during their "Blessings of the New Moon" service, I was turned down. They explained to me that since I was not bearded, they could not allow me to serve as cantor. Our travel agent, Menachem Elbaum, who had many connections with the Jewish communities of Eastern Europe, did some quiet negotiating. He then took me outside and I re-entered with my prayer shawl covering my head to such an extent that I could not see in front of me. No one knew who I was or whether I had a beard or not and I proceeded to chant the prayer.

Overall, our 1990 trip was not only an overwhelming emotional experience for all who took part, but also an historic occasion in terms of the re-establishment of genuine Jewish religious life in the Soviet Union. In fact, thanks to the seeds we planted on that trip, the OU was soon able to create an ongoing yeshiva program for Soviet Jewish youth in Kharkov, a large city in eastern Ukraine. Over the next several years, Kwestel would nurture this project into the huge success it later became. The only unfortunate thing concerning our trip to the Soviet Union was that due to the fact that the Union did not yet have a public relations department at that time, we were unable to share the significance of what we saw and accomplished on our trip with the rest of the world.

To Russia And Belarus

I took part in a second moving trip to Russia—a trip that included a visit to newly independent Belarus—as part of a delegation from the Conference of Presidents during the spring of 1995. During this visit we met not only with the Jewish communities, but also with top government leaders of both Russia and Belarus, which were two of the 15 independent states to have emerged after the collapse of the Soviet Union.

In Minsk, the capital of Belarus, we visited the enormous Soviet-era World War II memorials to the millions of citizens who died at the hands of the Nazis. While in Minsk we were invited by the Jewish community of the provincial town of Mogilev to take part in a celebration of Israel Independence Day. We drove for hours over terrible roads to reach our destination. In the exact center of town, we saw a large reviewing stand with a statue of Lenin that was a small-scale replica of the famous Moscow reviewing stand seen in Red Square. We asked the bus driver if, on the way home, we could stop for photos there.

The program in which we participated with the Mogilev Jewish community was of a very different sort. It comprised of Jewish childrens' choirs singing *"Hatikvah"* and religious songs like *"Adon Olam,"* a whirl of festive Jewish dancing, and speeches by the local Jewish leaders. In our own remarks, we simply expressed our deep love for Israel and *yiddishkeit*. Afterwards the city's Jewish leadership invited us for dinner. It was replete with flowing vodka and repeated toasts. I myself am a bourbon drinker and can easily handle a drink or two, but I must confess that my immersion in serious vodka drinking left me—and my fellow presidents as well—basically two sheets to the wind by the end of that long and festive dinner.

A very giddy bunch of "responsible adults" boarded the bus at about midnight for the long ride back to Minsk. As requested, the bus stopped at the reviewing stand in the center of Mogilev. After we snapped the photo on the reviewing stand, I tripped while climbing back down and might have done serious injury to myself if the president of the Women of Reform Jewry hadn't caught me and broken my fall. Referring to the often less-than-cordial Reform-Orthodox relations, my savior laughingly told me that a photo of my fall would be retained by the Reform Movement for potential blackmail purposes.

In St. Petersburg, formerly Leningrad, we stayed in the Grand Hotel on Shabbat and went to the city's main synagogue for services Saturday morning. However, on Friday night and Saturday afternoon, we held our services in our hotel; the same one that Hitler had once proclaimed would be the site of a grand party to celebrate Nazi Germany's military defeat over the Soviet Union. Although Malcolm Hoenlein and I were the only Orthodox members of the Presidents' Conference delegation, our services were held according to Orthodox standards in order to preserve the unity of the group. Because it was the middle of the summer at the height of St. Petersburg's white nights, we had to hold our *havdala* service at 1:30 in the morning. Malcolm and I decided between ourselves that whichever of us was awake at that hour would rouse the other in order for us to perform the service. It was Malcolm who woke me up.

Because of the nature of our group, we were given heavy security wherever we traveled in Russia and Belarus both by the local police and by Israeli Embassy personnel. Sometimes, though, there were snafus. For example, when we flew from Minsk into a small private airport outside of Moscow, we found that the small airport was empty and there was no one on the job to stamp our passports. At the end of our trip, when we arrived at the main Moscow airport to catch a commercial flight back to the United States, the Russian immigration officials at the airport demanded to know how we had entered the country without any Russian stamps in our passports. It took a great deal of agitated discussion with the immigration officials and, undoubtedly, a few phone calls from the airport officials to higher-ups in the Kremlin before they stamped our passports and allowed us to depart.

For me, one of the highlights of our stay in Moscow, along with our meetings with leading Russian Foreign Ministry officials and the U.S. and Israeli Ambassadors, was a surprise night visit with the famous Russian mafia. We met one night in a flashy nightclub on a deserted street. It was patrolled by a private security firm with Russian Jewish leaders from around the country—some of whom had come from as far away as Siberia. By choosing such an opulent locale, they wanted to impress upon us that there was now a Russian Jewish leadership with real clout and they were determined henceforth to run their own affairs without being further patronized by and dictated to by the leadership of world Jewry. Some of these leaders had become multi-millionaire tycoons in the wake of the introduction of capitalism in Russia, and now owned utilities, factories, automobile dealerships and television stations.

Their message to us was provocative in itself, but I found myself distracted by the nightclub, which resembled a speakeasy from the prohibition era in the U.S. There were security guards in striped or dark shirts standing around their respective bosses— wealthy businessmen who happened to be leaders of the Russian Jewish community—some of whom had been the subject of assassination attempts over the preceding months and years. When I stepped outside for a breath of fresh air, I noticed that the street was blocked at both ends by large black limousines. The sight felt like a scene from an old Elliot Ness movie. When I read about the Russian mafia today, I have a much more vivid sense of what it is about, having witnessed some of its machinations first hand.

Many of the people we met that evening have been in the news periodically as they battle the Putin administration.

Kazakhstan

Our February 2003 visit to Kazakhstan, under the auspices of the Presidents Conference, was as unique as any we had made. Kazakhstan, a country with 14 million inhabitants yet with a land mass ranking among the largest in the world, is rich with oil, gas, uranium, and other minerals. In fact, this Muslim, non-Arab, non-OPEC moderate nation should equal and possibly surpass Kuwait in energy production in ten years.

In addition to visiting the Jewish community of 20,000 to whom we brought a new Torah scroll, it was an opportunity to interact with President Nursultan Nazarbayev, who rolled out the red carpet for us.

Our first order of business was to attend the conclusion of an international conference on "Peace and Accord," whose declaration was signed by Kazakhstan, Krygzstan, Tajekistan, Afghanistan, Turkey, and Azerbaijan. They "absolutely and unconditionally condemned terrorism in all its forms, irrespective of motivation."

President Nazarbayev spent a great deal of time with our delegation, which carried a message to him from President Bush. We also met with Islamic leaders including the chief cleric, Absattar Derbisali, The Grand Mufti of Kazakhstan.

On Shabbat we were joined by Jewish leaders from throughout central Asian and Eastern European countries including Georgia, Armenia, Japan, Belarus, Australia, Russia, Ukraine, New Zealand, Azerbaijan, and Uzbekistan.

Our host in country was Alexander Machkovic, a successful businessman, leader of the Jewish community and friend of President Nazarbayev. Former Senator Rudy Boschwitz (R-Minn) and his wife were part of our delegation.

Our farewell dinner symbolically took place on the 14th day of the Hebrew month of Adar I, which normally is Purim. This year, since it was a leap year, Purim was celebrated one month later on Adar II. Thus our group commemorated "Minor Purim" (Purim Katan) with a storybook barbecue dinner in the snow-covered mountains in a heated yurt. The yurt is a unique structure that is a physical and metaphorical expression of Kazakh Nomadic life. To my eyes it was a cross between a heated igloo, teepee and succah, in rich harmonious color and carpeting.

One theme stands out and that is that our great grandparents in the shtetl and ghettoes were chased by Cossacks. We their progeny were given police escorts and respect; Kazakh soldiers and policemen stood often every 100 feet in the snow at attention saluting stiffly. The significance of a united Jewish American community was never more evident. As a reward, President Nazarbayev announced to us that he was naming a new ambassador to Israel, a post vacant for six months.

Scoring Big in the World Zionist Elections

Ever since Theodore Herzl convened the very first World Zionist Congress in Basle, Switzerland back in 1897, a Zionist Congress has been held every four years, preceded by elections for delegates in countries throughout the world. These elections not only determine the composition of the delegations to the upcoming Zionist Congress, but also the makeup of the Jewish Agency for the ensuing four-year period.

In 1996, the Reform Movement, angered by the stance of the Israeli government on "Who Is a Jew" and related issues, ran an aggressive and well-funded campaign in the Zionist elections in the United States. By making strenuous efforts to get its rank and file to vote, the triumphant Reform movement managed to capture 49.6 percent of the total vote in the U.S. In an informal coalition with the Conservative Movement, which also objects to the non-recognition of their movement in Israel and which garnered approximately 24 percent of the vote in the election, the Reform movement was able to swamp the combined Orthodox vote—(Mizrachi plus Amit and Emunah Women), which came to only 11 percent of the total.

To be sure, those dismal results could have been predicted given that the Reform movement is alleged to have spent somewhere between $1 to $2 million on its "get out the vote" effort, whereas the Orthodox side was totally disorganized and only spent a few hundred dollars. It was also unfortunate that the Aguda and Chabad-Lubavitch chose not to participate in the election. To have done so they would have had to sign a pledge that they endorsed the Zionist program, something they were not prepared to do. In any case, had these groups joined the OU and other groups in running a united, aggressive and well-funded Orthodox campaign, we might have won the election, since a total of only 114,000 American Jews voted.

The next Zionist elections were set for 2001-2002, and, stung by our embarrassing showing in 1996, the Mizrachi movement initiated a major effort to at least double our vote total in the United States. Late in 2000, as I was nearing the end of my term as president of the Union, I volunteered to head the orthodox drive for this election. This was more than nine months before I was offered and accepted a paid position at the Religious Zionists. Among the orthodox organizations that agreed to cooperate under the banner of Mizrachi were Amit, Emunah, the Religious Zionists, the Orthodox Union, National Council of Young Israel, Poale Aguda, Rabbinical Council of America, the alumni of Yeshiva University schools, the alumni of Touro College, as well as B'nei Akiva and Yavneh Olami. On paper, it looked like a formidable coalition and I was optimistic about what we could accomplish.

I drew up a master plan for the election campaign that included a budget for advertising, including radio spots in New York and Los Angeles and a national get-out-the-vote campaign. In a Zionist election it is relatively easy for all of the competing parties to monitor the number of their partisans who have registered to vote, since the rules specify that each voter must send a $4.00 check with a portion of their social security number to a central location. The entire registration process was to take place during the month of September 2001 with the actual voting to transpire during February 2002. I have always loved political campaigns and believed if we followed my master plan, we could pull off an upset that would turn heads in the Jewish world from Manhattan to Malibu—and in Jerusalem as well.

As the registration period began at the beginning of September, all of the religious and Zionist movements in the race, including our own, began sending out mailings to their constituents urging them to register to vote in order to impact the international zionist agenda. I noticed right away that the rhetoric from the Reform movement was marked by what I considered to be over-the-top hostility toward the orthodox. Reform ads were characterized by screaming headlines reading, "Ultra Orthodox Politicians Are Threatening Jewish Unity and the Jewish Community." One ad claimed, "Ultra-Orthodox politicians call our

rabbis clowns" and reminded potential Reform voters that a Reform Jewish synagogue in Jerusalem had been firebombed. Noting that Reform marriages, conversions and burials are not recognized in Israel, the ads asserted, "Registering and voting in this election will give you a voice in critical decisions concerning 'Who is a Jew" and not leave the decisions in the hands of ultra orthodox politicians."

I was incensed at both the tone and substance of the ad. On September 7th 2001, I wrote an op-ed article in the *Jerusalem Post* entitled "Reform Judaism's Intolerance" charging that the Reform had created a straw man; a hateful scapegoat they could blame everything on, namely the so-called "ultra-Orthodox." Pointing out that the dominant strain of Orthodoxy in both Israel and the U.S. was "mainstream" and not "ultra," I asked rhetorically, "Are there any ultra-Orthodox slates running in this election? Do the ultra Orthodox belong to the Zionist Congress?" Noting that the answer to these questions was "no," I then asked whether the pejorative term 'ultra-Orthodox' was not, in fact, a code word used for demonizing all Orthodox Jews.

I pointed out that if orthodox Jews decided to employ similar tactics, we could tar all non-orthodox Jews with the label "ultra liberal," a code word for rabbis who marry Jews and gentiles, perform same-sex marriages and do not observe the Sabbath. I asked our Reform adversaries to identify the Orthodox leaders who had called their rabbis clowns or encouraged firebombing the Reform synagogue in Jerusalem. I pointed out that the intention of the headline was to imply that these outrages were somehow the work of orthodox rabbis.

Having taken direct aim at the Reform movement's demonization of orthodox Jewry, I closed the article by reminding all Jews of the need for unity at a perilous moment. I asserted, "If I had my way I would forget the whole election, for as long as Jews are dying on the road to Modiin and in Hebron and as long as it is unsafe to sit in a pizza restaurant in Jerusalem, it is not time to be spending millions of dollars on a divisive campaign in America."

Nevertheless, it was clear that our opponents were not about to agree to a cancellation of the election or a scaling down of their get-out-the-vote drive, so neither could we. Our coalition held many meetings to build enthusiasm for the campaign. I arranged for each and every etrog box that was mailed from

Israel to the United States to have a message in it regarding the importance of the election.

Following the publication of my op-ed piece, I received a phone call from the head of the Reform zionist movement who lit right into me for what he characterized as the unfair nature of my attack on the Reform Movement, asking in an accusatory tone; "What has gotten into you?" I responded sharply that I had written the piece to expose the dirty campaign Reform was running, and told him that the Reform movement was capable of a campaign it could be proud of that would not incite Jew against Jew.

Not all of the reaction to my op-ed was negative. I received a congratulatory note from Avi Shafran, the spokesman for Aguda, informing me that he was extremely pleased with my piece. I responded that while I appreciated his good wishes, he could best help the cause by convincing adherents of Aguda and the yeshiva world to vote in the Zionist elections, noting that if they did so, they could provide our movement with 20,000-50,000 votes; enough to win the election for the Orthodox side. Alas, that was too large of a request for our friends at Aguda.

Only a few days later came September 11th, the momentous day that Islamic terrorists attacked the World Trade Center and the Pentagon, changing the landscape of America forever. One unfortunate effect of that traumatic event was that it threw into abeyance our plans to put together a winning campaign in the Zionist elections. Many rabbis were planning sermons for the High Holy Days regarding the need to register and vote in the Zionist elections. Such appeals seemed highly inappropriate at a moment when thousands of innocent victims lay under the rubble of the World Trade Center with little chance of recovery.

We had arranged a transcontinental conference phone call to all American orthodox rabbis from Rabbi Motti Alon, one of the luminaries in the religious world in Israel. He would explain the high stakes for orthodoxy in the upcoming Zionist elections and urge them to speak to their congregants about voting. The call had been scheduled weeks in advance for September 14. But the cataclysm of September 11 overshadowed everything and on the morning of the call I decided to cancel it. Electioneering simply felt improper in view of the tragedy.

Within days, President Bush declared war on the terrorists and those nations that supported them. At the same time, however, Secretary of State Colin Powell was placing ever–increasing pressure on Israel to make concessions in the peace process so as to make it easier for the U.S. to bring Syria and the Palestinian Authority into the so-called anti-terrorist coalition. Under the circumstances, I believed it was advisable to postpone the registration drive and the elections themselves. Because of the cataclysm of September 11, we simply had no time to register our voters. At a meeting held on September 13 the other organizations rejected our suggestion to cancel the registration and election, saying they saw no need to postpone the process.

There is no doubt that Orthodox registration for the Zionist election was severely impacted by the aftermath of September 11, leaving me, as campaign manager, in the position of a general without troops. I confess there were moments during those weeks when I felt tempted to give up. However, we had made a commitment to go all out to increase the Orthodox vote and therefore persevered despite the setbacks caused by September 11.

Ultimately, the key to our success in this endeavor had a lot to do with advances in the field of computer technology, as well as to the changed political climate in the aftermath of the collapse of Oslo and the new Palestinian intifada. While many fewer people, Orthodox and otherwise, registered for the Zionist elections than would have been the case if September 11 had never happened, we were able to make effective use of our computers. We were able to determine which of the 108,000 people who did register for the elections belonged to an Orthodox synagogue or organization. We found that 28,000 potential voters fell into these categories and barraged them with a series of special mailings and telemarketing calls. There were messages from Yeshiva University President Dr. Norman Lamm and myself as well as the presidents of Amit Women and the Rabbinical Council of America.

When the results were announced in late March 2002, we were delighted to find that our efforts and commitment of resources to the elections had paid off handsomely. We increased our share of the vote from eleven percent to twenty one percent and our total of delegates to the next World Zionist Convention from sixteen to twenty nine out of a total of 145 American seats. Our gains came at the expense of both the Reform and Conservative movements. Reform, which had hoped and expected to top fifty percent of the total vote this time, instead dropped closer to forty percent, and its number of delegates dropped from seventy to sixty one. The Conservative movement lost six delegates, dropping to thirty two, only three more than the resurgent Religious Zionist Movement.

While we were very pleased with our showing, it was frustrating to note that if Aguda and Chabad had taken part in our coalition, the Religious Zionist Movement could have secured a majority and won the election outright. Yet since the formation of such an evidently common-sense political alliance is unlikely to happen until the *Moshiach* (Messiah) comes, the mainstream religious Zionist organizations will redouble their efforts in future Zionist elections. This is to ensure that the Reform Movement does not unduly influence the Israeli political scene by a large victory in the U.S. elections.

CHAPTER SEVENTEEN
The Pluralism Wars

I n the fateful year of 1948, Prime Minister David Ben-Gurion had to accomplish more than simply turning back the eight Arab armies that sought to smother the newborn State of Israel in its cradle. He also had the complex and politically treacherous task of formulating the role of Judaism in the first Jewish state to exist in the world in 2000 years.

In trying to figure out what constituted a Jewish state, Ben-Gurion was torn between the ardent positions of such diametrically opposed factions as socialists and capitalists, ultra-Orthodox non-Zionists, religious Zionists, and secular Zionists, in addition to dozens of other philosophical approaches in between. Seeking guidance on what direction the Jewish state should take, B-G sent a letter to Jewish scholars, rabbis and intellectuals around the world, asking for their definition of "Who is a Jew?"

The answers were almost unanimous: there should be only one standard of Jewishness regarding the basic rites of continuity—namely, marriage, divorce, and conversion—and that standard should be the Orthodox one as administered by the Chief Rabbinate. The Chief Rabbinate is an institution that predated the state and is headed by two co-equal spiritual leaders, an Ashkenazic chief rabbi and a Sephardic chief rabbi, who are elected to represent all of its citizens.

In order to ensure a sense of one peoplehood, the scholars suggested to Ben-Gurion that Shabbat should be recognized as the day of rest for all Israelis. No public transportation would be allowed on the Sabbath in most of the country. Only kosher food would be served in the army, the new country's most universal public institution. Despite these rules, each individual Israeli Jew would have the right to decide whether to observe Judaism rigorously, in a more relaxed manner, or not at all.

Ben Gurion envisioned the Law of Return, which was one of the first laws passed by the new Knesset, to be one of the defining institutions of the State of Israel, and so it has remained to this day. Each and every Jew in the world is instantly entitled to citizenship in Israel. However it was only in the 1970's with the first great wave of Russian aliyah to Israel—several hundred thousand strong—that the somewhat loose definition of what constitutes Jewishness under the Law of Return became a deeply divisive issue in Israel. That was because the Russian Jews had been separated from Jewish observance by several generations. By most estimates, fifty percent or more of the Russian olim who poured into Israel were not Jewish according to *halacha*.

The first big battle over the Law of Return in both Israel and the Jewish communities of the diaspora began in 1986 when the Supreme Court of Israel ruled, in the famous Miller case, that conversions done outside of Israel by non-Orthodox rabbis should be considered valid. Nevertheless such conversions would still not be acceptable to the rabbinate. This decision was reaffirmed in 1989.

The Reform and Conservative movements began to bring additional cases to the Supreme Court, hoping that the Court, which tended to be supportive of liberal and secularist positions would go farther in legitimizing conversions inside the Jewish state. Orthodox members of the Knesset, fearing that the Supreme Court would do exactly that, threatened from time-to-time to introduce legislation in the Knesset that would, in affect, nullify such a decision by the court. They specified that only conversions performed *k'halacha* (according to Jewish law) would be recognized as valid in the Jewish state. Halacha, which is not observed by the Reform movement, would henceforth be the principle criteria for conversion to Judaism. In essence, this law, if enacted, ensured that Reform or Conservative conversions would not be recognized in Israel.

Both liberal movements smarted from what they described as prejudice against their rabbis and congregations in Israel in the areas of conversions, divorce and marriage. In general, they felt humiliated that their movements, which were so powerful in the United States, were not accepted in Israel on an equal footing to the Orthodox.

The Reform and Conservative movements have tried hard to build strong followings in Israel, but have met with indifferent success. The failure of the Conservatives to accept oral Torah and the Reform to accept neither oral nor written Torah and the latter movement's desecration of the Sabbath, acceptance and performance of intermarriage, adoption of patrilineal descent, and, in recent years, the acceptance of same-sex marriages, all have prevented these movements from managing to convert significant numbers of Israelis to their theologies.

Despite this failure, the Reform and Conservative movements have undertaken high decibel public relations campaigns to portray themselves as aggrieved and injured. They have used the High Holidays as a focal point to raise funds in the United States; publishing huge ads in the *New York Times* and the Jewish media charging that the Orthodox, in Israel and at home in the U.S. are "delegitimizing them and their rabbis." They have claimed that the Orthodox view the non-Orthodox Jews as not being Jewish. This, of course, is nonsense. We consider every person born to a Jewish mother or converted according to halacha to be Jewish. What we do not consider authentically Jewish are the non-halachic forms of Judaism practiced by their rabbis.

The Reform movement, which was officially anti-Zionist until well after the creation of the State of Israel, has in more recent years developed a strongly Zionist platform. For its part, the Conservative movement in Israel, with its successful Tali schools, has made some limited progress in attracting converts there. While the Orthodox have a number of political parties in Israel representing their various streams (from the modern Orthodoxy of the National Religious Party, to Agudah and Shas representing respectively, the more devoutly Orthodox Ashkenazi and Sephardi Jews) neither the Reform nor Conservative movements have political parties in Israel. Overall, their influence is quite limited in the Jewish state. Any success they have achieved has been a result of their public relations efforts in the press, the Knesset and the courts. In terms of membership, they constitute less than one percent of the Jewish population of Israel.

Despite their minimal presence in Israel, the Reform and Conservative movements are able to have a considerable effect in roiling Israeli politics and in complicating Israeli-diaspora relations. First of all, the overwhelming majority of the hundreds of millions of dollars funneled to Israel every year by the United

Jewish Appeal in the U.S. comes from non-Orthodox sources. Similarly, non-orthodox Jews are also the leaders of the Federation movements. Many of these same leaders serve on the board of diaspora-Israel bodies like the Jewish Agency, where there is a built in anti-orthodox lobby. Secondly, the opening of the gates of the former Soviet Union allowed hundreds of thousands of gentile Russians to make aliyah under the law of return. Not only were they not Jewish with no desire to become Jewish, but they have little feeling for the "Orthodox establishment." Indeed, the rapid growth of Russian Orthodox churches in Israel has been both telling and highly troubling.

In recent years the Reform and Conservative movements have focused their advocacy around the concept of pluralism, which argues that it is legitimate that there should be multiple streams within Judaism, and that none of them has the right to speak on behalf of all Jews. In real terms, however, the primary goal of these movements has been to force Israeli leaders to grant them equality with the Orthodox in the Jewish state. In effect they demand the right to marry, divorce and convert Jews in Israel according to their non-halachic standards. The issue they never address in this campaign is that their standards are unacceptable to the overwhelming majority of Israelis and that children produced by those Jews married according to Reform or Conservative standards would not be eligible according to halachic standards, to intermarry with other Jews. If the State of Israel accepts their premise, but the Orthodox establishment does not, as it surely never will, that would quickly lead to a situation where there are two or even three Jewish peoples inside the Jewish state.

Although the Reform and Conservative movements have been repeatedly rebuffed in their efforts to change the religious status quo in Israel, they have continued every year to cajole, threaten and bully the Jewish Agency and Knesset. Because their movements are based in the United States, they keep a steady pressure campaign on these shores on federations across the country to issue resolutions favoring pluralism. In addition, they have tried to influence national Jewish organizations, such as the Jewish National Fund, United Jewish Communities, and the American Zionist Movement to pass similar resolutions.

Local federations and temples in the U.S. have brought non-observant Knesset members to their cities on speaking engagements, and then have lobbied them intensely to address the supposedly aggrieved status of the non-Orthodox streams in Israel. Op-ed articles, ads, and new independent organizations of the Jewish left like the New Israel Fund all parrot the same demand for pluralism in Israel. During the recurrent "Who is a Jew" controversies of the 1980s and 1990's, some Reform Jews reportedly lobbied friendly members of Congress, urging them to threaten Israel with a withholding of U.S. aid if the Knesset dared to pass any change in the Law of Return their movement considered deleterious.

Threatening to decrease UJA funding to Israel is a more subtle utilized tool of the Reform leadership. For example, in 2001, one of the leaders of the Reform Movement is reported to have urged his followers prior to Passover not to contribute funds for matzos for poor Jews in Moscow because the fund would be administered by the Chabad Lubavitch movement. Chabad refuses to recognize the legitimacy of the Reform and Conservative rabbinate.

When I became President of the Orthodox Union in 1994, I had an opportunity to take on the advocates of pluralism head to head. For example, NJCRAC (the National Jewish Community Relations Council), a national umbrella organization of which we were a member organization, sought to pass resolutions in support of pluralism. I told them bluntly that if they did so, we would simply walk out of NJCRAC. Since the OU was the only Orthodox organization inside NJCRAC and since they could not claim to represent the entire community without Orthodox representation, our argument invariably carried the day. A similar dynamic was in play in other important umbrella bodies in which we sit side by side with the non-halachic streams—AIPAC and the Presidents' Conference, where these issues are "taboo" by mutual agreement.

Until the Lanner affair erupted in June of 2000, no other issue took up as much time and energy as the ongoing inter-Jewish controversy over "pluralism." In this struggle, I became the leading spokesmen on behalf of the organized Orthodox community. Particularly contentious were the three times a year meetings of the Jewish Agency in Jerusalem. The entire Reform and Conservative leadership invariably attended those events and aggressively pressed their agenda, which I believed to be a serious threat to the unity of the Jewish people.

Three confrontations over pluralism that took place during my years as OU President were particularly memorable. The first of these erupted on May 23, 1997, when the national UJA announced that they were launching a twenty million dollar campaign to "promote religious pluralism in Israel and to counter (Israeli) government moves that threaten to undermine the status of non-Orthodox movements." Richard Wexler, the national chairman of UJA, was quoted as saying that the government under Prime Minister Netanyahu was engaged in an effort "to de-legitimize Reform and Conservative rabbis in a myriad of ways."

Why would an avowedly denominationally neutral body like UJA, which was supposed to be fully focused on raising philanthropic money for Israel, get involved in promoting the agenda of the Reform and Conservative movements? It obviously did so because wealthy contributors to UJA-Federation who were also prominent Reform and Conservative Jews had intimated they might withhold their philanthropic giving on behalf of UJA unless the latter organization backed the liberal streams on the issue of promoting pluralism in Israel in a concrete manner.

Upon hearing of the UJA's new initiative, I immediately let their leadership know I was irate that the UJA was getting explicitly involved in the pluralism battle on behalf of the Reform and Conservative movements and had allocated a considerable sum of money to promote their agenda. Wexler and UJA vice chairman Bernard Moscovitz quickly dispatched a mollifying fax to me in which they expressed worry that "You might be justifiably concerned by news reports which make it appear as if the UJA is prepared to allocate ten million dollars each to Reform and Conservative movements. Nothing could be further from the truth."

The UJA leaders pointed out that at a meeting in Chicago the prior week to which they had been invited by the Reform and Conservative movements, they had offered to assist any of the movements "including the Orthodox" in raising "supplemental dollars over and above the annual campaign to assist in the areas of contributing to Jewish unity and pluralism in Israel." Needless to say, I was less than impressed with that offer given that neither the OU, nor any other Orthodox group, was likely to be initiating programs in support of a concept—pluralism in Israel—which we considered to be an anathema.

On June 2, 1997 I sent a letter to Wexler and Moscovitz specifying that "It is the opinion of the Orthodox movement that the UJA has no place in raising funds for political issues whether they be driven by theology or other sectarian belief. The focus should be on aiding the poor, the homeless and the impaired.

(The UJA) should inspire those throughout the world to come closer to their heritage and their homeland by supporting aliyah and religious education..."

I went on to contend that the linking by the UJA of the terms "unity and pluralism" represented an oxymoron. Jewish unity does not require the abdication of core principles by any of the denominational movements, but rather defines their ability to find shared principles that they can work for despite their sharp theological differences. Pluralism, on the other hand would demand the abdication of such core principles on the part of the Orthodox groups. Accepting pluralism meant accepting that Reform positions like patrilineal descent and same-sex marriage were legitimate Jewish expressions. That was something we could never accept.

I suggested in my letter that it was urgent that the UJA and the OU should meet as quickly as possible and try to find some resolution to the issue of the twenty million dollar allocation on behalf of pluralism. I noted that since the UJA had made its announcement concerning the twenty million dollars, I had been receiving inquiries from rabbis and congregations throughout the country asking whether, under the circumstances, they should go ahead with plans to sponsor appeals on behalf of UJA for the upcoming High Holidays.

I quickly got the impression in my ongoing discussions with Wexler and Moskovitz that our strongly expressed dissent from their new campaign and thinly veiled threats to cut our involvement in UJA fund raising efforts were indeed having a positive effect. On June 13, I received a response from Moskovitz confirming that the "top leadership of UJA has agreed to drop the use of the word "religious pluralism" or "pluralism" from our lexicon. We realize it means very different things to different people who hold different beliefs." Moscovitz wrote further that the UJA preferred to "disengage" from the battle over pluralism so as to concentrate on the needs of the Jewish people. About a week later the UJA issued a new statement stipulating that it would be spending the twenty million dollars in question in order to promote "Jewish unity." There was no longer any mention of the dreaded word "pluralism."

Yet no sooner had one crisis been resolved than another erupted. On June 16th, I arrived in Israel for a personal two-day visit to attend the wedding of my nephew. As I entered my hotel room I received a call from one of the leaders of the Orthodox leadership in Israel who informed me that the following day approximately thirteen leaders of the Reform and Conservative movement, mainly Americans, would testify before the Knesset Law Committee in opposition to legislation that would keep all conversions in Israel within the purview of the Chief Rabbinate. There were no American orthodox leaders available to testify and, therefore, he requested that I do so. Although I had no papers or briefing materials with me, I agreed to his request.

The following morning, I prepared my remarks in Hebrew with the aid of a friend. When I reached the parliamentary chambers, Knesset member Shaul Yahalom of the National Religious Party was presiding. On the other side of the room were Reform and Conservative rabbis, primarily American, who had already testified. I knew almost all of them. I was momentarily startled to see one of the most prominent reform rabbis wearing a *kippah*. That was something I seldom noticed him doing back home in New York. When I asked my friend why he thought the rabbi was looking so traditional, he pointed to the television cameras in the balcony. He conjectured that he wanted to project an image of faith and tradition on behalf of the Reform movement to the TV public.

The following is a transcription of the text of the remarks I delivered to the Knesset Law Committee that day:

"Honorable Chairman, Members of the Committee,

First let me say that the Conversion Law does not deal with conversions in the Jewish communities in the Diaspora, and we in the United States do not deal with internal Israeli matters. It is a recognized fact that in Israel most of the citizens are traditional or secular, with approximately twenty percent of the population identified as Orthodox. Reform and Conservative together constitute less than one-half of one percent of Israeli Jewry.

"I would like to speak from the heart. The Orthodox Union comprises many grassroots members that expend a great deal of effort advocating on behalf of Israel, particularly on the issue of the Israeli MIAs—Ron Arad, Zachary Baumel, Yehuda Katz, and Zvi Feldman—two of whom are Orthodox. While we believe in investing all our efforts in support of Israel, we still hold that American Jews who do not make aliyah and who do not pay taxes in Israel do not have the right to interfere in internal Israeli matters.

"I would also add that a very small percentage of Reform and Conservative Jews make aliyah to Israel, which is the reason they are few in number here. The Orthodox Union represents the majority of orthodox Jews in the United States, all of whom are zionists. Despite the fact that most of the olim to Israel from the United States are either religious or traditional, that still does not justify our trying to dictate Israeli policy.

"So, by what right do the Reform and Conservative have to interfere in internal Israeli religious affairs? When they make historical decisions such as endorsing patrilineal descent or ordaining a woman rabbi who does not keep mitzvoth and happens to be a lesbian, do they ask your permission? When they agree to perform intermarriages, thereby endangering the survival of the Jewish people, do they ask your permission? No. So why are they interfering in internal Israeli affairs?

"The truth is that the Conservative and Reform movements in America have failed. According to surveys, the Reform and Conservative movements do not succeed in preserving Jewish continuity. Those surveys reveal that out of 200 Reform and Conservative Jews, approximately fifty remain Jewish after four generations. Do you want to import those failed systems to Israel?

"Those whose testimonies preceded mine are paid to sound the alarms and cry that American Jewry is up in arms over this legislation. I have come to tell you that that is not the case. Wherever there is a large Jewish community—whether in England, Australia, France or any other country—most of the Jews are either traditional or secular. Only in America are there large numbers of Reform and Conservative Jews, the great majority of whom are not actively involved in their own movements. Most American Jews, including many who belong to Reform and Conservative synagogues, are not bothered by this (proposed) law. It just doesn't matter to them.

"In summation let me say:

One. The Orthodox Union and all the other Orthodox communities in the world support this legislation.

Two. If the supremacy of the Chief Rabbinate of Israel is maintained, then a compromise solution may be feasible.

Three. We are accused of claiming that Reform and Conservative are not Jews. As president of the largest Orthodox Jewish organization in the world, I declare that this is not so. The Reform and Conservative are Jews just like every member of the committee. Even so, this does not mean that the State of Israel should make the same tragic mistakes that American Jews have made. We in the United States do not know how to solve the difficulties and tragic problems that Reform conversions have wrought. We implore you, please do not make the same mistake!"

Needless to say, the Reform and Conservative leaders at the hearing were not pleased with my statement or my subsequent answers to questions posed by Knesset members. Clearly, my testimony had made an impact; especially in that they undercut the claims the Reform and Conservative leaders were making about opinion among American Jews.

Still, I might legitimately be asked, did not my decision to testify before the Knesset Committee violate a long-standing OU policy of strict non-interference in internal Israeli matters. The answer is obvious. I would definitely not have testified had the Reform and Conservatives not done so. But given that they were determined to force their agenda down the throats of Israelis, it was necessary for an American Orthodox spokesman to balance their testimony with an opposing point of view.

The pluralism debate heated up shortly thereafter during a visit to the United States by then-Prime Minister Netanyahu. In New York he met with the Reform and Conservative leadership and then separately with Orthodox leaders at the Park Lane Hotel. The prime minister's meeting with our own delegation was covered by the *New York Times* with a front-page story and picture. In the wake of his meetings here, Netanyahu decided to appoint a commission in Israel under the chairmanship of Finance Minister Yaakov Ne'eman, who was also a much respected Orthodox scholar and lawyer, to study the entire issue of "Who Is a Jew." The goal of the commission was to find a formula that would keep conversion acceptable to the Torah standards of the Orthodox but also be acceptable to Reform and Conservative leaders.

The committee, which was composed of six Orthodox members, one Conservative member, and one Reform member, held meetings over a period of seven months, and took testimony from an assortment of religious and organizational figures in the diaspora, including Dr. Norman Lamm, President of Yeshiva University and Rabbi Raphael Butler, Executive Vice President of the Orthodox Union. The Ne'eman Commission's final proposal called for the creation of an Institute of Torah Study, also known as the Conversion Institute, under the leadership of Professor Benny Ish Shalom and a coterie of Orthodox, Conservative, and Reform teachers. The Institute would provide an eighteen-month intensive program on Judaism aimed at Israeli citizens desiring conversion, most of them recent Russian immigrants. Nevertheless, the actual conversion process would be done before *batei din*, special courts under the aegis of the Chief Rabbinate.

The Reform and Conservative leadership was initially pleased with the recommendations of the Ne'eman Commission. They believed that if the Chief Rabbinate agreed to this proposal, it would be a victory for them since it would require the Orthodox establishment to consult and work together with Reform and Conservative rabbis for the first time in the country's history. For that very reason, the Chief Rabbis were not at all pleased with the Commission proposal. However, they hoped that the Reform and Conservative movements would reject the proposal as insufficient and therefore be the ones who took the blame for the failure.

In a beautiful, lawyerly move, Ne'eman informed the Chief Rabbinate that they would play no role in Part A of his proposal — the creation of the Conversion Institute— but would play the central and sole role in part B; namely that every graduate of the Institute would be examined by special courts run by the rabbinate. The court would be enjoined to consider each of the applicants for conversion without prejudice as to whether they had attended the new Conversion (or more correctly Jewish studies) Institute or another of the many conversion training programs under full Orthodox auspices that were already in existence.

It was clear that the Chief Rabbis were quite wary of cries of outrage from ultra Orthodox and Hasidic groups on its right flank if they were perceived as agreeing to cooperate with the Reform and Conservative movements in the creation of the new Institute.

Still, I thought it would be a good idea if they agreed to the idea. While at our OU convention, held that year in Jerusalem, I had meetings with Chief Rabbis Lau and Doron, and with Rav Simcha Kook, the Chief Rabbi of Rehovot, in the hope of convincing them that acceptance of the Ne'eman proposal would be a wonderful public relations move. It was obvious to discerning observers that there would not be enough Conservative and Reform instructors to teach in the branches of the new institute which eventually would be set up around the country after the pilot program proved its viability. Therefore the great majority of instructors who would take part in the hoped-for conversion of thousands of Russian olim would be Orthodox.

Meanwhile, mistakenly believing that the chief rabbis had been asked to accept both parts A and B of the Ne'eman recommendations, the Reform and Conservative leaders announced their own acceptance of the whole package. Then Rav Lau announced his acceptance of part B only, and accompanied that qualified acceptance with a verbal attack against the Reform Movement. Prime Minister Netanyahu issued a statement in which he publicly acclaimed the Chief Rabbis for what he characterized as a step forward.

Reform and Conservative leaders expressed fury at the Chief Rabbis' statement. They claimed they had been tricked into believing that both sides would fully accept the Ne'eman recommendations and the government would endorse it as well. Feeling double-crossed, they went back to their confrontational tactics of the pre-Ne'eman period; filing appeals before the Israeli Supreme Court to block pro-Orthodox legislation that was moving through the Knesset.

In this contentious atmosphere, the Board of Governors of the Jewish Agency met on June 25, 1998. There were two resolutions on the floor; the first sponsored by the Reform and Conservative movements and the second by the Orthodox. The first resolution urged the Knesset not to approve any legislation on the Law of Return. The second offered a deal whereby the Reform and Conservative movements would withdraw their litigation before the Supreme Court if the Orthodox withdrew their legislation before the Knesset. Other factions of the agency were not happy with the Reform and Conservatives for turning the floor of the Jewish Agency into a forum for their own ideological agenda.

Without prior notification, Professor Ne'eman appeared to address the Board of Governors meeting. His speech was received with extreme displeasure by the Conservatives, but more so by the Reform. Ne'eman began by citing his own family history and then made some reflections on Jewish history. Then he said, "Let me make it very clear. We are united because we have one religion, one G-d, one Torah, which we received from G-d, and nobody, no human being can change a word of the Torah. On this we are united. No matter how many *mitzvot* each one of us observes, something that is a personal question for each one of us, the glue of the Jewish nation is our Torah, our command-

ments. There is no other nation in the world that survived po-
groms, the Holocaust, except one nation, and that is the Jewish
nation. This is only because we have something in common, one
religion, one G-d and one Torah."

After speaking about Zionism and the importance of aliyah,
Ne'eman remarked, "I want to give you my personal opinion
about the conversion issue. If someone believes that issues will
be resolved by courts or by the legislature, let me tell you he is
driving the Jewish nation downhill . . . I blame anyone who will
continue either with court actions or with legislation. By doing
that, he is tearing apart the Jewish nation." Ne'eman concluded
forcefully by saying "Every Jew is an equal Jew. There is no
debate about that. There is no debate about who is a Jew."

Rabbi Yoffie rose to complain that Ne'eman had spoken as a
representative of the government and that the Reform and Conservative movements should therefore also be given a chance to
state their case. Ne'eman retorted, "I do not represent any group,
I only represent myself. I am a simple Jew from Jerusalem. Rabbi
Yoffie, you, too need to rise a little bit above this quarrel so as to
help lift us all a little bit above daily politics."

In response to a question, Ne'eman reminded his listeners that
he had asked the Chief Rabbinate to "give its opinion on only one
issue, which relates to the task of the Chief Rabbinate and that is
the establishment of the special courts. The Chief Rabbinate was
not asked by me to give its opinion on the issue of the establishment of the Institute for Jewish Studies."

After a few minutes interlude, Rabbi Yoffie got up to address
the body. He said, "I stand here now as the head of a movement
of 1.5 million Jews throughout the Jewish world. Some of them
are unhappy about recent developments in the religious area. I
am not sure that any of them are angrier than I am at this moment . . . Why should one particular strand of Torah be given a
monopoly at the expense of another?" He warned the Jewish
Agency not to become a sponsor of the Institute, and by doing
so, it had fallen into a trap."

Yoffie continued: "Now it can easily be said if we don't want
a crisis, if we don't want a law passed, let us just withdraw our
litigation and that is really the heart of the matter."

Yoffie then said that given that the Chief Rabbinate had not
fully accepted the Ne'eman Commission recommendations, the
Reform Movement had changed its mind and would not, after

all, withdraw its litigation before the Supreme Court. Because the litigation related to "thirty-five to forty-five cases of people who are "in real pain. In return for withdrawing our litigation last year, we have been abused by the Chief Rabbinate. We were misled by the leadership of the Ne'eman Commission. Now we are again asked to wait for two years for a process which is totally dependent on the same Rabbinate which has vilified us, defamed us, and refused to meet with us."

Yoffie contended that the concessions made by the Reform movement were very unpopular with his own constituency around the world. He remarked, "We were prepared to recognize the right of the Orthodox Rabbinate to be the only group that could perform registered conversions in the State of Israel." "The Rabbinate rejected any cooperation with us, [and] vilified us in the process. If the Chief Rabbinate won't participate, [in the process] how can you pass a law that will coerce them into doing what they choose not to do."

"This institute is a way for the Chief Rabbinate to circumvent us," he said. "It is a way for Reform and Conservative Jews to be given a very minor symbolic role in an essentially meaningless institution and the Chief Rabbinate retains total control over conversion without the need to come into contact with the Reform or Conservative Jews. . . That runs directly contrary to the spirit of the Ne'eman proposal after seven months of discussion." He concluded; "The Reform and Conservative movements are not going to withdraw their litigation."

I stood up and asked for equal time on behalf of the Orthodox side. "First of all," I said, "Rabbi Yoffie attacked the Chief Rabbinate in the most abusive manner. I think the Chief Rabbinate deserves to have someone to stand up and speak on its behalf. The Chief Rabbinate is not the Orthodox Rabbinate. It represents an official government agency. If 1.5 million Reform Jews would come here [on aliyah] and go to the ballot box as citizens, they could make Rabbi Yoffie the chief rabbi." But they don't do that; they come here to try to make political gains on the backs of Israeli society."

I continued,"Minister Ne'eman made it very clear here and in the Unity Committee. He never asked, [or] demanded that the Chief Rabbinate sign on to the concept of the Institute of Jewish Education. Never in its history has the Chief Rabbinate ever endorsed a school or an ulpan. The Chief Rabbinate has accepted that which we asked them to accept, namely the conversion court. Indeed, Rav Lau has said on a number of occasions that every single candidate that comes to this conversion institute will be considered in a double-blinded fashion, that is, that they will not be asked where they come from."

Becoming highly emotional, I stated: "20,000 Jewish Agency meetings, and 200,000 resolutions will never cause the Chief Rabbinate to accept Reform and Conservative clergy as legitimate halachic authorities. Those who have brought us patrilineal descent, intermarriage and same-sex marriages will never be recognized as true halachic authorities of the Jewish people. "It can never happen." I added, "We in the Orthodox movement were called about two weeks ago by the government and asked not to comment on the new issues by the Conservatives with the court cases in order not to inflame the passions. We have not. But if this resolution of Rabbi Yoffie passes, there is no possibility that the organized community, the Orthodox community will not rise up and say there must be legislation... Litigation is the sine qua non of legislation. As long as there is litigation there must be a counter-movement on the part of the Orthodox parties in the government for legislation."

Rabbi Jerome Epstein of the Conservative movement followed Yoffie and myself with relatively brief and far less controversial remarks in which he argued that contrary to popular opinion, the Conservative movement actually follows halacha (Jewish law).

At lunch, preceding the final vote, I schmoozed with a group of delegates from Hadassah, the Zionist Women's' Organization. They told me that although many of them were Reform Jews and none were Orthodox, they were all disgusted with the move by the Reform movement to force this contentious and needless battle between the streams. As soon as the proceedings were renewed, a Hadassah representative rose and spontaneously made a motion to table both the Reform and Orthodox resolutions. Since no debate is allowed on a tabling resolution, a vote was immediately taken, and the motion was passed thirty one to twenty four. I certainly had no problem with our own resolution getting tabled as long as the Reform one was similarly tabled. Following the vote, a motion was passed calling for the Jewish Agency to meet with the Chief Rabbis to try to begin a dialogue.

On December 19, 1998 the Unity Committee of the governing board of the Jewish Agency, of which I am a non-voting invitee, went to the offices of the Chief Rabbinate to meet with the two chief rabbis, Rav Lau and Rav Bakshi-Doron. Philip Meltzer of the Reform Zionist organization (Arza) opened the meeting by asking Rabbi Doron if the chief rabbinate would meet with the Unity Committee on an ongoing basis and if he would appoint a Beit Din for future conversion cases that would be sympathetic to Reform and Conservative concerns. I do not believe the Reform or Conservative leaders really understood the depths of our rejection of non-halachic "Judaism."

The Chief Sephardic Rabbi offered a quick word of praise for interdenominational Jewish unity in the "Diaspora," but made clear he found the efforts of the Reform and Conservative in Israel to be divisive. He pointed to a fifty to sixty percent intermarriage rate in U. S. Jewry and suggested that the liberal movements should concentrate on solving that problem before forcing themselves and their agenda onto the Israeli scene. The Chief Rabbi pointed out that conversion is an individual act, not a group one. Therefore, any individual who meets the criteria would be converted. He concluded that the Reform and Conservative Movements deserve credit for recognizing the importance of keeping people Jewish, but urged that they should insist that their adherents keep more mitzvot. Bakshi-Doron then left the meeting.

Rabbi Joel Meyers of the Conservative rabbinate then turned to Rav Lau, the Ashkenazi chief rabbi and asked if he would meet with the Conservative leaders, since, according to Meyers, the Conservatives had met six criteria that the Chief rabbinate had demanded of them to prove they upheld halacha. "Are you prepared to separate yourselves from the Reform"? Rav Lau asked bluntly. I glanced at the Reform leaders and could see they were quite distressed at this remark. Rabbi Lau then called upon Rabbi Meyers to make a break between his own movement and that of Reform Jewry. Rabbi Meyers sought to dodge the question; responding to Lau that his movement would like an official dialogue with the Chief Rabbinate." Rabbi Lau responded, "*Torah mishamayim* (belief in the Torah being given by God) is what is required. Tell your colleagues that you should join in the fight against Reform. Why don't you, the Conservative, and the Orthodox confront the Reform on such matters as patrilineal descent?"

Rabbi Richard Hirsch of the Reform movement rose to declare that he felt it was inappropriate for Rav Lau to try to separate the two non-Orthodox movements. Hirsch then told Lau that the Reform movement rejected his apparent premise that holding such a meeting with the Chief Rabbis required accepting their theological premises. Rav Lau said sternly: "It is I who speak for Soviet Jewry not you. You speak for two or three minor cases but I represent all the Soviet Jews. . . The Chief Rabbi of Hadera or the Chief Rabbi of Netanya do not ask for equality with the Chief Rabbinate of Israel. You come here and ask for a picture with us. Are we monuments? When the Reform Temple was built in New Orleans in the 19th Century, the 250 founding families said proudly; "We do not need Jerusalem; New Orleans is the center of Jewish life." Yet today not one descendant of those founding families is living as a Jew today. What does that say about the nature of the Reform movement?"

Rabbi Hirsch reminded the Chief Rabbi that only six percent of American Jews are Orthodox. Rav Lau responded, "Yes, maybe there are only six percent but what will happen in twenty and thirty years from now? The six percent will increase. Look at Boro Park, Williamsburg, and Teaneck. But as· to you Reform Jews, your own children will not be Jews." Staring directly into the eyes of Rabbi Hirsch, Rav Lau intoned, "You want to dismantle the Chief Rabbinate. You say we don't accept you as full Jews. Actually, we don't ask 'Who is a Jew.' That is not the question at all. The question is, 'Who is a Rabbi?' and the answer is very simple. We know that by looking at the Talmud Bavli (Babylonian Talmud). The opening words of the first tractate of the Babylonian Talmud states, "When do we commence to read the evening shemah ('Hear O Israel,' the central prayer of Judaism). There in the Talmud is the first time the word 'Rav' is used. A rabbi who doesn't observe Shabbos can be a leader, he can be a diplomat; but he cannot be a rabbi."

Lau noted that after 1948 the Reform movement had changed its previously hostile attitude toward Zionism, and then said, "I praise you for that change, but now do the same with Shabbat. Tell your congregations that the Chief Rabbinate demands a change, and I will come to your congregations to help you talk to them. We will not recognize as a Rav someone who doesn't follow the mitzvot of the *Shulchan Aruch* (legal authority on Jewish law) and the *Rambam* (Maimonides). The halacha is if you are Jewish you are a Jew, not a rabbi. The term rabbi is a halachic one." Lau concluded, "I am a student that stretches back more than 3,000 years. Moshe (Moses) said 'you shall not do work on the Shabbat' and yet you, the Reform movement, say it is permissible to work on the Shabbat. The Shulchan Aruch precedes the Reform movement."

Taking a more conciliatory pose, Rabbi Amiel Hirsch of the American Reform movement tried to convince Lau to agree to a follow up meeting with forty-five Reform rabbis in order to teach them. Lau responded sternly; "No, you are twisting my words." He then called upon the Reform rabbis to renounce any role in conducting marriages, divorces or conversions. He urged them to impress upon their followers the need to observe halachic norms.

The Reform and Conservative leaders were quite upset with the tenor of the meeting; telling waiting reporters that Rav Lau had been "unyielding." The Reform Movement representatives claimed that Lau had misrepresented them by saying they advocated the principle of patrilineal descent. Of course, they neglected to mention that it was only the very miniscule Reform branch in Israel that rejected patrilineal descent, but that the Reform movement in America, where the vast majority of Reform Jews reside, supported that principle. For my own part, I was quite proud of the performance of Rav Lau, who was articulate and strong and never yielded on matters of basic principle. He had made clear that the Chief Rabbinate would not enter into dialogue with the Reform and Conservative movements, nor recognize their legitimacy in Israel. It was probably the only meeting on this topic that I ever attended that I sat totally silent, taking very accurate notes.

The pluralism debate continues and will be with us for the foreseeable future. The Reform and Conservative movements are strong in America but weak in Israel. Their principle political allies in Israel are the left wing, secular, anti-religious parties. There is a bit of a contradiction there, since anti-religious Israelis would be no more prone to join a Reform temple than an Orthodox *shul*. The Meretz and Shinui parties are among the chief opponents of the established Orthodox rabbinate. Therefore those parties are drawn together with the Reform and Conservative movements, since both detest the Chief rabbinate and are working to erode the power of the Orthodox establishment in Israel.

The wealthy leaders of American fund raising organizations, like (UJC) UJA-Federation, look upon the Jewish Agency as their entrée to power in Israel. Many of them are fundamentally devoid of Jewish literacy, so their Judaism, as it applies to Israel, is the Jewish Agency and its worthwhile projects. These leaders tend to have ambivalent, even hostile feeling toward the Orthodox community, though few would acknowledge that openly. They would be more than happy to live in a world where groups like Mizrachi, Amit and Emunah did not exist. They are aware however, that they cannot credibly claim that the Jewish Agency is the parliament of the Jewish people unless they have Orthodox representation in that organization. Thus the Jewish Agency tolerates us. They throw us some bones and hope that we will be acquiescent enough so that they can carry out their work.

For our part, religious Zionists believe that our religion and our nationalism are part of one weltanschauung (world view). At the same time, we take very seriously the need for all Jews – religious and non-religious to present ourselves as one people to the outside world. Many times we have considered the possibility of leaving the Agency because of discrimination against us, but have concluded that we must not take action that increases the danger of splitting the Jewish people. Also, on a practical level we have seen some positive results from funds raised on behalf of the Jewish Agency that support the Torah cause in Israel and throughout the world. We realize it would be difficult to replicate the same level of funding for our institutions without this support.

The truth is that we have no fundamental argument with rank and file Reform, Conservative and secular Jews. Indeed, we hope we can be a positive influence to help them lead a more meaningful and spiritual life.

The Reform and Conservative movements were probably shocked that almost all the students of the first small class of the Neeman Commission Institute passed a course leading up to conversion, disproving their belief that Orthodox standards would be too rigorous for these candidates to master. Had the candidates failed, the cry would have been "See, I told you so." The major problem will be to duplicate these results across Israel. By 2001, there were 2000 candidates for conversion in classes around the country. By 2002, twenty five percent of army draftees were Russian immigrants. Of those, twenty five percent were Christians. The failure of the conversion courts to solve this problem is a major hurdle if we are to succeed in creating a united Jewish people.

Aryeh Deri, one of the organizers of the Shas movement and one of the brightest of Israeli politicians until he was tried and convicted on fraud charges, once warned me that there would come a time when thousands of Russian and Rumanian candidates for conversion would be turned down by the Beit Din, thereby triggering a revolution against the Rabbinate.

Some non-Orthodox members of the Knesset support the Reform movement under the premise that it would be better for the average Israeli to be a Reform Jew than be totally removed from our tradition. In taking this well-meaning position, they do not appreciate the devastating impact that Reform doctrines like patrilineal descent, intermarriage or same sex marriages are causing to Jews and Judaism in America and around the world.

My own solution in dealing with the Conservative and Reform movements in the United Sates has been to state forthrightly that our disagreement with them over their advocacy of pluralism is a disagreement over religious principle and, is therefore impossible to bridge. I believe we should stipulate that fact as a given and take pluralism off the table and the agenda of the organized American Jewish community. Let us allow Israelis to debate, discuss, and vote on those issues free of American interference. Meanwhile, let us work together as American Jews on important issues that unite us, such as assimilation, intermarriage, Jewish education, U.S.-Israel relations, the fight against terrorism, child abuse and Jewish poverty.

For the most part our collaboration with Reform and Conservative Jews inside umbrella bodies like AIPAC, UJC and the Presidents Conference, will continue even as we remain vigilant in opposition on the issue of pluralism in America. Yet, in comments I made to *U.S. News and World Report* and the *Los Angeles Times* not long ago, I asserted that the Reform movement's continuing aggressive "pluralism campaign" not only risks a further schism with Orthodox groups and quite possibly with the Conservative movement as well, but also may estrange them from their own Reform brethren in Israel. They have taken a more traditionalist position than their American counterparts on a number of issues, including patrilineal descent and same-sex marriage.

Indeed, in the last week of March 2000, the Reform movement officially sanctioned the union of gay couples. They did not use the word "marriage," but in essence gave a tacit blessing to that practice by refusing to condemn Reform rabbis who perform such ceremonies. At the same time, the Reform movement ruled that Reform clergy who do not wish to perform such unions are within their rights. Yet it is clearly written in Leviticus that homosexuality is an abomination. Apparently, the Reform movement feels that times have changed and that biblical precepts no longer apply. They have a right to believe that, of course, but we will not let them get away with preaching that acceptance of homosexuality as a legitimate lifestyle can be accepted under the umbrella of Judaism.

In short, there can be no mutual acceptance between halachic Judaism and the kind of "whatever feels good" ethic that is all too often the credo of the Reform movement. We will never accept the premise of pluralism that we should join the Reform and Conservative movements in forming a big tent and accepting positions diametrically opposed to basic Jewish precepts as legitimate. Authentic Judaism is not morally neutral.

CHAPTER EIGHTEEN

The Lanner Affair

I will never forget the moment the nightmare began.

The scene was the Ronald Reagan National Airport in Washington on June 21, 2000. I had just stepped off a shuttle from New York and was engaged in an animated chat with Stephen Solender, head of the United Jewish Communities (UJC) as the two of us walked briskly through the arrivals area. Steve and I were on our way to Blair House, opposite the White House, as part of a delegation from the Conference of Presidents of Major American Jewish Organizations that was going to hold an extended discussion that day with the King of Morocco. We were looking forward to querying the King forcefully about a downward trend in his country's previously warm relations with Israel. My phone rang.

It was Fran Breiner, my secretary at the Orthodox Union, alerting me that the internet edition of the New York *Jewish Week* had just posted a major story regarding Rabbi Baruch Lanner, the Director of Regions at the OU's National Council of Synagogue Youth (NCSY). The story concerning Lanner, who worked at OU headquarters in the NCSY offices, and who I saw around the office nearly every day, would be appearing the following day in the print edition of *The Jewish Week*. With a circulation of over 100,000 *The Jewish Week* is extremely influential in the Jewish community. I was shocked to hear even the barest outline of the story over the phone. Yet I was preoccupied by our business in Washington that day and did not attain a full appreciation of how huge was the scandal about to envelope the Union. The following morning I came to the office bright and early to read the massive 5000-word article in the *Jewish Week*.

What I read made me nauseous. In the lengthy special report entitled "Stolen Innocence" by the newspaper's editor in chief, Gary Rosenblatt, that began on page one and extended through four more pages, Rabbi Lanner was accused of mental, physical and sexual abuse of scores of male and female teenagers over a period of nearly three decades. This occurred at the OU's National Council of Synagogue Youth and at the Hillel High School in Deal, New Jersey, where he served as principal. The story carried accounts of alleged male and female victims, who charged Lanner had kissed and fondled scores of teenage girls and frequently kicked boys in the groin.

In the story, Rosenblatt asserted that "a number of rabbis, OU professionals and lay leaders sought to downplay Rabbi Lanner's behavior over the years" and had nevertheless promoted him to a higher position at NCSY. They had allowed him to continue working with youngsters, including attending NCSY shabbatons (weekend retreats) around the country, and leading NCSY groups to summer kollels in Israel.

The article said, "Rabbis Butler and Stopler (Executive V.P. and Senior Executive, respectively) say they never heard [of] specific allegations [against Lanner]" but they heard rumors for many years. Butler was quoted as saying that trying to track down the truth of the many "rumors" against Lanner was like "chasing shadows," but he had nevertheless decided, apparently in response to the renewal of the charges, that Lanner would not take part, as usual, in the OU kollel in Israel that summer. Calling this decision "a devastating loss" for the kollel program, Butler said that he had instead decided to move Lanner into adult education, a job in which he would work with college students, but not with those in high school. For his part, Stolper acknowledged that he had heard several complaints years earlier from young women about "improper behavior" by Lanner, but that he had found "no real substance to the charges." He had such a magnificent impact "on so many young people" said Stolper. In Lanner's defense Stolper said, "Despite some sickness that is not sexual but has to do with needing to be in control." Rabbi Stopler was also quoted as saying he cannot think of anyone "who has suffered as much as Rabbi Lanner."

Rosenblatt reported that several weeks before the article "two influentual lay leaders of the OU met personally with Rabbi Butler and urged the organization to remove Rabbi Lanner from working with youngsters."

Butler asserted in the article that a special Bet Din (court of Jewish law) had been convened in Teaneck, New Jersey at Lanner's request in 1989 over a dispute centering on Lanner and a young man named Elie Hiller who made a number of accusations against Lanner. The Bet Din had cleard Lanner of all charges made against him. According to Butler, the Bet Din has been consulted periodically and had permitted his youth work to continue. In reality, as Rosenblatt pointed out, the bet din had not really cleared Lanner, but rather ruled that Hiller had not proven his case.

One of the three members of the Bet Din, Rabbi Yosef Blau, believed that the assertion that the OU followed the guidance of the Bet Din regarding Lanner was technically correct. However, "it does not address many missteps along the way." He was quoted as saying that Rabbi Lanner "is unfit to work in Jewish education" and stressed; "The lack of action by the OU until now is a statement to the many victims that the Orthodox community condoned Baruch's actions and that they were the problem."

While Lanner had not returned his calls asking for an interview, Rosenblatt wrote, "a number of OU leaders and friends and colleagues of Rabbi Lanner" had called on his behalf and offered a deal whereby Lanner would promise to cease working with youngsters and instead go into adult education if the paper would withhold the article. As I read that, I felt stunned and infuriated to learn that even as these unnamed OU leaders engaged in frenzied behind-the-scenes lobbying on Lanner's behalf over a period of weeks, not one of them had breathed a word of any of it to me, as President of the Union or to Marcel Weber, our Chairman. Had I known what was going on, I would have immediately called an emergency officers meeting for the purpose of firing Lanner and would have taken other decisive steps to preserve the moral integrity and credibility of the Union. Yet because I was kept completely out of the loop, the scandal over Lanner had exploded in the most damaging way possible, and was now threatening to besmirch not only the reputations of some of our leading professionals, but the good name of the Orthodox Union itself.

The moment I finished reading the article, I got on the phone and began calling an ad-hoc group of former OU presidents, senior vice presidents, former chairmen of the board and asked them to come to the Union headquarters a few hours hence to grapple with a crisis unlike anything we had ever confronted.

Our Public Relations Department was being deluged with calls from major media ranging from the New York Times to WCBS-television. Many of our professionals were receiving calls, faxes and e-mails from grass roots supporters of the Union, especially in the northern New Jersey region where Lanner had been active as a NCSY leader for decades. The callers were expressing outrage at the shocking revelations and some were threatening to quit the OU unless we moved immediately to fire Lanner.

As I grappled with this onslaught, I was chagrined to read the proposed text of an official statement prepared in the words of the *Jewish Week* "by top OU professionals" the day before as part of a press release. I realized immediately that this proposed statement seemed more concerned about the fate of Lanner than with that of the youngsters he was alleged to have abused.

After ordering that the statement be brought before our officers' group, I convened an emergency meeting of our ad-hoc leadership group at about 12:30PM. About fifteen of our top lay leaders had managed to rearrange busy schedules in order make it to Union headquarters on short notice. One or two were on a phone connection. My first order of business was to insist that Lanner, who, unsurprisingly, had not come to work that day, should either resign immediately from his position at NCSY or be fired by the end of the day. They unanimously agreed with my position that Lanner must go immediately. Rabbi Butler left the conference room for a few minutes and later informed us that Lanner had agreed to resign effective immediately, and was faxing us a letter to that effect.

We then concluded that the text of the proposed press release was totally unacceptable and a revamped statement was released immediately after the meeting. The statement noted that Lanner had tendered his resignation after the Union concluded that "in light of the seriousness of the allegations made against him that he can no longer continue in his position with NCSY and its parent body, the Orthodox Union." The statement affirmed that NCSY had "a policy of zero tolerance of any inappropriate behavior," and that the OU was "initiating a thorough review of our existing procedures for monitoring our personnel" and would "immediately make such changes as the study may find necessary."

I returned to Monsey that night feeling sick at heart. I was deeply disturbed that, contrary to standard operating procedure in the fifth estate, Gary Rosenblatt had never called me for a comment before publishing his bombshell Lanner report. In fact, he did not call me until two weeks later when he was already preparing his second follow-up piece in the *Jewish Week*. I told him then that I would speak to him only on an off-the-record basis. I then asked why he had never called me or mentioned that there was an impending story in the works when we had lunch together about two months before the first Lanner story ran. Gary responded that he did not have the story at that point and that once he did have it, he was under the impression that I was aware of the impending release of the Lanner story.

One thing was clear; Rosenblatt had obviously vetted his article thoroughly before going to press. Nowhere in the article or in the accusatory follow up pieces that ran during the next several weeks was my name ever mentioned (except for having released the statement announcing Lanner's resignation), and there was not the slightest intimation in any of the *Jewish Week* articles that I had advance knowledge of the numerous charges of abuse against Lanner. In addition, I had never served either as a member or the chairman of the youth commission which oversees NCSY. This, at least, helped to convince many people that I had not been aware of the longstanding abuse charges against Lanner and had not been involved in protecting him.

Still, I was heartsick because I understood only too well that the eruption of the Lanner scandal six months before I was scheduled to complete my third term as president of the OU and step down from office, would almost certainly mean that my remaining time in office would largely be consumed with the scandal. I realized too that the Lanner Affair threatened to obscure much of the positive work I had done over six years to streamline the operation of the OU and to raise the profile of the organization within the councils of American Jewry, in Washington and in Israel. Angry and chagrined at the situation, I wracked my brains trying to understand how I had managed to miss telltale signs that there was something seriously amiss with our talented director of regions at NCSY.

Some people have painted a similarity between the Lanner

case and the far more extensive sexual abuse scandals of the Catholic Church. Looking back at the Lanner Affair from nearly two years removed, I believe such comparisons miss some essential differences. Intrinsic to the Church's problems are the complex issues of celibacy and homosexuality. Neither of these apply in our case. Nor was Lanner ever accused of statutory rape, but rather of physical, psychological, and sexual contact, as well as of language with sexual connotations and innuendos that were wrong, inappropriate, threatening, immoral and inconsistent with Torah values.

The Lanner case represented a tragic but isolated case in the sense that no other professional in NCSY or the OU was accused of any such acts. That there were people at the Union who failed the test of leadership had more to do with his perceived value as a professional. It was a failure to appreciate the severity and repetitious nature of the charges against him or a belief that his accusers lacked credibility. While none of these excuses is acceptable, they represent lapses regarding one individual and not a problem deeply rooted in our institutional culture.

At the time of the publication of the story in the *Jewish Week*, Baruch Lanner had been a prominent figure in the Orthodox community for nearly 30 years. A brilliant Talmudic scholar as a young man, he had been an ardent follower and student of the late Rav Joseph Soloveitchik, who was recognized in the late 20th century by all as the greatest leader of modern Orthodoxy in North America. From an early age, Lanner impressed all who knew him as a highly charismatic person and a mesmerizing teacher and youth leader. To listen to Baruch weave a story; lowering his voice and then raising it abruptly to deliver the greatest emotional impact, was to recognize an accomplished practitioner of an art form that fewer and fewer people master any more.

Wherever Baruch went to give a lecture, his audiences marvelled at his spell- binding speaking ability, his deep knowledge of Torah and evident talent as a teacher and a motivator. He was especially effective among teen-agers, and, over the years, had influenced large numbers of youngsters from non-religious backgrounds and troubled homes to embrace Torah Judaism.

Lanner worked his way up the ladder of leadership of the National Conference of Synagogue Youth (NCSY), and became one of its stars. He exhibited great skills as a planner and an innovator. He oversaw not only the regional directors of the youth movement, but also our Israel summer camps. Yet his influence within the Union extended far beyond NCSY. If one of the member synagogues of the OU complained that it was paying dues but receiving little from the Union in return, we would send Lanner there to be the scholar-in-residence over a Shabbat and weekend. Invariably, he wowed his audiences and many of them came to consider themselves his *"hasidim"* (followers). Lanner was like a pinch hitter, ready to jump into the fray at moments when the organization had a lot on the line, and belt a home run for the greater glory of the Union—and of his own growing legend.

Lanner was known within NCSY as someone who demanded loyalty from his subordinates. Unfortunately, as we found out once the *Jewish Week* story broke, Lanner also demanded "love" from the children in his care. For his part, he was extremely loyal to his superiors at the Union.

My presidential tenure started in November 1994 long after the Teaneck episodes took place. In general, I was content to leave youth affairs in what I presumed to be the capable hands of Rabbis Butler and Stolper and the youth commission. Without anyone even whispering to me any accusation against Lanner it is difficult to imagine what I could have done differently. My sons, Ari and Elli, both leaders in our local NCSY, never heard of one complaint against Lanner of the type mentioned in the *Jewish Week.*

Everything I heard from the NCSY leadership during my five and half years as OU president reinforced my impression that Lanner was doing a superb job as NCSY Director of Regions. In fact, I was so impressed by what I heard of Baruch's performance that I had suggested to Butler early in my term as OU president that NCSY should honor him at one of its dinners. Several days after I broached that idea, he informed me that he had checked with Lanner and the latter had told him that he and his wife did not want to be honored. I was a little surprised by Lanner's refusal, but it seemed to me at the time to be a sign of modesty. I even called Lanner and his wife at their home and urged Baruch to accept the award, but they told me emphatically that they were not interested.

Certainly, if I had even an inkling of the truth about Lanner, I would never have suggested to Butler (as I did in 1999), that we consider Lanner for the top position at NCSY. Butler immediately responded that this was a bad idea, and I dropped it, assuming that he must have his reasons—perhaps concern over Lanner's unpolished demeanor. Never did it occur to me that those reasons might have anything to do with allegations of improper behavior.

From the very day the first *Jewish Week* story broke, I had a strong feeling that at the end of the process the OU top professionals who had supervised Lanner and allowed him to remain in a high position at NCSY with access to young people would themselves have to go if the Union was to rebuild its credibility. Yet after consulting with a few of my closest friends and advisers as to whether I was in a position to clean house at the Union by firing the people in question, I quickly came to the conclusion that I could not follow that path. First, we could not be sure at that point what was true and false in the welter of charges against Lanner or as to which OU leaders had known of his pattern of abuse and had covered for him. Certainly, people who had given many years of dedicated service to the Union deserved due process. Secondly, as a practical matter, I simply did not have the political strength at that moment to make a move that would surely divide the leadership.

Yet, I also understood that if the OU were to have any hope of regaining the trust of the public, I would have to do far more than simply assign a few senior officers to investigate the Lanner affair. It was clear that under the circumstances we could not afford to be perceived as investigating ourselves. Rather, it was clear we would need to appoint an independent commission. They would require a mandate to undertake a "let the chips fall where they may" investigation that would pass the "reasonable man" standard—namely that a reasonable person would accept the commission's findings as fair and objective.

Before I could turn my attention to the crisis on a full-time basis, however, I had to leave for Israel on June 24 for the annual meeting of the Jewish Agency in Israel. Normally, I relish these meetings, but on this occasion I was badly distracted. I spent almost all of my time on the phone to New York with OU Chairman of the Board Marcel Weber and other Union officers. We discussed strategies for the creation of the independent commission. They reported that the situation was continuing to deteriorate as people inside and outside the Union denounced us for an unforgivable lapse of moral responsibility. Amidst this crescendo of bad news, Sheila and I celebrated our 38th wedding anniversary in Jerusalem on June 26. Even a dinner I had planned for the two of us at one of our favorite restaurants was interrupted by several urgent transatlantic calls from OU officers in New York. Sheila was not pleased to have our privacy intruded upon in that way, but the dire situation necessitated that I take those calls.

If any of our officers had any doubts that we urgently needed to appoint an independent commission to get back on top of events, they fell by the wayside when the June 30 edition of the *Jewish Week* hit the newsstands with a second Lanner story. This one, also penned by Rosenblatt, reported that the newspaper had received hundreds of letters, e-mails and phone calls in the week since the publication of the first story. The article expressed outrage with the OU for keeping Lanner in a leadership position for so long and allowing him to continue working with young-sters. It also noted that several days earlier Congregation Beth Aaron, a large and influential Orthodox synagogue in Teaneck, N.J., the town where the Lanner bet din had taken place, had voted overwhelmingly "to immediately withhold all monies to be paid to the Orthodox Union and to national and regional NCSY." This would be done until the synagogue's membership was satisfied that provisions for supervision of young people at NCSY events were improved. One board member at Beth Aaron said he believed other OU-affiliated synagogues in the region were considering similar steps. "The mood of the congregation was fighting mad. The OU and NCSY have zero credibility around here," he noted.

Meanwhile, the article reported, a split was developing within the OU between lay leaders who argued that only the resigna-tion of top OU personnel would adequately address the crisis of credibility, and "top professionals" who staunchly opposed any personnel changes. The latter expressed the belief that the Lan-ner Affair would eventually abate once the headlines surround-ing the case died down. Specifically, the professionals were said to oppose any firing of top personnel.

During that hellish week in Jerusalem, I had my eyes opened in a particularly jarring manner as to how pervasive Lanner's history of abuse had been.

On the very morning of my arrival in Jerusalem, I received a call from a young American dentist, a former NCSY'er who was angry and indignant. I asked him what was the matter, and was stunned when this young man responded emotionally that he had been abused by Baruch Lanner as a teenager, and that other members of his family had likewise been victims. I expressed shock and immediately arranged to meet with him. When we met, I assured him that there would be no cover up and that the special investigatory commission I planned to appoint in the coming days would have real independence to follow whatever leads emerged. He was interviewed about the Lanner controversy soon thereafter in the *Jerusalem Post*. The paper quoted him as angered over the abuses being "allowed to go on for so long." "I'm very disillusioned with the OU especially the two people who were responsible for NCSY."

For my own part, I was so shaken during that stressful week in Jerusalem, by my encounter with this young man and the stream of bad news I continued to receive on a daily basis from our office in New York, that I cancelled a vacation to Egypt that Sheila and I had planned after the end of the Jewish Agency meetings. I realized that I needed to get back immediately to the lion's den in New York and tie up the appointment of the independent commission. Before leaving Israel, I released a public letter in which I promised that such a "blue ribbon commission" would be set up within a few days and that the members of the commission, including "some now involved with the OU (and) others totally independent of it," would have "carte blanche to pursue their inquiries in any manner and any direction they wish."

In the same letter, I noted that the OU, at my direction, had set up a toll-free phone line for members of NCSY. They could call and discuss their concerns or report negative personal experiences with Lanner to an independent professional counselor or rabbi. But as a sign of the low level of trust in the OU among Orthodox youth in the wake of the Lanner revelations, Kedma, an association of observant college students, set up a separate 1-800 phone line to deal with anyone wishing to call for counselling.

Meanwhile, both the Jewish and mainstream media were focusing their lenses on the Lanner story. WCBS radio in New York seemed to be giving the story hourly mention. The *New York Times* ran two articles on the Lanner Affair and the story was also covered in the *Los Angeles Times* and other major dailies around the country. Several exhaustive articles appeared in New Jersey papers, particularly in the *Bergen Record*, which is the major paper of Bergen County, where Lanner resided. As noted, the

Jewish Week ran a second story filled with accounts of new charges against Lanner, and subsequently a third story which cast a critical light on what it presented as the pressure tactics on teenagers to become more observant allegedly used in some *kiruv* programs (bringing non-observant Jews into a halachically observant lifestyle) by Lanner and some other NCSY leaders. Finally, the Lanner Affair became a big story in the *Jerusalem Post* and other Israeli media, as a number of olim from the U.S. came forward with stories of how they had been abused by Lanner.

No doubt Lanner's apparent lack of remorse contributed to the sense of outrage in OU-affiliated synagogues and NCSY chapters. It was worse in New Jersey, where Lanner had served for many years, not only in NCSY but also as the principal of the Hillel Academy in Deal. Yet the outcry spread as far as Los Angeles. Ad hoc groups of NCSY parents were not only calling for meetings to discuss Baruch Lanner, but also sending out notices over the Internet and preparing resolutions calling for specific actions by the Union even before the meetings they called had met. In Washington three rabbis sent me a public letter. They charged that despite our statements of horror and stated determination to allow an independent investigation to go forward, the Union actually intended to carry out a cover-up. I never had a chance to discuss the charges with the rabbis, because they released the letter to the newspapers even before I received it.

The sensational quality of the charges against Lanner seemed to stir up a lamentable tendency among many people to play to the press. Quite a number of rabbis castigated the Union harshly in comments to the media, and then, after we complained about the unfairness of some of their charges, claimed to us that they had been misquoted. One rabbi at an OU-affiliated synagogue in New Jersey orchestrated a public meeting to which he invited the press. He subsequently turned around and disinvited them when I insisted that such a sensitive discussion should first be held within the Jewish community.

Needless to say, our public relations department was under severe pressure. With some outside assistance from Howard Rubenstein Associates, David Olivestone, our communications director, Stan Steinreich, lay chair of our public relations department and Sharyn Perlman, our public relations director, tried as best they could to reassure the public and the press. Yet the clamor kept getting worse. Not only was the media having a field day with the story, but, as noted, we were faced with a number of determined and irate individuals who were making expert use of the Internet to whip up synagogues and rabbis against the Orthodox Union and NCSY. It was clear that the only way to staunch the bleeding was to get the Special Commission up and running as quickly as possible.

The moment I arrived back in New York from Israel, I went into consultations with my ad-hoc group of OU wise men to commence an all-out-effort to assemble a commission that would be perceived as independent. Yet what sort of people could we find who would transmit that sense of independence? I was getting a wide range of advice on that question, both from OU insiders and from a wide spectrum of important outside figures in the Jewish world whose opinions I respected. Some argued that the commission should be made up exclusively of people with no ties to the OU or Orthodox Judaism, or "gentiles" as one advisor half-jokingly put it. Upon reflection, however, I decided that to do their difficult jobs fairly and judiciously, commission members needed to be knowledgeable of Orthodox doctrines that were central to the Lanner case such as *kiruv*. As much as we were determined to form a commission that was committed to finding the truth, we also wanted one that would endeavor to strengthen and rehabilitate the Union, rather than destroy it. At risk was the survival of a 100-year-old organization that had done so much to preserve and enhance orthodox Jewish life in the United States. Therefore, I decided that the composition of the commission should be a mix of top leaders of the OU and 'outsiders' who happened to be observant Jews.

When we began the process of vetting names, I was surprised to hear that quite a few people, including some prominent politicians who happened to be Orthodox, were eager to serve on the commission. From the beginning, I had a gut instinct that we should not select any individuals who were eager to be chosen. I also realized that politicians anxious to serve on the commission might have their own agendas.

In our search for quality people to serve on the commission, we sought to attain a mix of men and women and to find people known for their accomplishments in fields like finance, law, education, psychiatry, and pediatric medicine. We readily acknowledged to those to whom we reached out that serving on the commission would be a thankless and time consuming job, but appealed to their commitment to public service and to the well being of the orthodox community. Some of those we wanted to serve respectfully declined our offer, whereas others laid down conditions for serving which we endeavored to meet. The selection process took about two weeks. Finally, we had a commission we believed lived up to the stringent criteria we had set.

As chairman of the NCSY Special Commission, we selected Richard Joel, the national director of Hillel. Joel is a veteran Jewish leader with considerable experience in youth work, education and the administration of a large organization. I knew him to be tough but fair and extremely competent. Chosen to serve as members of the commission were Fred Ehrman, vice chairman of Brean Murray & Co., honorary president of the Lincoln Square Synagogue, co-chairman of the Orthodox Caucus, and a senior vice president of the OU; Allan Fagin, a partner and co-chairman of the labor and employment law department of Proskauer Rose LLP, and an OU officer; Rabbi Abraham Twerski, M.D., founder and medical director of the Gateway Rehabilitation Center and associate professor of psychiatry, University of Pittsburgh; and Susan K. Schulman, M.D., attending in pediatrics at Maimonides Medical Center and assistant clinical professor of pediatrics, SUNY Health Science Center in Brooklyn. Dr. Schulman had done a great deal of study concerning the problem of molestation of children in the Orthodox community.

Completing the list of those selected to serve on the commission were Jacob Yellin, vice president and counsel of the Walt Disney Company in charge of Disney's worldwide ethics compliance program; Matthew Maryles, a prominent investment banker who is active in UJA-Federation; Jules Polonetsky, a former New York City Commissioner of Consumer Protection, Mrs. Suzanne Stone, professor of Law at Cordoza Law School of Yeshiva University and Lydia Kess, an attorney who resigned on October 10, 2000.

Before we were able to announce the appointment of the Special Commission and the names of its members, however, I received a call from Richard Joel in which he said that he and other prospective commission members had caucused and had decided that in addition to appointing the Commission, the OU should also select a law firm. To conduct the actual investigation the commission would issue a public executive summary at the conclusion of the investigation. Richard asserted that this was the only way for the commission to assure the public of its independence. He told me explicitly that he and the other members would refuse to serve on the commission unless their demands were met.

Joel said he and the other members of the still-to-be-officially announced Special Commission had decided upon the law firm of Debevoise and Plimpton to represent them. To undertake the investigation, they wanted Bruce Yannett, a senior member of Debevoise and Plimpton and a former Assistant U.S. Attorney, who had earned a sterling reputation as a staff member of the Iran-Contra investigation. Yannett estimated that the total cost of the investigation would be $210-222,000, a hefty amount, but less than might be expected since the firm planned to use a large contingent of summer interns who would work pro-bono. Yannett told me the report would almost certainly be ready by Labor Day.

I knew that there would be plenty of grumbling about these demands from some members of the OU leadership. Yet after I discussed the matter with Marcel Weber, and other leaders, we came to the conclusion that we had no choice but to accede. Obviously, high-profile resignations from the commission by Joel and the other members would be a public relations disaster for the OU, and would almost certainly mean that we would not be able to obtain the services of other individuals of prominence.

Meanwhile, the Union had taken the precaution of choosing our own legal representative for matters related to the Lanner Affair. He was Charles Stillman, a well-known criminal attorney who in the course of a long and distinguished career had defended Clark Clifford and Mayor David Dinkins—the latter after he was charged with negligence by the Crown Heights Jewish community in the wake of the 1991 riots there that left a Torah scholar, Yankel Rosenbaum, dead. Stillman was known as "a lawyer's lawyer," but he was not only bright, talented and on top of the legal game, but he also possessed real common sense and *mentschlichkeit* (good character).

After my discussions with Richard Joel, Marcel and I were painfully aware that we needed to move forward immediately with the announcement of the special commission. While the two of us were in a position to speak and make policy in the name of the Union, technically we needed the endorsement of the Executive Board for the appointment of the special commission and for our agreement to also appoint a law firm to investigate the charges, as Joel had insisted upon. The Executive Board was to meet just before the July 4th holiday, and some 90-100 people, virtually the entire membership of the Board, were set to attend.

The word around the OU offices in the days immediately preceding the meeting was that members of the old guard faction, were angry at my insistence that the special commission should operate independent of Union control. Although Marcel and I knew that many members of the Executive Board would agree with the steps we had taken, including accepting the commission's insistence on bringing aboard Yannett and his law firm—with the attendant hefty price tag, we could not be certain that the overall Executive Board would endorse our position. At all times Marcel and I consulted with and kept our senior leadership up to date on our progress.

Knowing that time was of the essence, I therefore placed an ad in the upcoming issue of the *Jewish Week* announcing the creation of the commission and giving the names of its participants. That Internet edition of the paper was to appear on the afternoon of our meeting, only hours before the all-important Executive Board meeting. Waiting to place an ad until after the Executive Board meeting would have meant losing a valuable week (since the deadline would have passed) in public relations. We felt that the hemorrhaging must stop immediately and thus as soon as the commission was formed we announced it publicly. I felt then, as I do now that we had no choice. The survival of the Union was at stake.

The Executive Board meeting, which lasted nearly five hours, was not an easy affair. Rabbi Butler made an emotional speech. Afterwards, several members of the Executive Board invoked *halacha* in order to condemn *lashon ha'ra* (speaking ill of people) and *rechilut* (gossip). Others said we should ignore the press and simply hunker down in support of our staff. I noticed that not a single person discussed the implications of the gross violation of *halacha* involved in protecting those who abuse children.

Sentiment in the room was sharply divided and there seemed to be no guarantee Marcel and I would get even a bare majority of those present to support the steps I had taken. Finally, I took the floor and dropped my bombshell, explaining that I had placed an ad in the Jewish Week announcing the appointment of the commission and the Internet edition was already out. As I sat down I could hear a general hubbub as many expressed anger and incredulity at my action.

Yet after a few minutes of discussion, it became clear that my statement had taken the wind out of the sails of the opposition. Even those dead set against the commission realized that now that the commission had been officially announced by the President of the OU, they had no choice but to back me up. Soon a motion was made and passed unanimously supporting the establishment of the special commission and its use of a legal team. Certainly, as unhappy as many board members were about my decision to allow an independent commission to delve into the inner workings of the Union, none of them wanted to be on the record as appearing to support a cover-up. Some were less than pleased that the commission would deliver a public summary. My opponents realized that, at least for the moment, they had lost control of the debate.

I was pleased and more than a little relieved. The course that Marcel and I set had been sustained. We were able to announce to the public that we had an independent commission in place to investigate the Lanner Affair. I had also made clear to the top leadership of the OU that as long as I remained President, I would not tolerate an investigation that would amount to a whitewash. I felt that we had shown decisive leadership in getting the special commission up and running and ensuring that there would be a full and open investigation. Perhaps we could now get on top of the scandal, instead of always being in a reactive mode.

As a student of scandals going back to Watergate in the 70's and Tylenol in the 80's, I realized that if an organization in which there has been wrongdoing endeavors to come clean and get out the facts, the public will accept it, whereas those that go into a cover-up mode are the ones that end up getting clobbered. Yet for me, the obligation to undertake a "no holds barred" investigation was hardly only a matter of good public relations, but also our solemn moral obligation to root out wrongdoing. In the same statement announcing the establishment of the commission, I had pledged, "As a father and a grandfather, I promise that I will not rest until I am satisfied that our house is in order and NCSY's reputation is restored."

Yet while we had quelled the fires inside the Union leadership for the time being, we still had to contend with harsh criticism from the grass roots. We had hoped that the evident high quality of the commission members would bring praise even from our critics, but instead there were charges from many quarters that the commission was not independent enough because two members were OU officers and one was the wife of an OU board member—albeit a professor of law in her own right. Thankfully, the attacks abated after the *Jewish Week* ran an editorial in July urging that the commission should be judged by its actions, rather than on the connection of some members with the Union.

For my own part, I responded to such criticism by arguing that it would be next to impossible to find Orthodox community leaders who were totally removed from the Orthodox Union— people who hadn't written for us, spoken at a conference, or had some relatives who served on one of our boards. I pointed out that the commission was not a jury of the sort from which a woman might be excused from a malpractice case if her husband is a doctor. I argued that simply because someone had served in the positions of authority in the Orthodox community did not mean he or she could not honestly and fairly investigate the OU. I noted that former Senator John Danforth of Missouri had served in government for decades before he was appointed by President Clinton to investigate the FBI action at Waco that had resulted in the deaths of many Branch Davidians. Yet because of Danforth's reputation for ironclad integrity, no one charged that he had a conflict of interest and could not honestly investigate the U.S. government.

As part of my effort to quell the ongoing firestorm and to remind the public that the Union and its work far transcended the Lanner Affair, I wrote an op-ed article in the August 4th edition of the *Jewish Week*. In that piece, I wrote that the men and women we selected to serve on the special commission had "impeccable credentials" and were "respected for their honesty and integrity." I noted that the OU had instituted "a new and vigorous anti-harassment code in NCSY," that the NCSY staff would be receiving sensitivity training and NCSY was developing immediate plans to integrate the parents of NCSY members into decision-making and oversight capacities. I reminded readers that "the Orthodox Union is much more than that which is reflected in recent headlines, but was a vast network of people and programs for people of all ages and circumstances administered "by some 1000 talented, dedicated and ethical employees worldwide, supported by hundreds of committed lay leaders who devote their talent, time and energy to the betterment of the community."

Nevertheless, I pointed out, "There will always be individuals who act unethically and who will push the limits of their authority."

"Sometimes those in authority may fail the test of leadership by not acting decisively when confronted with the evidence of the improper actions of trusted colleagues. However, the true test of an organization's mettle is what it does when it learns of improper conduct by any of its employees. Does it deny the charges? Does it cover up the facts? Or does it act responsibly to investigate the matter and not rush to judge or condemn, while ensuring that the charges are brought out in the sunlight and that both redress and preventive measures are instituted? The latter is the course we have set for ourselves."

In conclusion, I appealed to the community "not to abandon (its) partnership" with the Orthodox Union, and said, "In return, we promise that we will do whatever it takes to regain your trust. Jewish tradition and moral imperative demand no less."

Several events that took place in July served as a vivid reminder as to just how serious was the moral imperative confronting the OU. On July 9th, I received a letter from Mrs. Shayndee Hiller. Her late son Jonah was the boy who Lanner had allegedly assaulted with a kitchen knife on August 7, 1987. This incident eventually led to the convening of the Bet Din two years later. In her letter, a copy of which was dispatched to the commission, Mrs. Hiller claimed that on August 9, 1987 she and her husband immediately contacted the Union after the alleged attack by Lanner on their son. On August 10, 1987 she received a call back from Rabbi Butler. Hiller said that Butler "acknowledged the severity of the situation," but said that before taking action he needed to corroborate their version of events. She said that he soon called back to say he had indeed "confirmed their story" and asked them what they wanted the Union to do. Hiller wrote me that she and her husband insisted that Lanner "should have no further contact" or involvement in NCSY in the *Etz Chaim* (northern New Jersey) region. (Lanner had long served as Regional Director for the New Jersey region, which included *Etz Chaim*).

Hiller said that the OU eventually agreed to these conditions. However, subsequently she claimed, "the OU reneged on the deal," allowing Lanner to speak at an NCSY weekend retreat in

Livingston, N.J. Hiller also said that "the incident that occurred on August 7 was denied" (by the OU). As a consequence, the Hillers' attorney, Sharon Stein, sent a tough letter to Butler on December 1, 1987, threatening to bring criminal and civil charges unless Lanner resigned as director of the New Jersey region by January 1, 1988. Stein wrote: "in preparation for litigation I will contact other youngsters who have informed the Hillers of physical and verbal abuse inflicted upon them by Rabbi Lanner." Hiller said the family then received a phone call from a high official of the OU Youth Commission, today in the top echelon of the Union lay leadership, advising her and her husband that "the Union had Alan Dershowitz on retainer should the family decide to continue with legal action." (The OU official in question denies he ever mentioned Dershowitz and therefore I do not mention his name). The *Jerusalem Post* in an article by Elli Wohlgelenter on February 8, 2001, quotes from the Sharon Stein letter which they possessed.

In any event, the Hillers, due to their son's recurrent illness and other family matters, decided not to push forward with their threat to sue Lanner. However, two years later, after the tragic death of Jonah Hiller from a chronic disease, his brother Elie, who had resigned as Director of Outreach Programs for New Jersey NCSY in outrage over what he felt was the OU's apparent coverup of Lanner's attack on his late brother, learned that a synagogue in nearby Teaneck was strongly considering Lanner as their rabbi. Elie Hiller then sent out a letter to the Teaneck Jewish community accusing Lanner of physical and verbal misconduct. That letter effectively put the kibosh on Lanner's chances of being hired by that or any other synagogue in Bergen County and caused Lanner to go to the Bet Din in a desperate effort to restore his good name. The Bet Din, after an eighteen hour session, concluded that most of the charges were not proven. The findings were never made public. Elie Hiller was told to make a public apology to Lanner, which he did. Rosenblatt reported that the Bet Din found some of Lanner's actions "were deemed inappropriate."

On July 21, Gary Rosenblatt ran another front page story in the *Jewish Week*. He wrote about a former female student at the Hillel High School, a co-ed yeshiva in Deal, N.J. where Lanner served as principal for 15 years until leaving in 1997. The girl gave a gut-wrenching account of how Lanner allegedly sexually molested her on multiple occasions in his office during 1995 when she was only 14. The girl said that the abuse she endured at Lanner's hands caused her to turn away from Judaism and get involved in drugs and juvenile delinquency. The girl who used a pseudonym in the article filed a criminal complaint against Lanner.

Meanwhile, a new crisis had erupted involving the Joel Commission. In late July, Joel called and asked for a meeting. When we met, he informed me that the investigation was becoming far more complicated than expected and would require considerably more time and money than had been anticipated a few weeks earlier. Richard explained that whereas the commission had originally expected to interview thirty witnesses, several hundred individuals had contacted the commission in less than a month to say they had information to give concerning the Lanner case. Also, new allegations—some involving alleged financial improprieties by Lanner with OU and NCSY funds—were coming to the forefront. Finally, he said the commission had determined that it would also require the services of a forensic accountant. He said that if we did not agree to that condition and to expand the commission's budget, the commission would be forced to discontinue its work. Joel emphasized that the commission members did not want their names associated with an investigation that was incomplete or which was not given the opportunity to root out all the facts.

As much as I was determined to give the commission full latitude to do its investigation, I was deeply distressed by what Joel told me. It appeared that he was raising the nightmare spectre of an open-ended investigation. After a good deal of back and forth, Joel and I agreed informally that there would be a reasonable cap on what the commission could spend on its investigation.

Nevertheless, I explained to Joel that I did not have the authority on my own to sanction such a payment by the Union. I therefore asked Richard if he and the other commission members would be willing to make a presentation to a group of seven or eight of the most senior people in the Union, including the treasurer and officials of the Finance Committee, to explain why the commission had concluded it needed more money than expected. The meeting, which was held in secret, was a success. The OU leaders, having been convinced by the commission of the need for a much wider investigation than originally expected, agreed to all of the commission's demands including the cap as a maximum cost for the investigation.

When word inevitably leaked out about our decision to sanction a much wider and more expensive commission investigation, a number of members of the Executive Board who had not been invited to the private meeting with the commission were angry with me. These were among the same people who wanted to end the independent investigation of the Lanner Affair. Frustrated by their inability to stop me from taking steps in support of the commission that they felt exceeded my mandate, a number of these leaders stridently criticized me. One sent a letter to each member of the Executive Board claiming that my decision to pay for the commission's legal counsel "could jeopardize the OU's financial ability" and force cancellation of programs" and asserting that I appeared to be "more concerned about (my) personal legacy than about the interests of the OU itself." A copy of the letter found its way into the *Jewish Week*. In response, I wrote each Board member a chronological outline of all the moves that I had made since the affair came to light and whom I had consulted at each step. I cited our constitution to show that I had not taken any steps that deviated from it. I asked for the support of the members and urged them to avoid personal attacks at a time of maximum tension. I never mentioned my attacker by name.

Given everything that was going on, it may seem remarkable to some that Rabbi Butler and I managed to maintain a collegial relationship and work together fruitfully to keep the day-to-day operations of the OU functioning despite our very different perspectives on the Lanner Affair. As in past years, our professional collaboration worked well because we were both committed to the well being of the OU and both were effective administrators and policy-makers. There was a certain sense of deja vu in the atmosphere. Only one year earlier Butler and I had forced the resignation of our top Israeli administrator because of a scandal that occurred on his "watch." In any case, I was satisfied to leave any personal decisions until after the Special Commission had thoroughly investigated all aspects of the Lanner Affair and had given us their report and recommendations.

Meanwhile, as the Union does every year a month or so before the High Holidays, we had sent out our membership renewal forms. Within a week, we were receiving an alarming number of responses from long time members informing us that they would not renew their membership until they were convinced the OU was doing a serious job of investigating Lanner and those inside the organization who had protected him. One long time supporter wrote: "As of this date, I have seen no accountability for the Baruch Lanner cover-up. No definite action has been taken. No one has been fired. Until there is definite, positive corrective action taken, we will not contribute anything to your organization. The 'one bad apple' rotted many other leaders. Shame on you!"

A couple from Maryland wrote, "We received the annual membership renewal form recently and will rejoin the OU once the OU comes clean on the 'Lanner Affair.' What is puzzling and most disturbing about the entire situation was his continued involvement with NCSY for the past several decades and the deafening silence from the OU."

Another couple wrote that they would honor a pledge they had already made to support our Torah Center in Kharkov, Ukraine, but added, "Please be informed that this is the last money we ever intend to give to the OU because you have demonstrated that your organization values protecting "its own" above protecting children. This is unconscionable.

"A woman from Los Angeles wrote that she considered Gary Rosenblatt's decision to publish the Lanner story to have been "both brave and according to Jewish law."

I realized that no matter how many statements I and other OU leaders made expressing contrition for what had occurred and promising that we would conduct an honest investigation, we would be unable to quell the continuing public clamor until the commission's report was finally delivered and made available to the media and to our membership. Unfortunately, because of the greatly expanded scope of the investigation, the commission's original deadline of Labor Day for delivering its report came and went without a clear sense of when they would actually finish their work. Those who at the time criticized the cost of the investigation never came forth and suggested "cleaning house" by firing four or five professionals and asking for a few lay resignations. This might have obviated the need for a commission. The alternative was to put our head in the sand and make believe that we were upset and proclaim that eventually we would get to the bottom of it. In essence saying let the public be damned.

Meanwhile, I, like all the top lay and professional leaders of the OU, had given testimony to the commission, which, in my case, lasted approximately five to six hours. Their questioning of me was extremely thorough and professionally done. For my part, I endeavored to be as open and honest as possible and give the fullest, most detailed testimony that I could. It turned out that much of what the commission asked was background material or corroboration of the stories and testimony of other witnesses. At the same time, the commission members attempted to shock me with a set of facts they knew I was unaware of, a technique they also apparently used with a number of other witnesses—primarily senior officers of the Union—to impress on them the gravity of the situation. It seemed that the commission felt that OU senior officers still did not fully appreciate the seriousness of the charges against Lanner.

Did I know, they asked, that Rabbi Lanner frequently slept overnight on the couch in my office? I was shocked. I frequently took 15-to 20-minute catnaps in the afternoon to refresh myself— a custom I had indulged in since my days as a resident in obstetrics and when I used to stay up all night providing emergency medical services to badly wounded G.I's in Vietnam. But where did Lanner get off thinking he had free run of my office?

Was I aware, they asked, that in May 2000, two lay leaders presented a written firsthand narrative of Rabbi Lanner's abuse to a senior OU professional and that after the meeting that professional phoned a group of senior OU lay leaders of which neither Marcel nor I were included? I answered in the negative. When Bruce Yannett asked how I felt about senior union officials not sharing their knowledge of Lanner's conduct with me. I answered that I felt as though "I had been assaulted." I had realized from the time of the first *Jewish Week* story that I had been kept in the dark concerning Lanner by our professional staff. Still, it was quite a shock and a cause for chagrin to have the commission explain to me the extent to which I had been played for a fool by our top professionals and was thereby denied the chance to deal with the Lanner matter in a way that might have limited the enormous damage the OU finally absorbed.

By mid October we had managed to assure that the Joel Commission would continue its work and definitely deliver a report. I had to do some hard decision-making about how the OU should respond to the report once it was finally ready and the process necessary to reach that goal.

As I mulled these difficult questions, I was acutely aware I was personally in a no-win situation. On the one hand, were I to try to play down the charges against Lanner and those who had supported and protected him inside the OU, I would be attacked by the families of the alleged victims, the community, and the press for whitewashing the very serious acts that had been committed. If, on the other hand, I followed my conscience and pressed for an honest and thorough Commission report and decisive OU response to its conclusions, I would be antagonizing a significant group of officers. It was a journey through a minefield. But I was determined to act in a clinically objective fashion. The patient, in this case the Union, must be saved and brought back to health. Only the truth could accomplish this.

The ongoing delays in the delivery of the Joel Commission report; first from Labor Day to November and finally to early December undercut my own position and those of others at the OU who insisted that the organization would need to make fundamental changes, including replacing top administrators, in order to begin the process of putting the scandal behind it.

This was especially true given that my term as President would come to an end on December 31, 2000 and the organization was scheduled to install a new president and new set of officers at our year-end convention. Many of us were acutely concerned that we should have the information from the commission as to whether some of the people being considered for officer positions had been implicated in protecting or supporting Lanner so our nominating committee could remove them from consideration. As it turned out, the nominating committee chairman stalled as long as possible. By late November, with the commission report still undelivered, he had to go forward with the organization's official nominations for officer positions.

Sensing the potential for disaster, some highly placed individuals came to me and asked me to consider whether we could amend the constitution so I and the slate of officers serving with me, could stay on for six to twelve months beyond the end of my term. After a period of introspection, I realized that such a step would not only violate our constitution, but would further aggravate the growing rifts within the Union. My main goal was to insure that continuity be preserved.

My preference was that in a short period of time after the coming election an entirely new slate of officers not connected to Lanner or the Youth Commission should be elected in a special election. I was concerned with the effect of individuals closely associated with the Youth Commission and NCSY leading the Union in post scandal period. This was not easily achieved. I could find no support for such an idea.

As I struggled with how best to move forward during those autumn days, I also had to deal with the fact that the Joel Commission had rebuffed my oft-repeated appeal that they not only lay out the facts in their report, but also to offer specific recommendations as to which personnel within the Union, if any, should be forced to resign as a result of their actions in regard to Lanner; which should be publicly censured, and which absolved of any involvement. The commission members emphatically rejected that approach; insisting that the evidence would speak for itself and that anyone who would read the report would come to the correct conclusions as to what needed to be done. I believed then they were wrong and was proven to be correct when, after the release of the report in late December, bitter debate ensued within the OU leadership, despite the tough language in the report.

Given all of these complex factors, I decided that I needed to create a high level group of thirteen senior officers that would accept and evaluate the Joel Commission report and make recommendations for a course of action. The group represented a cross-section of opinion on how the Union should respond. This included several people who were ardent supporters of Rabbi Butler and had been critical of my handling of the Lanner Affair.

I believed that the report would prove to be so definitive regarding Rabbi Lanner and the Union that this group would join in a unanimous report which the board would support. This would obviate the need for the full report to be released either to the board or the public.

I went ahead and set up the Committee of 13 without fanfare at the beginning of November 2000. As noted, I tried hard to make the Committee of Thirteen a balanced group, but inevitably I was attacked for not including each former living president and senior vice presidents. Others blasted me for not appointing any women or pulpit rabbis to the committee. Unless the thirteen managed to reach a unanimous decision as to how to respond to the Joel Commission report, we were in for a rocky road. I believed this group could do it.

The commission had committed itself to releasing an executive summary to the public, but not the report itself. The executive summary would not include names of Lanner's victims, nor of every rabbi and NCSY professional who had crossed Lanner's path over 30 years. We were concerned that if we released the full report that completely innocent people who had worked with Lanner in projects over the years but had no idea of his abusive activities would find their names unfairly blackened. The summary would also not include the sort of sexual specifics that had made the Starr Report on President Clinton's affair with Monica Lewinsky read like a smutty novel.

I was convinced that we could unmistakably define the nature of Lanner's activities without going into degrading details. Yet within a few weeks I came to realize that I had made a profound mistake in believing that an executive summary would have enough punch to force personnel changes highly unpopular with many in our hierarchy.

At last the Joel Commission concluded its report. On December 7, 2000, three weeks before the opening of the OU annual convention and the end of my administration, the commission delivered to me, via our attorney, Stillman, a 332-page report with 104 exhibits. The Committee of 13 agreed that neither the report nor our notes would be allowed to be taken out of Stillman's office and would not be released to the Executive Board or any other group unless there was a vote by the board to overturn this decision.

The Joel Commission had been extremely thorough in covering events from 1972 to the present. They identified 800 potential witnesses and interviewed more than 175 of them. The Debevoise team had used over 6,000 hours to investigate and prepare the report. Even though I thanked them publicly, I privately sent each of the members of the commission a letter in appreciation of their commitment. I truly appreciated firsthand the seriousness and thoroughness of the report. In addition, I released a statement to the media, affirming; "We are distressed that behavior like this could have occurred within our organization. We sincerely apologize for the pain and suffering these young people experienced as a result of Rabbi Lanner's actions. We also want to apologize to the families of these young people who entrusted their children to us. We promise to use this sad event as an opportunity to ensure that behavior such as this will never again occur within this organization."

The report and executive summary put an end to any speculation or discussion that the Commission's efforts would be a cover-up or whitewash. The report concluded that Lanner had "engaged in a pattern of inappropriate and abusive behavior, emotional, physical, and sexual, towards a number of NCSY students, causing enormous pain and suffering." The report further reached the conclusion that though Lanner alone had engaged in a pattern of abuse, some members of the lay and professional leadership of the OU and NCSY "made profound errors of judgement in their handling of Lanner throughout his career with NCSY." The report gave twelve examples of what it called "red flags" that should have warned the Union leadership of serious problems. No cover-up was found, but the report contended that Lanner's "inappropriate and crude behavior" should have led to his firing, yet there was no investigation.

The Joel Commission found that "a senior official misrepresented the 1989 Beit Din as being an affirmative approval for Lanner to continue his employment at NCSY." The commission further stated, "The description of the Beit Din (September 1989) . . . as a complete exoneration . . . was simply not true. . . .These inaccurate representations . . . continued over the course of the next ten years." It was suggested that the bet din was monitoring Lanner's employment. "In fact," said the commission, "the bet din, which ceased to exist as an institution after sending its psak (rabbinic ruling), did not have any continuing jurisdiction over the matter." In the commission report obviously the senior official was named.

The commission found that, over the years, the Union's professional staff had become the repository of accumulated information about Lanner and did not share it in a relevant manner with the lay officers. Different lay leaders knew bits and pieces, but there is no evidence to show that they were informed of the situation by the professionals.

The report found:
• Lanner engaged in emotional, physical and sexual inappropriate behavior toward NCSY students causing them "pain and suffering."

• Ten women testified that Lanner engaged in sexually abusive behavior toward them during his NCSY career.

• Lanner operated an unauthorized bank account in New Jersey, which he used for his sole discretion. He instructed donors that he solicited for NCSY programs to send the checks to his home. The report did not determine what became of the money.

• During working hours and with full knowledge of his superiors he engaged in financial transactions involving other OU employees and NCSY advisors and students through which he stood to profit personally.

• Members of the OU leadership knew or should have known of his conduct but took no effective action. This included four incidents in 1972, 1977, 1984 and 2000, when OU and NCSY officials were informed of specific sexual misconduct.

The commission report did offer some specific recommendations. It urged the organization to take "decisive and appropriate action" against those it specified as being responsible; and address "serious weaknesses" in the area of "overall management structure; procedures for staff selection, development, training, supervision and evaluation; procedures for financial accountability and internal audit; and lay oversight."

The committee of thirteen had two weeks to read and study the complete unabridged report. The Joel Commission planned to place the executive summary, which was fifty four pages long on the Internet on December 21. Our goal was to come to the executive board with specific recommendations before that date.

The commission refused to meet with us regarding the report until we had it in our hands. They maintained an extreme arms-length relationship with us, fearing that otherwise they would be accused of having been compromised in their conclusions. In truth, the only thing missing in the Executive public summary that was in the full report were the names of the OU personnel involved in their investigation and the narrative of salacious material.

The multifaceted issues raised by the Lanner episode carried many ethical ramifications under Jewish law, especially with regard to making the report public and engaging in possible "gossip" or "speaking ill of people." The Commission members were extremely concerned about these ramifications. They consulted with a noted OU rabbi, scholar, and professor of law, Yitzchak Breitowitz, who provided halachic guidance. He read the completed draft of the report and agreed to allow his name to be used in this regard.

One Executive Board member who opposed the work of the Commission publicly challenged me on at least two occasions to produce an opinion by a halachic leader concerning the issue of the possible spread of gossip about OU employees or lay leaders. Marcel Weber and I were equally concerned about that possibility, but were no less troubled by the fact that no Union leader had publicly considered the halachic implications of tolerating year after year of alleged abuse of children. During the long run up to the release of the Joel Commission report, Marcel and I had discussed these issues with my own Rav and spiritual adviser, Rabbi Dr. Moshe Tendler of Yeshiva University. Tendler knew about the Lanner Affair in considerable detail; from newspaper accounts and through his relationship with former students, who were now coming forward with information.

Rabbi Tendler agreed to write a halachic opinion, which basically stated that when individuals had "knowledge of physical or sexual abuse of NCSY participants (they) cannot remain in the organization." Similarly, he found that employees who "violated their fiduciary obligations should . . .be given the opportunity to resign," and then the Commission findings should "be sealed." During the course of the deliberations of the committee of thirteen, Avi Blumenfeld, a member of the group, and I met with an advisory panel of the Monsey Beit Din that in essence reinforced the goals laid down by Rabbi Tendler.

Despite these strong feelings, which I fully shared, those of us in the committee of thirteen decided during our study of the commission report that it contained no smoking gun, at least in the sense that there was nothing there that could be the basis for action against any former or present member of the Union professional staff, except, of course, Lanner himself. As for the two principal players, Rabbi Stolper was about to retire, so his situation was basically moot. The big issue was whether or not Rabbi Butler should be allowed to continue as executive vice president given the circumstances concerning Lanner that had taken place under his professional command. The committee of thirteen was not able to agree on a course of action concerning him.

The committee of thirteen did decide that there was nothing in the report that disqualified President-elect Harvey Blitz, a former youth commission chairman, or any of the new officers from assuming office on January 1, as planned.

While Butler's partisans were putting up a stiff fight from within the Union to help him retain his position, we were coming under tremendous pressure from the outside to take a decisive act to show that someone inside the organization was accountable for what had happened. Every day in the wake of the release of the executive summary, I was receiving dozens of e-mails, letters, and phone calls. Some were unsigned, but all were extremely angry. Their anger was directed at the OU, but more specifically, at our two senior employees, Butler and Stolper. The *Jewish Week* ran a front page article by Gary Rosenblatt entitled "Fate of Top OU Leaders In Limbo," speculating as to whether Butler or any other OU leader would be dismissed as a result of the findings.

For my part, I was determined that these public demands not be the cause for irrational or unjustified actions against Rabbi Butler or any other individuals, but also that we look the facts as presented by the Joel Commission and do what was best for the organization. Yet try as I could to complete the deliberations of the committee of thirteen by December 31, the late issuance of the report and the closeness to the biannual convention, which ran from Dec 28-30 in Rye Brook, NY, made that impossible. Furthermore, as noted, my hopes that the committee of thirteen would be able to come to a unanimous decision proved naïve, as did my hopes that we would be able to keep our deliberations secret.

Had this occurred in private industry probably four or five professionals and a few lay people would have voluntarily submitted their resignations or be fired as soon as the newspaper story came out. However, absent specific Joel Commission recommendations, such was not the case.

In the end no lay person was ever asked to retire and the committee of thirteen wound up discussing two main issues – the fate of Rabbi Butler and the fate of the full report. As I noted Rabbi Stolper retired December 31, 2000.

While I initially felt that it would not be in the interests of the Union or the general community to release the full report I was concerned that the total failure to hold any top professionals accountable would cost us dearly.

There was talk of a compromise with Rabbi Butler taking on a new role. However, I realized no new top administrator could enter the Union and function with Butler holding the title of Executive Vice-President as was suggested by some.

The *Jewish Week* and other papers kept up the pressure for a change in leadership. "If OU leaders stay, critics may leave" was the January 5, 2001 headline. Some of Butler's friends allegedly were whispering in his ear to hang tough. If so, I believe they misled him. They felt that once I left the presidency the story would die down. However, it was not that simple. Synagogue groups, rabbinical groups and the press maintained the pressure incessantly via e-mail, phone and community meetings.

On January 3, 2001, Murray Sragow, a leader of the New Jersey region of NCSY and an activist in an e-mail campaign told the Jewish Telegraphic Agency "I don't think that this philosophy (of turning a blind eye because of Lanner's ability to inspire) is going to change as long as Rabbi Butler continues to be around." He continued,"I'm very concerned that at the end of the day, it's all going to be like moving deck chairs on the Titanic."

The discussions and caucusing within the committee of thirteen continued throughout the biennial convention and beyond as I assumed the title of Chairman of the Board.

I looked upon my role as president not in a personal sense but as one who had at the end of the day to answer to the broad Orthodox Jewish community, and, specifically, to the leadership of the synagogues and individual members of the OU. My job was to save the Union and not allow further *chilul hashem* (desecration of God's name). I could not allow my personal feelings to absolve me of my responsibilities. I cannot say everyone followed that approach.

As the convention ended and my presidency over, I was sad that we did not complete the task of reporting to the Board. The committee of thirteen was deadlocked.

Finally I went to a member of the Joel Commission and asked bluntly "could the Union survive the publication of the entire report?" He answered affirmatively.

On January 6, 2001, hours before leaving on a long-delayed two-week trip to Hong Kong with Sheila, I finally bit the bullet. I sent a fax to each member of the committee of thirteen, calling for the immediate release of the full Joel Commission report. It made clear that if the committee of thirteen refused to take that step I was prepared upon my return from vacation to make a formal presentation either to the Executive Board or to the Board of Directors, which I now headed.

In the fax, I noted that I had received two anguished phone calls from a woman who had two children who had allegedly been abused by Lanner. The woman had informed me that despite being devoutly Orthodox and a supporter of OU-affiliated institutions in her community, she had agreed to be interviewed by an ABC video magazine about what Lanner had done to her children and had decided to join in legal action against the OU unless there was a change at the top of the professional staff of the Union.

By the time I returned to New York two weeks later, Rabbi Butler had resigned as executive director. Butler's resignation took the steam out of the political pressure the new President faced, thereby making it possible for the OU to avoid releasing the full commission report.

In his letter of resignation, Rabbi Butler wrote, "I firmly believe that the appropriate recommendations of the NCSY special commission must be implemented within a movement wholly united in its resolve to rise above the fray. The pursuit of that resolve must begin at the top." Butler said that his decision to resign was intended "to prevent the divisiveness and rancor that threaten the mission of the OU. To my mind, the mission is paramount and far outweighs any personal considerations."

The small cadre of top officers running the show at the OU after January 1, 2001 were furious at me firstly for forming and supporting the Joel Commission and for Rabbi Butler's subsequent resignation. They quickly moved to make me pay a steep personal price for what many considered my treachery in going public with a call for full disclosure. They did this by cold-shouldering me for the next two years and preventing me from exercising any responsibility at the OU. Even though I had just officially become chairman of the Board of Directors, a prestigious post that is customarily given to OU presidents upon their retirement, I quickly discovered that for two years I had been almost totally cut out of the OU organizational loop. I was never informed of a single committee meeting, nor consulted on any but a few issues in which I happened to have been involved in before.

Many of my friends who had worked closely with me and supported the work of the Joel Commission during the frenzied final six months of my presidency, such as Marcel Weber, were similarly isolated. This would not have mattered so much if the new leadership had shown vision or leadership. Unfortunately, after witnessing Butler's resignation, the new leaders seemed animated by a desire for revenge against those long time loyal backers of the Union who had supported the Joel Commission and urged leadership change if the organization was to survive. I was number one on that list.

Several days after meeting with Blitz in February 2001, in which I offered to undertake any assignment he required for the Union, I sent him a letter that read: "I am disturbed by our conversation in which you point out the hard feelings of a group of officers regarding Rabbi Butler's disposition. While I acknowledge this problem, I believe it is your task as our president not to (divide) the Union leadership into two camps, but to force everyone to work together for a common goal. The war is over... The world must see a united, vigorous Union leadership working on reorganization and the strengthening of programs."

In the wake of Butler's resignation, there was no effective professional leadership at the helm of the OU for twelve months and little evident sense of urgency about finding someone. Initially, when I first approached Blitz and asked whether in my role as chairman of the board and former president, I could join the search committee for a successor to Butler, he agreed. But in mid-March, when I told him—as a courtesy—that I had been selected to be executive vice president of the Religious Zionists of America, and would assume that position on July 1, 2001, he responded that he had already been informed of this by others. They had also recommended that I should not be allowed to serve on the search committee, since this would constitute a "conflict of interest."

I asked Blitz if the people who made that statement had wanted me to serve on the search committee before my choice as RZA executive vice president. He answered candidly that they had not. Nevertheless, I was taken off the committee, even though its report was initially intended to be ready in six weeks—long before I began my tenure at RZA. As it happened, when the new executive vice president, Rabbi Dr. Tzvi Hersh Weinreb of Baltimore, was finally chosen in January 2002, I was not informed about the selection until hours before the announcement ran in the *Jewish Week*.

At the May, 2001 meeting of the Executive Board, two senior

officers stood up and asked that I resign as chairman of the board of the OU because of the conflict with my new position which I was to assume July 1, 2001. When I asked what the conflict was, since I had not been given a single assignment by the OU president that could possibly conflict with that position, they had no answer. Julius Berman took the floor and totally demolished the arguments of the two individuals, who dropped their planned onslaught against me. Therefore, I remained as Chairman of the Board even though much of the top leadership of the OU continued to refuse to have any contact with me beyond saying "hello."

At the annual Orthodox Union Dinner in May 2001, honoring our dear friends Naomi and Harvey Wolinetz, my sole assignment was reading the plaque to the Wolinetzes—at their request. I felt like singing out loud, "What a Difference a Year Makes." At the previous annual dinner, held May 21, 2000, I had been the guest of honor and Keter Shem Tov awardee and received numerous accolades from the dais. It was only one month later, on June 23, that the *Jewish Week* article entitled "Stolen Innocence" started a chain of events that turned the Union and many lives topsy-turvy.

In retrospect, I consider the two steps I took: a) the appointment of the Joel Commission, and b) faxing the fateful memo to the committee of thirteen on January 6, 2001 to have been well worth the price I have had to pay. I have the solace of following the dictates of my conscience. I know in my heart that I did the right thing; not only for myself but for the whole Orthodox community. This was especially true for those young people who were physically violated by Lanner and the much larger number of people whose faith in the moral integrity of the OU was shaken by the terrible revelations in the *Jewish Week*.

As I look back over the last tumultuous six months of my presidency, I feel both sadness and pride. I believe that the decisions I made saved the Orthodox Union by stabilizing a terrible situation. Though many will never completely trust the Union again, others will come back and get involved. I know that the thoroughness and openness of the commission's report enabled many angry individuals, including some exposed to Lanner, to greet the report with a sense of closure and to look to the future in a new light. Wherever I go in the orthodox or non-orthodox community, the secular or chasidic world, people I barely know come over to me to congratulate me and thank me for living up to my conscience as President of the OU and saving it. Ultimately,

I would rather be ethical than popular. People are incredulous when told that the current leadership has treated me thusly.

I believe NCSY has the potential to be a much-greater organization than it has been in the past. From the very beginning, as soon as news of Lanner's alleged misconduct came to the fore, we instituted new guidelines and set up committees to train our personnel properly at every level. Within weeks, we had a new set of codes and guidelines for our summer camps regarding the interaction of counselors and teachers with students at every level. We also began arranging our programs so that students would have an ombudsman—and be able to complain immediately and on an ongoing basis should they feel they've been harassed.

On the financial level, the Lanner Affair motivated us to hasten the centralization of our fiscal program for all our regions. This process had been worked on even before the scandal broke, but after it did I was determined that the process be completed. No longer would an individual have a checkbook that he or she could control without the knowledge of the national office.

While some charges against Lanner and some in the OU hierarchy who knew of his behavior were reasonably proven, it was saddening to witness the reactions of a large section of the public. They were prepared to attack a major organization with a hundred year record of accomplishment on the basis of innuendo and a newspaper story without waiting for clarifications or the other side of the story. Despite the fact that thousands upon thousands of young people had come through NCSY better people, and despite all of the major accomplishments of the Union, one or two stories in the *Jewish Week* caused people to turn against us and for sources of major funding to dry up. The public showed little willingness to allow individuals or the larger organization to prove their innocence or to have their day in court. The written word in our society has the ability to charge, indict, and convict—and there is a certain sadness to that.

The Union is made up of so many wonderful people and volunteers who give their time for a worthwhile cause at great personal expense in time and finances. They surely deserve better. I do not know how many institutions, Jewish or secular, private or public, could have undergone the scrutiny we did for eight months—to have a team made up of individuals such as Bruce Yannett going through bank records and conducting

6,000 hours of examination of witnesses, against a backdrop of newspaper articles attacking us with innuendos and half-truths. Despite it all, I believe the Union came out tarnished but whole. There is no doubt in my mind that had we not appointed the Commission, we would have been left with a festering sore that would have made it all but impossible for the OU to function.

On March 21, 2001, Rabbi Lanner was indicted by a grand jury in Monmouth County, N.J. Two female students charged that he sexually molested them while principal at the Hillel High School in Deal. Nothing in the trial related to his function at NCSY or the OU. As I write these words in late June 2002, Lanner has just been found guilty of endangering the welfare of both girls, the most serious charge. In addition, he was convicted of aggravated criminal sexual contact and sexual contact against one of the girls, but was acquitted of those charges against the other.

He is now awaiting sentencing as well as the outcome of appeals in the case. He faces a maximum of twenty years in prison on the two endangering convictions, as well as up to $300,000 in fines. However, court experts said they expect Lanner's eventual prison term will be considerably less, given that this is a first offense and given his standing as a clergyman. As the sentencing date comes closer, I hope that Lanner, an individual with a troubled personality, will not receive a sentence that is harsher than warranted because of the impact of the Catholic Church scandals.

Meanwhile, at the OU, not even one lay leader has been forced to give up his or her position as a result of the Commission report. It seems to me that the appointment of Rabbi Dr. Tzvi Hersh Weinreb of Baltimore in January 2002 as new Executive Vice President presents the organization with an opportunity for healing and coalescence, provided that the new top professional moves quickly to bring together the various factions, including those made outcasts since the 2000 convention.

Weinreb must reverse a downward cycle begun in 2001 characterized by a marked drop in contributions to the Union. During that year, the Development and Public Relations departments lost their directors, and as noted before, a number of gifted and renowned lay people resigned from leadership positions at the OU and NCSY. How rapidly Weinreb masters the professional bureaucracy will determine whether he is successful. The fiscal success of the Union these past two years is predicated on Kashruth income rather than individual contributions.

Certainly Weinreb has a tough road ahead of him although his talents as a psychologist and a master teacher may help smooth his way. Sadly, he has so far chosen not to speak with me assumably out of a sense of "Union political correctness" regarding Union issues even though as president for six years I have much knowledge and insight about the organization. He has concentrated on issues that he feels are his strengths such as "parenting" and "family values." Perhaps we will have to wait until a future OU administration realizes that its mandate must include confronting the issues that only a national organization such as the OU can undertake, ie Jewish Unity, Israel, World Jewry, and the future of Orthodoxy (to name a few). Their leadership and vision is critical for the success of the our people. For the Orthodox Union, the jury is still out but the clock is rapidly ticking.

Normally immediate past presidents are nominated and elected for three two-year terms as Chairman of the Board. I chose not to stand for re-election in December 2002, for it would have been ludicrous to serve under the conditions that existed in 2001-2.

CHAPTER NINETEEN
Summing Up

I have been truly blessed with a wonderful life, and I thank G-d every day for what he has allowed me to accomplish. Still, without wishing to sound conceited, I feel that I have made the most of the opportunities that presented themselves. From childhood on, I always aimed high in my life striving towards goals and ambitions, yet stayed in touch with the realities of the world around me. To some who knew me in my youth, my goals appeared exalted and even unobtainable. Yet I never sought to perform miracles, but instead followed a coherent, well-thought-through "feet on the ground" path to success.

While I have worked hard to achieve financial success, I have also endeavored to broaden my horizons beyond that goal. Knowledge and intellectual stimulation have always been important to me. For example, when I was in Yeshiva College as a pre-med student I requested permission to sign up for a course in English Constitutional and Political History that was only open to pre-law students. Dr. Simeon Gutterman, the college dean and teacher of that course initially turned down my request to register for his class, but then inquired as to why I wanted to take a course that was unrelated to my field of study. I responded by citing a Latin aphorism, "Nil Humani A Me Alienum Puto" (Nothing human do I consider alien). When he heard that, Professor Gutterman's demeanor changed instantly from perplexed disapproval to warm acceptance, and he abruptly reversed his decision. "You are going to love this course Mr. Ganchrow!" he said enthusiastically. In fact, I did love the course, learned a great deal, and received two A's in the process.

Ever since I was a child, I have been aware of the problems and injustices of the world around me. As I matured, I focused my energy and my will to make the world a better place (tikkun olam) through my work as a practicing physician and as an activist and leader within the American Jewish community. Early on, I realized that even though our community is composed of many individuals who are sophisticated, articulate and intelligent, most of us have become so caught up in the rat race of daily life that we have delegated to Jewish organizational leaders—people we did not elect and whose names we rarely even know—to speak on our behalf on issues of public policy. Unfortunately, this tendency often accrues to the detriment of true community needs.

I have gone through life as an "Orthodox Jew;" a label that has never felt like a burden to me. To the contrary I am extremely proud to be a "modern Orthodox Jew."

I have been fortunate to maintain a loving, warm and open relationship with Sheila and my children. In doing so, I was simply mimicking the love and warmth I experienced from my own parents as a child. I was blessed that I was able to marry a girl who was confident and intelligent enough in her own right that she gave me not only the space but the encouragement to fulfill my desire to become an activist and leader at the highest levels of Jewish communal life.

Although I was fortunate to achieve a modicum of success as well as entree into the highest levels of political power, it never occurred to me to try to emulate the contemporary mores of secular American society—as presented on MTV—or to encourage my own children to do so. I have tried to be friendly with every individual I have met throughout my career as a physician or activist, but I have never felt the need to add to the small group of close friends I have maintained all of my life.

Still sometimes I have a sense of disbelief about the exciting places I have visited and the extraordinary people I have had the privilege to meet during my career as a pro-Israel advocate. As a young man, I would never have imagined that some day I would be sitting opposite the President of Turkey discussing his government's policy toward Israel, or that I would have the opportunity to travel to Uzbekistan to meet with that country's president and his cabinet. Forty years ago, I would never have dared to dream that I would one day be invited by the Governor of New York to march alongside him down Fifth Avenue in the annual Salute to Israel parade.

If anyone had told me at the height of the Cold War that during the 1990's I would visit the Kremlin and at a particular meeting sit as the head of a delegation of American Jewish leaders opposite the Foreign Minister of Russia, I surely would have laughed my head off at the implausibility of it all. As it turned out, I laughed even harder when, in the course of that meeting, the Russian Foreign Minister asked me if I was a Reform Jew. When I responded that I was the President of the Orthodox Union, the Foreign Minister apologized but explained that my lack of a beard and the fact that I was wearing a light colored suit and shirt rather than what he considered the black uniform of Orthodoxy totally confused him. Obviously, much of the world still has a lot to learn about the varied makeup of American Orthodoxy.

Sheila and I have been blessed with bright, respectful and loving children, Malkie, Ari and Elli; each of whom in their individual ways has followed the calling of service to the Jewish community as well as the teachings of our Torah in their private and public lives. Paul, our son-in-law, is a neurosurgeon who brings the entire family great pride each year when he completes a Tractate in Talmud and invites the family, friends and his rabbi to share in this event. He and Malkie are active in both their local yeshiva, where she serves as president of the PTA and the board of the synagogue. Our sons Ari and Elli learn Talmud together despite the time pressures of their respective law practices. Ari's wife Banji is the president of the synagogue sisterhood and both Banji and Ari are active in their new elementary day school. Ari, likewise, is active in the synagogue and on the Boards of the OU and the Religious Zionists. Immediately upon starting to earn salaries, Elli and his wife Brina, who recently became a CPA, have as our other children dedicated ten percent of their combined salary to charity. I am confident that Brina and Elli, our young newlyweds, will follow in their older siblings' footsteps and become very involved in their new community, North Woodmere.

My wife and I have also been blessed with wonderful friends. Every Saturday afternoon for as long as I can remember, a group of our closest friends have gathered together at the home of Naomi and Harvey Wolinetz for an informal get together at Shalos Seudot, the meal between afternoon and evening services. The affection and camaraderie of this group has helped me keep a sense of proportion about my dealings in the corridors of power in Washington and Manhattan. In addition to the talk about Torah, there is a general easiness and conviviality among the participants in those wonderful get-togethers that can only take place among old and trusted friends.

Often I am the target of much good natured ribbing and kibitzing, that is done in an affectionate way that reminds me that, with all that I have witnessed and accomplished in the world of politics, I am still simply one of the guys. I will always treasure the friendship of Murray Appelbaum, Avi Blumenfeld, Shishie Fein, Shaya Gordon, Steve and Ralph Rothschild, Elliot Schreiber, and Jack Siegel who are regulars at this Shabbos afternoon get together at Naomi and Harvey's.

Lois Blumenfeld is a close friend who deserves special mention. Over the years, whenever my name was mentioned in the *Rockland Journal News*, she conscientiously collected all of the clippings. She did this ostensibly to send the articles to my mother, but even after my mother became blind Lois continued to provide the clippings to me for my personal scrapbook. Nowadays, Lois sends me an email every day that is an amalgam of jokes and serious news items about Israel.

I have always wanted to share with others the knowledge and expertise I have acquired during my life. Over the years I wrote 19 papers for surgical magazines and periodicals. I have also enjoyed writing on Jewish themes and have especially enjoyed writing and publishing my books on sheva brochas and circumcision. The first book was especially well received by the Orthodox public and I was happy that all earnings from the two books have been donated to NCSY.

I love teaching as well as writing. Many of those who attended my lectures in medicine or Jewish issues complimented me for transmitting complicated material in a logical and illuminating way. I brought the same approach to my teaching of Jewish themes, which I sometimes was able to share with my fellow physicians. When Rabbi Adin Steinsaltz's Talmudic commentary was published in English by Random House, I volunteered to teach his works to a small group of physicians at Good Samaritan Hospital; a Catholic institution in Suffern, New York where I served for two years as chief of surgery. I teach my Talmud class once a week to eight physicians; of whom only three can read Hebrew.

I retired from surgery after I had been teaching my Talmud class for two years and naturally stopped giving those early morning classes. On the occasion of our last class, my students were kind enough to present me with a set of cufflinks as a token of appreciation. A few months later, however, a member of the group called me and said that all of them badly missed their study of Talmud and wanted to continue it. I found it impossible to reject their request and have been going to Good Samaritan one morning a week ever since to teach them. It has been a labor of love for me to prepare for my Talmud instruction each week as well as to discuss the weekly Torah portion with my students. Hopefully, I am successful in making them understand that our ancient faith is also a living religion and totally relevant to modern life. My students, Drs. Bernie Berson, Beatrice Bloom, Lewis Bobroff, Harry Boltin, Larry Katz, Richard Kroll, Harvey Peck, and Michael Resnick have allowed me to perform the mitzvah of teaching others Torah.

I have invited such rabbinical luminaries as Rabbi Moses Tendler, Rabbi Yaacov Haber, and Rabbi Nachum Muschel to teach my group in our Succah during the Succot holiday. Last year, I presented to each student a knitted *kippah* from Israel, with their individual names in Hebrew which they wear to class.

To be sure, I have had disappointments in my life as well as successes, although many of those setbacks later turned out to be for the better. Being compelled to serve in Vietnam and to confront the horrifying face of war felt like a disaster to Sheila and myself when I was first shipped off to the conflict. In retrospect, however, my year in the war zone ultimately helped to shape my life in many positive ways.

Sheila helped me to deal with my sense of betrayal of post Lanner by offering me a perspective that made sense to me. She said, "Make believe the OU was your first wife but the marriage broke down. You did love her very much, but now the time has come to move on." I am doing so, with the hope that in the near future new leadership will re-inspire the loyalty of the lay backers who have been the backbone of the organization for decades.

After leaving the OU, I soon realized that I have too much talent and energy to allow myself to sit passively on the sidelines. My arthritis would not allow me to return to surgery.

Therefore, when the opportunity came to lead the Religious Zionist of America (RZA) in a professional position, under the presidency of Rabbi Simcha Krauss, an organization that is many times smaller and less well known than the OU, I felt that this was a challenge I could not refuse to take on. Perhaps my reasons for taking on the Executive Vice Presidency of the RZA, an organization that has been described as virtually moribund by many people, are best summed up in my response to a letter I received from my dear old friend, Rabbi Maurice Wohlgelenter, a former professor of English at Yeshiva and City College. Upon hearing that I had taken that position he wrote me a letter consisting of the following sentence: "Dear Mendy, Why? Why? Why? Fondly, The Reb." My answer was "Dear Reb, Why Number One; Sheila told me to get out of the house and get a job. Why Number Two; I have never participated in the mitzvah of *tchiyat hamaytim* (resurrection of the dead). Why, Number Three; I love a challenge." And then I added a Why Number Four; "Why not?" and closed with "Fondly Mendy."

How long I decide to serve as Executive Vice President of the RZA will depend on the state of my health and the satisfaction I am getting from the job, as well as the level of support I receive from the organization's lay leadership. I feel that the organization retains relevance because I believe there is a need to build an umbrella for religious Zionism in the United States that consists of education, youth camping, aliyah and adult services. I never forget that the Religious Zionist movement is one hundred years old and has a great tradition. The first eighteen months have witnessed a much needed reorganization, renaissance and growth of the RZA.

On September 11, 2001 the world changed forever. That terrible event made vividly clear— although to many of us there had never been much doubt—that it is not possible for Orthodox Jews to wrap themselves in a cocoon and avoid getting involved in the world that we live in, as flawed and imperfect as it is. Not only must we do our part to help protect this country—and Israel as well—but we must rededicate ourselves to embracing and loving our fellow human beings and reaching out to our fellow Jews. Our goal must be to elevate our brethren to even a minimal attachment to our traditions. Perhaps many will reject our effort to share with them the beauty of *yiddishkeit*. Some however, will appreciate the gift we are offering and understand that there can be a better tomorrow based upon Jewish education. Those of us who are Orthodox should never exhibit a sense of smugness or triumphalism toward our less observant Jewish brothers and sisters. There but for the grace of G-d go I.

Our grandchildren, now 4th generation Americans, are absorbing the sweet waters of Torah in their homes, synagogues, day schools and communities. This is what King Solomon referred to as the bond of continuity that speaks to an unbroken chain of tradition. It is our secret weapon.

Our rabbis teach that each of us has been given an assignment in this world; a very specific assignment that can be carried out by no other person. I hope that I have carried out my own assignment according to the instructions of my maker. I pray that our grandchildren Zachary, Jake, Carlie and Tamara Ratzker and Jack, Jonah, Matthew and Rachel Ganchrow, will find value and direction for their own lives in the events I have described.

Selected Writings

THE JERUSALEM POST
JULY 28, 1991

A Taste of Their Own Medicine for Boycotters
Mandell Ganchrow, Marvin Jacob, and William Rapfogel

The Arab economic boycott continues to hurt Israel economically. But world Jewry can help fight the boycott by using its own economic clout, as was illustrated recently in the case of Baxter International, a major U.S. supplier of health-care products.

In 1988, Baxter agreed to build a facility in Syria, and divested itself of its Israeli plant. The company was thus removed from the Arab boycott list.

Baxter has been accused of surrendering to the Arab boycott, a charge which it vigorously denies. A report by independent counsel, commissioned by Baxter's board of directors, allegedly found nothing illegal or improper with the company's decision. But Baxter refused to release the full report to its own stockholders or to Jewish organizations. The allegations are under investigation by the U.S. Commerce and Justice Departments. Numerous Jewish organizations and individuals protested publicly and attended stockholders meetings.

The Institute of Public Affairs of the Orthodox Union became involved because we felt that a different approach should be tried, mainly economic pressure. A hospital that one of us is affiliated with purchases $3.5 million worth of Baxter products a year. The administration of this Catholic hospital enthusiastically promised to aid any effort to defeat the Arab boycott.

This hospital is a member of a large buying group of about 40 hospitals with huge contracts with Baxter. The buying group's administrator likewise was prepared to cooperate in a joint effort to send a message to Baxter regarding its treatment of Israel. These feelings were intensified after The Wall Street Journal published an article on the Baxter affair. Baxter International has total annual sales of $8.01 billion.

We organized a campaign to educate physicians regarding Baxter's actions. The campaign was to start out in the New York metropolitan area and eventually include the entire U.S.

Physicians are free to act in accordance with their own moral interests. American law permits an individual to boycott a product for moral reasons, such as participation by a major corporation in an illegal boycott of a U.S. ally. Such was the case when American Jews acted against Mexico, after it voted in favor of the UN Zionism-is-Racism resolution. Tourism to Mexico was greatly hampered and it did not take long for Mexico to renounce its vote.

Last May, on the day after Shavuot, the Orthodox Union's Institute for Public Affairs scheduled a meeting with 100 physicians, from the New York metropolitan area, representing most area hospitals, to discuss the Baxter issue. The participants were to be educated as to the economic opportunities available to those who wished to protest the boycott in a meaningful way.

But the meeting was cancelled at Baxter's request and a delegation of the Institute met instead with senior management of Baxter International. Our intentions were made quite clear to Baxter in a very open, informal and frank meeting.

A few weeks later, we received official notification, in advance of the public anouncement, that Baxter would withdraw its plans to build a plant in Syria. We do not know precisely how much impact our actions had on Baxter's decision, but, in our opinion, Baxter was aware of the potential economic power of our considerable membership across America, which includes a large number of practicing physicians.

We applaud Baxter's decision. More importantly, what happened with Baxter is an example to other companies that entertain the idea of submitting to the Arab boycott. It demonstrates that American citizens; who support Israel, will not permit companies that they patronize, to harm Israel's vital economic interests without protesting by word and deed.

It is time that a list of those who boycott Israel be made public and periodically published and updated: Organizations such as Hadassah,B'nai B'rith and others should send out a quarterly update to their members. Select companies should be singled out on an ongoing basis. The world Jewish public needs to make its own choice as to whether it will sit idly by or force such companies to reconsider.

A famous marketing slogan in the U.S. is "an educated consumer is our best customer." That is correct, The pro-.Israel consumer should be made fully aware of who is willing to stand up to the Arab boycott and who "plays along." History has shown that if the pro-Israel community is educated in the proper manner, it will make the right decisions. Educated consumers are not the boycotter's best customers.

Marvin Jacob chairs its Law and Legislation Commission. William Rapfogel is the Institute's executive director.

Letter to Yitzhak Rabin, Prime Minister of Israel
AUGUST 28, 1995

Dear Mr. Prime Minister:

We write to you out of the sense of connection that we all feel with you as the elected leader of the State of Israel. Yehuda HaLevi lamented: *Libi Ba'Mizrach V'Ani B'Sof Maarav - My heart is in the East as I stand far to the West.* Whenever we stand in prayer we face our homeland and Yerushalayim, our center of spirituality, sanctity, and national sovereignty. No news report regarding Israel goes unheard throughout the Jewish world. Israel is mentioned and a silence descends upon the listeners. . . a silence that has in recent times led all too often to anguish, tears, and grief. Certainly your pain as the leader of our Jewish state, Mr. Prime Minister, extends to depths that exceeds all other. You have valiantly defended our state and have devoted your life to its security.

But our common grief seems to know no bounds. We stood together on the White House lawn in support of the search for peace. We stood together in the Jordanian-Israeli desert in support of the search for peace. Yet the cause so dear to all has come at a price so high to the people of Israel.

* We stood together in the belief that all Israel would finally find peace after the long reign of terror. Instead, many of our brethren, modern-day-pioneers, have been portrayed as pariahs in their own land. Is this the price for peace?

* We stood together in the belief that the soldiers and police of Israel would cease to be in harms way. Instead, they have been exposed to greater danger. Is this the price for peace?

* We stood together in the belief that Yerushalayim Hashlaima would be a permanent reality. Instead, we have witnessed the burgeoning Palestinian governmental presence throughout the holy city. Is this the price for peace?

* We stood together in the belief that Yassir Arafat in shaking hands with you, had indeed changed and would live up to his commitments contained in the Declaration of Principles and subsequent agreements.

Instead, we hear him speak to his people in rallying cries of Jihad-Holy War. Is this the price for peace?

*   We stood together in the belief that the agreement process would bring protection. Instead, Israel has given and given and protection seems to be a dream of the past. Is this the price for peace?

Od Lo Avdah Tikvateinu - we have not lost our hope. We will never lose hope.

Increasingly we ask ourselves, *what are we to do? How are we to react?* We have always respected the government position on the security and safety of the State of Israel. That unwavering support continues as we lobby our Congress and Administration to maintain the strong U.S.-Israel relationship and a militarily secure State of Israel.

But Mr. Prime Minister, should we not feel the searing threat of civil strife? How can we silently witness the pain of a citizenry whose national fabric and vital interests are being torn asunder? Do we dare not express our concern for the 150,000 residents who followed the pleas of your and previous governments to till the soil *b'eretz lo zruah - in the barren, implanted area of the Holy Land?*

President Weizman has repeatedly called for a pause in the process and a reevaluation of the process. While our hearts cry, we have no right to decide the fate of Israel. We do, however, have the right – indeed, the duty - to express concern for Acheinu Bnai Yisrael - our brothers and sisters.

We therefore respectfully urge you to heal the wounds of a fractured nation as you continue your search for peace. Bring your people alongside you in your quest. Slow your process as you reach out to a nation in despair. In the name of Jewish unity and destiny, we plead with you to use your resolve and to unite our nation through a dialogue with all elements of Israeli society in order to bring about a sense of unity that the Jewish people so desperately require before proceeding further.

Shlomo Hamelech spoke of men of strength as those who were victorious on the battlefield, then compassionate with their nemesis after the battle had been won. Imagine the strength he would ascribe to a man who wins in the field, settles with the vanquished, and at the same time shows the wisdom and strength to galvanize his own people.

May G-d give you the strength to achieve these ends.

Respectfully,

Mandell I. Ganchrow, MD, President
Rabbi Raphael B. Butler, Executive Vice President

HOUSE COMMITTEE ON INTERNATIONAL RELATIONS
SEPTEMBER 20, 1995

Written Statement to the Committee

Mr. Chairman, Members of the Committee, I wish to express my sincerest appreciation to you for inviting me to testify on this most important topic. My name is Dr. Mendy Ganchrow. I am the President of the Union of Orthodox Jewish Congregations. I am here to represent seven Orthodox organizations: Amit Women, Emunah of America, National Council of Young Israel, Poale Agudath Israel, Rabbinical Council of America, Religious Zionists of America and the Union of Orthodox Jewish Congregations of America.

We are all members of the Conference of Presidents of Major American Jewish Organizations, as well as active members of AIPAC. We have all supported the search for Middle East peace. We stood together on the White House Lawn a little over two years ago in support of the search for peace. We stood together in the Jordanian-Israeli desert in support of the search for peace. Yet, this search has come at a cost so dear to the people of Israel. The continued call for jihad in Arabic by Mr. Arafat, the poor performance of the Palestinian Authority, including its failure to return even one terrorist requested by the Israeli authorities in accordance with the Oslo Accord, the continued political activities of Palestinian Authority affairs in Jerusalem and Orient House in contradiction to the Oslo Accord, the failure to disarm the members of Hamas, the continued increase in horrendous terrorist attacks all require and demand that we place the tightest restrictions on U.S. aid to the Palestinians.

A newly published American Jewish Committee study indicates that two-thirds of American Jews are opposed to any American aid to the Palestinians. This is despite the fact that the overwhelming majority support the peace process.

The majority of our organizations have joined the Conference of Presidents of Major American Jewish Organizations in supporting Helms-Pell, which strengthens the Middle East Peace Facilitation Act. However, we believe that there are some major loopholes which weaken this act and that require strengthening on the part of Congress. We have joined the Conference of Presidents in stressing the need for stronger language and additional safeguards to guarantee that the bill's intentions are carried out to the fullest.

We recommend that all the money that has been recommended by the Administration be placed into an escrow account for a period of six months during which the Palestinians and Mr. Arafat may prove their compliance with the Oslo agreement. If they live up to the accords, they could then be able to obtain the aid.

Our testimony is in the spirit of the AIPAC resolutions that call for total compliance on the part of Mr. Arafat before receiving U.S. funds. I quote the AIPAC policy statement of 1995 that "continues to support the Spector-Shelby-Lowey Amendment which ties U.S. funding to the Palestinians, to PLO compliance with its commitments.

AIPAC will be working with Congress to renew and greatly strengthen the Middle East Peace Facilitation Act in order to maximize its effectiveness as a tool in pressing for PLO compliance with its commitment to renounce and condemn terrorism recognize Israel and negotiate differences peacefully, prevent terrorism and prosecute terrorists, prevent incitement to violence, bar unauthorized forces, "Extradite terrorists to Israel, ensure that the Palestinian police cooperate with Israel's security forces, and amend the Palestinian covenant."

We must make the PLO accountable. The following should take place in order for the money to be appropriated. The failure to carry out these obligations would be cause for withholding aid, by law, not by "sense of Congress".

1- The PLO Charter must be renounced and repealed definitively. Declaring that it is superseded by events on the ground is not sufficient. We equate this charter with the "Zionism is Racism" resolution which was repealed at the insistence of the Congress of the United States and the citizens of this country, even though it was insinuated that the resolution was irrelevant. The PLO charter must be repealed. Each sentence and each word of it calls for the destruction of the State of Israel.

2- The failure to disarm Hamas, the presence of huge numbers of weapons held by individuals in the area controlled by the Palestinian Authority and the failure to stop new smuggling of arms into these areas cannot be tolerated. This should not be considered a violation of the "sense of Congress," but should be considered a legal cause for American aid to be terminated.

3- The Palestinian Authority must carry out the mandate of the Oslo Accord that terrorists who escape Israel must be returned when requested by Israel. To date, not a single terrorist has been returned.

4- Mr. Arafat and the members of his cabinet must stop talking of jihad, the destruction of Israel, the killing of Jews and the glorification of those who have killed Jews. Recent tapes of these statements by Arafat are available to every member of Congress. Arafat may not continue this incendiary rhetoric and still receive U.S. aid.

5- All Palestinian offices in Jerusalem, especially Orient House, which are there in contravention of the Oslo Accord should be closed. There is no reason why all political activity cannot take place in Jericho and Gaza as stated in the agreement.

6- The length of time that this act should be considered active should be 12 months or less in order to provide full opportunity to evaluate compliance. The time limit should not be placed at any point after the American or Israeli elections.

7- We believe that the Congress of the United States should investigate whether money given to the Palestinian Authority for housing and other purposes in Gaza and Jericho have been used illegally to buy housing and land within Jerusalem to create facts on the ground.

8- Finally, we believe that the GAO report which was commissioned to investigate whether or not the British claim that the PLO currently has $8 billion or more of illegal funds in various countries should be made public so that every member of Congress may have this information prior to voting. If it is found that the PLO has these illegal assets, we would strongly oppose any further financial assistance by the United States to the Palestinian Authority.

Mr. Chairman, we support the road to peace, but it cannot be won with American taxpayers' money going to support continued terrorism, jihad, and the undermining of the stability in this volatile area.

Finally, we would ask the Congress that any attempt by the Palestinian Authority to declare a Palestinian State should be automatic cause for cutting off all funds to them, runs contrary to the interests of America and would also destabilize the Middle East region.

Mr. Chairman, I thank you for your courtesy and your time.

THE JEWISH TELEGRAPHIC AGENCY
NOVEMBER 13, 1995

An Orthodox Response

Jewish tradition tells us that one should experience inner trepidation on the eve of Yom Kippur, that period of soul-searching when one's fate is in the hands of the Supreme Being. Since the horrible moment when I learned of the assassination of Prime Minister Rabin, I have experienced that same anguish.

The Orthodox Union's position is clear and unequivocal: We felt "shock and horror at the murder of Israeli Prime Minister Yitzhak Rabin. This reprehensible deed violates all principles of Torah and *Halakah,* Jewish Law, and constitutes a desecration of the name of the Almighty, *Chillul HaShem.* There is absolutely no way to justify such an act. It is unequivocally condemned by the Torah."

What is needed now is not finger pointing, but national soul searching, *Cheshbon Hanefesh.* We must find the crossroads where we parted

ways, where brothers ceased speaking the same language or appreci-
ating common goals and principles.

The Orthodox community, far from monolithic, has always encouraged debate. Every reasoned shade of political opinion is welcome. At
the last National Convention of the Orthodox Union, our guest speakers
Yossi Beilin and Ariel Sharon, represented both sides of Israel's political
spectrum. It is worthwhile to note that despite their diverse views, our
1,200 delegates listened respectfully to both presentations.

We have always supported the search for peace. Political discourse
and understanding are the keystones of our existence. We joined Prime
Minister Rabin on the White House lawn in 1993 and in the Arava with
King Hussein in 1994.

Along that road we grappled with many questions and concerns,
raising them in face to face discussions with Israeli officials from the
Prime Minister down. Our principle has always been never to attack
the Israeli government or its leaders personally. Any dissent on our
part has always been respectful, never yielding to extremism.

It was the Orthodox Union that issued repeated calls to lower the
tone of the inflammatory rhetoric; to avoid a kulturkampf that would
split our people. In order to make peace with Egypt, Menachem Begin
ordered the withdrawal from Sinai. It was the Orthodox Union that
called for unity.

More recently, we publicly condemned the statements of Rabbi
Hecht. In personal discussions with the Prime Minister we stressed
that the overwhelming majority of Orthodox Jews are not in any way
associated with such extremist and anti-Torah polemics.

This past August, we wrote an open letter to Prime Minister Rabin
acknowledging him as one who "valiantly defended our State and...
devoted (his) life to (its) security." In that letter, published in many
American Anglo-Jewish newspapers, as well as in the Jerusalem Post
and Ha'aretz in Israel, we lamented the "fractured nation" and endorsed President Ezer Weizman's call for a healing process.

"We plead with you," we wrote, "to unite our nation to dialogue
with all elements of Israeli society." Not one of those papers considered it newsworthy enough to comment on our effort to unite *all* segments of society. Our call to CNN informing them of our effort was
greeted with: "Call back when you are prepared to throw rocks." Are
only fringe elements of Orthodoxy worthy of coverage?

We have much to be proud of. . .

The leaders of Israel have repeatedly called for Aliyah. The Orthodox responded well out of proportion to their numbers.

They called on young people to visit Israel. We have responded by
sending our children for at least a year of study.

They called for tourism. There are few Orthodox Jews who haven't visited, many annually.

The leaders of world Jewry called for a battle against the 70% intermarriage rate. Fewer than 4% of Orthodox Day School students intermarry.

The most recent call is for "continuity." A study of Jewish history will show that we would not exist today without our rabbis and teachers.

Perhaps we did not do all we could have done. Did we pressure the extremist rabbis in our midst? Have we allowed the inflammatory headlines and radical accusations of our Orthodox press to go unchallenged? Just last week I was personally attacked in a full page "open letter" for refusing to promote civil disobedience in Israel and for promoting the Jerusalem 3000 celebration.

Have we failed to drive home to our children that the observance of mitzvot requires sensitivity?... that no one ever became a Sabbath observer by having stones thrown at his car?... that we must rather continue to open our homes to our fellow Jews to showcase the beauty, warmth and spirituality of Shabbat?

Have we failed to insist on moderation and civility in public discourse and condemn the tiny, but vocal minority who might actually condone murder without the knowledge and consent of their constituency?

There are enough challenges for all to confront. No one group is the sole repository of political wisdom, the vision of peace and security, or the only ones who have a claim to Eretz Yisrael. The cemeteries of Israel are filled with the remains of brave soldiers who knew no dogmas - just the love of the State of Israel and the people of Israel.

For the Jewish people to survive we must resolve to dialogue. Two days before the assassination, sitting with Gideon Meir, Assistant to the Foreign Minister, we discussed methods to create fruitful and effective dialogue.

Responding to this terrible act we have:

Scheduled a memorial to Prime Minister Rabin on the thirtieth day of his passing, the "Shloshim."

Pledged to work with acting Prime Minister Peres in an effort to bridge our "fractured" nation.

Extended an offer to dialogue to all elements in the political arena.

Begun work on an educational curriculum stressing our responsibility to fellow human beings, "Bein adam lechavero"

We reserve the right to continue to speak out in a responsible manner on issues of national and international importance. We will not refrain from responsible comment and redress.

The unity of the Jewish people remains our primary concern, above all else. We are prepared to look seriously at our shortcomings and take on added responsibility. We call on all of the segments of the House of Israel to join us.

WASHINGTON JEWISH WEEK
OCTOBER 23, 1997

Another view of the Zionist elections
An Orthodox bloc could have eclipsed the registered vote

The headlines trumpeted a Reform/Conservative victory in the Zionist elections. Indeed, a superficial reading of the results indicated that 48 percent of all registrants (identified as Reform) and 26 percent of all registrants (identified as Conservative) did vote for their respective slates. Now Reform and Conservative leaders are claiming that these results indicate a push for pluralism. But is that really the message? Could the headlines just have easily read, "Five million American Jews proclaim pluralism a non-issue?" or "Reform fall short of projected one million disgruntled voters?"

Last month, 80,000 Orthodox Jews gathered at various locations throughout the United States to participate in the Siyum Hashas (the celebration of the end of the 7 ½ year cycle of reading a page of the Talmud every day). Had these Jews chosen to register and vote, their bloc would have yielded more votes than the Reform and Conservative slates combined.

The agenda of the 80,000, plus spouses and adult children, many of whom were not present, just does not include pluralism. On the contrary, theirs is a unanimous vote for the 3,500-year-old Torah tradition. So why should the media assume that the 75,000 Reform and Conservative voters, who signed up as the result of an expensive voter registration campaign that included the hiring of a professional electoral consultant, represent the future of the Jewish people more than the 80,000 who sat and studied the Talmud but who did not register to vote?

In its coverage, the New York Times pointed out that out of some six million Jews in America, only 150,000 registered, and of those only 110,000 actually voted. Despite a massive campaign, the majority of the American Jewish community knows little about, and probably cares less, for the workings of the Jewish Agency. And of those who are in the know, some wonder privately, and sometimes even publicly, whether there is even a need for this government within a government.

The biggest losers in this election are, of course, the Labor and Likud parties that mistakenly allowed this election to take place. What a waste of millions of dollars that could have, and should have, been used for Jewish education.

The absence of Hadassah from the slate allowed the Reform leaders to fashion an expensive, one-issue campaign—claiming that the Orthodox are trying to delegitimize American Jewry. It is interesting that at a recent luncheon in Washington for Israeli President Ezer Weizman, I was approached by Reconstructionist and Reform Jews who wanted to know why the Orthodox are not answering the charges that they are trying to delegitimize Reform and Conservative Jews.

These non-Orthodox Jews heard their respective rabbis deride the Orthodox during High Holy Day sermons for claiming that Reform and Conservative Jews are not Jews. This is an unfair claim. While the Orthodox cannot accept revisions enacted by the Reform and Conservative movements, we never once questioned the authenticity of any halachically Jewish person, regardless of his or her affiliation.

The campaign of the religious Zionists was actually a non-campaign with expenditures totaling about $20,000. There were a few meetings attended by representatives of groups who felt that the costs of running a professional campaign could not be justified in the light of the needs of the Israeli and U.S. communities that they represent.

The Orthodox groups did not send videos to prospective registrants, import speakers from Israel or set up booths at shopping malls to register voters. If, as some people believe, the Reform spent $2 million on their campaign, then each vote cost $40.

The Reform and Conservative leadership has tried to convince the Israeli government that American Jewry is aflame over the conversion issue, that it is a source of tremendous anguish to millions of American Jews. But when given the opportunity to express themselves, where were these anguished millions? Apparently, the Reform and Conservative leadership has failed to convince its own constituents. How can it expect to convince the Israelis?

INTERMOUNTAIN JEWISH NEWS
NOVEMBER 28, 1997

The Oslo Peace Agreements—Have They Worked?

Approximately three days after Israel and the PLO announced their Oslo agreement, US Senator Harris Wofford (D-PA) led a small delegation, of which I was part, that met privately with then Prime Minister Yitzhak Rabin.

In the course of the discussion I asked Mr. Rabin what his rationale was in receiving Yassir Arafat at a time when he seemed to be politically "on the ropes."

I posited that three years down the road Mr. Arafat could be out of the picture and Rabin would then be positioned to deal with responsible members of the indigenous Palestinian leadership.

Rabin answered very simply: first and most important, left unchecked for three years the Hamas—terrorists with whom he could not reason—would defeat the PLO.

Rabin's hope was that he could deal faithfully with the PLO and Arafat.

Second, in three years, Hezbollah, another intransigent group, would likewise overcome the Lebanese.

Third, the prime danger to the Middle East is not from its immediate neighbors, but rather from Islamic fundamentalists and, as he referred to it, "Khomeinism without Khomeini."

For all these reasons, Rabin thought that the Oslo Accords were in the short and long-term best interests of the State of Israel.

After the meeting with the Prime Minister, our group visited the American Consulate in Jerusalem where we met with a select group of Palestinian Arabs.

Some of the Arabs expressed the belief that following the signing of the agreement, Arafat and the PLO would be able to "take care" of the Hamas in a way that the Israelis could never get away with.

They felt that the PLO could and would eliminate Hamas as a political and military force.

Shortly thereafter, as I sat on the White House lawn and witnessed "the handshake," I wasn't sure whether to cry or to applaud. Although I had great misgivings, I prayed that just maybe we were living in a new era that would try to bring peace to Israel and the region. Perhaps I was witnessing history in the making.

How have the suppositions of the Oslo Accords played out?

The PLO and Hamas

Hamas has not been destroyed. To the contrary, according to an agreement made two years ago by Arafat, the Palestinian Authority (PA) and Hamas are partners.

Hamas is now the military counterpart to Arafat's political party.

The de facto agreement between Hamas and the PA seems to indicate that Hamas terrorism can exist as long as it does not emanate from land controlled by Arafat.

It is still beyond belief for most of the world that Hamas and the PLO are indeed partners. They physically and politically embrace one another.

We hear Arafat say that he will redeem Jerusalem with blood and jihad (holy war). Yet we refuse to comprehend that Arafat speaks the language of Hamas in Arabic and that of conciliation in English.

The PA and the Oslo Accords

Arafat has not lived up to any of the provisions of the Oslo Accord, with the exception, when pressured, of an occasional arrest.

The PLO charter calling for the destruction of Israel is still part of its credo.

Not a single terrorist has been extradited.

The language of jihad has not been squelched. Rather, it has flourished and is now spoken in schools, universities and the press.

Arms continue to be smuggled into the territories. It is frightening to learn from off-the-record conversations with Israeli intelligence of fears regarding the enormous amounts of munitions, including anti-tank weapons, being smuggled by the PA.

Arafat has violated the Hebron Agreement by tripling the number of troops-policemen allowed under the agreement

Additionally, huge numbers of militia exist throughout the territories. He clearly uses terror as an instrument of diplomacy.

Arafat's goal is to appeal to segments of the American and Israeli communities and thereby, together with Russia and Europe, create a formidable bloc to pressure Netanyahu in order to gain concessions and statehood.

Those who still believe that Arafat is a partner in peace should hear his words on the Arafat tapes and watch his actions.

It is quite clear that his long-term plan is to dismantle Israel piece by piece, stage by stage. The map in his office clearly shows his ultimate aim—a Middle East without Israel.

Hezbollah and Lebanon

Unfortunately, Lebanon is still under Syria's thumb. Israel's soldiers are attacked daily. Katyusha rockets, launched from Lebanon by the Hezbollah, routinely land in Israel.

Arafat and Islamic Fundamentalists

Terror exported from Iran is responsible for the bombing of the World Trade Center, the massacres in Algeria, the threat to Egypt.

Arafat has failed to curb Islamic extremists in areas under PA rule.

Even if Israel were to grant Arafat a Palestinian state—with Jerusalem as its capital—and an airport, seaport and anything else he desires, there is no reason to believe that Hamas and other fundamentalist groups would accept Israel's right to exist.

It is time to stop worrying about being politically correct and begin to recognize Arafat for what he is—a duplicitous, de facto terrorist.

As American Jews we have two options.

The first is to wait quietly and patiently to see what future steps our government will take and how it will exert its pressure on Israel. This wait-and-see attitude leads to an inability to respond as challenges evolve.

The second option is to take a far more proactive approach, to meet with representatives in Congress and the Senate now. Our message should be:

1. America must not pressure Israel into making concessions contrary to her best interests.
2. Aid to the Palestinians must be suspended until they meet the obligations to which they agreed in the Oslo Accords.
3. Arafat must unequivocally live up to all of his Oslo obligations.

Rabin signed the Oslo Accords because they were based on certain conditions and expectations. It is time to acknowledge that these have not been met. Israel cannot continue to be the sole party living up to its agreements.

Unless the Palestinians keep their part of the bargain, peace will have no chance.

OU DINNER
JUNE 7,1998

Speech By Dr. Mendy Ganchrow, President

Mr. Chairman, worthy rabbis, honored guests, members of the dais, ladies and gentlemen:

I am honored to welcome so many dignitaries on this our 100th Anniversary, but I must make special reference to Ambassador Dore Gold, Senator Patrick Moynihan and Governor Pete Wilson of California.

Allow me to welcome you on this auspicious occasion. Shehechyanu, v'kiymanu, v'higiyanu lazman hazeh. I wish to extend ' our appreciation to our Chairman Elliot Gibber and our entire staff for an outstanding job.

On this signal occasion, the Centennial of the Orthodox Union, I have the great honor of introducing our special guest and honoree, the Vice President of the United States, the Honorable Albert Gore, Jr.

Mr. Vice President, it is our pleasure to welcome you here tonight. Your presence at our Centennial dinner has great significance to our community. Exactly 100 years ago tomorrow, on June 8, 1898, the Orthodox Union's founders gathered in New York City. They met under the cloud of a hostile environment that was threatening to destroy the small Orthodox Jewish community. Having come to this great country to escape religious persecution, and for a better economic existence, their concerns were very real. How could Jews survive in America and yet remain Sabbath observers? How could they keep kosher? By what means could they give their children a proper Jewish education?

These pioneers were often told, even by their co-religionists, either reform your traditions or face extinction. By what leap of faith could our founders ever imagine that their children could become Sabbath observing doctors, lawyers, or even a United States Senator?

Tonight, despite all the odds, we proclaim proudly that the Orthodox Union of 1998 is a Torah community of 1,000 synagogues and hundreds of thousands of individuals who share a unity of purpose. We set the standard for kashruth operating in 56 countries and certifying over 220,000 products. NCSY, our youth movement reaches out to some 40,000 teenagers throughout the United States. We are a national resource for thousands of developmentally disabled, deaf and hard of hearing. The Union has a major presence in the former Soviet Union and a burgeoning youth movement in Israel. Our web site welcomes thousands upon thousands of individuals, from the-four corners of the earth, enabling them to learn Torah on the internet. And, as you know, Mr. Vice President, because you have been kind enough year after year to greet our Washington summer interns, we are the only internship program on Capitol Hill run by any Jewish organization, secular or religious.

Our founders children, grandchildren, and great-grandchildren have indeed become Sabbath observing physicians, lawyers, accountants, business people, two members of Congress from Florida, Peter Deutsch and Robert Wexler both members of Orthodox Union synagogues, and even a United States Senator, who happens to be a member of our Board of Directors our mutual friend, Joe Lieberman.

Mr. Vice President, your presence here this evening sends a clear message to the world that the Orthodox Jewish community, which, like its co-religionists was an insecure, isolated group until after the Holocaust and the creation of the State of Israel, is proud to be part of today's political process. We have surely fulfilled our mission to represent our community by discharging G-d's charge of Tikkun Olam, perfecting the world and bettering our society.

The Orthodox Union is delighted to bestow its National Humanitarian Centennial Award on Albert Gore, Jr., son of a great American senator, whose entire life has been devoted to public service.

Jewish survival, the welfare of the American Jewish community, Soviet Jewry, the safety and security of Israel, and the special U.S.-Israel relationship are issues that have always been paramount throughout your career.

I recall visiting your Congressional office, wishing you well as you made your bid for the Senate. I can vividly remember standing behind you in 1988, in Rockland County, as the co-chairman of the Gore for President campaign. Mr. Vice President, this sign, which has been in my home since then (showing a sign of Gore for President), is more than personal memorabilia. It is a symbol of our faith in you as a human being, a leader, and as a friend to the Jewish community. That does not mean that we will always see eye to eye with you on every issue, but, as Prime Minister Netanyahu has reiterated, both publicly and privately, these are disagreements within the family and around the dinner table.

I had the privilege of hearing you speak two weeks ago at the AIPAC meeting in Washington. You spoke with passion and conviction about your lifelong association and affiliation with Jewish people and the Jewish State. You pointed out so beautifully how Jewish existence has always been guided by the principle of, as you so eloquently quoted the Torah, *"Tzedek, tzdek tirdof."*

Mr. Vice President, our community also has its passions. We passionately support Israel, its need to be free of outside pressure, whether European or American, and, in your words, its ability to be the sole determinant of its own security needs. We are passionate about the role and the centrality of Jerusalem and its neighborhoods, including Har Homa, in our prayers, our hopes and in our aspirations, as the eternal, undivided capital of the State of Israel, and of no other entity or country.

Mr. Vice President, allow me to deviate from my prepared remarks to add one sentence. We beseech you, Mr. Vice President, to convey to President Clinton the prayers of this assemblage and those we represent, that he speedily free Jonathan Pollard on humanitarian grounds.

Mr. Vice President, tonight we re-commit ourselves to continue to work together with you for a morally strong America, based upon equality and justice and a continuation of the very special relationship that exists between our government, its leadership, and the State of Israel. It is to you that we look for this leadership. You have never let us down.

It is therefore my privilege, as President of the Orthodox Union, to present this special award to you not only as the representative of our government, but as a friend of the Union and that of the entire Jewish community, and as one who has devoted so much of your distinguished public service career to our causes and betterment.

THE JERUSALEM POST
AUGUST 13, 1998

Where is the Strength?

A congregation's new rabbi gave an impassioned sermon on his first Shabbat. It included many areas of concern that he shared with his new community.

On the second Shabbat, he gave the same sermon.

The membership, though confused, attributed this to the rabbi's inexperience. When, on the third, fourth and fifth Shabbatot, the rabbi repeated the same sermon, a committee visited him to discuss the matter.

The rabbi's answer was simple, "Until you act on the issues I raised in the first sermon, what is the point of going on to the second?"

Last month, during a conference call between the leadership of the American Jewish community and a high-level Israeli official, we were informed of the seriousness of the Palestinian move to upgrade their status to near-statehood at the United Nations. "Gross violation of Oslo" and "dangerous" were some of the milder descriptions applied to the Palestinian initiative.

I asked a simple question: "If this is such a fundamental violation of Oslo, why would Israel continue to prepare, for a peace package as though nothing occurred?"

What can be accomplished by signing a new document with the same provisions the PLO has accepted and violated in the past? The recent impasse at the crossroad in Gaza, the murder of two Israelis at Yitzhar, and the repeated ultimatums by the Palestinian Authority during negotiations do not paint an encouraging picture of peaceful coexistence.

A few months ago, at the AIPAC policy conference, I asked Assistant Secretary of State Martin Indyk for one example of PLO compliance with the Oslo Accords. He told me that I wouldn't like his answer. "'They have declared their support for peace," he said after a long pause.

"Peace in our time" is a familiar cry of many tyrants, dictators and do-gooders.

Why should Israel withdraw from 13.1 percent of its precious land if a final and "true" peace is not attainable? Even if an agreement could be reached soon, Palestinian intractability on issues such as Jerusalem, water, Palestinian statehood and the Palestinian Diaspora still remains.

Israel should heed the examples of Britain and the US, which left Hong Kong and Panama, respectively, long after agreements were reached and ratified.

The situation in Israel becomes more puzzling every day. At the very moment the media announced an impending decision on 13 percent withdrawal over not more than a 12-week period, the Palestinian Authority announced that it would reject Israel's demand to convene a PNC meeting where issues such as amending the PLO charter and disarming Hamas would be addressed.

The prime minister's two recent trips to the United States were marked by triumphant encounters with Congress, Jewish leadership and Christian groups. As we approach the November elections in the US, grassroots sentiment indicates that the ability of the Clinton administration to pressure the Netanyahu government will decrease.

In the long run, American pressure on Israel is not sustainable.

Israel has been subjected to US pressure before, with minimal effect. Israel should not be forced to choose between a battle of wills with the president of the United States or her safety and security. Perhaps the administration's chief foreign policy spokesperson, Secretary of State Madeleine Albright, might be willing to cross the line from threat to actual policy change, but she is not a free agent. The president and the vice president are the final arbiters of American foreign policy. They are advised by experts, many of whom, unfortunately, are not sympathetic to the current Israeli government. A strong resolve on the part of Prime Minister Netanyahu will serve Israel well by enabling her to resist US pressure.

In the final analysis, Israel can only rely upon herself, world Jewry and the Almighty. Israel understands all too well that no American president is prepared to recognize Jerusalem as the eternal capital of Israel no matter how many concessions Israel makes. Israel must therefore act in her own long-term interests.

In spite of all the criticism, the Netanyahu government has done more than one would have ever expected to try to live up to Israel's Oslo commitments. The prime minister has abandoned many initiatives that he wished to implement in the hope of creating a climate conducive to co-existence, including stopping illegal Palestinian political activity in Jerusalem, closing Orient House, or insisting on limiting Palestinian police to the agreed-upon number. Despite spending much political capital on Har Homa, the building project is still on hold. These acts of self-restraint are being interpreted by many as a response to American pressure.

Israel must insist on total reciprocity. She must send the clear message of staunch adherence to her principles. Israel's leadership must rise to the occasion and find the strength to resist external pressure. Too much is at stake for a hurried, rushed decision.

THE LONG ISLAND JEWISH WORLD
SEPTEMBER 18, 1998

America's Challenge
To Regain Respect, The Nation Must
Take the Moral High Ground

The month of Elul is traditionally one of introspection. This year it is not only members of the Jewish community who must search their souls, but the American people. That immorality has occurred is without question. That our president is weakened, whether or not he survives the ensuing few weeks is likewise agreed upon, and there are many who feel that the president should save the country the trauma of an impeachment process by resigning.

But there is a much larger and more disturbing issue here. If we step back and look at our country, our despair should not only be directed at the president and what he has done, but at the society we have created a society that also gave rise to a young woman who felt no sense of wrong or shame in enticing and cavorting with a married man.

The concept of public versus private morality is antithetical to Torah tradition. One cannot be called a Torah-observant Jew, regardless of garb or synagogue attendance, if he or she cheats in business, whether the victim be Jew or gentile. This is true even if the crime is perpetrated privately.

Leaders—of academia, local communities, national organizations and, certainly, our nation—have a higher responsibility. They are, by definition, role models. To seek leadership yet deny that responsibility, undermines the foundation to which members of a community or nation are entitled.

Our society understands imperfection and temptation, but can we acquiesce when the actions represent a pattern of conduct that brings about charges of womanizing, infidelity, lying and obstruction of justice?

Our society tolerated the "rehabilitation" of Dick Morris, who as a White House aide disgraced himself by cavorting with a prostitute while speaking on the telephone to the president. He now appears on cable television as an "expert," which casts him as a quasi role model. Does shame no longer exist in the American lexicon?

If we judge a person by the company he or she keeps, we have to wonder where the president's moral compass was pointed when he called Morris on the night that the Monica Lewinsky story broke and inquired whether he should tell the truth. Morris, after some private polling, advised the president that the truth wouldn't work. The president took the path of least resistance—he lied.

What has happened to America? The public demands the return of

Marv Albert because he's a good sportscaster. People bought tickets to Mike Tyson's comeback, even though he is a convicted rapist (it was only biting off his opponent's ear that caused revulsion). MTV, sports and situation comedies produce Hollywood "heroes" that do little to instill family values in our young people. The moral climate on television and in movies and magazines is dedicated to nihilistic pleasure.

Instant gratification without commitment is the hallmark of our society. Even the Reverend Jesse Jackson pointed out that the president only violated one commandment. What's bad? There are nine others.

What is most disconcerting is the lack of a single resignation from the Cabinet White House. Does no one's conscience bother them?

Equally upsetting is the cast of spinmeisters who regularly appear on television stations, stalwarts on both sides of the aisle giving pat answers devoid of intellect or conviction. Where are political independence and personal integrity? We have lost them as a people because we are concerned about our own narrow agendas.

As human beings we have the ability to forgive wrongs committed against us even as we seek forgiveness for our sins against others. Being contrite, sorrowful and tearful is not, however, a formula for legal forgiveness. Crimes against society must be redressed in a legal forum. As a taxi driver interviewed on television said, "If the president can get   away with lying before a grand jury, why can't I get away with my parking tickets?"

It is this moral atmosphere that prompted Senator Joseph Lieberman (D-Conn.) to step forward. He articulated what many felt. We cannot divide ourselves into two parts-an ethical public persona and an unethical private one. On behalf of the Orthodox Union, I sent a letter to Lieberman, commending him, within hours of his speech. His point, which should have been obvious, is that as a nation, we are so accustomed to lowering our standards that we haven't yet realized that we've hit bottom.

The prayer for our country is recited in synagogues across the country every Shabbat. We need a strong America with a powerful president who can concentrate on leadership, but America is not only a seat of political power; it is also a major influence on the world's culture, style and mores. Let Clinton instruct his lawyers to halt their dissection of the English language and allow the president to simply tell the truth. Perhaps, just perhaps, we Americans can put this episode behind us. Let us hope that the meaningful introspection of our New Year's prayers will lead us toward a new horizon in ethics and morality.

ORTHODOX UNION 102ND ANNIVERSARY DINNER
MAY 21, 2000

Address upon receiving the Keter Shem Tov Award

Tonight is neither the time nor the place for speeches or policy statements. Rather just for a few thoughts.

On occasion, during moments of frustration I muse on the amount of time and effort that I have put in as a full-time President of the Union. However, when I come in contact with an NCSY youth from a home devoid of Torah, a Yachad or Our Way child integrated into society, the smiling children whose lives we have really literally saved in Kharkov, the Ethiopian and Russian children in Bet NCSY in Lod in Israel, and so on, tears always come to my eyes as I realize that this is what we are working for, this is what we have been accomplishing, it is something historical and monumental. The Or Hachayim has forty different explanations for the first sentence in this week's portion in Bechukothai talacho. Among his thoughts are that the use of the word talacho from Halicha to walk reminds us that to be amalim ba'Torah, to be engrossed in Torah is not only sitting at the table learning or praying but it involves all of our activities of life. We can never divorce ourselves from our Torah personality, secondly, there is no shiur, no quantitative amount given that will satisfy this mitzvah that requires us to walk in the path of the statutes of Hashem. The Union's multifaceted activities fit the mold of all forty of his elucidations. But none of what we have accomplished could happen by itself or by one person.

Tonight I pay tribute to those who deserve the honor along with me. Tonight's dinner could not have been accomplished without the efforts of three of my closest friends, our Chairman and Co-Chairmen, Harvey Wolinetz, Ralph Rothschild and Tzvi Friedman as well as the professional staff Rabbi Pinchas Stolper, Steve Karp, Malka Laks, and their staff and Shelly Fliegelman, our director. The professionalism of the videos by Ricky Magder and his staff make the award process so interesting and different. The activities of the Union are coordinated on a day-to-day basis by my fellow officers, especially Marcel Weber, our lay volunteers, and the chairman of each commission, working hand in hand with our professional staff and especially the directors of each department. They are the most dedicated, competent and loyal group of individuals that one could ever assemble in one organization. I have a very special relationship with each and every one of them. And of course, Rabbi Butler, our Executive Vice-President whose great vision and energy serves as an inspiration for all of us Our efforts and our visions have complemented each other. It has been a wonderful partnership.

But above all I could never have put in the effort, I could never have been as successful without my ezer kanegdi. my wife, my partner, my crutch, my conscience, my advisor, my wonderful wife Sheila, whose intellect and common sense allow me to maintain a semblance of stability. She reminds me of the *pusuk in Shir ha Shirim* (Song of Songs), "You are completely beautiful my companion and you have no blemish."

The Netziv refers to the unity of the Jewish people especially during the chagim' when all Jews came to Jerusalem and are called chaverim. This Jewish unity is portrayed to us as beauty, but for me it is the simple understanding of the words that refers to the inner and outer beauty of Sheila, my beloved wife who has been at my side for 38 wonderful years. Her intellect, outlook on life, and common sense place all issues into a sense of proper perspective. I am deeply grateful to her and our children, Malkie and Paul, Banji and Ari, Brina and Elli and our grandchildren Zachary, Jake, and Carlie, Jack and Jonah for making life so beautiful for me that I have been able to devote my time for the Union with a clear mind.

Finally, I want to say that I have been involved in many projects over the last fifteen years, including some which I have had the honor to initiate. One project that I have worked on harder than most has been to take the historic efforts of George Falk, who started our Israel Center, and accommodate the needs of our next generation with new headquarters. Three years ago we started NCSY in Israel and that added pressure on us to create a true world headquarters. Today, I am happy to report that our new building in Jerusalem to be known as the Seymour Abrams Center will be open in September. Sheila and I are proud to announce this evening that we join our dear friends, the chairman of tonight's event and his wife, Naomi and Harvey Wolinetz, who have dedicated the Bais Hakneseth. Tonight we dedicate the bais hamedrash in this beautiful building in memory of three individuals who have had such impact on our lives, Sheila's parents Anna and Jack Weinreb, and my father, Rabbi Morris Ganchrow, aleyhem Hashalom, all of whom dedicated their lives to Torah and Torah study and were embodiments of our way of life. They devoted themselves towards the enhancement of their children's growth in Torah. It is sad that they cannot be here tonight except in spirit and Tibadli Lechaim Mrs. Kate Ganchrow, my mother, who is here tonight, who at the age of 89 has such spirit, clear intellect and drive, and a wonderful warm personality that only looks at life in a positive sense. She is an inspiration to all who know her. My mother has just returned from Israel this Pesach where she went to visit her grandchildren and great-grandchildren. I think nothing would make her happier than when she, with G-d's help, visits Israel next *Pesach* and will walk into a *bais medrash* that bears her name and that of her late husband, my father *olav hashalom*, for they were always involved in *Harbazat Torah*. I believe it an appropriate tribute to them. I thank each and every one of you for coming here tonight to honor me and moreover I thank you for allowing me the privilege and for giving me the honor of serving you as your President these past years.

UNITED PRESS INTERNATIONAL
SEPTEMBER 5, 2000

Nation's Values Based on Faith

NEW YORK— If the Founding Fathers were alive today, they would be shocked to observe a debate brewing not on freedom of religion, but on fear of religion.

While they would surely applaud the Anti-Defamation League for its vigilance in protecting the rights of all Americans to believe as they wish, they would at the same time question the effort to trample upon a guiding American principle of faith.

It appears to me that the initiators of this debate have misconstrued the thrust of Senator Joseph Lieberman's remarks on faith by equating a "reaffirmation of faith" with crossing that critically important, invisible threshold of separation of church and state.

I am well aware that, historically, minority faiths are at greatest peril when church and state unite, and I believe firmly that a separation must be maintained. Therefore, I have a far greater issue with the setting of the speech than with the message, which I find commendable. Political candidates who preach from the pulpit, even without invoking religion, do a disservice to church/state separation: delivering a sermon or homily as part of a religious service stretches the borders of the critical church-state divide.

I am equally displeased with practicing members of the clergy endorsing political candidates.

But let us examine the alleged violations of Senator Lieberman's speech. In his personal expressions on the role faith plays in his life, did the senator advocate a state-sponsored religion? Did he call for federal funding of church-synagogue activities? Did he urge legislation based upon Torah principles? No. He spoke of God, faith, morality and an implicit spirituality within man.

He spoke of the same God whose name is inscribed on our coins, the same deity to whom the chaplains of the Senate and House pray on behalf of our nation. From early childhood, we are taught the pledge of allegiance, which refers to "one nation under God," and it is on the Bible that our leaders place their hands as they take the oath of office.

Our pluralistic society allows each of us to believe or deny, to practice or to abstain. But the ethics and morality of our society are surely nurtured by a deeply rooted American devotion to the divine. Whether we, as individuals, opt to believe or not, the underpinnings of the "one nation under God" society in which we live sets the tenor of our lives.

The electorate is entitled to hear the source of the passions that ignite our candidates on the major issues of the day. In Senator Lieberman's case, he does not invoke a religious point of view on any policy issue; rather he expresses the fact that faith-based teachings help in molding his personality and framing his judgment. At the same time, he assiduously avoids casting his decisions as religious doctrine.

It is therefore not the adherence to God's laws that has occasioned such an upsurge of appreciation of so many Americans for the Lieberman candidacy, but rather the presence of faith as a guiding hand in navigating national decisions. Our national debate should not be limited to taxes or prescription drug prices, but should focus as well on the state of our society.

The presence of violence in our streets, shootings in our schools, drugs in our neighborhoods, abuse in our homes, call us to task for moving our society away from its moorings of faith. In fact, over the years, Joe Lieberman has spoken out against the entertainment industry that glorifies these ills of society. He speaks against this abuse of cultural freedom on behalf of millions of Americans who are fed up with these excesses — and he speaks in the name of decency, not religious law.

It is Lieberman's perspective that Americans applaud, not his personal religious beliefs.

His perspective rings familiar because it is that of the Founding Fathers, upheld for generations. We always have been a faith-based nation of upright values and moral strength. The glory of our nation rests in its ability to preserve that faith while defending the individual's right to demur. God may have no place in politics, but He has a secured place within the body of American life that cannot be ignored. To invoke God's mission is far from a departure from our American tradition; rather it is deeply rooted in that tradition and restores it to a position of honor.

THE INTERNET JERUSALEM POST
SEPTEMBER 7, 2001

Reform Judaism's Intolerance

This week saw the opening of registration for the World Zionist Congress elections. As mortars fell in Gilo, it seemed surreal to serve as the chairman of the Orthodox effort for this election. On the very day that I received calls from the Jewish Community Relations Council and the Presidents' Conference on the need for unity, strength, diligence and an all-out effort for our September 23 solidarity rally for Israel, I also received a fax from Artza, the World Union of Reform Judaism.

The Reform leaflet starts off with: "Ultra-Orthodox politicians are threatening Jewish unity and the Jewish community." Let us look at this headline and other charges that the Reform movement makes in this document.

Firstly, it creates a straw man - someone you always love to hate, namely "the ultra-Orthodox."

We ask the question: Are there any ultra-Orthodox slates running in this election? Do the "ultra-Orthodox" belong to the Zionist Congress? Or, in fact, is "ultra-Orthodox" code for all Orthodox parties, Modern, Left, and Center?

Secondly, if there is such an entity as "ultra-Orthodox," then there must be a group of "ultra-liberal" Jews. Does this refer to those clergy who marry gentiles, who do not observe the Sabbath, who recognize patrilineal descent and perform same-sex marriages? Are these members of the "Jewish" clergy, who divorce themselves from Torah and tradition?

Isn't it time to declare "ultra-Orthodox," a pejorative term and discard it from our vocabulary?

"Reform marriages, conversions and burials are not yet recognized," the leaflet declares. Does the Zionist Congress decide these issues? Wouldn't the proper forum for the solution of the Reform Movement's problems be to take 100,000 American Reform Jews, convince them to migrate to Israel and then run Reform candidates for the Knesset, where these decisions are made?

"Registering and voting in this election will give you a voice in critical decisions to defining 'who is a Jew' and not leave the decisions to ultra-Orthodox politicians," the leaflet continues. Again, these decisions are in the hands of the Supreme Court of the State of Israel and the Knesset. The declarations on these issues from the World Zionist Congress are mere words.

"Ultra-Orthodox politicians call our rabbis 'clowns,'" it cries.

In these elections, which member of any slate running against Reform is guilty of such a crime? Who are these so-called politicians? In fact, this is another example of subjecting the reader to inflammatory and biased suggestions in the hope that they will get angry, rather than understand the issues and the need to vote as good Jews. It is a campaign of hate - hate against all Orthodox Jews.

"A Reform Jewish kindergarten was firebombed."

Who did it? Isn't the intention of this headline for readers to assume that it was the same people who labeled their rabbis "clowns," those "ultra-Orthodox politicians," who threaten Jewish unity by burning reform institutions?

These innuendoes are meant to inflame and incite. Why is it that we hear nothing regarding Orthodox schools and synagogues in Israel which are damaged by vandals, such as in Efrat? If they are not suggesting a culprit, why raise the issue?

"The future of our Movement remains in doubt."

It is clear that voting for the Reform slate for the Zionist Congress will not change the status of the Reform Movement in Israel. The Reform Movement's problem is that the Israeli people are not ready to adapt to a religion that is so radically different from the Judaism of our Torah and of their parents. They understand that, whereas Reform Jewry in Israel does not practice patrilineal descent, or approve of same-sex marriages, the American movement does. When the Israeli movement has gained some credibility they, too, will adopt these changes. It is no wonder that there is only an infinitesimal number of Israelis who have become Reform Jews.

How sad that the Reform movement was the only movement to cancel its Israel programs this summer. This week, thousands of young Orthodox students arrived here to spend at least a year of study. The contrast speaks for itself.

If I had my way, I would forget these whole elections. As long as Jews are dying on the road to Modi'in and in Hebron, and it is unsafe to sit in a pizza restaurant in Jerusalem, it is not the time to be spending millions of dollars on a divisive campaign in America. But if we are going to have an election, let's stop the character assassination.

There is only one line in the Reform Movement's message that should be taken note of. . . "we can instill tolerance." Reform should practice what it preaches.

THE JEWISH PRESS
APRIL 4, 2003

Jews Must Support The War In Iraq

In what I consider a naive and theologically simplistic attempt to substitute slogans and emotions for facts, a group called the Shalom Center placed a full page ad in the Friday, March 21, New York Times calling on Jews to "oppose the war."

While arguing that "disarming a dangerous dictator is a just end," the group fails to inform us as to how, after 12 years of intransigence accompanied by Iraq's mockery of the world's disarmament demands, this impasse could ever come to a successful conclusion. Security Council Resolution 1441 called for a total disarmament, not a cat and mouse game with public relations efforts to imply acquiescence as the world prays that weapons of mass destruction are not transferred to terrorists around the world. (To wit: the Ricin found in the Paris subway last week.) The ad claims:

 * "War will kill innocent. . . children." Unlike Islamic suicide murderers who target innocents and civilians, the "shock and awe" campaign is a combination of psychological and military efforts to avoid civilian casualties. Within technological possibilities the attack is aimed at combatants and leadership only.

 * "War will kill and wound countless American soldiers in battle." American casualties in Gulf War I and to date have been minimal. But every human life is precious and these heroes give their lives so that our society can live and function in freedom and to ensure that any citizen can protest government policies, with full-page ads and/or marches.

 * "War will subject Americans, Israelis .. to hellish terrorist reprisals." There is no proof this will occur. Daily terror against Israel, and the attacks of 9/1 1, occurred absent our invasion of Iraq. To the contrary, in Israel terrorist casualties decrease as pre-emptive military action against terrorist groups increases. Further, American inaction would in no way guarantee our safety from terrorism.

 * "War will give spurious legitimacy to further attacks on our civil rights."

What kind of double talk is this? If the FBI intensifies its search for Al Qaeda sleeper cells, then G-d bless the FBI. Even with all our alerts and safeguards at airports, etc., I'll compare our civil liberties favorably with any other democracy in the world. By the way, who is concerned with the civil liberties of the Iraqis?

 * "War will diminish the lives of all Americans, divest hundreds of billions of dollars needed for health, etc." Talk about dollar waste! Jewish education could certainly have benefited from the nearly $100,000 cost of a full page New York Times ad. Sept. 11 and its aftermath cost us thousands of lives and untold billions in property and economic loss. Our security needs will cost additional billions because we avoided dealing with these problems five and ten years ago. But the ultimate cost of waiting to clean up after a terrorist attack on our soil with weapons of mass destruction, possibly supplied by Iraq, would be far greater.

Jews must support this war on geopolitical, moral and theological grounds.

Judaism does not teach us to turn the other cheek. Yes, we strive for justice, but evil has a penalty that must be meted out. Justice does not imply or mean the absence of war. We are not pacifists. War is an instrument — albeit a final one - for Jewish survival.

The war against Amalek is one of the 613 mitzvot. We are commanded to destroy, remember and never forget the Hitlers, Arafats, Saddams, Assads, and Osamas - the Amalekites of our generation.

Yes, King Solomon said in Psalm 34 (as quoted in the Shalom Center ad), "Seek peace and pursue it." However, he also wrote (Ecclesiastes 3.1): "Everything has its season and there is a time for everything under the heaven. A time to be born and a time to die ... And time to kill and time to heal ... A time for war and a time for peace."

Moreover, the Talmud Sanhedrin 72.1 exclaims, "He who comes to kill you, arise first and kill him."

Had George W. Bush been president in 1939, 6 million Jews might have been saved from the crematoria.

President Bush tried every possible means to bring peace. The Iraqis, encouraged by the French and Germans, were able to mouth the words and express a positive intent, but refused to comply with total disarmament. This from a regime that killed its own people with poison gas, attempted to assassinate the first President Bush, occupied Kuwait, attacked Iran, fired scuds at Israel and developed weapons of mass destruction.

The ad concludes with a call to pursue justice peace and Tikkun Olam healing the planet.

If one examines the 613 commandments, the writings of Maimonides, Nachmonides, Mishna Brura, etc., there is no mitzvah of Tikkun Olam per se. Tikkun Olam requires a moral society in order to thrive. Thus, many thinkers pointed out that during the Holocaust when Jews were threatened with destruction,Tikkun Olam could not be on our agenda..When we have the ability to live in tranquility and harmony with the environment and our neighbors, then we can shine as we perfect our efforts on behalf of Tikun Olam in medicine, the arts, technology, human relations and so on.

The war, please G-d, will soon end victoriously. Sadly, the ad never mentions the safety of our soldiers. Hopefully the Middle East may change immeasurably for the better and perhaps—just perhaps—Israel and Jews will be able to breathe a little easier as we prepare for the next crisis in the "peace process" that will once again require Jewish unity, strength and fortitude.

Index

A

Abbas, Mahmoud 219, 238. *See also* Abu Mazen
Abdullah, King 292
Abrams, Seymour 170
Abu Mazen 225, 238. *See also* Abbas, Mahmoud
ADL 187, 288
Adler, Dr. Shelly 100
Adolph Schreiber Hebrew Academy 102, 111
Agudath Israel of America 142, 193, 198, 200
American Israel Public Affairs Committee (AIPAC) 108–110, 116, 118, 127, 131, 134–135, 141–144, 151, 157, 160, 165, 194, 196, 208, 213, 217, 229–231, 245, 250, 262, 264, 266, 317, 332
Akins, James 116
Al Qaeda 140
Albright, Madeline 246, 264
Allen, Mark 278
American College of Surgeons 107
Americans for Peace Now 150, 251, 256
Amir, Yigal 233
Amit Women 125, 311
Anti-Defamation League 186
APN 150, 251
Arad, Ron 320

Arafat, Yasser 110, 114, 124, 126, 152, 216–217, 219–220, 225–226, 229–230, 245, 252, 257, 259, 264, 277
ARZA *See* Reform Zionist Organization
Asaraf, Rabbi Shlomo 175
Ashe, Arthur 79
Ashrawi, Hanan 217
Ateret Kohanim 124
Avital, Colette 227

B

Ball, George 116
Bar-Ilan University 233
Barak, Ehud 253–259, 270–272, 275, 278
Baumel, Zachary 320
Begin, Binyamin (Benny) 254
Beilin, Yossi 215, 222–225, 238, 240, 243, 258
Ben-Gurion, David 313
Ben-Zohar, Israel 186
Berger, Sandy 248
Berlin, Mo 97
Berman, Julius 227, 366
Berman, Rabbi Saul 211–214
Bernstein, Rabbi Louis 69
Bettencourt, Andre 186
Bin-Laden, Osama 259
Bingaman, Jeff 112
Bitter Scent 186

Blitz, Harvey 362
Bloomfield, Doug 231
Blumenfeld, Avi 170, 362
Boesky, Ivan 132, 136–137
Boschwitz, Rudy 145
Breger, Marshall 122
Breiner, Fran 334
Breitowitz, Yitzchak 361
Breslin, Jimmy 282
Brief, Dr. Donald 93
Bronfman, Charles 223
Bronfman, Edgar 241, 243, 253
Brooklyn Museum 190, 191–192
Brozan, Nadine 172
Bryan, Richard 132–133
Burdick, Quentin 120, 285
Burg, Avrum 187
Burian, Lawrence 129–130
Bush, George H.W. 158–159, 259,
    266–267, 271
Bush, George W. 152, 259–260,
    264–265, 286
Butler, Rabbi Raphael 164–165,
    170–174, 206, 213, 277–278,
    280, 322, 335–337, 340, 348,
    351, 354, 358, 362–363, 365–366

C

Carlebach, Rabbi Shlomo 299
Chabad 136, 307, 312, 317. *See also*
    Lubavitch
Christopher, Warren 246
Churchill, Winston 258
Cleland, Max 115
Clifford, Clark 347
Clifton, Sweetwater 33
Clinton, Bill 113, 124, 126, 142,
    188–189, 213, 216, 219, 221,
    230, 244–246, 248–249, 251–
    252, 256, 263–273, 275, 282,
    286, 295, 350, 359
Clinton, Hillary 172–173, 252,
    270–271, 274–283

CNN 278
Coats, Dan 115
Cobrin, Jerry 101
Cohen, Mike 167
Cohen, William 113
Colman, Sam 180
Colonel Cohen 71
Conference of Presidents of Major
    Jewish Organizations 81, 127,
    198, 291, 302, 334
Cox, Monsignor 112–113
Cranston, Alan 134
Curtiss, Richard 116

D

Danforth, John 350
Davis, Arthur 152
De Clerk, F.W. 296
De Sapio, Carmine 19
Denise, Judge Majette 152
Deri, Aryeh 332
Dershowitz, Professor Alan
    In high school 25
    Lanner Affair 352
Dewey, Thomas 19
Diament, Nathan 169, 278
Dichter, Adam 172
Dine, Tom 141–142, 144, 160, 262
Dinkins, David 347
Don Nickles 282
Donaldson, Sam (ABC) 140
Dorgan, Byron 117
Doron, Chief Rabbi Bakshi 168,
    323, 328
Dukakis, Michael 285
Durbin, Dick 110–112, 122, 152, 158

E

Edah 193, 210–212, 214
Ehrenberg, Betty 169
Ehrman, Fred 170, 346
Eisenstat, Sandy 135, 157
Eisner, Dr. Joel 84

Ettinger, Yoram 244
Ewing, Oscar 39

F

Fein, Shishie 374
Feldman, Dr. Shelly 84
Feldman, Zvi 320
Ferguson, Dr. James 96–98, 166
Ferraro, Geraldine 114
Findley, Paul 110, 116, 122
Fishman, Rabbi Joshua 200
Fliegelman, Shelly 185
Ford, Wendell 144
The Forward 126–127, 172, 231, 248, 276, 278, 282
Foxman, Abe 251
Friedman, Tsvi 165, 245
From Time Immemorial 219
Fuinsz, Dr. Richard 179
Fuji Plan 81
Furillo, Carl 21

G

Ganchrow, Ari 94, 97, 124, 157, 340, 373
   Marriage 106, 228
   Work on Capitol Hill 120, 146
Ganchrow, Banji 106, 228, 373
Ganchrow, Brina 106, 373
Ganchrow, Elli 94, 101–102, 146, 152, 157, 163, 247, 286, 340, 373
   Marriage 106, 373
   Work on Capitol Hill 120, 124
Ganchrow, Jacob 13, 16, 47
Ganchrow, Kate 10, 12, 14–17, 42–43, 46–48, 374
Ganchrow, Malkie 2, 54–56, 59–61, 69, 82–83, 86, 88, 95–98, 106, 372–373
Ganchrow, Mendy
   in AIPAC 108–111, 140–141
   in RZA 376–377
   and Baseball 14, 20–23
   Basic training in Army 58–62
   Birth 8
   Birth of children 54, 94, 97
   Courtship and engagement 41–44
   Early years 8–18
   in Grand Rapids 95–98
   in HUVPAC
      Founding HUVPAC 111–114,
      HUVPAC dealings 115–120
      Leaving HUVPAC 148–151
   Marriage 6, 46–49
   Medical practice in Monsey 98–107
   in Medical school 37–40, 45–47
   in Orthodox Union
      Election to OU presidency 152, 163–165
      Lanner Affair 163, 334–370
      OU presidency tenure 165–177
   Poetry by 86–90
   Parents, relationship with 10–14, 17–18
   in School 19–20, 23–28, 31–36, 371
   in Vietnam 1–7, 63–94, 128
Ganchrow, Morris 8, 9, 11, 14, 36, 46
Ganchrow, Saul 13, 16, 40, 47, 69
Ganchrow, Sheila 2, 11, 32, 56, 59, 91, 99, 104, 114, 151, 162, 169, 277–278
   Courtship with 14, 35, 40–43
   Marriage 6, 46–49
   Poetry to 86–90
   Family life with 54–55, 61, 86, 101, 106, 286, 341, 372–375
   Foreign travels 174, 216, 228, 239, 242-243, 291-292
   Meetings at the White House 266, 270–273
Gibbons, Sam 121
Gilman, Ben 125, 245
Giuliani, Rudolph 190–191, 271, 277–279, 282–283

Gold, Dore 251
Gootman, Elissa 172
Gordon, Shaya 374
Gore, Al 115, 235, 246, 256, 284–286
Gore, Karenna 247, 286
Gotel, Marty 181
Greenberg, David 19
Greenwald, Jerry 233
Gribetz, Ken 267
Gutterman, Simeon 371

H

Haber, Rabbi Yaacov 375
Hadassah 327
Hamas 125, 217, 218, 227, 229
Hammond, Colonel 1
Hanks, Richard 116
Hartstein, Sam 168
Harvey, Dr. Peck 130
Hasten, Hart 136, 138
Hecht, Chic 112, 131–132, 136
Hecht, Marty 132, 136, 139
Hecht, Rabbi Abraham 234
Heinz, John 129
Helms, Jesse 40, 115, 117, 120, 122–127, 131, 134–135, 231
Herut-America 138
Herzog, Yitzhak 256
Hezbollah 217
Hier, Rabbi Marvin 187
Hilliard, Earl 152
Hoenlein, Malcolm 136–137, 198, 244, 283, 303
Hollings, Ernest 121
Holzman, Elizabeth 179
Hornblass, Dr. Albie 85
Hunt, Governor Jim 115, 122
Hurwitt, Dr. Elliot 52
Husseini, Feisel 217
Hudson Valley Political Action Committee (HUVPAC) 11, 108–153, 222

I

Ifshin, David 266
Indyk, Martin 244, 250
Inouye, Daniel 129, 146
Israel Bonds 102, 146
Israel Policy Forum 257

J

Jacob, Marvin 182–183
Jacobs, Robert 122, 135
Jepson, Roger 109
Jerusalem Post 150, 235
Jewish Community Relations Council of New York 136
Jewish Press 228, 231, 232
Jewish Theological Seminary 137
Joel Commission 173, 352, 356–360, 362–368
Joel, Rabbi Meyers 328
Johnson, President Lyndon 39
Johnson, Tim 115
Jotkowitz, Seymour "Skippy" 33
Jutkowitz, Dr. Arnold 66

K

Kahn, Jacques 242
Kamin, Lawrence 117–118
Kaminetsky, Rabbi Yakov 102
Kanotopsky, Rabbi Harold 24
Kaplan, Dr. Joel 85
Karimov, Islam 294
Kasten, Robert 123
Katz, Yehuda 320
Kennedy, John F. 39
Kennedy, Joseph 39
Kessler 172
Kessler, Eve 172
Killgore, Andrew 116
Knesset 194, 247, 254, 258, 269, 292, 314–317, 320, 322, 324, 332
Kohn, Baruch 195
Kramer, Marsha 278

Krupka, Rabbi Moshe 169
Kwestel, Shimmy 33, 78, 156, 158–159, 161, 165, 175, 204, 209, 223, 297, 299, 302

L

Lamm, Rabbi Norman 198, 200, 236, 311, 322
Landau, David 142
Lanner Affair 165–166, 169, 171, 177, 334–370
Lanner, Rabbi Baruch 174, 293, 334–370
Latkin, Dr. Richard and Eita 106
Lau, Yisrael 235
Lavenson, Colonel George 84
Levine, Joshua 117
Levine, Mel 120
Levy, Leon 187
Levy, William 84
Lewinsky, Monica 188–189, 252, 267–270, 273, 359
Lewis, John 148
Lieberman, Joseph 113
Long, Clarence 115
Long Island Jewish World 172
L'Oreal 185–188
Loucks, Vernon R. Jr. 185
Love Story 23
Lubavitch 8, 12–13, 136, 307, 317. *See also* Chabad
Luchins, David 184, 276

M

Mack, Connie 149–150
Maldonado, Colonel 71
Marcos, Dr. Katz 222
Maryles, Matthew 346
McCain, John 94, 115
McGuire 33
McKinney, Cynthia 152
Meltzer, Philip 328
Mendes, Dr. Henry Pereira 155, 169

Miller, Rabbi Israel 118, 314
Miller, Rhoda 159
Mitchell, George 112
Mizrachi 307, 308
Mnookin, Seth 172
Mohammed, King VI 293
Mubarak, Hosni 292
Muschel, Rabbi Nachum 102, 375
Muskie, Edwin 112

N

Nachtomi, Morris 105
Nadler, Jerry 295
National Council of Synagogue Youth (NCSY) 157, 165, 167, 169, 170–171, 173–176, 205, 223, 255, 300, 334–335, 337–344, 346, 350–353, 355, 357–362, 364–365, 367–369, 374
National Council of Young Israel 196, 203, 207, 236, 297, 308
Neeman Convention 331
Netanyahu, Prime Minister Binyamin (Bibi) 168, 187, 197, 236, 238–241, 243–245, 248, 251–254, 318, 322, 324
New York Medical College 107
New York Times 140, 142, 227
National Jewish Committee Relations Council (NJCRAC) 184, 194, 213, 317

O

Ofili, Chris 191
Olmert, Ehud 168, 278–279
O'Malley, Walter 21
Orthodox Union *See* Union of Orthodox Jewish Congregations
Oslo Peace Accords 124
OU *See* Union of Orthodox Jewish Congregations
Our Way 157

P

Pan-Am Flight *103* 159
Parker, Orin 116
Peck, Dr. Harvey 129
Percy, Charles 114, 115, 127
Peres, Shimon 124, 126, 168, 209, 215, 219–220, 234–236, 238–239, 241, 243–245, 248, 254–256
Perlman, Sharyn 167, 278, 344
Perlow, Rav (the Novominsker Rebbe) 201
Pletka, Danielle 124
PLO 114, 126, 215–222, 226, 229–230, 238, 250, 257, 277
Podres, Johnny 22
Poindexter, Admiral 136
Porush, Rabbi Menachem 194
Powell, Colin 259, 265, 272, 311
Pressler, Larry 94, 115

R

Rabbinical Council of America (RCA) 125, 194, 197, 199, 200, 202, 208, 213–214
Rabin, Yitzhak 130, 142, 209, 215–217, 219–222, 226–228, 232–236, 238–239, 244–245, 248, 253–254, 256, 263
Rabinovitch, Itamar 144
Ratzker, Malkie. *See* Ganchrow, Malkie
Ratzker, Paul 106
Rausman, Sam 106
Reagan, Ronald 109, 123, 128–129, 132–136, 138–139, 157, 259, 271, 334
Reform Zionist Organization (ARZA) 328
Regan, Sister Joan 113, 180, 181
Reid, Harry 146
Religious Zionists of America (RZA) 81, 125, 197, 230, 233, 366, 376
Rice, Condaleeza 152

Ripstein, Dr. Charles 49, 51, 54, 55, 57
Riskin, Rabbi Shlomo 25
Robinson, Tommy 115
Rockefeller, Jay 146
Rothschild, Ralph 374
Rudoff, Sheldon 159, 161
Rumsfeld, Donald 152

S

Savitsky, Steve 169
SCA 207–208, 212
Schachter, Rabbi Herschel 214
Schaechter, Rabbi Aaron 201
Schmidt, Harrison 112
Schreiber, Elliot 108, 374
Schreiber, Sylvia 108
Schuller, Eugene 186
Schuster, Arnold 26
Schwartz, William 180
Schwinn, Douglas 90–91
Segal, Erich 23
Shapiro, Lenny 32
Sharansky, Natan 187
Sherer, Rabbi Moshe 142, 195, 196–197, 199–202
Sholom, Rabbi Klass 232
Shomrim Society 10
Shultz, George 136, 140
Siegel, Jack 374
Silver, Shelly 172
Simcha, Rabbi Krauss 376
Simcha, Rav Kook 323
Simon, Paul 114
Singer, Saul 150
Singer, Wendy 150
Smith, Larry 120
Snapper, Dr. Isidore 49–51
Solarz, Steven 128
Soloveitchik, Rabbi Joseph B. 197, 339
Sontag, Shimon 101
Spector, Arlen 149
Stark, Abe 12

Steinreich, Stan 167, 344
Stewart, Jimmy 79
Stolper, Rabbi Pinchas 206, 212, 335, 340, 362–363
Stone, Professor Richard 165
Strauss, David 120
Sturm, Rabbi Frank 205, 206, 297
Sutton, Willie 26
Svei, Rabbi Elya 198–202
Symms, Steve 117, 122, 127, 131, 134

T

Tendler, Rabbi Moshe (Moses) 50, 98, 362, 375
The Haj 146
Thurm, Max 102
Tisch, James 119
Tokayer, Rabbi Marvin 81, 295
Torah u'Madah 27, 31, 203
Torricelli, Bob 120
Trible, Paul 133–134
Truman, President Harry 19
Twerski, Rabbi Abraham 346

U

UN Conference on Racism 264
Union of Orthodox Jewish Congregations 33, 55, 85, 104, 106, 124–125, 127, 129, 132–133, 141, 144, 148, 152, 154–160, 162–168, 170, 172–173, 175–178, 180, 183–188, 190–202, 204–214, 222–224, 226–228, 231–232, 234–236, 240–242, 246, 253, 258, 268–269, 271, 275–278, 280–283, 285–286, 288, 293, 296–297, 299, 302, 308, 317–323, 334–369, 373, 375–376
United Jewish Communities (UJC) 330, 332, 334
Uris, Leon 146

V

Victor, Chaplain Solomon 81

Vietnam 1–7, 30, 34, 63–95, 115–116, 128, 138, 147–148
Votta, Johnny 12

W

Wallace, Henry 19
Wallace, Mike 118
Wallach, Jacob 15
Wasserman, Rabbi Harold "Chico" 1–2, 5, 68–69, 71, 83–85
Weber, Marcel 165, 201, 204, 280, 336, 341, 347, 361, 365
Weber, Vin 119, 285
Weinberg, Rabbi Joseph 188
Weinreb, Ann and Jack 41
Weinreb, Rabbi Dr. Tzvi Hersh 366, 369
Weinreb, Sheila 35, 40–47. *See also* Ganchrow, Sheila
White House 31, 114, 122–123, 132, 135–138, 141, 149, 158, 216–217, 219–221, 244, 246, 248, 256, 263–264, 267–274, 281, 284–285, 334
Wofford, Harris 129, 130
Wolinetz, Harvey 170, 367, 374

Y

Yeshiva College 31–35, 68, 84
Yeshiva University 9–10, 17, 19, 23, 27, 31, 84–85, 106, 118
Yoffie, Rabbi Erich 213, 325–327
Yogel, Rabbi Peretz 24, 25
Young Israel 9, 24, 26, 125

Z

Zackheim, Dov 151
Zimmerman, Dr. 45
Zionist Organization of America (ZOA) 125, 236, 248
Zises, Seymour 118
Zlatlow, Dr. 40
Zwiebel, Rabbi Chaim Dovid (David) 202